THE
100
BEST
MUTUAL
FUNDS
YOU CAN BUY
2004

▲

Gordon K. Williamson

Adams Media Corporation
Avon, Massachusetts

Also by Gordon K. Williamson
Big Decisions, Small Investor
Low Risk Investing
Making the Most of Your 401(k)

DEDICATION
This book is dedicated to all of my clients.
I would be nowhere without their trust and support.

ACKNOWLEDGMENTS
Special thanks (again) to Cynthia Shaffer for her computer skills. This is a truly
thankless job, and I appreciate everything she has done.

Published by Adams Media Corporation
57 Littlefield Street, Avon, MA 02322

ISBN: 1-58062-927-X
ISSN: 1521-7787

Printed in Canada.

J I H G F E D C B A

This publication is designed to provide accurate and authoritative information with regard to
the subject matter covered. It is sold with the understanding that the publisher is not engaged
in rendering legal, accounting, or other professional advice. If legal advice or other expert
assistance is required, the services of a competent professional person should be sought.
—From a *Declaration of Principles* jointly adopted by a Committee of the
American Bar Association and a Committee of Publishers and Associations

While due care has been taken to ensure accurate and current data, the ideas, principles, conclusions, and general suggestions contained in this volume are subject to the laws and regulations of local, state, and federal authorities, as well as to court cases and any revisions of
court cases. Due to the magnitude of the database and the complexity of the subject matter,
occasional errors are possible; the publisher assumes no liability direct or incidental for any
actions or investments made by readers of this book, and strongly suggests that readers seek
consultation with legal, financial, or accounting professionals before making any investment.

The data used to analyze the funds is current through December 31, 2002.

This book is available at quantity discounts for bulk purchases.
For information, call 1-800-872-5627 (in Massachusetts, 508-427-7100).

Visit our home page at *www.adamsmedia.com*

Contents

I.   About This Book 1
II.   What Is a Mutual Fund? 3
III.   How to Invest in a Mutual Fund 5
IV.   How a Mutual Fund Operates 7
V.   Different Categories of Mutual Funds 8
VI.   Which Funds Are Best for You? 26
VII.   Fund Features 33
VIII. Reading a Mutual Fund Prospectus 37
IX.   Commonly Asked Questions 38
X.   How the 100 Best Funds Were Determined 43
XI.   The 100 Best Funds 45

AGGRESSIVE GROWTH FUNDS 48
     Ariel 51
     ARK Small Cap Equity A 53
     Bjurman, Barry Micro-Cap Growth 55
     Fidelity Low-Priced Stock 57
     Pennsylvania Mutual Investor 59
     Quaker Aggressive Growth A 61
     Royce Micro-Cap 63
     Royce Opportunity 65
     Royce Total Return 67
     Smith Barney Aggressive Growth A 69

BALANCED FUNDS 71
     American Funds American Balanced A 73
     Calamos Convertible Growth & Income A 75
     Dodge & Cox Balanced 77
     First Eagle Global A 79
     FPA Crescent Institutional 81
     Franklin Income A 83
     MFS Total Return A 85
     Oakmark Equity & Income I 87
     Vanguard Wellesley Income 89

CORPORATE BOND FUNDS **91**
   Dodge & Cox Income............................94
   Fidelity Short-Term Bond.......................96
   Fremont Bond 98
   Janus Short-Term Bond 100
   TIAA-CREF Bond Plus 102
   Vanguard Intermediate-Term Bond Index 104

FINANCIAL FUNDS **106**
   FBR Small Cap Financial A 108
   Hancock Regional Bank B 110

GLOBAL EQUITY (STOCK) FUNDS **112**
   American Funds Capital World Growth & Income A 116
   American Funds New Perspective A 118
   First Eagle Overseas A 120
   Julius Baer International Equity A 122
   Matthews Asian Growth & Income................124
   Matthews Pacific Tiger 126
   Tweedy, Browne Global Value 128

GOVERNMENT BOND FUNDS **130**
   American Century Ginnie Mae Investor 132
   ING GNMA Income A 134
   Sit U.S. Government Securities.....................136
   Vanguard GNMA 138
   Vanguard Short-Term Federal 140

GROWTH FUNDS **142**
   Calamos Growth A 145
   Clipper.....................................147
   Hartford Midcap A 149
   Longleaf Partners 151
   Lord Abbett Mid-Cap Value A 153
   Mairs & Power Growth 155
   Merger.....................................157
   Meridian Value...............................159
   Yacktman 161

GROWTH AND INCOME FUNDS **163**
   American Century Equity Income 165
   American Funds Capital Income Builder A 167
   Ameristock 169
   Dodge & Cox Stock 171
   FPA Perennial 173
   Franklin Rising Dividends A 175

Prudential Jennison Equity Opportunities A 177
Scudder Dreman High Return Equity A 179
Van Kampen Equity and Income A 181

HEALTH CARE FUNDS 183
Eaton Vance World Health A 185
Vanguard Health Care 187

HIGH-YIELD CORPORATE BOND FUNDS. 189
Janus High-Yield 192
Lord Abbett Bond-Debenture A 194
T. Rowe Price High-Yield 196
Vanguard High-Yield Corporate 198
Waddell & Reed Advisor High-Income A 200

METALS AND NATURAL RESOURCES FUNDS 202
American Century Global Gold Investments 205
First Eagle Gold 207
Oppenheimer Gold & Special Minerals A 209
State Street Research Global Resources A 211

MONEY MARKET FUNDS 213
Dreyfus Basic Money Market. 216
Federated Liquid Cash Trust. 217
Federated Short-Term Government Trust 218
Strong Municipal Money Market 219
Scudder Tax Exempt Money. 220
Scudder Yieldwise Money 221
TIAA-CREF Money Market 222
USAA Tax-Exempt Money Market 223
Vanguard Federal Money Market. 224
Vanguard Prime Money Market 225
Wells Fargo National Tax-Free Money Market Fund 226

MUNICIPAL BOND FUNDS 227
American Century California High-Yield Municipal
    Investor 230
American Funds Limited-Term Tax-Exempt
    Bond Fund of America 232
American Funds Tax-Exempt Bond A 234
Fidelity Advisor Municipal Income T. 236
Franklin Federal Tax-Free Income A 238
USAA Tax Exempt Intermediate-Term. 240
Vanguard Intermediate-Term Tax-Exempt 242
Vanguard New York Long-Term Tax-Exempt Investor 244
Vanguard Short-Term Tax-Exempt 246

REAL ESTATE FUNDS **248**
  Security Capital U.S. Real Estate 250
  Vanguard REIT Index 252

TECHNOLOGY FUNDS **254**
  Icon Information Technology 256
  Seligman Communications & Information A 258

UTILITY STOCK FUNDS **260**
  AXP Utilities A 263
  Morgan Stanley Global Utilities B 265
  Prudential Utility A 267
  Strong Dividend Income 269

WORLD BOND FUNDS **271**
  Credit Suisse Global Fixed-Income..................... 274
  Fidelity New Markets Income........................ 276
  Payden Global Fixed-Income R 278
  T. Rowe Price Emerging Markets Bond 280

XII.   Summary **282**
Appendix A Glossary of Mutual Fund Terms **284**
Appendix B Who Regulates Mutual Funds? **289**
Appendix C Dollar-Cost Averaging **290**
Appendix D Systematic Withdrawal Plan **292**
Appendix E Load or No-Load—Which Is Right for You? **294**
Appendix F The U.S. Market Compared to Foreign
            Markets **298**
Appendix G Growth Stocks versus Value Stocks **299**
Appendix H Stock Market Declines **300**
Appendix I A Reason Not to Index **303**
Appendix J A Benefit of Balanced Funds. **305**
Appendix K Asset Categories:
            Total Returns for the Past 16 Years **306**
Appendix L Stock Gains, Losses, and Averages **307**
Appendix M Individual Stocks versus Mutual Funds **308**
Appendix N Decades at a Glance (1930–1999) **309**
About the Author. **312**

I.
About This Book

There are roughly 6 million business entities operating in the United States; close to 15,000 of these businesses are publicly held (meaning they have issued stock to the public). Of the 15,000 publicly traded companies, fewer than 4,000 are listed on the New York Stock Exchange (NYSE). The world's total stock market capitalization is approximately $18 trillion, almost one-half of which is represented by U.S. equities.

There are more than 13,000 mutual funds. There are well over three times as many mutual funds as there are stocks listed on the NYSE! The mutual fund industry is now the second largest financial institution in the nation, with assets exceeding $7 trillion, up from $1 trillion in 1991. By the beginning of the year 2000, U.S. households held 81 percent of mutual fund assets, up from 74 percent in 1990. Individual stocks and mutual funds accounted for 38 percent of U.S. households' financial assets, surpassing the previous all-time high of 34 percent in 1968. As of the middle of 2003, close to 55 million households (52 percent of all households) own shares of one or more mutual funds, up from 4.6 million in 1980.

Mutual funds are the *best* investment vehicle that has been developed in the twentieth century. When properly selected, these vehicles combine professional management, ease of purchase and redemption, simple record-keeping, risk reduction, and superb performance, all in one type of investment. There are dozens of other types of investments, but none match the overall versatility of mutual funds.

A mutual fund is simply one method of investing. When you invest in a fund, your money is pooled with thousands of other investors' monies. This large pool of money is overseen by the fund's management, who place it in one or more types of investments. The universe of investments includes common stocks, preferred stocks, corporate bonds, tax-free municipal bonds, U.S. government obligations, zero-coupon bonds, convertible securities, gold, silver, foreign securities, and even real estate. The amount of money invested in one or more of these categories depends on the fund's objectives and restrictions and on management's perception of the economy.

The beauty of mutual funds is that once the investor decides on the *type* of investment desired, there are several funds that fulfill that criterion. As an example, someone who needs current income would be attracted to bond funds (or a series of equity-oriented funds coupled with what is known as a "systematic withdrawal plan"—a monthly income program described in Appendix D). A person interested in appreciation would focus on an aggressive growth, growth and income, and/or international stock fund. A person who wanted some current income plus some growth to offset the effects of inflation should consider a balanced fund.

The track records of these funds can easily be obtained, as contrasted to the track records of stockbrokers, who are not ranked at all. A few mutual fund sources even look at a fund's risk-adjusted return, a standard of measurement that has not been sufficiently emphasized in the past.

This book was written to fill a void. There are already several mutual fund books and directories, but none deal exclusively with the very best funds. More important, *none of these publications measure risk properly*.

This is the fourteenth edition of this book. If you have read one or more of the previous editions, you will notice that this edition includes many funds not previously listed and that several of the previous "100 Best" are not included here. This does not mean that you should sell or transfer from a previous recommendation to one that appears in this edition. For the most part, mutual funds described in past editions are still excellent choices and should not be moved. There are a number of reasons a fund no longer appears in this, or previous, editions. These reasons are detailed in Chapter X.

Moving from one fund to another can often spell trouble. Since 1970, the average holding period for mutual funds has been reduced from over 11 years to just over two years. More recent studies indicate that it may now be closer to one year. Although the period from 1984 through 2000 was one of the strongest periods in history, many investors experienced significantly less performance than the market offered. While the Standard & Poor's 500 (S&P 500) Index returned an average of 16.3 percent per year from January 1984 through December 2000, the typical equity investor earned only 5.3 percent per year during the same period. The lesson from these numbers is simple: By jumping from investment to investment, investors lose out on the solid performance they are seeking.

Other sources give almost endless numbers and performance statistics for hundreds and hundreds of mutual funds, leaving readers to draw their own conclusions about what are the best funds. This book will save you a great deal of time because it has taken more than 13,000 existing funds and narrowed them down to the best 100, ranked by specific category and risk level. Even money market funds are included, a category rarely covered by any other publication.

Investors and financial advisors are not concerned with mediocre or poor performers; they simply want the best funds, *given certain parameters*. Personal investment considerations should include (in order of priority) your time horizon, risk tolerance, financial goals, existing portfolio, and tax bracket. Parameters within a given fund category include risk, performance, and consistency.

Current books and periodicals that cover funds focus on how a fund has performed in the past. Studies clearly point out that a fund whose performance is in the top half one year has a 50-50 chance of being in the bottom half the next year, or the year after that. Since there is little correlation between the past and the future when it comes to market returns, this book concentrates on consistency in management and the amount of risk assumed.

The model used to rank the 100 best is fully described in Chapter X. It is a logical, common-sense approach that cuts through the statistical jargon; it is also easy to understand. As my dad used to say, "There is nothing as uncommon as common sense."

II.
What Is a Mutual Fund?

A mutual fund is an investment company: an entity that makes investments on behalf of individuals and institutions that share common financial goals. The fund pools the money of many people, each with a different amount to invest. Professional money managers then use this pool of money to buy a variety of stocks, bonds, or money market instruments that, in their judgment, will help the fund's shareholders achieve their financial objectives.

Each fund has an investment objective, described in the fund's prospectus, that is important both to the manager and to the potential investor. The fund manager uses this objective as a guide when choosing investments for the fund's portfolio. Prospective investors use it to determine which funds are suitable for their own needs. The investment objectives of mutual funds cover a wide range. Some follow aggressive investment policies, involving greater risk, in search of higher returns; others seek current income from more conservative investments.

When the fund earns money, it distributes the earnings to its shareholders. Earnings come from stock dividends, interest paid by bonds or money market instruments, and gains from the sale of securities in the fund's portfolio. The dividends and capital gains produced are paid out in proportion to the number of fund shares owned. Thus, shareholders who invest a few hundred dollars get the same investment return per dollar as those who invest hundreds of thousands.

Mutual funds remain popular because they are convenient and efficient investment vehicles that give all individuals—even those with small sums to invest—access to a splendid array of opportunities. Mutual funds are uniquely democratic institutions. They can take a portfolio of giant blue-chip companies such as IBM, General Electric, and General Motors and slice it into small enough pieces so that almost anyone can buy.

Mutual funds allow you to participate in foreign stock and bond markets that might otherwise demand too much time, expertise, or expense to be worthwhile. International funds make investing across national borders no more difficult than investing across state lines. Over the next decade, as securities markets develop in the former Iron Curtain countries, mutual funds will no doubt give investors many opportunities to participate in those markets as well.

Mutual funds have opened up a world of fixed-income investing to people who, until recently, had few choices apart from passbook accounts and savings bonds. Through bond funds, shareholders can tap into the interest payments from any kind of fixed-income security they can imagine—and many they have never heard of. The range goes from U.S. Treasury bonds (T-bonds) to collateralized mortgage obligations (CMOs), adjustable-rate preferred stock, floating-rate notes, and even to other countries' debts—denominated both in U.S. dollars and in other currencies.

What is heavily marketed is not necessarily what is appropriate for you to invest in. A global biotechnology fund may be a great investment, but it may not be the right mutual fund for you. Buying what is "hot" rather than what is appropriate is one of the most common mistakes made by investors and an issue that is addressed throughout this book.

A reason to invest is to offset the effects of inflation. Over time, inflation can erode individuals' purchasing power. Mutual funds that invest primarily in common stocks may help keep you ahead of inflation over the long term.

	year	amount
first-class stamp	1934	3 cents
	1980	15 cents
	2002	34 cents
	Increase	1,133%
a new car	1934	$1,436
	1980	$6,200
	2002	$19,175
	Increase	1,335%
a day in the hospital	1934	$12
	1980	$344
	2002	$2,854
	Increase	23,783%

Sources: U.S. Postal Service, U.S. Census Bureau, and the *Wall Street Journal*, April 30, 2002.

III.
How to Invest in a Mutual Fund

Investing in a mutual fund means buying shares of the fund. An investor becomes an owner of shares in the fund just as he or she might be an owner of shares of stock in a large corporation. The difference is that a fund's only business is investing in securities, and the price of its shares is directly related to the value of the securities held by the fund.

Mutual funds continually issue new shares for purchase by the public. The price per share for existing fund investors is not decreased by the ongoing issuance of new shares, since each share created is offset by the amount of new money coming in. Phrased another way, new money that comes into the fund is used to purchase additional securities in order not to dilute the income or value for existing shareholders.

A fund's share price can change from day to day, depending on the daily value of the securities held by the fund. The share price is called the net asset value, which is calculated as follows: The total value of the fund's investments at the end of the day, after expenses, is divided by the number of shares outstanding.

Newspapers report mutual fund activity every day. An example from the *Wall Street Journal* is shown here.

Everett Funds:

Evrt r	12.38	NL	-.01
MaxRtn	18.39	NL	+.06
ValTr	12.33	NL	-.01
LtdSl	17.71	NL	-.14
ExtrMid	2.82	2.95	-.02
ExJY p	7.24	7.60	+.01
FBK Gth t	11.06	11.06	..

FJA Funds:

Capit f	14.67	15.69	-.02
NwHrz	9.65	10.10	..
Permt	12.91	13.81	..
Perrin	20.96	22.42	-.02

The first column in the table is the fund's abbreviated name. Several funds under a single heading indicate a family of funds.

The second column is the net asset value (NAV) per share as of the close of the preceding business day. In some newspapers, the NAV is identified as the sell or the bid price; that is, the amount per share you would receive if you sold your shares. Each mutual fund determines its net asset value every business day by dividing the market value of its total assets, less liabilities, by the number of shares outstanding. On any given day, you can determine the value of your holdings by multiplying the NAV by the number of shares you own.

The third column is usually the offering price or, in some papers, the buy or the asked price; that is, the price you would pay if you purchased shares. The buy price is the NAV plus any sales charges. If there are no sales charges, an NL for no load appears in this column. In such a case, the buy price would be the same as the NAV.

The next column shows the change, if any, in the NAV from the preceding quotation—in other words, the change over the most recent one-day trading period. Thus, if you see a "+.06" in the newspaper next to your fund, *each* of your shares in the fund went up in value by six cents during the previous day.

A *p* following the abbreviated name of the fund denotes a fund that charges a fee that is subtracted from assets for marketing and distribution costs, also known as a 12b-1 plan (named after the federal government rule that permits such an expense). If the fund name is followed by an *r*, the fund has a contingent deferred sales load (CDSL) or a redemption fee. A CDSL is a charge incurred if shares are sold within a certain period; a redemption fee is a cost paid whenever shares are sold. An *f* indicates a fund that habitually enters the previous day's prices, instead of the current day's. A *t* designates a fund that has both a CDSL or a redemption fee and a 12b-1 plan.

IV.
How a Mutual Fund Operates

A mutual fund is owned by all of its shareholders, the people who purchased shares of the fund. The day-to-day operation of a fund is delegated to a management company.

The management company, often the organization that created the fund, may offer other mutual funds, financial products, and financial services as well. The management company usually serves as the fund's investment advisor.

The investment advisor manages the fund's portfolio of securities. The advisor is paid for its services in the form of a fee that is based on the total value of the fund's assets; fees average 0.5 percent. The advisor employs professional portfolio managers who invest the fund's money by purchasing a number of stocks or bonds or money market instruments, depending on what type of fund it is.

These fund professionals decide where to invest the fund's assets. The money managers make their investment decisions based on extensive, ongoing research into the financial performance of individual companies, taking into account general economic and market trends. In addition, they are backed up by economic and statistical resources. On the basis of their research, money managers decide what and when to buy, sell, or hold for the fund's portfolio, in light of the fund's specific investment objective.

In addition to the investment advisor, the fund may also contract with an underwriter that arranges for the distribution of the fund's shares to the investing public. The underwriter may act as a wholesaler, selling fund shares to security dealers, or it may retail directly to the public.

V.
Different Categories of Mutual Funds

Aggressive Growth. The investment objective of aggressive growth funds is maximum capital gains, with little or no concern for dividends or income of any kind. What makes this category of mutual funds unique is that fund managers often have the ability to use borrowed money (leverage) to increase positions. Sometimes they deal in stock options and futures contracts (commodities). These trading techniques sound, and can be, scary, but such activities represent only a minor portion of the funds' holdings.

Because of their bullish dispositions, these funds will usually stay fully invested in the stock market. For investors, this means better-than-expected results during good (bull) markets and worse-than-average losses during bad (bear) market periods. Fortunately, the average bull market is almost four times as long as the typical bear market.

Do not be confused by economic conditions and stock market performance. There have been eight recessions since World War II. During seven of those eight recessions, U.S. stocks went up. During all eight recessions, stocks posted impressive gains in the second half of every recession. By the same token, do not underestimate the impact of a loss. A 20 percent decline means that you must then have a gain of 25 percent just to break even.

A loss of 20 percent does not happen very often to aggressive growth funds, particularly on a calendar year basis, but you should be aware that such extreme downward moves are possible, as was the case in 2001. Often brokers like to focus on the plus 45 percent, plus 50 percent, and plus 60 percent years, such as 1980, 1991, and 1999, while glossing over bad years, such as 1984, 2001, and 2002, when aggressive growth funds were down 13 percent, 20 percent, and 28 percent, respectively, on average.

One of the great wonders of the stock market is how volatility of returns is reduced when the investor's holding period is increased. Because of this, aggressive growth funds should only be owned by one of two kinds of investors: those who can live with high levels of daily, monthly, quarterly, and/or annual price per share fluctuations, and those who realize the importance of a diversified portfolio that cuts across several investment categories. The second kind of investor looks at how the entire package is performing, not just one segment.

The typical price-earnings (p/e) ratio for stocks in this category is 28, roughly 10 percent more than the S&P 500 Index, which has an average p/e ratio of 25. This group of funds has an average beta of 1.1, making its *market-related* risk 10 percent higher than the S&P 500 (which always has a beta of 1.0, no matter what market conditions or levels are).

The standard deviation for aggressive growth funds is 27 percent. This means that the expected return for any given year would typically vary either way by 27 percent. In other words, since aggressive growth funds have annually averaged -20 percent over the past three years (ending December 31, 2002), annual returns are expected to range from *negative* 47.0 percent (-20 – 27) to *positive* 7 percent (-20 + 27). This would represent one standard deviation. A single standard deviation accounts for what you can expect two out of every three months (67 percent of the time or roughly two out of every three years). If you are looking for greater assurance, then two standard deviations must be used (multiply 27 percent times 2 in this case). This means that returns for about 95 percent of the time (two standard deviations) would be -20 percent plus or minus 54 percent; in other words, a range of -74 percent to +34 percent.

Small-company stocks have an average p/e ratio of 25. (The price-earnings ratio refers to the selling price of a stock in relation to its annual earnings. Thus, a fund category that has a p/e ratio of, say, 10 is comprised of mutual funds whose typical stock in the portfolio is selling for 10 times what the corporation earnings are for the year.) Small-company stock funds have a standard deviation of 25 percent and a beta of 0.9, figures that support the view that this category is less volatile than aggressive growth funds.

Historical returns over the past three, five, ten, and 15 years for aggressive growth and small-company stock funds are shown here. All of the figures shown are *compound annual* rates of return (all periods ending December 31, 2002).

category	3 years	5 years	10 years	15 years
aggressive growth funds	-19.9%	-2.3%	5.2%	9.0%
small company stock funds	-7.2%	0.4%	8.1%	11.1%
S&P 500	-14.6%	-0.6%	9.3%	11.5%
T-bills	3.8%	4.2%	4.4%	5.0%
CPI (rate of inflation)	2.4%	2.3%	2.5%	3.0%

Health care and consumer service stocks dominate the aggressive growth fund category. Health care alone represents just over 21 percent of the typical aggressive growth fund's portfolio, followed by 14 percent in consumer services and 13 percent in financial services. Small-company stocks are also dominated by health care (15 percent) and financial service issues (15 percent).

Balanced. This kind of fund invests in common stocks and corporate bonds. The weighting given to stocks depends on the fund manager's perception of, or belief in, the market. The more bullish the manager is, the more likely the portfolio will be loaded up with equities. Yet, no matter how strongly management feels about the stock market, it would be very rare to see stocks equal more than 67 percent of the portfolio. Similarly, no matter how bearish one becomes, it would be unlikely for a balanced fund to have more than 67 percent of its holdings represented by bonds. Often a fund's prospectus will outline the weighting ranges: The fund's managers must stay within these wide boundaries at all times. A small portion of these funds is made up of cash equivalents (T-bills, CDs, commercial paper, etc.), with a very small amount sometimes dedicated to preferred stocks and convertible securities.

Three other categories—multiasset global, convertible, and asset allocation— have been combined with balanced funds for the purposes of this book. This grouping is logical; because their overall objectives are largely similar, the general portfolio composition can be virtually identical in many cases, and the fund managers in each of these categories have the flexibility to load up heavily on stocks, bonds, preferreds, or convertible securities.

Multiasset global funds typically emphasize bonds more than stocks or cash. It is not uncommon to see a multiasset global fund that has 60 percent of its holdings in bonds, with 10 to 20 percent in stocks, and the remainder in foreign equities, preferred stocks, and cash. For the *stock* portion of this category, the average p/e ratio is 22. On the bond side, the average maturity of debt instruments in the portfolio is eight years. The standard deviation for this narrow category is 14 percent.

Convertible funds, as the name implies, are made up mostly of convertible preferred stocks and convertible bonds. The conversion feature allows the owner, the fund in this case, to convert or exchange securities for the corporation's common stock. Conversion and price appreciation take place during bull-market periods. Uncertain or down markets make conversion much less likely; instead, management falls back on the comparatively high dividend or interest payments that convertibles enjoy. The typical convertible fund has roughly half of its holdings in convertibles; the balance is in cash, stocks, and preferreds. For the stock portion of this category, the p/e ratio averages 31 and the standard deviation is 16 percent. On the bond side, the average maturity of debt instruments in the portfolio is seven years.

Asset allocation funds, like other categories that fall under the broad definition of "balanced," are hybrid in nature—part equity and part debt. These funds have a tendency to emphasize stocks over bonds. A fund manager who wants to take a defensive posture may stay on the sidelines by converting moderate or large parts of the portfolio into cash equivalents. The average asset allocation fund has roughly 55 percent of its portfolio in common stocks, with the remainder in bonds, foreign stocks, and cash. For the stock portion of this category, the typical p/e ratio is 24 and the standard deviation is 11 percent. On the bond side, the average maturity of debt instruments in the portfolio is nine years.

This group of funds has an average beta of 0.5, making its *market-related risk* 50 percent less than the S&P 500. Keep in mind that beta refers to a portfolio's *stock market-related risk*; it is not a meaningful way to measure bond or foreign security risk.

The standard deviation for balanced funds is 11 percent, which is under one-third the level of aggressive growth funds. This means that the expected return for any given year will vary by 11 percent. (For example, if you were expecting an annualized return of 7 percent, your actual return would range from -4 percent to 18 percent most of the time.)

Historical returns over the past three, five, ten, and 15 years for balanced, multiasset global, convertible, and asset allocation funds are shown here. All of the figures are *compound annual* rates of return (all periods ending December 31, 2002).

category	3 years	5 years	10 years	15 years
balanced funds	-4.6%	1.5%	7.4%	9.3%
multiasset global funds	-4.0%	1.8%	6.3%	6.5%
asset allocation funds	-4.3%	1.6%	7.2%	8.7%
convertible funds	-5.2%	2.9%	7.9%	9.7%
utility funds	-13.2%	-2.0%	4.8%	7.8%

Financial services and health care stocks dominate the equity portion of the balanced fund category. These two groups represent over one-third of the typical balanced fund's stock portfolio. The other major equity sectors are industrial materials, consumer goods, and consumer services stocks.

Like other hybrid funds, balanced funds provide an income stream. The average yield of balanced funds is 2.7 percent (3.2 percent for asset allocation, 3.7 percent for convertibles, and 1.8 percent for multiasset global). High-tax-bracket investors who want to invest in these funds should consider using tax-sheltered money, if possible. Balanced, multiasset global, asset allocation, and convertible bond funds are particularly attractive within an individual retirement account (IRA), other qualified retirement plans, or variable annuities. (For more information about both fixed-rate and variable annuities, see two of my other books, *The 100 Best Annuities* and *Getting Started in Annuities*.)

Corporate Bonds. These funds invest in debt instruments (IOUs) issued by corporations, governments, and agencies of the U.S. government. Perhaps the typical corporate bond fund should be called a "government-corporate" fund.

All bonds have a maturity date: a date when the issuer (the government, municipality, or corporation) pays back the *face value* of the bond (which is almost always $1,000 per bond) and stops paying interest. There are often hundreds of different securities in any given bond fund. Each one of these securities (bonds in this case) has a maturity date; these maturity dates can range from a few days up to 30 years.

Bond funds have a wide range of maturities. The name of the fund will often indicate whether it is made up of *short-term* or *medium-term* obligations. If the name of the fund does not include the words "short-term" or "intermediate," then the fund most likely invests in bonds with average maturities over 10 years. The greater the maturity, the more the fund's share value can change. There is an inverse relationship between interest rates and the value of a bond; when one moves up, the other goes down.

The weighted maturity date of the bonds within this group averages seven years, with a typical coupon rate of 5.7 percent and an average yield of 3.8 percent. "Weighted maturity" refers to the time left until the average bond in the portfolio comes due (matures). The coupon rate represents the interest that the corporation or government pays out annually on a per-bond basis. The standard deviation for corporate bonds is 3.7 percent, approximately two-thirds less than that found with balanced funds. This means that the expected return for any given month, quarter, or year will be more predictable than almost any other category of mutual funds.

Using a beta measurement for bonds is of little value, because beta defines *stock market* risk and has nothing to do with interest-rate or financial risk.

Corporate bonds are rated in terms of their safety. The two major rating services are Moody's and Standard & Poor's. By reading the fund's prospectus or by telephoning the mutual fund company, you can find out how safe a corporate bond fund is, at least as far as financial or default risk is concerned. The vast majority of these funds are extremely conservative and safety (default) is not really an issue. U.S. government bonds are not rated since it is believed that there is no chance of default; unlike a corporation, the federal government can print money.

Historical returns over the past three, five, ten, and 15 years for corporate bond funds are shown here. All of the figures shown are *compound annual* rates of return (all periods ending December 31, 2002).

category	3 years	5 years	10 years	15 years
corporate bond funds	7.6%	5.8%	6.4%	7.7%
government bond funds	8.8%	6.4%	6.3%	7.4%
municipal bond funds	7.4%	4.7%	5.6%	6.8%
world bond funds	6.7%	4.7%	6.2%	6.2%
CPI (rate of inflation)	2.4%	2.3%	2.5%	3.0%

Like income funds, corporate funds provide a high yield that is fully taxable and should be sheltered whenever possible. The average yield of these bond funds is 4.4 percent.

Financial Services. Financial sector funds invest in the common stock of banks, brokerage firms, insurance companies, consumer credit providers, as well as savings and loan associations. A large number of the portfolios in this industry group focus on a particular type of financial company, with banking being one of the more popular.

During the 2001 and 2002 calendar years, the normally defensive financial services sector was affected by the volatility of the overall stock market. Although the group as a whole outperformed the S&P 500, the typical financial fund turned in negative results for the year. Despite short-term weakness, this sector remains one of the strongest.

Financial funds underperformed the S&P 500 by 17 percentage points during the last bull market (September 1998 to August 2000), but outperformed the S&P 500 by 29 percentage points during the last bear market (August 2000 to September 2001). Over the past 20 years, ending January 31, 2002, the average annualized return of financial funds was 17.3 percent versus 15.2 percent for the S&P 500. During the past 15 years, the best year for this sector was 1991 (59 percent) and the worst year was 1990 (-16 percent). Over the past five years, the best year was 2000 (28 percent) and the worst year was 2002 (-11 percent).

The typical p/e ratio for stocks in this category is 18 versus 25 for the S&P 500. This group of funds also has an average beta of 0.7, which means that it has 30 percent less *market risk* than the S&P 500.

The standard deviation for financial funds is 22 percent. Historical returns over the past three, five, ten, and 15 years for financial stock funds are shown here. All of the figures shown are *compound annual* rates of return (all periods ending December 31, 2002).

category	3 years	5 years	10 years	15 years
financial funds	3.7%	2.9%	12.6%	16.0%
utility funds	-13.2%	-2.0%	4.8%	7.8%
S&P 500	-14.6%	-0.6%	9.3%	11.5%
growth & income funds	-10.2%	-0.6%	8.6%	10.3%
health care funds	-0.3%	4.8%	10.0%	15.3%

Global Stock. This category of mutual funds invests in equities issued by domestic and foreign firms. 15 of the 20 largest corporations in the world are located outside the United States. It makes sense to be able to invest in these and other corporations and industries—to be able to take advantage of opportunities wherever they appear. Global, also known as world, stock funds have the ability to invest in any country. Conceptually the more countries a fund is able to invest in, the lower its overall risk level can be; often return potential can also increase.

For the purposes of this book, the global stock category includes foreign and international equity funds. When it comes to investing in mutual funds, the words *foreign* and *international* are interchangeable. A foreign, or international, fund invests in securities outside the United States. Some foreign funds are broadly diversified, including stocks from European as well as Pacific Basin economies. Other international funds specialize in a particular region or country. A global fund invests in domestic as well as foreign securities. The portfolio manager of a global fund generally has more latitude in selecting securities, since either domestic or foreign securities can end up representing 50 percent or more of the portfolio, depending on management's view of the different markets, whereas a foreign or international fund is not allowed to invest in U.S. stocks or bonds.

The typical p/e ratio for global stock funds is 23, a figure that is lower than that of the S&P 500 (p/e ratio of 25). This group of funds has an average beta of 0.8, meaning that its U.S. *market-related* risk is about 20 percent less than that of the general market, as measured by the S&P 500. The standard deviation for global stock funds is 17 percent, versus 21 percent for growth funds.

Foreign stock funds, which are exclusive of U.S. investments, have a p/e ratio of 20. Their standard deviation over the past three years has been 16 percent. Pacific Basin funds, a more narrowly focused type of foreign fund, have an average p/e ratio of 21 and a standard deviation of 18 percent. European funds, another type of specialized international fund, have a p/e ratio of 18 and a standard deviation of 19 percent.

Historical returns over the past three, five, ten, and 15 years for global stocks are shown here. All of the figures shown are *compound annual* rates of return (all periods ending December 31, 2002).

category	3 years	5 years	10 years	15 years
global stock funds	-15.0%	-0.6%	6.4%	8.6%
foreign stock funds	-17.5%	-2.1%	5.0%	6.6%
emerging markets funds	-14.0%	-4.6%	0.3%	N/A
Pacific Basin funds	-19.9%	-2.1%	-0.4%	1.8%
European funds	-15.1%	-1.2%	6.4%	4.8%

The four areas that dominate global (world) stock funds are the United States (50 percent of a typical fund's holdings), Europe (34 percent), and the Pacific Rim (16 percent).

Government Bonds. These funds invest in securities issued by the U.S. government or one of its agencies (or former affiliates), such as the Government National Mortgage Association (GNMA), the Federal Home Loan Mortgage Corporation (FHLMC), or the Federal National Mortgage Association (FNMA). Investors are attracted to bond funds of all kinds for two reasons. First, bond funds have monthly distributions; individual bonds pay interest only semiannually. Second, effective management can control interest-rate risk by varying the average maturity of the fund's portfolio. If management believes that interest rates are moving downward, the fund will load up heavily on long-term obligations. If rates do decline, long-term bonds will appreciate more than their short- and medium-term counterparts. Conversely, if the manager anticipates rate hikes, average portfolio maturity can be pared down so there will be only modest principal deterioration if rates do go up.

Bond funds have portfolios with a wide range of maturities. Many funds use their names to characterize their maturity structure. Generally, "short term" means that the portfolio has a weighted average maturity of less than five years. "Intermediate" implies an average maturity of five to 10 years, and "long term" is over 10 years. The longer the maturity is, the greater the change in the fund's price per share (your principal) when interest rates change. Longer-term bond funds are riskier than short-term funds but tend to offer higher yields. The top holdings of government bond funds are GNMAs and U.S. Treasury notes (T-notes) of varying maturities.

The weighted maturity date of the bonds within this group averages seven years, with a typical coupon rate of 5.7 percent (the coupon rate represents the interest that the corporation or government pays out annually on a per-bond basis)—figures that are virtually identical to the corporate bond category. The current yield of the typical government bond fund is 3.9 percent. These funds have a standard deviation of 3.7 percent—again the figure is almost identical to that for corporate bonds. This means that corporate and government bonds have similar volatilities.

Historical returns over the past three, five, ten, and 15 years for government bond funds are shown here. All of the figures shown are *compound annual* rates of return (all periods ending December 31, 2002).

category	3 years	5 years	10 years	15 years
government bond funds	8.8%	6.4%	6.3%	7.4%
high-yield bond funds	-2.7%	-1.3%	4.7%	6.2%
CPI (rate of inflation)	2.4%	2.3%	2.5%	3.0%
convertible funds	-5.2%	2.9%	7.9%	9.7%
utility funds	-13.2%	-2.0%	4.8%	7.8%

Like corporate bond funds, government funds provide a high yield that is fully taxable on the federal level and should be sheltered whenever possible. Interest from direct obligations of the U.S. government—T-bonds, T-notes, T-bills, EE bonds, HH bonds, and I bonds—are exempt from state and local income taxes. This means that a part of the income you receive from funds that include such securities is exempt from *state* taxes.

Growth. These funds seek capital appreciation with dividend income as a distant secondary concern. Investors who are attracted to growth funds are aiming to sell stock at a profit; they are not normally income oriented. If you are interested in current income you will want to look at Appendix D, "Systematic Withdrawal Plan."

Growth funds are attracted to equities from large well-established corporations. Unlike aggressive growth funds, growth funds may end up holding large cash positions during market declines or when investors are nervous about recent economic or market activities. The typical p/e ratio for stocks in this category is 26, virtually the same as the S&P 500. This group of funds also has an average beta of 1, which means that it has the same *market risk* as the S&P 500.

The standard deviation for growth funds is 21 percent. This means that the expected return for any given year will vary by 21 percentage points. As an example, if you were expecting a 12 percent annual return, annual returns would probably range between negative 9 percent and positive 33 percent (12 percent plus or minus 21 percent).

Historical returns over the past three, five, ten, and 15 years for growth and small-company stock funds are shown here. All of the figures shown are *compound annual* rates of return (all periods ending December 31, 2002).

category	3 years	5 years	10 years	15 years
growth funds	-13.8%	-0.8%	7.4%	10.1%
small company stock funds	-7.2%	0.4%	8.1%	11.1%
S&P 500	-14.6%	-0.6%	9.3%	11.5%
growth & income funds	-10.2%	-0.6%	8.6%	10.3%
global stock funds	-15.0%	-0.6%	6.4%	8.6%

Financial services (18 percent of the typical portfolio), health care (17 percent), consumer services (12 percent), and hardware (10 percent) dominate the composition of growth funds.

Growth and Income. With a name like this, you would think that this category of mutual funds is almost equally as concerned with income as it is with growth. The fact is, growth and income funds have an average dividend yield of just 1.3 percent. This boost in income is due to the small holdings in bonds and convertibles possessed by most growth and income funds.

The typical p/e ratio for stocks in this category is 24, versus 25 for the S&P 500. This group of funds has an average beta of 0.9, meaning that its *market-related risk* is 10 percent less than that of the general market, as measured by the S&P 500.

The standard deviation for growth and income funds is 17 percent, compared to 21 percent for the average growth fund. This means that, as a group, growth and income funds have slightly more predictable returns than growth funds.

For the purposes of this book, a second category, "equity-income funds," has been combined with growth and income. Equity-income funds have a lower standard deviation (15 percent), a higher yield (2.2 percent), and a lower beta (0.7 percent).

The typical growth and income fund is divided as follows: 90 percent in common stocks (3 percent of which is in foreign stock), 4 percent in cash, 3 percent in bonds, and 3 percent in other assets. The typical equity-income fund is divided as follows: 80 percent in common stocks (4 percent of which is in foreign stock), 10 percent in bonds, 5 percent in cash, and 5 percent in other assets. The typical p/e ratio for stocks in this category is 23.

Historical returns over the past three, five, ten, and 15 years for growth and income funds are shown here. All of the figures shown are average *annual* rates of return (all periods ending December 31, 2002).

category	3 years	5 years	10 years	15 years
growth & income funds	-10.2%	-0.6%	8.6%	10.3%
equity-income funds	-5.0%	0.3%	8.5%	10.3%
growth funds	-13.8%	-0.8%	7.4%	10.1%
balanced funds	-4.6%	1.5%	7.4%	9.3%
foreign stock funds	-17.5%	-2.1%	5.0%	6.6%

Financial services, industrial materials, and health care dominate growth and income funds, representing close to half of the typical portfolio.

Health Care. Health-care funds can invest in biotechnology, HMOs, pharmaceuticals, hospitals, nursing home care, and medical-device makers. A small number of the funds in this sector concentrate on one or two areas such as the riskier biotech or the more conservative service providers.

For the 12 months ending January 2003, the average health-care fund lost 29 percent and underperformed the S&P 500 by more than 7 percentage points during this period. The past year was mixed-to-negative for this sector. At the beginning of 2001, pharmaceutical and biotechnology issues suffered as investors shifted money into more cyclical than value-oriented sectors. During the final months of 2001, the sector rallied but then fell again throughout 2002. The most recent decline was most likely due to investors shying away from the more speculative biotech segment of health care, FDA delays in new-drug approval, as well as lost sales from generic competition.

Despite these short-term negatives, this sector offers tremendous promise in the future.

Over the past 15 years, ending January 31, 2002, the average annualized return of health-care funds was 15.3 percent versus 11.5 percent for the S&P 500. During the past 15 years, the best year for this sector was 2000 (56 percent) and the worst year was 2002 (-29.0 percent).

The typical p/e ratio for stocks in this category is 28, a figure that is about 10 percent higher than the p/e ratio for the S&P 500. This group of funds also has an average beta of 0.4, which means that it has 60 percent less *market risk* than the S&P 500.

The standard deviation for health-care funds is 29 percent. Historical returns over the past three, five, ten, and 15 years for health-care stock funds are shown here. All of the figures shown are *compound annual* rates of return (all periods ending December 31, 2002).

category	3 years	5 years	10 years	15 years
health-care funds	-0.3%	4.8%	10.0%	15.3%
technology funds	-37.3%	-3.2%	6.8%	12.1%
S&P 500	-14.6%	-0.6%	9.3%	11.5%
aggressive growth	-19.9%	-2.3%	5.2%	9.0%
real estate funds	12.8%	2.8%	8.9%	10.1%

High-Yield. These funds generally invest in lower-rated corporate debt instruments. Bonds are characterized as either "bank quality," also known as "investment grade," or "junk." Investment-grade bonds are bonds rated AAA, AA, A, or BAA; junk bonds are instruments rated less than BAA: BA, B, CCC, CC, C, and D. High-yield bonds, also referred to as junk bonds, offer investors higher yields in exchange for the additional risk of default. High-yield bonds are subject to less interest-rate risk than regular corporate or government bonds. However, when the economy slows or people panic, these bonds can quickly drop in value.

The average weighted maturity date of the bonds within this group is just seven years, a figure similar to that for high-quality corporate and government bond funds. The typical coupon rate is 9 percent. (The coupon rate represents what the corporation pays out annually on a per-bond basis.) When it comes to high-yield bonds, investors would be wise to accept a lower yield in return for more stability of principal and appreciation potential. As with income funds, corporate funds provide a high yield that is fully taxable and should be sheltered whenever possible. The current yield for the typical high-yield bond fund is 8.5 percent.

The standard deviation for high-yield bond funds is 9 percent, a figure that is more than twice the rate of corporate or government bond funds as a whole but less than balanced (11 percent) and more than global bond funds (8.0 percent). Historical returns over the past three, ten, and 15 years for high-yield corporate bond funds are shown here. All of the figures shown are *compound annual* rates of return (all periods ending December 31, 2002).

category	3 years	5 years	10 years	15 years
high-yield bond funds	-2.7%	-1.3%	4.7%	6.2%
corporate bond funds	7.6%	5.8%	6.4%	7.7%
government bond funds	8.8%	6.4%	6.3%	7.4%
world bond funds	6.7%	4.7%	6.2%	6.2%
balanced funds	-4.6%	1.5%	7.4%	9.3%

Metals and Natural Resources. Metals funds invest in precious metals and mining stocks from around the world. The majority of these stocks are located in North America; South Africa and Australia are the only other major players. Most of these companies specialize in gold mining. Some funds own gold and silver bullion outright. Direct ownership of the metal is considered to be a more conservative posture than owning stocks of mining companies; these stocks are more volatile than the metal itself.

Metals funds, also known as gold funds, are the most speculative group represented in this book. They are considered to be a sector or specialty fund in that they are only able to invest in a single industry or country. Metals funds enjoy international diversification but are still narrowly focused; the limitations of the fund are what make it so unpredictable. Usually, fund management can invest in only three things: mining stocks, direct metal ownership (bullion or coins), and cash equivalents.

Despite their volatile nature, gold funds are included in the book because they can actually reduce portfolio risk. Why? The answer is that gold and other investments often move in opposite directions. For example, when government bonds are moving down in value, gold funds often increase in value. What could otherwise be viewed as a wild investment becomes somewhat tamer when included as part of a diversified portfolio.

The typical dividend for metal funds is 3.7 percent. The typical p/e ratio for stocks in this category is 39, about 60 percent more than the S&P 500 (p/e ratio of 25).

This group of funds has an average beta of 0.2, meaning that its stock market-related risk is modest—but do not let this fool you. We are only talking about stock market risk. Beta focuses on that portion of risk that investors cannot reduce by further diversification in U.S. stocks. Metals funds, as shown by their wild track record, are anything but conservative. A 0.2 beta indicates that movement in this category has little to do with the direction of the S&P 500; therefore, portfolio risk may be reduced by diversification into this category. The standard deviation for metals funds is 40 percent, versus a standard deviation of 37 percent for technology funds.

Another category, natural resources, has been combined with metals funds for this book. As the name implies, natural resources funds are commodity-driven, just as metals funds are heavily influenced by two commodities: gold and silver. In the case of natural resources funds, the prices of oil, gas, and timber are the driving force. Natural resources funds invest in companies that are involved with the discovery, exploration, development, refinement, storage, and transportation of one or more of these three natural resources. The standard deviation for natural resources funds is 27 percent, beta is 0.7, and the p/e ratio is 30.

Historical returns over the past three, five, ten, and 15 years for metals and natural resources funds are shown here. All of the figures shown are *compound annual* rates of return (all periods ending December 31, 2002).

category	3 years	5 years	10 years	15 years
metals funds	17.2%	7.6%	3.0%	-0.8%
natural resources funds	4.2%	2.1%	9.1%	7.9%
aggressive growth funds	-19.9%	-2.3%	5.2%	9.0%
emerging markets funds	-14.0%	-5%	0%	N/A
CPI (rate of inflation)	2.4%	2.3%	2.5%	3.0%

Money Market. These funds invest in short-term money market instruments such as bank CDs, T-bills, and commercial paper. By maintaining a short average maturity and investing in high-quality instruments, money market funds are able to maintain a stable $1 net asset value. Since money market funds offer higher yields than a bank's insured money market deposit accounts, they are a very attractive haven for savings or temporary investment dollars. Like bond funds, money market funds come in both taxable and tax-free versions. Reflecting their tax-free status, municipal money market funds pay lower before-tax yields than taxable money market funds but can offer higher returns on an after-tax basis.

Since the price per share of taxable money market funds always stays at $1, interest is shown by the accumulation of additional shares. (For example, at the beginning of the year you may have 1,000 shares, and by the end of the year, 1,025. The 25-share increase, or $25, represents interest.) There are no such things as capital gains or unrecognized gains in a money market fund. The entire return, or yield, is fully taxable (except in the case of a tax-free money market fund where your gain or return would always be exempt from federal taxes and possibly state income taxes as well).

These funds are designed as a place to park your money for a relatively short period, in anticipation of a major purchase such as a car or house, or until conditions appear more favorable for stocks, bonds, and/or real estate. There has only been one money market fund, now defunct, that has ever lost money for its investors (most of whom were bankers).

The standard deviation for money market funds is lower than any other category of mutual funds and is well under 1 percent. Historical returns over the past three, five, ten, and 15 years for taxable and tax-free money market funds are shown here. All of the figures shown are *compound annual* rates of return (all periods ending December 31, 2002).

category	3 years	5 years	10 years	15 years
money market funds	3.5%	4.1%	4.3%	5.0%
tax-free money market funds	2.2%	2.5%	2.6%	N/A
gov't money market funds	3.5%	4.0%	4.2%	N/A
government bond funds	8.8%	6.4%	6.3%	7.4%
CPI (rate of inflation)	2.4%	2.3%	2.5%	3.0%

Municipal Bonds. Also known as tax-free, these funds are made up of tax-free debt instruments issued by states, counties, districts, or political subdivisions. Interest from municipal bonds is normally exempt from federal income tax. In almost all states, interest is also exempt from state and local income taxes if the portfolio is made up of issues from the investor's state of residence, a U.S. territory (Puerto Rico, the U.S. Virgin Islands, etc.), or the District of Columbia.

Until the early 1980s, municipal bonds were almost as sensitive to interest rate changes as corporate and government bonds. During the past several years, however, tax-free bonds have taken on a new personality. Now when interest rates change, municipal bonds exhibit only one-half to one-third the price change that occurs with similar funds comprised of corporate or government issues. This decreased volatility is due to a smaller supply of municipal bonds and the elimination of almost all tax shelters, which has increased the popularity of tax-free bonds.

Three kinds of events may result in tax liability for every mutual fund except money market funds. The first two events described are ones that cannot be controlled by the investor, while the final event is determined solely by the shareholder or investor (you).

First, when bonds or stocks are sold in the fund portfolio for a profit (or loss), a capital gain (or capital loss) occurs. These gains and losses are passed down to the shareholder. Tax-free bond funds are not immune from capital gains taxes (or capital losses).

Second, interest and/or dividends paid by the securities within the fund are also passed on to shareholders (investors). As already mentioned, interest from municipal bonds is free from federal income taxes and, depending on the fund, may also be exempt from state income taxes. Municipal bond funds do not own stocks or convertibles, so they never throw off dividends.

Third, a taxable event may occur when you sell or exchange shares of a fund for cash or to go into another fund. As an example, suppose you bought into the fund at X dollars and cents per share. If you sell or exchange shares for X plus Y, then there will be a taxable gain (on Y, in this example). If you sell or exchange shares for a loss (X minus Y), then there will be a capital loss. Municipal bond funds are subject to such capital gains or losses. Fortunately, you are never required to sell off shares in any mutual fund, the decision about when and how much is always yours.

The standard deviation for municipal bond funds is 4 percent, meaning that this category's volatility is virtually identical to corporate bonds and government securities. Historical returns over the past three, five, ten, and 15 years for municipal funds are shown here. All of the figures shown are *compound annual* rates of return (all periods ending December 31, 2002).

category	3 years	5 years	10 years	15 years
municipal bond funds	7.4%	4.7%	5.6%	6.8%
Calif. municipal bond funds	7.8%	4.9%	5.9%	7.0%
N.Y. municipal bond funds	7.9%	5.0%	5.8%	7.1%
government bond funds	8.8%	6.4%	6.3%	7.4%
CPI (rate of inflation)	2.4%	2.3%	2.5%	3.0%

Real Estate. This specialized group of mutual funds mostly invests in real estate investment trusts (REITs) of various types (e.g., equity, mortgage-backed, and hybrid). There are a number of different types of REITs that are categorized by type and geographical location. The most common REITs are apartment, factory-outlet, health care, hotel, industrial, office, and shopping centers.

One of the more interesting ongoing debates is whether an investor should own real estate outright (rental property, strip shopping center, apartments, etc.) or indirectly through a mutual fund and/or REIT. Advocates of REITs point out that they have outperformed direct real estate investing over the past 20 years, although most of the difference is because REITs carry leverage of 30 percent or more, which adds to risk. Yet, even if the returns were the same, which they were from 1991 to 2001 according to a study by Wilshire Associates, direct ownership includes the following negatives: possible employees to manage the property, illiquidity (buying and selling can take months), lack of accountability (the appraisal process masks the volatility of direct investing), and lack of transparency of a public company.

For the 12 months ending December 31, 2002, the average real-estate fund gained just under 4 percent. The sector outperformed the S&P 500 by 26 percentage points during this period. The bear market along with a low-interest-rate environment translated into an almost ideal environment for real estate and real estate investment trusts (REITs). Within the sector there was quite a bit of return disparity, the more conservative segment of the real-estate market rallied sporadically while the more speculative issues experienced large gains. During the first part of 2002 and 2003, the sector was led by REITs that provided high income. Outlook for the next year or so remains mixed. Economic recovery should be a positive influence on rents while possible overbuilding by developers and the threat of rising interest rates are potential negatives. Regardless of one's outlook, REITs and real-estate funds remain a meaningful way to diversify a portfolio while enjoying a high current income stream.

Over the past 10 years, ending December 31, 2002, the average annualized return of real estate funds was 8.9 percent versus 9.3 percent for the S&P 500. During the past 15 years, the best year for this sector was 1991 (32 percent) and the worst year was 1998 (-16 percent). Over the past five years, the best year was 2000 (27 percent).

The typical p/e ratio for stocks in this category is 21, a figure that is about 20 percent lower than the p/e ratio for the S&P 500. This group of funds also has an average beta of 0.2, which means that it has 80 percent less market risk than S&P 500.

The standard deviation for real estate funds is 14 percent. Historical returns over the past three, five, ten, and 15 years for real estate funds are shown here. All of the figures shown are *compound annual* rates of return (all periods ending December 31, 2002).

category	3 years	5 years	10 years	15 years
real estate funds	12.8%	2.8%	8.9%	10.1%
equity-income funds	-5.0%	0.3%	8.5%	10.3%
S&P 500	-14.6%	-0.6%	9.3%	11.5%
aggressive growth funds	-19.9%	-2.3%	5.2%	9.0%
health-care funds	-0.3%	4.8%	10.0%	15.3%

Technology. It is difficult to identify a segment of the economy that has not been profoundly influenced by technology. From traditional manufacturers developing e-commerce strategies to emerging companies with revolutionary new products, technology is changing businesses and creating unprecedented opportunities for investors. Technology represents nearly half of all business equipment spending by U.S. companies. Consumer spending on information technology as a percentage of disposable income has nearly tripled in the past 12 years. Today, just under 24 percent of the S&P 500 Index is made up of "information economy" stocks.

Historically, because of its volatility, most investors have considered the technology sector a "speculative sector play." Consequently, they have either limited their holdings in this area to a small portion of their overall portfolios or avoided them altogether.

Having perfect 20-20 hindsight, this strategy would not have appeared to be misplaced for the years 2000, 2001, and 2002 when technology funds had returns of -31 percent, -37 percent, and -43 percent, respectively. Keep in mind though, that avoiding this sector during the 1990s would have meant missing out on spectacular performance and nothing but positive returns, including 54 percent and 135 percent in 1998 and 1999, respectively.

These funds invest in common stocks of all aspects of technology, including computer hardware and software, telecommunications, semiconductor, networking, data storage, data security, fiber optics, wireless, and the Internet.

Technology is changing the way we work, live, and think. As the computer revolution evolves into the Internet and the wireless revolution, technology continues to amaze and dazzle us. This is true for investors in technology stocks as well. However, this excitement comes with significant risk.

The typical p/e ratio for stocks in this category is 38, versus 25 for the S&P 500. This group of funds has an average beta of 2.0, meaning that its market-related risk is over double that of the general market, as measured by the S&P 500. The standard deviation for technology funds is 37 percent, a figure that is significantly higher than any other category in the book except metals funds, which have a standard deviation of 40. The next closest category, aggressive growth funds, has a standard deviation of 27. This means that, as a group, technology funds are expected to have less predictable returns than almost any other fund or category in the book.

Historical returns over the past three, five, ten, and 15 years for technology funds are shown here. All of the figures shown are *compound annual* rates of return (all periods ending December 31, 2002).

category	3 years	5 years	10 years	15 years
technology funds	-37.3%	-3.2%	6.8%	12.1%
aggressive growth funds	-19.9%	-2.3%	5.2%	9.0%
growth funds	-13.8%	-0.8%	7.4%	10.1%
S&P 500	-14.6%	-0.6%	9.3%	11.5%
metals funds	17.2%	7.6%	3.0%	-0.8%

Utilities. These funds invest in common stocks of utility companies. A small percentage of the funds' assets are invested in bonds. Investors opposed to or in favor of nuclear power can seek out funds that avoid or buy into such utility companies by reviewing a fund's semiannual report or by telephoning the fund using its toll-free phone number.

If you like the usual stability of a bond fund but want more appreciation potential, then utility funds are for you. Since these funds are interest-rate sensitive, their performance somewhat parallels that of bonds but is also influenced by the stock market. The large dividend stream provided by utility funds makes them less risky than other categories of stock funds. Recession-resistant demand for electricity, gas, and other utilities translates into a comparatively steady stream of returns.

Since a healthy portion of the total return for utility funds (dividends) cannot be controlled by the investor, these funds are best suited for retirement plans or as part of some other tax-sheltered vehicle. But even if you do not have a qualified retirement plan such as an IRA, pension plan, or tax-sheltered annuity (TSA), utility funds can be a wise choice to lower overall portfolio volatility.

The average p/e ratio for this category is 18, with a standard deviation of 15 percent, a figure that is lower than that of growth and income funds. Utility funds have a beta of 0.6.

Historical returns over the past three, five, ten, and 15 years for utilities funds are shown here. All of the figures shown are *compound annual* rates of return (all periods ending December 31, 2002).

category	3 years	5 years	10 years	15 years
utility funds	-13.2%	-2.0%	4.8%	7.8%
balanced funds	-4.6%	1.5%	7.4%	9.3%
multiasset global funds	-4.0%	1.8%	6.3%	6.5%
asset allocation funds	-4.3%	1.6%	7.2%	8.7%
convertible funds	-5.2%	2.9%	7.9%	9.7%

World Bonds. Although the United States leads the world in outstanding debt, other countries and foreign corporations also issue IOUs as a way of financing projects and operations. As high as our debt seems, it is not out of line when compared to our gross national product (now called gross domestic product, GDP). The ratio of our debt to GDP is lower than any other member of the group of seven. (The other G-7 members are Germany, Japan, Canada, Italy, the United Kingdom, and France.)

International, also known as foreign, bond funds invest in fixed-income securities outside the United States. Global, or world, bond funds invest around the world, including the United States. Foreign bond funds normally offer higher yields than their domestic counterparts but also provide additional risk. Global bonds, on the other hand, provide less risk than a pure U.S. bond portfolio and also enjoy greater rates of return.

Global diversification reduces risk because the major economies around the world do not move up and down at the same time. As the United States climbs out of a recession, Japan may be just entering one, and Germany may still be in the middle of one. When Italy is trying to stimulate its economy by lowering interest rates, Canada may be raising its rates to curtail inflation. By investing in different world bond markets, you ensure that you will not be at the mercy of any one country's political environment or fiscal policy.

The weighted maturity date of the bonds within this group is just over nine years, about three years longer than U.S. government bond funds. Global bond funds have an average coupon rate of 6 percent. As with any investment that throws off a high current income, global and foreign bond funds should be part of a qualified retirement plan or variable annuity whenever possible.

The standard deviation for world bond funds is 8 percent, a low figure but still over twice the typical U.S. government bond fund. Historical returns over the past three, five, ten, and 15 years for world bond funds are shown here. All of the figures shown are *compound annual* rates of return (all periods ending December 31, 2002).

category	3 years	5 years	10 years	15 years
world bond funds	6.7%	4.7%	6.2%	6.2%
government bond funds	8.8%	6.4%	6.3%	7.4%
high-yield bond funds	-2.7%	-1.3%	4.7%	6.2%
convertible funds	-5.2%	2.9%	7.9%	9.7%
utility funds	-13.2%	-2.0%	4.8%	7.8%

All Categories. An inescapable conclusion we can draw from these different tables is that patience usually pays off. The most important thing left out of all of these tables is risk. However, we could make the case that stocks are not much riskier than bonds when the holding period is 10 to 15 years. The tables also do not take into account the tax advantages of certain investments. Government bonds are exempt from state and local income taxes. (Note: This is only true with direct obligations of the United States. It does not apply to GNMAs, FNMAs, or other government-agency issues.) Municipal bonds are exempt from federal income taxes and, depending on the type of tax-free fund as well as your state of residency, may also be exempt from any state or local taxes.

You should never consider money market funds as an investment. Money market funds, T-bills, and bank CDs are places to park your money temporarily. These accounts are best used to earn interest before you make a major purchase, while you are learning about investing in general, or until market conditions change. Almost all investors should avoid metals funds. The track record of this category is wild and usually negative. It is doubtful that a strong case can be made for metals. You can diversify and reduce your risk by owning other categories such as money market, one or more of the bond categories, and even possibly natural resources.

Compound Annual Returns for the 15-Year Period
Ending December 31, 2002

category	15-year returns	category	15-year returns
aggressive growth	9.0%	high-yield bonds	6.2%
asset allocation	8.7%	metals	-0.8%
balanced	9.3%	money market	5.0%
convertibles	9.7%	multiasset global	6.5%
corporate bond	7.7%	municipal bond	6.8%
equity-income	10.3%	natural resources	7.9%
European stocks	4.8%	Pacific Basin stocks	1.8%
financial stocks	16.0%	real estate	10.1%
foreign stocks	6.6%	technology	12.1%
global stocks	6.7%	utilities	7.8%
government bonds	6.6%	world bond	6.2%
growth	10.1%		
growth & income	10.3%	*S&P 500*	11.5%
health-care stocks	15.3%	*CPI (inflation)*	3.0%

A common theme throughout this book is that, given time, equity (the different stock categories) always outperforms debt (the different bond categories). This does not mean that all of your money should be in the equity categories. Not everyone has the same level of patience or time horizon. It does mean that the great majority of investors need to review their portfolios and perhaps begin to emphasize domestic and even foreign stocks more.

VI.
Which Funds Are Best for You?

When asked what they are looking for, investors typically say, "I want the best." This could mean that they are looking for the most safety and greatest current income or the highest total return. There is no single "best" fund. The top-performing fund may have incredible volatility, causing shareholders to redeem their shares at the first sign of trouble. The "safest" fund may be devastated by risks not previously considered: inflation and taxes.

As you have already seen, there are several different categories of mutual funds, ranging from tax-free money market accounts to precious metals. During one period or another, each of these categories has dominated some periodical's "ten best funds" list. These impressive scores may only last a quarter, six months, or a year. The fact is that no one knows what the next best-performing category or individual fund will be.

For some fund groups—such as international stocks, growth, growth and income, and aggressive growth—the reign may last for several years. For other categories—such as money market, government bond, and precious metals—the glory may last a year or even less. Trying to outguess, chart, or follow a financial guru in order to determine the next trend is a fool's paradise. The notion that anyone has special insights into the marketplace is sheer nonsense. Countless neutral and lengthy studies attest to this fact. If this is the case, what should we do?

Step 1: Categories That Have Done Well Historically
The first step is to look at those generic categories of investments that have done well over long periods. A time frame of at least 15 or 20 years is recommended. True, your investment horizon may be a fraction of this, but keep in mind two points. First, 15 or 20 years includes good as well as bad times. Second, bad results cannot be hidden when you are studying the long term. Even the investor looking at a one- or two-year holding period should ask, "Do I want something that does phenomenally well one out of every five years, or do I want something that has a very good return in eight or nine out of every 10 years?" Unless you are a gambler, the answer is obvious.

All investments can be categorized as either debt or equity instruments. Debt instruments in this book include corporate bonds, government bonds, high-yield bonds, international bonds, money market accounts, and municipal bonds. Equity instruments include growth, growth and income, international stocks, metals, and utility funds. Four other categories are hybrid instruments: asset allocation; and balanced, convertible, and multiasset global funds. In this book, these four categories are combined under the heading "balanced."

26

Throughout history, equity has outperformed debt. The longer the time frame reviewed, the better equity vehicles look. Over the past half century, the worst 15-year holding period performance for stocks (+4.3 percent per year) was very similar to the average 15-year holding period performance for long-term government bonds (+4.9 percent per year). For 20-year holding periods, the worst period for common stocks has been more than 40 percent better than the average for long-term government bonds. Indeed, stocks have outperformed bonds in every decade. Look at it this way: Would you rather have loaned Henry Ford or Bill Gates the money to start their companies, or would you rather have given them money in return for a piece of the action?

Step 2: Review Your Objectives

Decide what you are trying to do with your portfolio. Everyone wants one of the following: growth, current income, or a combination of growth and income. Don't assume that if you are looking for current income, your money should go into a bond or money market fund. There is a way to set up an equity fund so it will give you a high monthly income. This is known as a "systematic withdrawal plan" and is discussed in Appendix D. The growth-oriented investor, on the other hand, should consider certain categories of debt instruments or hybrid securities to help add more stability to a portfolio.

Objectives are certainly important, but so is the element of time. The shorter the time frame and the greater the need for assurances, the greater the likelihood that debt instruments should be used. A growth investor who is looking at a single-year time frame and wants a degree of safety is probably better off in a series of bond and/or money market accounts. On the other hand, the longer the commitment, the better equities look. Thus, even a cautious investor who has a life expectancy (or whose spouse has a life expectancy) of 10 years or more should seriously consider having at least a moderate portion of his or her portfolio in equities.

A retired couple in their sixties should realize that one or both of them will probably live at least 15 more years. Since this is the case, and since we know that equities have almost always outperformed bonds when looking at a horizon of 10 years or more, their emphasis should be in this area.

The conservative investor may say that stocks are too risky. True, the day-to-day or year-to-year volatility of equities can be quite disturbing. However, it is also true that the medium- and long-term effects of inflation and the resulting diminished purchasing power of a fixed-income investment are even more devastating. At least with an equity there is a better than 50-50 chance that it will go up in value. In the case of inflation, what are the chances that the cost of goods and services will go down during the next one, three, five, or 10 years? The answer is "not likely."

Step 3: Ascertain Your Risk Level

No investment is worthwhile if you stay awake at night worrying about it. If you do not already know or are uncertain about your risk level, contact your financial advisor. These professionals usually have some kind of questionnaire that you can answer. Your responses will give a good indication of which investments are proper for you and which should be avoided. If you do not deal with a financial advisor, take the following test. Your score, and what it means, are shown at the end of the questionnaire.

Test for Determining Your Risk Level

1. "I invest for the long term, five to 10 years or more. The final result is more important than daily, monthly, or annual fluctuations in value."

(10) Totally disagree. (20) Willing to accept some volatility, but not loss of principal. (30) Could accept a moderate amount of yearly fluctuation in return for a good total return. (40) Would accept an occasional negative year if the final results were good. (50) Agree.

2. Rank the importance of current income.

(10) Crucial, the exact amount must be known. (20) Important, but I am willing to have the amount vary each period. (30) Fairly important, but other aspects of investing are also of concern. (40) Only a modest amount of income is needed. (50) Current income is unimportant.

3. Rank the amount of loss you could tolerate in a single quarter.

(10) None. (20) A little, but over a year's time the total value of the investment should not decline. (30) Consistency of total return is more important than trying to get big gains. (40) One or two quarters of negative returns are the price you must pay when looking at the total picture. (50) Unimportant.

4. Rank the importance of beating inflation.

(10) Factors such as preservation of principal and current income are much more important. (20) I am willing to have a slight variance in my returns, on a quarterly basis only, in order to have at least a partial hedge against inflation. (30) Could accept some annual volatility in order to offset inflation. (40) I consider inflation to be important, but have mixed feelings about how much volatility I could accept from one year to the next. (50) The long-term effects of inflation are devastating and should not be ignored by anyone.

5. Rank the importance of beating the stock market over any given two- to three-year period.

(10) Irrelevant. (20) A small concern. (30) Fairly important. (40) Very important. (50) Absolutely crucial.

Add up your score from questions 1 through 5. Your risk, as defined by your total point score, is as follows: 0–50 points = extremely conservative; 50–100 points = somewhat conservative; 100–150 points = moderate; 150–200 points = somewhat aggressive; 200–250 points = very aggressive.

Step 4: Review Your Current Holdings

Everyone has heard the expression, "Don't put all your eggs in one basket." This advice also applies to investing. No matter how much we like investment X, if a third of our net worth is already in X, we probably should not add any more to this investment. After all, there is more than one good investment.

Since no single investment category is the top performer every year, it makes sense to diversify into several fundamentally good categories. By using proper diversification, we have an excellent chance of being number one with a portion of our portfolio every year. Babe Ruth may have hit more home runs than almost anyone, but he also struck out more. As investors, we should be content with consistently hitting doubles and triples.

Trying to hit a homer every time may result in financial ruin. Never lose track of the fact that losses always have a greater impact than gains. An investment that goes up 50 percent the first year and falls 50 percent the next year still has a net loss of 25 percent. This philosophy is emphasized throughout the book.

Step 5: Implementation

There is no such thing as the perfect time to invest. No matter how strongly you or some "expert" individual or publication believes that the market is going to go up or down, no one actually knows.

After you have properly educated yourself is the right time to invest. If you are afraid to take the big plunge, consider some form of dollar-cost averaging (see Appendix C). This is a disciplined approach to investing; it also reduces your risk exposure significantly.

Do read investment books and attend classes. Some people, however, may be tempted to remain on the sidelines indefinitely. For such people, there is no perfect time to invest. If the stock market drops 200 points, they are waiting for the next 100-point drop. If stocks or bonds are up 15 percent, they say things are peaking and they will invest as soon as it drops by 10 percent. If the stock or bond market does drop by that magical figure, these same investors are now certain that it will drop another 10 percent.

This "strategy" is frustrating. More important, it is wrong. You can look back in history and find lots of reasons not to have invested. But the fact is that all of the investments in this book have gone up almost every year. The "wait and see" approach is a poor one; the same reasons for not investing will still exist in the present and throughout the future.

Remember, your money is doing something right now. It is invested somewhere. If it is under the mattress, it is being eaten away by inflation. If it is in a "risk-free" investment, such as an insured savings account, bank CD, or U.S. Treasury bill, it is being subjected to taxation and the cumulative effects of reduced purchasing power. Do not think you can hide by having your money in some safe haven. Once you understand that there can be things worse than market swings, you will become an educated investor who knows there is no such thing as a truly risk-free place or investment.

If you are still not convinced, consider the story of "Louie the loser." There is only one thing you can say about Louie's timing: It is always awful. So, it is no surprise that when he decided to invest $10,000 a year in Investment Company of America, he managed to pick the worst possible times. Every year for the past 20 years (1983–2002), he has invested on the very day that the stock market peaked. How has he done? He has over $653,930, which means his money has grown at an average rate of 10.9 percent a year (a cumulative investment of $200,000; 20 years times $10,000 invested each year).

If Louie had had "perfect timing," meaning he invested $10,000 on the worst day of the market each year for the past 20 years, his cumulative $200,000 investment would have grown to $802,100, or 12.2 percent annualized.

After asking you a series of questions, your investment advisor can give you a framework within which to operate. Investors who do not have a good advisor may wish to look at the different sample portfolios given here. These general recommendations will provide you with a sense of direction.

The Conservative Investor
15 percent balanced
10 percent utilities
15 percent growth and income (value oriented)
10 percent world bond
20 percent money market or short-term bonds
30 percent intermediate-term municipal or government bonds
  (depending on your tax bracket)

This portfolio would give you a weighting of 33 percent in equities (stocks) and 67 percent in debt instruments (bonds and cash equivalents). Investors who are not in a high federal income tax bracket may wish to avoid municipal bonds completely and use government bonds instead.

If your tax bracket is such that you are not sure whether you should own tax-free or taxable bonds (if, that is, the after-tax return on government bonds is similar to what a similarly maturing high-quality municipal bond pays), lean toward a municipal bond fund. These funds are almost always less volatile than a government bond fund that has the same or a similar average maturity.

The Moderate Investor
10 percent small-company growth (value oriented)
 5 percent balanced/convertibles
10 percent growth (value oriented)
15 percent growth and income (value oriented)
10 percent high-yield
10 percent short-term bonds
10 percent world bonds
15 percent global equities (value oriented)
10 percent health care
 5 percent financial

This portfolio would give you a weighting of 67 percent in equities (common stocks) and 33 percent in debt instruments. The figures are a little misleading since high-yield bonds are more of a hybrid investment: part stock and part bond. The price, or value, of high-yield bonds is influenced by economic (macro and micro) news as well as interest rate changes. Whereas government, municipal, and high-quality corporate bonds often react favorably to bad economic news such as a recession, increases in the jobless rate, a slowdown in housing starts, and so on; high-yield bonds have a tendency to view such news positively. Thus, taking into account that high-yield bonds are about halfway between traditional bonds and stocks, the weighting distribution is more in the range of 72 percent equities and 28 percent bonds.

The Aggressive Investor
15 percent aggressive growth
20 percent small-company growth (value oriented)
20 percent growth (value oriented)
10 percent growth and income
15 percent health care
10 percent financial
10 percent real estate

This portfolio would give you a weighting of 100 percent in equities. Bond fund categories, with the possible exception of high-yield and international, are not recommended for the aggressive investor because they usually do not have enough appreciation potential.

Readers of the previous editions of this book may notice that this edition weighs equities (the different stock categories) less than it has in the past. This is because stock valuations as a whole are grossly out of line. The price-earnings ratios of the typical growth fund are at, or slightly higher than, the levels seen at the market's peak during the first quarter of 2000. Value-oriented equities are a much more attractive alternative to growth stocks, using current as well as historical comparisons.

Step 6: Review

After implementation, it is important that you keep track of how you are doing. One of the beauties of mutual funds is that, if you choose a fund with good management, managers will do their job and you can spend your time on something else. Nevertheless, review your situation at least quarterly. Once you feel comfortable with your portfolio, review it only semiannually or annually.

Daily or weekly tracking is pointless. If a particular investment goes up or down 5 percent, that does not mean you should rush out and buy more or sell off. That same investment may do just the opposite the following week or month. By watching your investments too closely, you will be defeating a major attribute of mutual funds: professional management. Presumably these fund managers know a lot more about their particular investments than you do. If they do not, you should either choose another fund or start your own mutual fund.

Step 7: Relax

If you do your homework by reading this book, you will be in fine shape. There are several thousand mutual funds. Some funds are just plain bad. Most mutual funds are mediocre. And, as with everything else in this world, a small portion are truly excellent. This book has taken those thousands of funds and eliminated all of the bad, mediocre, and fairly good. Only excellent mutual funds remain.

If you would like help designing a portfolio or picking a specific fund, telephone the Institute of Business & Finance (1-800-848-2029). The institute will be able to give you the names and telephone numbers of Certified Fund Specialists (CFS) in your area. To become a CFS, an individual must complete a rigorous, one-year educational program, pass a comprehensive exam, adhere to a professional code of ethics, and meet annual continuing education requirements.

VII.
Fund Features

Advantages of Mutual Funds

Listed here are some of the features of mutual funds—advantages not found in other kinds of investments.

Ease of Purchase. Mutual fund shares are easy to buy. For those who prefer to make investment decisions themselves, mutual funds are as close as the telephone or the mailbox. Those who would like help choosing a fund can draw on a wide variety of sources.

Many funds sell their shares through stockbrokers, financial planners, or insurance agents. These representatives can help you analyze your financial needs and objectives and recommend appropriate funds. For these professional services, you may be charged a sales commission, usually referred to as a "load." This charge is expressed as a percentage of the total purchase price of the fund shares. In some cases, there is no initial sales charge, or load, but there may be an annual fee and/or another charge if shares are redeemed during the first few years of ownership.

Other funds distribute their shares directly to the public. They may advertise in magazines and newspapers; most can be reached through toll-free telephone numbers. Because there are no sales agents involved, most of these funds, often called "no loads," charge a much lower fee or no sales commission at all. With these funds, it is generally up to you to do your investment homework.

In order to attract new shareholders, some funds have adopted 12b-1 plans (named after a federal government rule). These plans enable the fund to pay its own distribution costs. Distribution costs are those costs associated with marketing the fund, either through sales agents or through advertising. The 12b-1 fee is charged against fund assets and is paid indirectly by existing shareholders. Annual distribution fees of this type usually range between 0.1 percent and 1.25 percent of the value of the account.

Fees charged by a fund are described in the prospectus. In addition, a fee table listing all transactional fees and all annual fund expenses can be found at the front of the prospectus.

Access to Your Money (Marketability). Mutual funds, by law, must stand ready on any business day to redeem any or all of your shares at their current net asset value (NAV). Of course, the value may be greater or less than the price you originally paid, depending on the market.

To sell shares back to the fund, all you need to do is give the fund proper notification, as explained in the prospectus. Most funds will accept such notification by telephone; some funds require a written request. The fund will then send your check promptly. In most instances, the fund will issue a check when it receives the notification; by law, the fund must send you the check within seven business days. You receive the price your shares are worth on the day the fund gets proper notice of redemption from you. If you own a money market fund, you can also redeem shares by writing checks directly against your fund balance.

Disciplined Investment. The majority of funds allow you to set up what is known as a "check-o-matic plan." Under such a program, a set amount of money is automatically deducted from your checking account each month and sent directly to the mutual fund of your choice. Your bank (or credit union) will not charge you for this service. Mutual funds also offer such programs free of charge. Automatic investment plans can be changed or terminated at any time, again at no charge.

Exchange Privileges. As the economy or your own personal circumstances change, the kinds of funds you hold may no longer be the ones you need. Many mutual funds are part of a "family of funds" and offer a feature called an exchange privilege. Within a family of funds there may be several choices, each with a different investment objective, varying from highly conservative funds to more aggressive funds that carry a higher degree of risk. An exchange privilege allows you to transfer all or part of your money from one of these funds to another. Exchange policies vary from fund to fund. The fee for an exchange is nominal, five dollars or less. For the specifics about a fund's exchange privilege, check the prospectus.

Automatic Reinvestment. You can elect to have any dividends and capital gains distributions from your mutual fund investment turned back into the fund, automatically buying new shares and expanding your current holdings. Most shareholders opt for the reinvestment privilege. There is usually no cost or fee involved.

Automatic Withdrawal. You can make arrangements with the fund to automatically send you, or anyone you designate, checks from the fund's earnings or principal. This system works well for retirees, families who want to arrange for payments to their children at college, or anyone needing monthly income checks. See Appendix D for a more detailed example of how a systematic withdrawal plan works.

Detailed Record Keeping. The fund will handle all the paperwork and record keeping necessary to keep track of your investment transactions. A typical statement will note such items as your most recent investment or withdrawal and any dividends or capital gains paid to you in cash or reinvested in the fund. The fund will also report to you on the tax status of your earnings. If you lose any paperwork, the fund will send you copies of current or past statements.

Retirement Plans. Financial experts have long viewed mutual funds as appropriate vehicles for retirement investing; indeed, they are quite commonly used for this purpose. For retirees over the age of 70½, mutual fund companies will recompute the minimum amount that needs to be taken out each year, as dictated by the IRS. Mutual funds are ideal for Keoghs, IRAs, 401(k) plans, and other employer-sponsored retirement plans. Many funds offer prototype retirement plans and standard IRA agreements. Having your own retirement plan drafted by a law firm would cost you thousands of dollars, not to mention the fees for the updates that would be needed every time the laws change. Mutual funds offer these plans and required updates for free.

Accountability. There are literally dozens of sources that track and monitor mutual funds. It is easy to determine a fund's track record and volatility over several different time periods. Federal regulatory bodies such as the NASD (National Association of Securities Dealers) and the SEC (Securities and Exchange Commission) have strict rules concerning performance figures and what appears in advertisements, brochures, and prospectuses.

Flexibility. Investment choices are almost endless: domestic stocks, foreign debt, international equities, government obligations, money market instruments, convertible securities, short- and intermediate-term bonds, real estate, gold, and natural resources. You are only limited by the choices offered by the fund family or families you are invested in. And because you can move part or all of your money from one mutual fund to another fund within the same family, usually for a minimal transfer fee, your portfolio can become more aggressive, conservative, or moderate with a simple phone call.

Economies of Scale. As a shareholder (investor) in a fund, you automatically get the benefit of reduced transaction charges. Since a fund often buys or sells thousands of shares of stock at a time, it is able to conduct its transactions at dramatically reduced costs. The fees a fund pays are far lower than what you would pay even if you were buying several hundred shares of a stock from a discount broker. The same is true when it comes to bonds. Funds are able to add them to their portfolio without any markup. When you buy a bond through a broker, even a discounter, there is always a markup; it is hidden in the price you pay and sell the bond for. The savings for bond investors ranges anywhere from less than 1 percent all the way up to 5 percent.

Risk Reduction: Importance of Diversification

If there is one ingredient to successful investing that is universally agreed on, it is the benefit of diversification. This concept is also backed by a great deal of research and market experience. The benefit provided by diversification is risk reduction. Risk to investors is frequently defined as volatility of return; in other words, how much an investment's return might vary. Investors prefer returns that are relatively predictable, which is to say, less volatile. On the other hand, they want returns to be high. Diversification eliminates most of the risk without reducing potential returns.

A fund's portfolio manager(s) will normally invest the fund's pool of money in 50 to 150 different securities to spread the fund's holdings over a number of investments. This diversification is an important principle in lessening the fund's overall investment risk. Such diversification is typically beyond the financial capacity of most individual investors. The following table shows the relationship between diversification and investment risk, defined as the variability of annual returns of a stock portfolio.

number of stocks	risk ratio
1	6.6
2	3.8
4	2.4
10	1.6
50	1.1
100	1.0

Note that the variability of return, or risk, associated with holding just one stock is more than six times that of a 100-stock portfolio. Yet, the increased potential return found in a portfolio made up of a small number of stocks is minimal.

VIII.
Reading a Mutual Fund Prospectus

The purpose of the fund's prospectus is to provide the reader with full and complete disclosure. The prospectus covers the following key points:

- The fund's investment objective: what the managers are trying to achieve
- The investment methods it uses in trying to achieve this objective
- The name and address of its investment advisor and a brief description of the advisor's experience
- The level of investment risk the fund is willing to assume in pursuit of its investment objective
- Any investments the fund will not make (for example, real estate, options, or commodities)
- Tax consequences of the investment for the shareholder
- How to purchase shares of the fund, including the cost of investing
- How to redeem shares
- Services provided, such as IRAs, automatic investment of dividends and capital gains distributions, check writing, withdrawal plans, and any other features
- A condensed financial statement (in tabular form, covering the past 10 years, or the period the fund has been in existence, if less than 10 years) called "Per-Share Income and Capital Changes." (The fund's performance may be calculated from the information given in this table.)
- A tabular statement of any fees charged by the fund and their effect on earnings over time

IX.
Commonly Asked Questions

Q Are mutual funds a new kind of investment?

No. In fact, they have roots in eighteenth-century Scotland. The first U.S. mutual fund was organized in Boston in 1924. This fund, Massachusetts Investors Trust, is still in existence today. Several mutual fund companies have been in operation for over half a century.

Q How much money do you need to invest in a mutual fund?

Literally anywhere from a few dollars to several million. Many funds have no minimum requirements for investing. A few funds are open to large institutional accounts only. The vast majority of funds require a minimum investment of between $250 and $1,000.

Q Do mutual funds offer a fixed rate of return?

No. Mutual funds invest in securities such as stocks, bonds, and money market accounts whose yields and values fluctuate with market conditions.

Mutual funds can make money for their shareholders in three ways. First, they pay their shareholders dividends earned from the fund's investments. Second, if a security held by a fund is sold at a profit, funds pay their shareholders capital gains distributions. And third, if the value of the securities held by the fund increases, the value of each mutual fund share also increases.

In none of these cases, however, can a return be guaranteed. In fact, it is against the law for a mutual fund to make a claim as to its future performance. Ads quoting returns are based on past performance and should not be interpreted as a fixed rate yield. Past performance should not be taken as a predictor of future earnings.

Q What are the risks of mutual fund investing?

Mutual funds are investments in financial securities with fluctuating values. The value of the securities in a fund's portfolio, for example, will rise and fall according to general economic conditions and the fortunes of the particular companies that issue those securities. Even the most conservative assets, such as U.S. government obligations, will fluctuate in value as interest rates change. These are risks that investors should be aware of when purchasing mutual fund shares.

Q How can I evaluate a fund's long-term performance?

You can calculate a fund's performance by referring to the section in the prospectus headed "Per-Share Income and Capital Changes." This section will give you the figures you need to compute the annual rates of return earned by the fund each year for the past 10 years (or for the life of the fund if less than 10 years). There are also several periodicals that track the performance of funds on a regular basis. Or, you can telephone the fund, and they will give you performance figures.

Q What's the difference between yield and total return?

Yield is the income per share paid to a shareholder from the dividends and interest over a specified period. Yield is expressed as a percentage of the current offering price per share.

Total return is a measure of the per-share change in total value from the beginning to the end of a specified period, usually a year, including distributions paid to shareholders. This measure includes income received from dividends and interest, capital gains distributions, and any unrealized capital gains or losses. Total return looks at the whole picture: appreciation (or loss) of principal plus any dividends or income. Total return provides the best measure of overall fund performance; do not be misled by an enticing yield.

Q How much does it cost to invest in a mutual fund?

A mutual fund normally contracts with its management company to provide for most of the needs of a normal business. The management company is paid a fee for these services, which usually include managing the fund's investments.

In addition, the fund may pay directly for some of its costs, such as printing, mailing, accounting, and legal services. Typically, these two annual charges average 1.5 percent. In such a fund you would be paying $10 to $15 a year on every $1,000 invested.

Some fund directors have adopted plans (with the approval of the fund's shareholders) that allow them to pay certain distribution costs (the costs of advertising, for example) directly from fund assets. These costs may range from 0.1 percent to 1.25 percent annually.

There may also be other charges involved—for example, for exchanging shares. Some funds may charge a redemption fee when a shareholder redeems his or her shares, usually within five years of purchasing them. All costs and charges assessed by the fund organization are disclosed in its prospectus.

Q Is the management fee part of the sales charge?

No, the management fee paid by the fund to its investment advisor is for services rendered in managing the fund's portfolio. An average fee ranges from 0.5 percent to 1.0 percent of the fund's total assets each year. As described earlier, the management fee and other business expenses generally total somewhere between 1.0 percent and 1.5 percent. These expenses are paid from the fund's assets and are reflected in the price of the fund shares. In contrast, most sales charges are deducted from your initial investment.

Q Is my money locked up for a certain period in a mutual fund?

Unlike some other types of financial accounts, mutual funds are liquid investments. That means that any shares an investor owns may be redeemed freely on any day the fund is open for business. Since a mutual fund stands ready to buy back its shares at their current net asset value, you always have a buyer for your shares at current market value.

Q How often do I get statements from a mutual fund?

Mutual funds ordinarily send immediate confirmation statements when an investor purchases or redeems (sells) shares. Statements alerting shareholders to reinvested dividends are sent out periodically. At least semiannually, investors also receive statements on the status of the fund's investments. Tax statements, referred to as "substitute 1099s," are mailed annually. Some funds automatically send out quarterly reports.

Q I've already purchased shares of a mutual fund. How can I tell how well my investment is doing?

Figuring out how well your fund is faring is a two-step procedure. First, you need to know how many shares you now own. The *now* is emphasized because if you have asked the fund to plow any dividends and capital gains distributions back into the fund for you, it will do so by issuing you more shares, thereby increasing the value of your investment. Once you know how many shares you own, look up the fund's net assets value (sometimes called the sell or bid price) in the financial section of a major metropolitan daily newspaper. Next, multiply the net asset value by the number of shares you own to figure out the value of your investment as of that date. Compare today's value against your beginning value.

You will need to keep the confirmation statements you receive when you first purchase shares and as you make subsequent purchases in order to compare present value to the original purchase value. You will also need these statements for tax purposes.

Q Do investment experts recommend mutual funds for IRAs and other qualified plans?

Financial experts view many mutual funds as compatible with the long-term objectives of saving for retirement. Indeed, fund shareholders cite this reason for investing more than any other. Many kinds of funds work best when allowed to ride out the ups and downs of market cycles over long periods.

Funds can also offer the owner of an IRA, Keogh, pension plan, 401(k), or 403(b) flexibility. By using the exchange privilege within a family of funds, the investor can shift investments from one kind of security to another in response to changes in personal finances or the economic outlook, or as retirement approaches.

Q Are money market funds a good investment?

No. If I were to recommend an investment to you that lost money in 17 of the past 25 calendar years (adjusted for income taxes and inflation), you would probably balk. Yet, this is the track record of CDs, money market accounts, and T-bills. Money market funds are an excellent place to park your money for the short-term; that is, some period less than two years.

Q Why don't more people invest in foreign (international) securities?

Ignorance. The reality is that foreign securities (stocks and bonds), when added to domestic investments, actually reduce the portfolio's level of risk. Stock and bond markets around the world rarely move up and down at the same time. This random correlation is what helps lower risk and volatility: When U.S. stocks (or bonds) are going down, securities in other parts of the world may well be moving sideways or going up.

Q Is standard deviation the correct way to measure risk?

No. Standard deviation measures volatility (or predictability) of returns. The standard deviation for each of the mutual funds in this book is ranked under the star system next to the heading "predictability of returns." The system used in this book for measuring risk is different, punishing funds for performance that is less than that offered by T-bills, a figure commonly referred to as the "risk-free rate of return." To me, this makes more sense than a system that punishes a fund for volatility by translating its high standard deviation figure as "high risk." This is what most financial writers do, whether the volatility the fund experienced was upward or downward volatility. I have yet to meet an investor who is upset that he or she did better than expected. No one minds upward volatility.

Q Why not simply invest in those funds that were the best performers over the past one, three, five, or 10 years?

This would be a big mistake. There is little relationship (or correlation) between the performance of one fund or fund category from one year to the next. This, by the way, is the way most investors and advisors select investments— making this one of the biggest and costliest mistakes one could make. Unfortunately, no one knows what the next best-performing fund or category will be.

Q What are you referring to when you talk about "common stocks"?

Whenever you see the words *common stocks*, they refer to the Standard & Poor's 500 (S&P 500). The S&P 500 is comprised of 500 of many of the largest corporations in the United States, representing several industry groups. As of the middle of 1998, there had been 75 changes made to the S&P 500 since the beginning of 1995. The purpose of these changes is to make the index more representative of the U.S. economy and the stock market. As an example, financial stocks now represent 15 percent of the S&P 500 capitalization, up from 8 percent in 1990; technology stocks represent 14 percent, up from 7 percent in 1990 (Microsoft, which was added to the index in 1994, makes up 2.3 percent of the index). In short, the S&P 500 is higher growth, more global, less cyclical, and more diversified than it has ever been (and therefore deserves a higher p/e ratio than in the past).

Q Speaking of common stocks, what are the odds of making money in the market?

If you think investing in the market is too risky, consider what the odds are for the following.

You will win a state lottery?	1 in 4 million
You will be dealt a royal flush poker hand?	1 in 649,739
Earth will be struck by a huge meteor during your lifetime?	1 in 9,000
You will be robbed this year?	1 in 500
The airlines will lose your luggage?	1 in 186
You will be audited by the IRS?	1 in 100
You will roll dice and get snake eyes?	1 in 36
You will go to Disney World this year?	1 in 9
The next bottled water you buy will be nothing more than tap water?	1 in 4
You will eat out today?	1 in 2
An investment in stocks will make money in any given year?	7 in 10
You will regain the weight you lost by dieting?	9 in 10

Source: What the Odds Are, by Les Krantz (Harper Perennial, 1992)

X.
How the 100 Best Funds Were Determined

With an entry field that numbers more than 13,000, it is no easy task to determine the 100 best mutual funds. Magazines and newspapers report on the "best" by relying on performance figures over a specific period, usually one, three, five, or 10 years. Investors often rely on these sources and invest accordingly, only to be disappointed later.

Studies from around the world bear out what investors typically experience: that there is no correlation between the performance of a stock or bond from one year to the next. The same can be said for individual money managers—and sadly, for most mutual funds.

The criteria used to determine the 100 best mutual funds are unique and far-reaching. For a fund to be considered for this book, it had to pass several tests. First, all stock and bond funds that have had managers for less than five years were excluded; in the case of money market funds, the only remaining category, the criterion was liberalized since overhead costs have a much greater bearing on net returns than management's expertise.

This first step alone eliminated well over half the contenders. The reason for the cutoff is simple: A fund is often only as good as its manager. An outstanding 10-year track record may be cited in a periodical, but how relevant is this performance if the manager who oversaw the fund left a year or two ago? This criterion was liberalized in selecting money market funds because this category of funds normally requires less expertise.

Second, any fund that places in the bottom (worst) half of its category's risk ranking is excluded. No matter how profitable the finish line looks, the number of investors will be sparse if the fund demonstrates too much negative activity. In most cases, a little performance was gladly given up if a great deal of risk was eliminated. This reflects the book's philosophy that returns must be viewed in relation to the amount of risk that was taken. In most cases the funds described in the book possess outstanding risk management. Those few selected funds where risk control has been less than stellar have shown tremendous performance, and their risky nature has been highlighted to warn the reader.

Virtually all sources measure risk by standard deviation. Determining an investment's standard deviation is not as difficult as you might imagine. First, you calculate the asset's average annual return. Usually, the most recent three years are used, updated each quarter. Once an average annual rate of return is determined, a line is drawn on a graph, representing this return.

Next, the monthly returns are plotted on the graph. Since three years is a commonly accepted time period for such calculations, a total of 36 individual points are plotted—one for each month over the past three years. After these points are plotted, the standard deviation can be determined. Quite simply, standard deviation measures the variance of returns from the norm (the line drawn on a graph).

There is a problem in using standard deviation to determine the risk level of any investment, including a mutual fund. The shortcoming of this method is that standard deviation punishes good as well as bad results. An example will help expose the problem.

Suppose there were two different investments, X and Y. Investment X went up almost every month by exactly 1.5 percent but had a few months each year when it went down 1 percent. Investment Y went up only 1 percent most months, but it always went up 6 percent for each of the final months of the year. The standard deviation of Y would be substantially higher than X. It might be so high that we would avoid it because it was classified as "high risk." The fact is that we would love to own such an investment. No one ever minds upward volatility or surprises; it is only negative or downward volatility that is cause for alarm.

The system used for determining risk in this book is not widely used, but it is certainly a fairer and more meaningful measurement. The book's method for determining risk is to see how many months over the past three years a fund underperformed what is popularly referred to as a "risk-free vehicle," such as a bank CD or U.S. Treasury bill. The more months a fund falls below this safe return, the greater the fund will be punished in its risk ranking.

Third, the fund must have performed well for the past three and five years. A one- or two-year time horizon could be attributed to luck or nonrecurring events. A 10- or 15-year period would certainly be better, if not for the reality that the overwhelming majority of funds are managed by a different person today than they were even six years ago. More disturbing is the fact that investors do not stay with a fund for five years or more.

Finally, the fund must either possess an excellent risk-adjusted return or have had superior returns with no more than average levels of risk. It is assumed that most readers are equally concerned with risk and reward. Thus, the foundation of the text is based on which mutual funds have the best risk-adjusted returns.

Sadly, some funds were excluded, despite their superior performance and risk control, because they were either less than five years old, had new management, or were closed to new investors. A few funds in this edition have excellent returns with poorer-than-average levels of risk or had a risk level that was lower than its respective category average. The reasons that a handful of these funds were still included are evident when you read about them later in the book.

XI.
The 100 Best Funds

This section describes the 100 very best funds. As discussed, the methodology used to narrow down the universe of funds is based on performance, risk, and management.

Every one of these 100 funds is a superlative choice. However, there must still be a means to compare and rank each of the funds within its peer group. Each fund is first categorized by its investment objective. The category breakdown is as follows:

category of mutual fund	number
aggressive growth	10
balanced	9
corporate bond	6
financial	2
global equity	7
government bond	5
growth	9
growth & income	9
health care	2
high-yield bonds	5
metals/natural resources	4
money market	11
municipal bonds	9
real estate	2
technology	2
utilities	4
world bonds	4
total	**100 funds**

There are five areas to be ranked: total return, risk/volatility, management, tax minimization (current income in the case of bond, hybrid, and money market funds), and expense control. Of these five classifications, management, risk/volatility, and total return are the most important.

The track record of a fund is only as good as its management, which is why extensive space is given to this section for each fund. The areas of concern are the length of time the manager, or team, has overseen the fund, and management's background and investment philosophy.

The risk/volatility of the fund is the second biggest concern. Investors like to invest in things that have somewhat predictable results—that aren't up 60 percent one year and down 25 percent the next. A few such highly volatile funds are included, but the risk associated with such a fund is clearly highlighted, informing the prospective investor.

Total return was the third concern. When all is said and done, people like to make lots of money with an acceptable level of risk, or at least get decent returns by taking little, if any, risk. This is also known as the risk-adjusted return. So, although the very safest funds within each category were preferred, this safety had to be combined with impressive returns.

The fourth category, current income, was of lesser importance. Income is important to a lot of people but often gets in the way of selecting the proper investment; preservation of capital should also be considered. There is a better way to get current income than to rely on monthly dividend or interest checks. This is known as a systematic withdrawal plan (SWP). A 66-year example of a SWP is shown in Appendix D. Current income-oriented investors will truly be amazed when they see how such a system works.

In the case of equity funds, "tax minimization" was substituted for the category "current income." This was done for two reasons. First, there is no reason a fund whose objective is capital appreciation should be punished simply because it does not throw off a high dividend. Once you are familiar with the benefits of using a systematic withdrawal plan, you will no longer care whether a certain aggressive growth or even growth and income fund pays much in the form of dividends. Second, unless your money is sheltered in a qualified retirement plan (IRA, pension plan, etc.), income taxes are a real concern. Funds should be rewarded for minimizing shareholder tax liability. This is why every mutual fund in the book is rated, one way or another, when it comes to personal income taxes.

Tax-conscious investors want to downplay current income as much as possible. For them, a high current income simply means paying more in taxes. For other categories—such as growth and income, utilities, and balanced—a healthy current income stream often translates into lower risk. And for still other categories—such as corporate bonds, government bonds, international bonds, money market, and municipal bonds—current income is, and rightfully should be, a major determinant for selection.

The final category, expenses, rates how effective management is in operating the fund. High expense ratios for a given category mean that the advisors are either too greedy or simply do not know or care about running an efficient operation. The actual expenses incurred by a fund are not directly seen by the client, but such costs are deducted from the portfolio's gross returns, which is important.

In addition to looking at the expense ratio of a fund, the turnover rate is studied. The turnover rate shows how often the fund buys and sells its securities. There is a real cost when such a transaction occurs. These transaction costs, also known as commissions, are borne by the fund and eat into the gross return figures. Expense ratios do not include transaction costs incurred when management decides to replace or add a security. Thus, expense ratios do not tell the whole story. By scrutinizing the turnover rate, the rankings take into account excessive trading. A fund's turnover rate may represent a larger true cost to the investor than the fund's expense ratio.

Each fund is ranked in each of these five categories. The rating ranges from zero to five points (stars) in each category. The points can be transcribed as follows: zero points = poor, one point = fair, two points = good, three points = very good, four points = superior, and five points = excellent.

All of the rankings for each fund are based on how the fund fared against its peer group category in the book. Thus, even though a given rating may only be fair or even poor, it is within the context of the category and its peers that have made the book—a category that only includes the very best. There is a strong likelihood that a fund in the book that is given a low score in one category would still rate as great when compared to the entire universe of funds or even compared to other funds within the same category but not included in this book.

Do not be fooled by a low rating for any fund in any of the five areas. All 100 of these funds are true winners. Keep in mind that only about one in 100 funds can appear in the book. The purpose of the ratings is to show the best of the best.

Aggressive Growth Funds

These funds focus strictly on appreciation, with no concern about generating income. Aggressive growth funds strive for maximum capital growth, frequently using trading strategies such as leveraging, purchasing restricted securities, or buying stocks of emerging growth companies. Portfolio composition is almost exclusively U.S. stocks.

Aggressive growth funds can go up in value quite rapidly during favorable market conditions. These funds will often outperform other categories of U.S. stocks during bull markets but suffer greater percentage losses during bear markets.

Over the past 15 years (ending December 31, 2002), small stocks, which are included in the aggressive growth category, have *outperformed* common stocks by 0.8 percent per year, as measured by the Standard & Poor's 500 Stock Index. From 1988 through 2002, small stocks averaged 12.3 percent, while common stocks averaged 11.5 percent compounded per year. A $10,000 investment in small stocks grew to $56,663 over the past 15 years; a similar initial investment in the S&P 500 grew to $51,020.

During the past 20 years, there have been sixteen 5-year periods (1983–1987, 1984–1988, etc.). The Small Stock Index, made up from the smallest 20 percent of companies listed on the NYSE, as measured by market capitalization, outperformed the S&P 500 in just four of those sixteen 5-year periods. During these same 20 years, there have been eleven 10-year periods (1983–1992, 1984–1993, etc.). The Small Stock Index has only outperformed the S&P 500 three of those eleven 10-year periods (1992–2001).

During the past 30 years, there have been eleven 20-year periods (1973–1992, 1974–1993, etc.). The Small Stock Index outperformed the S&P 500 in six of those eleven 20-year periods.

Over the past 50 years, there have been forty-six 5-year periods (1953–1957, 1954–1958, etc.). The Small Stock Index outperformed the S&P 500 in 19 of those forty-six 5-year periods. Over the past 50 years, there have been forty-one 10-year periods (1953–1962, 1954–1963, etc.). The Small Stock Index outperformed the S&P 500 in 29 of those forty-one 10-year periods, the last such period being 1992–2001.

Ten thousand dollars invested in small stocks for the past 50 years grew to $7,072,431 by the end of 2002 (versus $1,901,608 for $10,000 invested in the S&P 500). For small stocks, this translates into an average compound return of 14.0 percent per year (vs. 11.1 percent for the S&P 500). Over the past 50 years, the worst year for small stocks was 1973, when a loss of 31 percent was suffered. Two years later, these same stocks posted a gain of almost 53 percent in one year, followed by a gain of more than 57 percent the year after. The best year so far has been 1967, when small stocks posted a gain of 84 percent. The best five years in a row were 1975 to 1979, when the compounded annual rate of return was 39.8 percent per year. The worst five-year period over the past half-century has been 1969 to 1973, when this group lost an average compounded rate of -12.3 percent per year. For 10-year periods, the best has been 1975 to 1984 (compounded average rate of 30.4 percent per year); the worst has been 1965 to 1974 (compounded average rate of 3.2 percent per year).

To obtain the kinds of returns described here, investors would have needed quite a bit of patience and understanding. During the 1990s, small-company stocks had a standard deviation (variation of return) of 20.2 percent, compared to 15.8 percent for common stocks and 8.9 percent for long-term government bonds.

During the past three years, aggressive growth funds have underperformed the S&P 500 by 5.3 percent per year. Over the past five years, this fund category has underperformed the S&P 500 by an average of 1.8 percent per year. Average turnover during the past three years has been 150 percent.

The price-earnings (p/e) ratio is 28 for the typical aggressive growth fund, versus 25 for the S&P 500. The typical stock in these portfolios is only 21 percent the size of the average stock in the S&P 500. The average beta is 1.1, which means the group has a market-related risk that is 10 percent higher than the S&P 500. As a group, the average aggressive growth and small company fund has an average annual dividend yield of 0.1 percent. The typical annual expense ratio for this group is 1.6 percent.

The p/e ratio for the typical small-company fund is 25, the same as the S&P 500. The typical stock in these portfolios is only about 2 percent the size of the average stock in the S&P 500. The average beta is 0.9, which means the group's market-related risk is 10 percent less than the S&P 500. There is a little over $1 trillion in all small-company funds combined. The typical annual expense ratio for this group is 1.6 percent.

There are 260 funds that make up the aggressive growth category. The small-company stock category, which has 1,000 funds, has been combined with aggressive growth funds. Thus, for this section, there were a total of 1,260 possible candidates.

Over the past three years, aggressive growth funds combined with small-company stock funds have had an average compound return of *negative* 9.7 percent per year (-7.2 percent for small-company stock funds alone). The annual return has been *negative* 0.1 percent for the past five years (0.4 percent for small-company stock funds), 7.3 percent for the past decade (8.1 percent for small-company stock funds), and 10.4 percent for the past 15 years (11.1 percent for small-company stock funds).

The standard deviation for this combined category (aggressive growth and small-company stock funds) has been 26 percent over the past three years, versus 16 for the S&P 500. This means that these funds have been more volatile than any other category except metals (standard deviation of 40), technology (standard deviation of 37 percent), health care (standard deviation of 29 percent), and natural resources (standard deviation of 27). Aggressive growth funds are certainly not for the faint of heart.

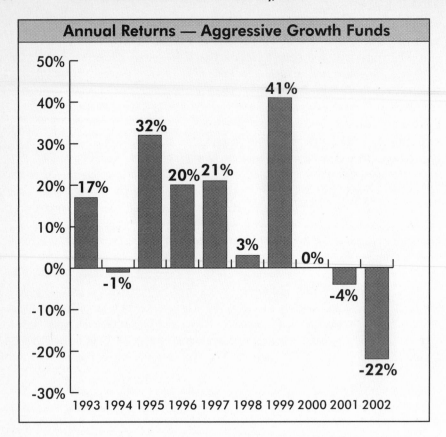

Annual Returns — Aggressive Growth Funds

Ariel

200 E Randolph Street, Suite 2900
Chicago, IL 60601
(800) 292-7435
www.arielmutualfunds.com

total return	★★★
risk reduction	★★★★
management	★★★★
tax minimization	★★★
expense control	★★★★★
symbol ARGFX	19 points
up-market performance	poor
down-market performance	excellent
predictability of returns	very good

Total Return   ★★★

Over the past five years, Ariel has taken $10,000 and turned it into $14,440 ($13,940 over three years and $30,050 over the past 10 years). This translates into an annualized return of 8 percent over the past five years, 12 percent over the past three years, and 12 percent for the decade. Over the past five years, this fund has outperformed 98 percent of all mutual funds; within its general category it has also done better than 98 percent of its peers. Aggressive growth funds have averaged less than 1 percent annually over these same five years.

Risk/Volatility   ★★★★

Over the past five years, Ariel has experienced below average risk for its category. Over the past decade, the fund has had three negative years, while the S&P 500 has had three (off 9 percent in 2000, 12 percent in 2001, and 22 percent in 2002); the Russell 2000 fell four times (off 2 percent in 1994, 3 percent in 1998, 3 percent in 2000, and 20 percent in 2002). The fund has underperformed the S&P 500 five times and the Russell 2000 four times in the past 10 years. Consistency of *over-performance* for this fund has been very good.

	last 5 years		last 10 years	
worst year	-5.8%	1999	-5.8%	1999
best year	28.8%	2000	36.4%	1997

In the past, Ariel has only done better than 10 percent of its peer group during the most recent bull market but outperformed 96 percent of its peer group during the most recent bear market. Consistency, or predictability, of returns for Ariel can be described as very good. This fund's risk-adjusted return over the past three/five years ranks in the top quintile.

Management   ★★★★

There are 45 stocks in this $1 billion portfolio. The average aggressive growth fund today is $190 million in size. Close to 100 percent of the fund's holdings are in stocks. The stocks in this portfolio have an average p/e ratio of 30 and a median market capitalization of $1 billion. The 10 largest holdings compose 40 percent of the fund's total assets. The three largest sector weightings are services (35 percent), industrial cyclicals (35 percent), and consumer staples (20 percent). The portfolio's equity holdings can be categorized as small-cap and a blend of growth and value stocks.

John W. Rogers Jr. has managed this fund for the past 16 years. Management seeks companies selling at intrinsic value discounts of 40 percent or more. Rogers also leans towards corporations and industry groups that have strong barriers to entry, clean balance sheets, and strong cash flow. The fund's price movement has a low correlation to that of the S&P 500. There are three funds besides Ariel within the Ariel family. Overall, the fund family's risk adjusted performance can be described as very good.

Tax Minimization   ★★★
During the past five years, a $10,000 initial investment grew to $13,200 after taxes, assuming a 40 percent income tax bracket (state and federal combined) and a capital gains rate of 20 percent. This means that investors in this fund were able to preserve 72 percent of their total returns. Compared to other funds in its category, this fund's tax savings are considered to be good.

Expenses   ★★★★★
Ariel's expense ratio is 1.2 percent; it has averaged 1.2 percent annually over the past three calendar years. The average expense ratio for the 1,265 funds in this category is 1.6 percent. This fund's turnover rate over the past year has been 24 percent, while its peer group average has been 113 percent.

Summary
Ariel scores well in every category, particularly when it comes to overhead costs. Its expense ratio is about a third less than its peer group and its turnover rate is about 80 percent less. The fund's return figures are even more impressive—positive, and high, numbers for the past three and five years, versus negative numbers for its category averages. Management does a very good job of blending growth and value.

Profile

minimum initial investment $1,000	*IRA accounts available* . . . . yes
subsequent minimum investment . . . $50	*IRA minimum investment* $250
available in all 50 states. . . . . yes	*date of inception* . . . . Nov. 1986
telephone exchanges. . . . . yes	*dividend/income paid* . . . . annually
number of funds in family 4	*largest sector weighting* . . . . . . services

ARK Small Cap Equity A

P.O. Box 8525
Boston, MA 02266
(800) 275-3863
www.arkfunds.com

total return	★★★★
risk reduction	★★★
management	★★★
tax minimization	★★★
expense control	★★★
symbol ARPAX	16 points
up-market performance	poor
down-market performance	good
predictability of returns	fair

Total Return   ★★★★

Over the past five years, ARK Small Cap Equity A has taken $10,000 and turned it into $18,690 ($6,290 over three years). This translates into an annualized return of 13 percent over the past five years and -14 percent over the past three years. Over the past five years, this fund has outperformed 99 percent of all mutual funds; within its general category it has done better than 98 percent of its peers. Aggressive growth funds have averaged less than 1 percent annually over these same five years.

Risk/Volatility   ★★★

Over the past five years, ARK Small Cap Equity A has experienced average risk for its category. Over the past decade, the fund has had three negative years, while the S&P 500 has had three (off 9 percent in 2000, 12 percent in 2001, and 22 percent in 2002); the Russell 2000 fell four times (off 2 percent in 1994, 3 percent in 1998, 3 percent in 2000, and 20 percent in 2002). The fund has underperformed the S&P 500 seven times and the Russell 2000 seven times in the past 10 years. Consistency of *overperformance* for this fund has been excellent.

	last 5 years		last 10 years	
worst year	-27.9%	2002	-27.9%	2002
best year	149.8%	1999	149.8%	1999

During the past five years, the fund's three worst months have been August 1998 (-18 percent), September 2001 (-15 percent), and November 2000 (-11 percent). During the same period, the three best months have been February 2000 (12 percent), October 1998 (11 percent), and February 1998 (10 percent). In the past, ARK Small Cap Equity A has only done better than 20 percent of its peer group during the most recent bull market but outperformed 50 percent of its peer group during the most recent bear market. Consistency, or predictability, of returns for ARK Small Cap Equity A can be described as very good. This fund's risk-adjusted return over the past three/five years ranks in the top-two quintiles.

Management   ★★★

There are 65 stocks in this $50 million portfolio. The average aggressive growth fund today is $190 million in size. Close to 90 percent of the fund's holdings are in stocks. The stocks in this portfolio have an average p/e ratio of 21 and a median market capitalization of $690 million. The 10 largest holdings compose 30 percent of the fund's total assets. The three largest sector weightings are services (35 percent), health (20 percent), and industrial cyclicals (20 percent). The portfolio's equity holdings can be categorized as small-cap and growth-oriented issues.

H. Giles Knight has managed this fund for the past seven years. Management employs a momentum-driven approach to equity selection. Knight is quick to sell stocks of companies whose revenue growth begins to decline or if there are concerns about corporate management. The fund's price movement has a very low correlation to that of the S&P 500. There are 16 funds besides Small Cap Equity within the Ark family. Overall, the fund family's risk adjusted performance can be described as good.

Tax Minimization   ★★★

During the past five years, a $10,000 initial investment grew to $16,430 after taxes, assuming a 40 percent income tax bracket (state and federal combined) and a capital gains rate of 20 percent. This means that investors in this fund were able to preserve 74 percent of their total returns. Compared to other funds in its category, this fund's tax savings are considered to be good.

Expenses   ★★★

ARK Small Cap Equity A's expense ratio is 1.3 percent; it has averaged 1.3 percent annually over the past three calendar years. The average expense ratio for the 1,265 funds in this category is 1.6 percent. This fund's turnover rate over the past year has been 267 percent, while its peer group average has been 113 percent.

Summary

ARK Small Cap Equity A has a low expense ratio but an extremely high turnover rate. Still, annualized performance figures over the past five years are some of the best on record. This would be a good complement with a value-oriented portfolio.

Profile

minimum initial investment $500	*IRA accounts available* . . . . yes
subsequent minimum investment . . $500	*IRA minimum investment* $500
available in all 50 states . . . . yes	*date of inception* . . . . May 1996
telephone exchanges . . . . yes	*dividend/income paid* . . . . annually
number of funds in family 17	*largest sector weighting* . . . . . . services

Bjurman, Barry Micro-Cap Growth
10100 Santa Monica Boulevard, Suite 1200
Los Angeles, CA 90067-4103
800-227-7264
www.bjurmanbarry.com

total return	★★★★★
risk reduction	★★★
management	★★★★
tax minimization	★★★★★
expense control	★★
symbol BMCFX	19 points
up-market performance	fair
down-market performance	very good
predictability of returns	poor

Total Return ★★★★★

Over the past five years, Bjurman, Barry Micro-Cap Growth has taken $10,000 and turned it into $24,600 ($14,350 over three years). This translates into an annualized return of 20 percent over the past five years and 13 percent over the past three years. Over the past five years, this fund has outperformed 99 percent of all mutual funds; within its general category it has also done better than 99 percent of its peers. Aggressive growth funds have averaged less than 1 percent annually over these same five years.

Risk/Volatility ★★★

Over the past five years, Bjurman, Barry Micro-Cap Growth has experienced above average risk for its category. Over the past decade, the fund has had one negative year, while the S&P 500 has had three (off 9 percent in 2000, 12 percent in 2001, and 22 percent in 2002); the Russell 2000 fell four times (off 2 percent in 1994, 3 percent in 1998, 3 percent in 2000, and 20 percent in 2002). The fund has underperformed the S&P 500 six times and the Russell 2000 four times in the past 10 years. Consistency of *overperformance* for this fund has been excellent.

	last 5 years		last 10 years	
worst year	-17.5%	2002	-17.5%	2002
best year	53.3%	1999	53.3%	1999

During the past five years, the fund's three worst months have been August 1998 (-24 percent), November 2000 (-13 percent), and March 2000 (-10 percent). During the same period, the three best months have been February 2000 (39 percent), June 2000 (24 percent), and November 1999 (21 percent). In the past, Bjurman, Barry Micro-Cap Growth has only done better than 35 percent of its peer group during the most recent bull market but outperformed 70 percent of its peer group during the most recent bear market. Consistency, or predictability, of returns for Bjurman, Barry Micro-Cap Growth can be described as poor. This fund's risk-adjusted return over the past three/five years ranks in the top quintile.

Management   ★★★★
There are 155 stocks in this $340 million portfolio. The average aggressive growth fund today is $190 million in size. Close to 95 percent of the fund's holdings are in stocks. The stocks in this portfolio have an average p/e ratio of 29 and a median market capitalization of $260 million. The 10 largest holdings compose 15 percent of the fund's total assets. The three largest sector weightings are services (30 percent), consumer durables (20 percent), and health (20 percent). The portfolio's equity holdings can be categorized as small-cap and growth-oriented issues.

O. Thomas Barry III has managed this fund for the past six years. What makes this fund different from many of its peers is Barry's concern with price multiples: He frequently sells stocks that demonstrate worse-than-expected earnings and buys those that have posted better-than-expected profits. The fund's price movement has a very low correlation to that of the S&P 500. There is one other fund besides Bjurman, Barry Micro-Cap Growth within the Bjurman, Barry "family." Overall, the fund family's risk adjusted performance can be described as very good.

Tax Minimization   ★★★★★
During the past five years, a $10,000 initial investment grew to $24,450 after taxes, assuming a 40 percent income tax bracket (state and federal combined) and a capital gains rate of 20 percent. This means that investors in this fund were able to preserve 99 percent of their total returns. Compared to other funds in its category, this fund's tax savings are considered to be excellent.

Expenses   ★★
Bjurman, Barry Micro-Cap Growth's expense ratio is 1.8 percent; it has averaged 1.8 percent annually over the past three calendar years. The average expense ratio for the 1,265 funds in this category is 1.6 percent. This fund's turnover rate over the past year has been 105 percent, while its peer group average has been 113 percent.

Summary
Bjurman, Barry Micro-Cap Growth boasts the best three- and five-year track record within its category. Predictability has not been good, but for the patient investor, the wait is certainly worth the payoff. Tax-conscious investors will also be extremely happy with their returns.

Profile
minimum initial investment $5,000	*IRA accounts available* . . . . yes
subsequent minimum investment . . $100	*IRA minimum investment* $2,000
available in all 50 states . . . . yes	*date of inception* . . . . Mar. 1997
telephone exchanges . . . . yes	*dividend/income paid* . . . . annually
number of funds in family 2	*largest sector weighting* . . . . . . services

Fidelity Low-Priced Stock

82 Devonshire Street
Boston, MA 02109
(800) 544-8888
www.fidelity.com

total return	★★★★
risk reduction	★★★★★
management	★★★★★
tax minimization	★★★★
expense control	★★★★★
symbol FLPSX	23 points
up-market performance	good
down-market performance	excellent
predictability of returns	excellent

Total Return   ★★★★

Over the past five years, Fidelity Low-Priced Stock has taken $10,000 and turned it into $14,920 ($14,120 over three years and $37,760 over the past 10 years). This translates into an annualized return of 8 percent over the past five years, 12 percent over the past three years, and 14 percent for the decade. Over the past five years, this fund has outperformed 98 percent of all mutual funds; within its general category it has done better than 92 percent of its peers. Aggressive growth funds have averaged less than 1 percent annually over these same five years.

Risk/Volatility   ★★★★★

Over the past five years, Fidelity Low-Priced Stock has experienced low risk for its category. Over the past decade, the fund has had one negative year, while the S&P 500 has had three (off 9 percent in 2000, 12 percent in 2001, and 22 percent in 2002); the Russell 2000 fell four times (off 2 percent in 1994, 3 percent in 1998, 3 percent in 2000, and 20 percent in 2002). The fund has underperformed the S&P 500 four times and the Russell 2000 twice in the past 10 years. Consistency of *overperformance* for this fund has been very good.

	last 5 years		last 10 years	
worst year	-6.2%	2002	-6.2%	2002
best year	26.7%	2001	26.9%	1996

During the past five years, the fund's three worst months have been August 1998 (-15 percent), September 2001 (-12 percent), and September 2000 (-11 percent). During the same period, the three best months have been April 1999 (7 percent), January 2001 (7 percent), and March 2001 (7 percent). In the past, Fidelity Low-Priced Stock has done better than 50 percent of its peer group during the most recent bull market and outperformed 92 percent of its peer group during the most recent bear market. Consistency, or predictability, of returns for Fidelity Low-Priced Stock can be described as excellent. This fund's risk-adjusted return over the past three/five years ranks in the top quintile.

Management ★★★★★

There are 895 stocks in this $16 billion portfolio. The average aggressive growth fund today is $190 million in size. Close to 85 percent of the fund's holdings are in stocks. The stocks in this portfolio have an average p/e ratio of 17 and a median market capitalization of $980 million. The 10 largest holdings compose 10 percent of the fund's total assets. The three largest sector weightings are services (35 percent), industrial cyclicals (30 percent), and consumer durables (20 percent). The portfolio's equity holdings can be categorized as small-cap and a blend of growth and value stocks.

Joel C. Tillinghast has managed this fund for the past 13 years. Management has done a superb job of buying into areas on weakness. Tillinghast is one of the very few managers who has been able to handle a portfolio of close to a thousand different issues while being able to constantly beat out his small- and mid-cap peers. There are 76 funds besides Low-Priced Stock within the Fidelity family. Overall, the fund family's risk adjusted performance can be described as between good and very good.

Tax Minimization ★★★★

During the past five years, a $10,000 initial investment grew to $14,180 after taxes, assuming a 40 percent income tax bracket (state and federal combined) and a capital gains rate of 20 percent. This means that investors in this fund were able to preserve 85 percent of their total returns. Compared to other funds in its category, this fund's tax savings are considered to be very good.

Expenses ★★★★★

Fidelity Low-Priced Stock's expense ratio is 0.9 percent; it has averaged 0.9 percent annually over the past three calendar years. The average expense ratio for the 1,265 funds in this category is 1.6 percent. This fund's turnover rate over the past year has been 26 percent, while its peer group average has been 113 percent.

Summary

Fidelity Low-Priced Stock receives a near-perfect score. Virtually every seasoned investment advisor is familiar with this fund's legendary and long-term greatness. This Fidelity offering is particularly well suited for the conservative investor who wants the best of all worlds: low cost, high returns, low risk, and quarter-to-quarter peace of mind.

Profile

minimum initial investment $2,500	*IRA accounts available* . . . . yes
subsequent minimum investment . . $250	*IRA minimum investment* $500
available in all 50 states . . . . yes	*date of inception* . . . . Dec. 1989
telephone exchanges . . . . yes	*dividend/income paid* . . . . semiannually
number of funds in family 77	*largest sector weighting* . . . . . . services

Pennsylvania Mutual Investor
1414 Avenue of the Americas
New York, NY 10019
(800) 221-4268
www.roycefunds.com

total return	★★★
risk reduction	★★★★★
management	★★★★
tax minimization	★★★
expense control	★★★★★
symbol PENNX	20 points
up-market performance	fair
down-market performance	excellent
predictability of returns	very good

Total Return   ★★★
Over the past five years, Pennsylvania Mutual Investor has taken $10,000 and turned it into $14,040 ($12,720 over three years and $25,960 over the past 10 years). This translates into an annualized return of 7 percent over the past five years, 8 percent over the past three years, and 10 percent for the decade. Over the past five years, this fund has outperformed 95 percent of all mutual funds; within its general category it has done better than 87 percent of its peers. Aggressive growth funds have averaged less than 1 percent annually over these same five years.

Risk/Volatility   ★★★★★
Over the past five years, Pennsylvania Mutual Investor has experienced low risk for its category. Over the past decade, the fund has had two negative years, while the S&P 500 has had three (off 9 percent in 2000, 12 percent in 2001, and 22 percent in 2002); the Russell 2000 fell four times (off 2 percent in 1994, 3 percent in 1998, 3 percent in 2000, and 20 percent in 2002). The fund has underperformed the S&P 500 six times and the Russell 2000 four times in the past 10 years. Consistency of *overperformance* for this fund has been very good.

	last 5 years		last 10 years	
worst year	-9.2%	2002	-9.2%	2002
best year	18.4%	2001	25.0%	1997

During the past five years, the fund's three worst months have been December 2000 (-13 percent), August 1998 (-13 percent), and September 2001 (-12 percent). During the same period, the three best months have been April 1999 (9 percent), February 1998 (7 percent), and April 2001 (6 percent). In the past, Pennsylvania Mutual Investor has done better than 40 percent of its peer group during the most recent bull market and outperformed 86 percent of its peer group during the most recent bear market. Consistency, or predictability, of returns for Pennsylvania Mutual Investor can be described as very good. This fund's risk-adjusted return over the past three/five years ranks in the top quintile.

Management   ★★★★

There are 200 stocks in this $550 million portfolio. The average aggressive growth fund today is $190 million in size. Close to 90 percent of the fund's holdings are in stocks. The stocks in this portfolio have an average p/e ratio of 25 and a median market capitalization of $460 million. The 10 largest holdings compose 10 percent of the fund's total assets. The three largest sector weightings are industrial cyclicals (45 percent), consumer durables (30 percent), and services (20 percent). The portfolio's equity holdings can be categorized as small-cap and a blend of growth and value stocks.

Charles M. Royce and W. Whitney George have managed this fund for the past 30 years. Management favors micro-cap and small-cap securities. The co-managers look for companies trading well below their estimated net worths. There are seven funds besides Pennsylvania Mutual Investor within the Royce family. Overall, the fund family's risk adjusted performance can be described as very good.

Tax Minimization   ★★★

During the past five years, a $10,000 initial investment grew to $12,790 after taxes, assuming a 40 percent income tax bracket (state and federal combined) and a capital gains rate of 20 percent. This means that investors in this fund were able to preserve 69 percent of their total returns. Compared to other funds in its category, this fund's tax savings are considered to be good.

Expenses   ★★★★★

Pennsylvania Mutual Investor's expense ratio is 1 percent; it has averaged 1 percent annually over the past three calendar years. The average expense ratio for the 1,265 funds in this category is 1.6 percent. This fund's turnover rate over the past year has been 39 percent, while its peer group average has been 113 percent.

Summary

Pennsylvania Mutual Investor scores very well in every area, particularly when it comes to low risk and high risk-adjusted returns. The fund has outperformed more than 95 percent of all mutual funds while keeping a low profile when it comes to volatility. It also has done an excellent job of keeping expenses and turnover low.

Profile

minimum initial investment $2,000
subsequent minimum investment . . . $50
available in all 50 states . . . . yes
telephone exchanges . . . . yes
number of funds in family 8

IRA accounts available . . . . yes
IRA minimum investment $500
date of inception . . . . Dec. 1962
dividend/income paid . . . . annually
largest sector weighting . . . . . industrial cyclicals

Quaker Aggressive Growth A

1288 Valley Forge Road, Suite 87
Valley Forge, PA 19482
(800) 220-8888
www.quakerfunds.com

total return	★★★★★
risk reduction	★★★★★
management	★★★★★
tax minimization	★★★★
expense control	★
symbol QUAGX	20 points
up-market performance	poor
down-market performance	excellent
predictability of returns	excellent

Total Return ★★★★★

Over the past five years, Quaker Aggressive Growth A has taken $10,000 and turned it into $22,640 ($8,800 over three years). This translates into an annualized return of 18 percent over the past five years and -4 percent over the past three years. Over the past five years, this fund has outperformed 99 percent of all mutual funds; within its general category it has also done better than 99 percent of its peers. Aggressive growth funds have averaged less than 1 percent annually over these same five years.

Risk/Volatility ★★★★★

Over the past five years, Quaker Aggressive Growth A has experienced low risk for its category. Over the past decade, the fund has had two negative years, while the S&P 500 has had three (off 9 percent in 2000, 12 percent in 2001, and 22 percent in 2002); the Russell 2000 fell four times (off 2 percent in 1994, 3 percent in 1998, 3 percent in 2000, and 20 percent in 2002). The fund has underperformed the S&P 500 five times and the Russell 2000 five times in the past 10 years. Consistency of *overperformance* for this fund has been excellent.

	last 5 years		last 10 years	
worst year	-17.1%	2002	-17.1%	2002
best year	97.0%	1999	97.0%	1999

During the past five years, the fund's three worst months have been December 2000 (-11 percent), June 1999 (-11 percent), and August 1998 (-7 percent). During the same period, the three best months have been February 2000 (18 percent), March 1999 (14 percent), and December 1998 (10 percent). In the past, Quaker Aggressive Growth A has only done better than 10 percent of its peer group during the most recent bull market but outperformed 85 percent of its peer group during the most recent bear market. Consistency, or predictability, of returns for Quaker Aggressive Growth A can be described as excellent. This fund's risk-adjusted return over the past three/five years ranks in the top quintile.

Management ★★★★★
There are 40 stocks in this $140 million portfolio. The average aggressive growth fund today is $190 million in size. Close to 45 percent of the fund's holdings are in stocks. The stocks in this portfolio have an average p/e ratio of 19 and a median market capitalization of $22 billion. The 10 largest holdings compose 20 percent of the fund's total assets. The three largest sector weightings are industrial cyclicals (40 percent), health (30 percent), and services (20 percent). The portfolio's equity holdings can be categorized as large-cap and a blend of growth and value stocks.

Manu Daftary has managed this fund for the past six years. In the past, management has been known to do massive trading all over the board. Daftary maintains a realistic view of the market and has not been taken in by Wall Street's overly optimistic predictions. He has no problem keeping large portions of the portfolio in cash equivalents. There are four funds besides Aggressive Growth within the Quaker family. Overall, the fund family's risk adjusted performance can be described as very good.

Tax Minimization ★★★★
During the past five years, a $10,000 initial investment grew to $20,490 after taxes, assuming a 40 percent income tax bracket (state and federal combined) and a capital gains rate of 20 percent. This means that investors in this fund were able to preserve 83 percent of their total returns. Compared to other funds in its category, this fund's tax savings are considered to be very good.

Expenses ★
Quaker Aggressive Growth A's expense ratio is 2.2 percent; it has averaged 2 percent annually over the past three calendar years. The average expense ratio for the 1,265 funds in this category is 1.6 percent. This fund's turnover rate over the past year has been 524 percent, while its peer group average has been 113 percent.

Summary
Quaker Aggressive Growth A has higher expenses than most of its peers, but, as they say, "you get what you pay for." Returns over the past five years have been absolutely stunning. This is even more amazing when you consider how low the fund's risk level has been over the past three and five years. This is an excellent defensive play for the investor who wants predictable returns plus a combination of both value and growth equities.

Profile
minimum initial investment $2,000
subsequent minimum investment . . $100
available in all 50 states . . . . yes
telephone exchanges . . . . yes
number of funds in family 5

IRA accounts available . . . . yes
IRA minimum investment $1,000
date of inception . . . . Nov. 1996
dividend/income paid . . . . annually
largest sector weighting . . . . . industrial cyclicals

Royce Micro-Cap
1414 Avenue of the Americas
New York, NY 10019
(800) 221-4268
www.roycefunds.com

total return	★★★
risk reduction	★★★★
management	★★★★
tax minimization	★★★★
expense control	★★★★
symbol RYOTX	19 points
up-market performance	very good
down-market performance	very good
predictability of returns	good

Total Return   ★★★
Over the past five years, Royce Micro-Cap has taken $10,000 and turned it into $13,670 ($12,440 over three years and $30,020 over the past 10 years). This translates into an annualized return of 6 percent over the past five years, 8 percent over the past three years, and 12 percent for the decade. Over the past five years, this fund has outperformed 95 percent of all mutual funds; within its general category it has done better than 85 percent of its peers. Aggressive growth funds have averaged less than 1 percent annually over these same five years.

Risk/Volatility   ★★★★
Over the past five years, Royce Micro-Cap has experienced average risk for its category. Over the past decade, the fund has had two negative years, while the S&P 500 has had three (off 9 percent in 2000, 12 percent in 2001, and 22 percent in 2002); the Russell 2000 fell four times (off 2 percent in 1994, 3 percent in 1998, 3 percent in 2000, and 20 percent in 2002). The fund has underperformed the S&P 500 five times and the Russell 2000 four times in the past 10 years. Consistency of *overperformance* for this fund has been very good.

	last 5 years		last 10 years	
worst year	-13.4%	2002	-13.4%	2002
best year	23.1%	2001	24.7%	1997

During the past five years, the fund's three worst months have been August 1998 (-16 percent), September 2001 (-13 percent), and March 1999 (-8 percent). During the same period, the three best months have been February 2000 (10 percent), January 2001 (9 percent), and April 1999 (9 percent). In the past, Royce Micro-Cap has done better than 70 percent of its peer group during the most recent bull market and also outperformed 70 percent of its peer group during the most recent bear market. Consistency, or predictability, of returns for Royce Micro-Cap can be described as good. This fund's risk-adjusted return over the past three/five years ranks in the top-two quintiles.

Management   ★★★★
There are 190 stocks in this $330 million portfolio. The average aggressive growth fund today is $190 million in size. Close to 95 percent of the fund's holdings are in stocks. The stocks in this portfolio have an average p/e ratio of 13 and a median market capitalization of $220 million. The 10 largest holdings compose 15 percent of the fund's total assets. The three largest sector weightings are industrial cyclicals (35 percent), consumer durables (30 percent), and services (20 percent). The portfolio's equity holdings can be categorized as small-cap and a blend of growth and value stocks.

W. Whitney George has managed this fund for the past nine years. Management invests in very tiny companies. George particularly favors financially healthy companies that trade at low prices compared to their cash balances. There are seven funds besides Micro-Cap within the Royce family. Overall, the fund family's risk adjusted performance can be described as excellent.

Tax Minimization   ★★★★
During the past five years, a $10,000 initial investment grew to $13,120 after taxes, assuming a 40 percent income tax bracket (state and federal combined) and a capital gains rate of 20 percent. This means that investors in this fund were able to preserve 85 percent of their total returns. Compared to other funds in its category, this fund's tax savings are considered to be very good.

Expenses   ★★★★
Royce Micro-Cap's expense ratio is 1.5 percent; it has averaged 1.5 percent annually over the past three calendar years. The average expense ratio for the 1,265 funds in this category is 1.6 percent. This fund's turnover rate over the past year has been 30 percent, while its peer group average has been 113 percent.

Summary
Royce Micro-Cap is one of three Royce funds to appear in this book under the small-cap and aggressive fund banner. This fund group clearly dominates the category. This particular offering scores well or very well in every single category. It is one of the few funds out there that has done a good job in both a bull and bear market.

Profile

minimum initial investment $2,000	*IRA accounts available* . . . . yes
subsequent minimum investment . . . $50	*IRA minimum investment* $500
available in all 50 states . . . . yes	*date of inception* . . . . Dec. 1991
telephone exchanges . . . . yes	*dividend/income paid* . . . . annually
number of funds in family 8	*largest sector weighting* . . . . . industrial cyclicals

Royce Opportunity
1414 Avenue of the Americas
New York, NY 10019
(800) 221-4268
www.roycefunds.com

total return	★★★★
risk reduction	★★
management	★★★
tax minimization	★★★★
expense control	★★★★★
symbol RYPNX	18 points
up-market performance	excellent
down-market performance	very good
predictability of returns	excellent

Total Return   ★★★★
Over the past five years, Royce Opportunity has taken $10,000 and turned it into $16,200 ($11,670 over three years). This translates into an annualized return of 10 percent over the past five years and 5 percent over the past three years. Over the past five years, this fund has outperformed 98 percent of all mutual funds; within its general category it has done better than 99 percent of its peers. Aggressive growth funds have averaged less than 1 percent annually over these same five years.

Risk/Volatility   ★★
Over the past five years, Royce Opportunity has experienced high risk for its category. Over the past decade, the fund has had one negative year, while the S&P 500 has had three (off 9 percent in 2000, 12 percent in 2001, and 22 percent in 2002); the Russell 2000 fell four times (off 2 percent in 1994, 3 percent in 1998, 3 percent in 2000, and 20 percent in 2002). The fund has underperformed the S&P 500 six times and the Russell 2000 four times in the past 10 years. Consistency of *over-performance* for this fund has been good.

	last 5 years		last 10 years	
worst year	-17.0%	2002	-17%	2002
best year	32.3%	1999	32.3%	1999

During the past five years, the fund's three worst months have been August 1998 (-16 percent), September 2001 (-15 percent), and February 1999 (-9 percent). During the same period, the three best months have been April 1999 (16 percent), January 2001 (14 percent), and November 1998 (10 percent). In the past, Royce Opportunity has done better than 90 percent of its peer group during the most recent bull market and outperformed 70 percent of its peer group during the most recent bear market. Consistency, or predictability, of returns for Royce Opportunity can be described as excellent. This fund's risk-adjusted return over the past three/five years ranks in the top-three quintiles.

Management   ★★★

There are 285 stocks in this $890 million portfolio. The average aggressive growth fund today is $190 million in size. Close to 95 percent of the fund's holdings are in stocks. The stocks in this portfolio have an average p/e ratio of 12 and a median market capitalization of $250 million. The 10 largest holdings compose 10 percent of the fund's total assets. The three largest sector weightings are consumer durables (50 percent), industrial cyclicals (40 percent), and services (25 percent). The portfolio's equity holdings can be categorized as small-cap and value-oriented issues.

Boniface Zaino has managed this fund for the past five years. Management seeks out companies that have low valuation based on traditional metrics. Zaino has no problem with venturing outside of traditional value issues. There are seven funds besides Opportunity within the Royce family. Overall, the fund family's risk adjusted performance can be described as excellent.

Tax Minimization

During the past five years, a $10,000 initial investment grew to $15,460 after taxes, assuming a 40 percent income tax bracket (state and federal combined) and a capital gains rate of 20 percent. This means that investors in this fund were able to preserve 88 percent of their total returns. Compared to other funds in its category, this fund's tax savings are considered to be very good.

Expenses

Royce Opportunity's expense ratio is 1.2 percent; it has averaged 1.2 percent annually over the past three calendar years. The average expense ratio for the 1,265 funds in this category is 1.6 percent. This fund's turnover rate over the past year has been 44 percent, while its peer group average has been 113 percent.

Summary

Royce Opportunity is the second of three Royce offerings to be listed in this category and has the best five-year record of the group. The fund has turned in positive returns for the past three and five years, dramatically outperforming its category averages. This is the most aggressive offering, but those with patience will be quite pleased.

Profile

minimum initial investment $2,000	*IRA accounts available* . . . . yes
subsequent minimum investment . . . $50	*IRA minimum investment* $500
available in all 50 states . . . . yes	*date of inception* . . . . Nov. 1996
telephone exchanges . . . . yes	*dividend/income paid* . . . . annually
number of funds in family 8	*largest sector weighting* . . . . consumer durables

Royce Total Return
1414 Avenue of the Americas
New York, NY 10019
(800) 221-4268
www.roycefunds.com

total return	★★★
risk reduction	★★★★★
management	★★★★
tax minimization	★★★★
expense control	★★★★★
symbol RYTRX	21 points
up-market performance	poor
down-market performance	excellent
predictability of returns	excellent

Total Return ★★★
Over the past five years, Royce Total Return has taken $10,000 and turned it into $14,350 ($13,490 over three years). This translates into an annualized return of 7 percent over the past five years and 10 percent over the past three years. Over the past five years, this fund has outperformed 96 percent of all mutual funds; within its general category it has done better than 95 percent of its peers. Aggressive growth funds have averaged less than 1 percent annually over these same five years.

Risk/Volatility ★★★★★
Over the past five years, Royce Total Return has experienced low risk for its category. Over the past decade, the fund has had one negative year, while the S&P 500 has had three (off 9 percent in 2000, 12 percent in 2001, and 22 percent in 2002); the Russell 2000 fell four times (off 2 percent in 1994, 3 percent in 1998, 3 percent in 2000, and 20 percent in 2002). The fund has underperformed the S&P 500 five times and the Russell 2000 three times in the past 10 years. Consistency of *overperformance* for this fund has been very good.

	last 5 years		last 10 years	
worst year	-1.6%	2002	-1.6%	2002
best year	19.4%	2000	26.9%	1995

During the past five years, the fund's three worst months have been September 2001 (-11 percent), August 1998 (-10 percent), and February 1999 (-5 percent). During the same period, the three best months have been March 1999 (8 percent), November 2001 (5 percent), and April 2001 (5 percent). In the past, Royce Total Return has only done better than 15 percent of its peer group during the most recent bull market but outperformed 96 percent of its peer group during the most recent bear market. Consistency, or predictability, of returns for Royce Total Return can be described as excellent. This fund's risk-adjusted return over the past three/five years ranks in the top quintile.

Management   ★★★★

There are 350 stocks in this $880 million portfolio. The average aggressive growth fund today is $190 million in size. Close to 90 percent of the fund's holdings are in stocks. The stocks in this portfolio have an average p/e ratio of 24 and a median market capitalization of $960 million. The 10 largest holdings compose 10 percent of the fund's total assets. The three largest sector weightings are industrial cyclicals (45 percent), consumer durables (30 percent), and financials (25 percent). The portfolio's equity holdings can be categorized as small-cap and value-oriented issues.

Charles M. Royce and W. Whitney George have managed this fund for the past nine years. The portfolio is considered one of the least volatile small-cap value offerings. Volatility is reduced by management's almost insistence that the vast majority of its holdings include dividend-paying issues while spreading the risk over several hundred different stocks. Management feels that the ability of a company to pay a dividend is a sign of stability. There are seven funds besides Total Return within the Royce family. Overall, the fund family's risk adjusted performance can be described as excellent.

Tax Minimization   ★★★★

During the past five years, a $10,000 initial investment grew to $13,520 after taxes, assuming a 40 percent income tax bracket (state and federal combined) and a capital gains rate of 20 percent. This means that investors in this fund were able to preserve 81 percent of their total returns. Compared to other funds in its category, this fund's tax savings are considered to be very good.

Expenses   ★★★★★

Royce Total Return's expense ratio is 1.2 percent; it has averaged 1.2 percent annually over the past three calendar years. The average expense ratio for the 1,265 funds in this category is 1.6 percent. This fund's turnover rate over the past year has been 24 percent, while its peer group average has been 113 percent.

Summary

Royce Total Return is the third of three Royce funds to appear in this category. It also sports the best three-year record of the group. The fund's risk level is lower than any other aggressive or small company growth in the book. As you might have guessed, predictability of returns (volatility) is superb. Turnover is also impressively low.

Profile

minimum initial investment $2,000	*IRA accounts available* . . . . yes
subsequent minimum investment . . . $50	*IRA minimum investment* $500
available in all 50 states . . . . yes	*date of inception* . . . . Dec. 1993
telephone exchanges. . . . . yes	*dividend/income paid* . . . . quarterly
number of funds in family 8	*largest sector weighting*. . . . . industrial cyclicals

Smith Barney Aggressive Growth A
750 Washington Boulevard, 11th Floor
Stamford, CT 10048
(800) 451-2010
www.smithbarney.com

total return	★★★★
risk reduction	★★★
management	★★★★
tax minimization	★★★★★
expense control	★★★★★
symbol SHRAX	21 points
up-market performance	excellent
down-market performance	poor
predictability of returns	good

Total Return   ★★★★
Over the past five years, Smith Barney Aggressive Growth A has taken $10,000 and turned it into $16,840 ($7,620 over three years and $35,980 over the past 10 years). This translates into an annualized return of 11 percent over the past five years, -9 percent over the past three years, and 14 percent for the decade. Over the past five years, this fund has outperformed 99 percent of all mutual funds; within its general category it has also done better than 99 percent of its peers. Aggressive growth funds have averaged less than 1 percent annually over these same five years.

Risk/Volatility   ★★★
Over the past five years, Smith Barney Aggressive Growth A has experienced above average risk for its category. Over the past decade, the fund has had three negative years, while the S&P 500 has had three (off 9 percent in 2000, 12 percent in 2001, and 22 percent in 2002); the Russell 2000 fell four times (off 2 percent in 1994, 3 percent in 1998, 3 percent in 2000, and 20 percent in 2002). The fund has underperformed the S&P 500 five times and the Russell 2000 three times in the past 10 years. Consistency of *overperformance* for this fund has been very good.

	last 5 years		last 10 years	
worst year	-32.8%	2002	-32.8%	2002
best year	63.7%	1999	63.7%	1999

During the past five years, the fund's three worst months have been August 1998 (-22 percent), September 2001 (-13 percent), and November 2000 (-10 percent). During the same period, the three best months have been December 1999 (17 percent), June 2000 (14 percent), and December 1998 (14 percent). In the past, Smith Barney Aggressive Growth A has done better than 91 percent of its peer group during the most recent bull market but outperformed just 15 percent of its peer group during the most recent bear market. Consistency, or predictability, of returns for Smith Barney Aggressive Growth A can be described as good. This fund's risk-adjusted return over the past three/five years ranks in the top quintile.

Management   ★★★★
There are 75 stocks in this $2 billion portfolio. The average aggressive growth fund today is $190 million in size. Close to 100 percent of the fund's holdings are in stocks. The stocks in this portfolio have an average p/e ratio of 32 and a median market capitalization of $14 billion. The 10 largest holdings compose 55 percent of the fund's total assets. The three largest sector weightings are health (50 percent), consumer durables (15 percent), and financials (15 percent). The portfolio's equity holdings can be categorized as large-cap and growth-oriented issues.

Richard A. Freeman has managed this fund for the past 20 years. Management is known as a "quintessential buy-and-hold investor." Freeman's long-term success has proven that his patience has greatly rewarded investors. There are 64 funds besides Aggressive Growth within the Smith Barney family. Overall, the fund family's risk adjusted performance can be described as good.

Tax Minimization   ★★★★★
During the past five years, a $10,000 initial investment grew to $16,770 after taxes, assuming a 40 percent income tax bracket (state and federal combined) and a capital gains rate of 20 percent. This means that investors in this fund were able to preserve 99 percent of their total returns. Compared to other funds in its category, this fund's tax savings are considered to be excellent.

Expenses   ★★★★★
Smith Barney Aggressive Growth A's expense ratio is 1.2 percent; it has averaged 1.2 percent annually over the past three calendar years. The average expense ratio for the 1,265 funds in this category is 1.6 percent. This fund's turnover rate over the past year has been 0 percent, while its peer group average has been 113 percent.

Summary
Smith Barney Aggressive Growth A has had overall negative returns over the past three years, but well less than half its peer group average. Moreover, five-year return figures have not only been positive, they are some of the very best in the industry. The fund's expenses are even lower than they appear—turnover, which has been virtually nonexistent with this fund over the years, can end up being greater than published expense ratios (which do not include the cost of buying and selling securities).

Profile

minimum initial investment $1,000	*IRA accounts available* . . . . yes
subsequent minimum investment . . . $50	*IRA minimum investment* $250
available in all 50 states. . . . . yes	*date of inception* . . . . Oct. 1983
telephone exchanges. . . . . yes	*dividend/income paid* . . . . annually
number of funds in family 65	*largest sector weighting* . . . . health

Balanced Funds

The objective of balanced funds, also referred to as total return funds, is to provide both growth and income. Fund management purchases common stocks, bonds, and convertible securities. Portfolio composition is almost always exclusively U.S. securities. The weighting of stocks compared to bonds depends on the portfolio manager's perception of the stock market, interest rates, and risk levels. It is rare for less than 30 percent of the fund's holdings to be in either stocks or bonds.

Balanced funds offer neither the best nor the worst of both worlds. These funds will often outperform the different categories of bond funds during bull markets but suffer greater percentage losses during stock market declines. On the other hand, when interest rates are on the rise, balanced funds will typically decline less on a total return basis (current yield plus or minus principal appreciation) than a bond fund. When rates are falling, balanced funds will also outperform bond funds if stocks are also doing well.

Over the past 10 years, the average balanced fund had 79 percent of the return of growth funds (7.4 percent versus 9.3 percent) with only 52 percent of the risk. Balanced funds are the perfect choice for the investor who cannot decide between stocks and bonds. This hybrid security is a middle-of-the-road approach, ideal for someone who wants a fund manager to determine the portfolio's weighting of stocks, bonds, and convertibles.

More than 1,155 funds make up the entire balanced category, which consists of balanced only (520 funds), asset allocation (470 funds), multiasset global (90 funds), and convertibles (75 funds). The price-earnings (p/e) ratio for stocks in a typical balanced fund is 22, roughly 10 percent lower than the S&P 500's p/e ratio of 25. The average beta is 0.5, which means that this group has only half of the market-related risk of the S&P 500. During the past three years, balanced funds have surpassed the performance of the S&P 500 by slightly more than 10 percent annually. The gap drops down to over 2 percent on an annualized basis for the past five years. However, over the past decade, the S&P 500 has outperformed balanced funds by an average of 2 percent per year. Average turnover during the past three years has been 98 percent per annum. Balanced funds throw off an income stream of approximately 2.1 percent annually. The typical annual expense ratio for this group is 1.3 percent.

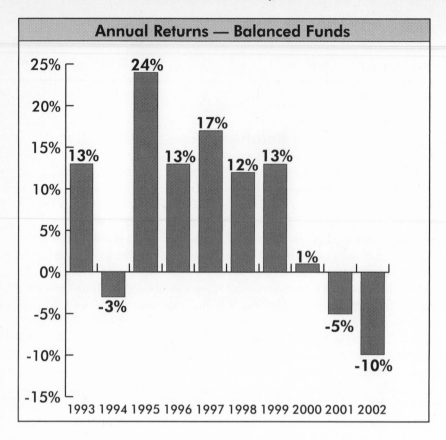

American Funds American Balanced A

333 South Hope Street
Los Angeles, CA 90071
(800) 421-4120
www.americanfunds.com

total return	★★★
risk reduction	★★
management	★★★
current income	★★★★
expense control	★★★★★
symbol ABALX	17 points
up-market performance	excellent
down-market performance	very good
predictability of returns	good

Total Return ★★★

Over the past five years, American Funds American Balanced A has taken $10,000 and turned it into $13,510 ($11,750 over three years and $26,270 over the past 10 years). This translates into an annualized return of 6 percent over the past five years, 6 percent over the past three years, and 10 percent for the decade. Over the past five years, this fund has outperformed 94 percent of all mutual funds; within its general category it has done better than 96 percent of its peers. Balanced funds have averaged 2 percent annually over these same five years.

During the past five years, a $10,000 initial investment grew to $11,720 after taxes, assuming a 40 percent income tax bracket (state and federal combined) and a capital gains rate of 20 percent. This means that investors in this fund were able to preserve 49 percent of their total returns. Compared to other funds in its category, this fund's tax savings are considered to be good.

Risk/Volatility ★★

Over the past five years, American Funds American Balanced A has experienced average risk for its category. Over the past decade, the fund has had one negative year, while the S&P 500 has had three (off 9 percent in 2000, 12 percent in 2001, and 22 percent in 2002); the Lehman Brothers Aggregate Bond Index fell twice (off 3 percent in 1994 and 1 percent in 1999). The fund has underperformed the S&P 500 six times and the Lehman Brothers Aggregate Bond Index twice in the past 10 years. Consistency of *overperformance* for this fund has been good.

	last 5 years		last 10 years	
worst year	-6.3%	2002	-6.3%	2002
best year	15.9%	2000	27.1%	1995

During the past five years, the fund's three worst months have been August 1998 (-7 percent), December 1999 (-7 percent), and December 1998 (-5 percent). During the same period, the three best months have been March 2000 (7 percent), April 1999 (5 percent), and October 1998 (5 percent). In the past, American Funds

American Balanced A has done better than 90 percent of its peer group during the most recent bull market and outperformed 70 percent of its peer group during the most recent bear market. Consistency, or predictability, of returns for American Funds American Balanced A can be described as good. This fund's risk-adjusted return over the past three/five years ranks in the top-two quintiles.

Management   ★★★

There are 110 stocks and 450 fixed-income securities in this $12 billion portfolio. The average balanced fund today is $270 million in size. Close to 60 percent of this fund's holdings are in stocks and 30 percent in bonds. The stocks in this portfolio have an average p/e ratio of 25 and a median market capitalization of $22 billion. The weighted coupon rate of the bonds in the portfolio averages 7 percent. The portfolio's equity holdings can be categorized as large-cap and value-oriented issues. The portfolio's fixed-income holdings can be categorized as intermediate-term, high-quality debt.

A team has managed this fund for the past 28 years. Management has consistently been more prudent than the majority of its competitors when it comes to security selection. The team that oversees this fund concentrates on established corporations. For the fixed-income portion of the portfolio, only investment-grade issues are purchased. There are 27 funds besides Balanced within the American Funds family. Overall, the fund family's risk adjusted performance can be described as very good.

Current Income   ★★★★

Over the past year, American Funds American Balanced A had a 12-month yield of 3.0 percent. During this same 12-month period, the typical balanced fund had a yield that averaged 2.2 percent.

Expenses   ★★★★★

American Funds American Balanced A's expense ratio is 0.7 percent; it has averaged 0.7 percent annually over the past three calendar years. The average expense ratio for the 1,150 funds in this category is 1.3 percent. This fund's turnover rate over the past year has been 50 percent, while its peer group average has been 98 percent.

Summary

American Funds American Balanced A is one of those funds that you love more the longer you own it. The fund has dramatically outperformed its peer group average over the past three and five years (outperforming 96 percent of its competitors), yet its risk level is in line with the overall category.

Profile

minimum initial investment $250	*IRA accounts available* . . . . yes
subsequent minimum investment . . . $50	*IRA minimum investment* $250
available in all 50 states . . . . yes	*date of inception* . . . . Jan. 1993
telephone exchanges . . . . yes	*dividend/income paid* . . . . quarterly
number of funds in family 28	*average credit quality* . . . . AA

Calamos Convertible Growth & Income A

1111 East Warrenville Road
Naperville, IL 60563
(800) 823-7386
www.calamos.com

total return	★★★★★
risk reduction	★★★
management	★★★★
current income	★★
expense control	★★★
symbol CVTRX	17 points
up-market performance	poor
down-market performance	excellent
predictability of returns	poor

Total Return   ★★★★★

Over the past five years, Calamos Convertible Growth & Income A has taken $10,000 and turned it into $17,840 ($9,910 over three years and $36,940 over the past 10 years). This translates into an annualized return of 12 percent over the past five years, 0 percent over the past three years, and 14 percent for the decade. Over the past five years, this fund has outperformed 99 percent of all mutual funds; within its general category it has also done better than 99 percent of its peers. Balanced funds have averaged 2 percent annually over these same five years.

During the past five years, a $10,000 initial investment grew to $16,350 after taxes, assuming a 40 percent income tax bracket (state and federal combined) and a capital gains rate of 20 percent. This means that investors in this fund were able to preserve 81 percent of their total returns. Compared to other funds in its category, this fund's tax savings are considered to be excellent.

Risk/Volatility   ★★★

Over the past five years, Calamos Convertible Growth & Income A has experienced average risk for its category. Over the past decade, the fund has had three negative years, while the S&P 500 has had three (off 9 percent in 2000, 12 percent in 2001, and 22 percent in 2002); the Lehman Brothers Aggregate Bond Index fell twice (off 3 percent in 1994 and 1 percent in 1999). The fund has underperformed the S&P 500 five times and the Lehman Brothers Aggregate Bond Index four times in the past 10 years. Consistency of *overperformance* for this fund has been excellent.

	last 5 years		last 10 years	
worst year	-4.1%	2002	-5.3%	1994
best year	52.9%	1999	52.9%	1999

During the past five years, the fund's three worst months have been November 2000 (-16 percent), August 1998 (-11 percent), and September 2001 (-7 percent). During the same period, the three best months have been December 1999 (17 percent), February 2000 (15 percent), and August 2000 (10 percent). In the past,

Calamos Convertible Growth & Income A has only done better than 12 percent of its peer group during the most recent bull market but outperformed 95 percent of its peer group during the most recent bear market. Consistency, or predictability, of returns for Calamos Convertible Growth & Income A can be described as poor. This fund's risk-adjusted return over the past three/five years ranks in the top quintile.

Management   ★★★★
There are 60 stocks and 80 fixed-income securities in this $470 million portfolio. The average balanced fund today is $270 million in size. Close to 20 percent of this fund's holdings are in stocks and 45 percent in bonds. The stocks in this portfolio have an average p/e ratio of 30 and a median market capitalization of $7 billion. The average maturity of the bonds in this account is four years; the weighted coupon rate averages 3 percent. The portfolio's equity holdings can be categorized as mid-cap and growth-oriented issues. The portfolio's fixed-income holdings can be categorized as short-term, low-quality debt.

John P. Calamos and Nick P. Calamos have managed this fund for the past 14 years. Management is very flexible with this offering; a large portion of fund assets are invested in stocks and low-quality convertibles. The name "Calamos" is almost synonymous with "convertibles." There are six funds besides Convertible Growth & Income within the Calamos family. Overall, the fund family's risk adjusted performance can be described as excellent.

Current Income   ★★
Over the past year, Calamos Convertible Growth & Income A had a 12-month yield of 1.9 percent. During this same 12-month period, the typical balanced fund had a yield that averaged 2.2 percent.

Expenses   ★★★
Calamos Convertible Growth & Income A's expense ratio is 1.4 percent; it has averaged 1.5 percent annually over the past three calendar years. The average expense ratio for the 1,150 funds in this category is 1.3 percent. This fund's turnover rate over the past year has been 82 percent, while its peer group average has been 98 percent.

Summary
Calamos Convertible Growth & Income A has outperformed 99 percent of its category and 99 percent of all mutual funds. It also has the best five-year track record of any balanced portfolio. The fund has consistently done better than its benchmark. The name "Calamos" is finally starting to get the recognition and praise it has long deserved.

Profile

minimum initial investment $1,000	*IRA accounts available* .... yes
subsequent minimum investment ... $50	*IRA minimum investment* $500
available in all 50 states .... yes	*date of inception* .... Sept. 1988
telephone exchanges .... yes	*dividend/income paid* .... quarterly
number of funds in family 7	*average credit quality* .... BB

Dodge & Cox Balanced
One Sansome Street, 35th Floor
San Francisco, CA 94104
(800) 621-3979
www.dodgeandcox.com

total return	★★★
risk reduction	★★★
management	★★★
current income	★★★★
expense control	★★★★★
symbol DODBX	18 points
up-market performance	very good
down-market performance	poor
predictability of returns	good

Total Return   ★★★
Over the past five years, Dodge & Cox Balanced has taken $10,000 and turned it into $14,710 ($12,300 over three years and $30,950 over the past 10 years). This translates into an annualized return of 8 percent over the past five years, 7 percent over the past three years, and 12 percent for the decade. Over the past five years, this fund has outperformed 97 percent of all mutual funds; within its general category it has done better than 98 percent of its peers. Balanced funds have averaged 2 percent annually over these same five years.

During the past five years, a $10,000 initial investment grew to $12,970 after taxes, assuming a 40 percent income tax bracket (state and federal combined) and a capital gains rate of 20 percent. This means that investors in this fund were able to preserve 63 percent of their total returns. Compared to other funds in its category, this fund's tax savings are considered to be very good.

Risk/Volatility   ★★★
Over the past five years, Dodge & Cox Balanced has experienced average risk for its category. Over the past decade, the fund has had one negative year, while the S&P 500 has had three (off 9 percent in 2000, 12 percent in 2001, and 22 percent in 2002); the Lehman Brothers Aggregate Bond Index fell twice (off 3 percent in 1994 and 1 percent in 1999). The fund has underperformed the S&P 500 five times and the Lehman Brothers Aggregate Bond Index twice in the past 10 years. Consistency of *overperformance* for this fund has been good.

	last 5 years		last 10 years	
worst year	-2.9%	2002	-2.9%	2002
best year	15.1%	2000	28%	1995

During the past five years, the fund's three worst months have been August 1998 (-8 percent), September 2001 (-6 percent), and December 2000 (-5 percent). During the same period, the three best months have been April 1999 (7 percent), November 2001 (5 percent), and October 1998 (4 percent). In the past, Dodge &

Cox Balanced has done better than 65 percent of its peer group during the most recent bull market and outperformed 86 percent of its peer group during the most recent bear market. Consistency, or predictability, of returns for Dodge & Cox Balanced can be described as good. This fund's risk-adjusted return over the past three/five years ranks in the top quintile.

Management   ★★★

There are 80 stocks and 140 fixed-income securities in this $8 billion portfolio. The average balanced fund today is $270 million in size. Close to 60 percent of this fund's holdings are in stocks and 30 percent in bonds. The stocks in this portfolio have an average p/e ratio of 26 and a median market capitalization of $10 billion. The average maturity of the bonds in this account is nine years. The portfolio's equity holdings can be categorized as large-cap and value-oriented issues. The portfolio's fixed-income holdings can be categorized as intermediate-term, high-quality debt.

A team has managed this fund for the past 36 years. Management is particularly strong when it comes to disciplined valuations and stock selection. The incredibly lengthy tenure of the management team, coupled with their low turnover and low overhead have only enhanced their reputation as "investor friendly." There are two funds besides Balanced within the Dodge & Cox family. Overall, the fund family's risk adjusted performance can be described as excellent.

Current Income   ★★★★

Over the past year, Dodge & Cox Balanced had a 12-month yield of 3.1 percent. During this same 12-month period, the typical balanced fund had a yield that averaged 2.2 percent.

Expenses   ★★★★★

Dodge & Cox Balanced's expense ratio is 0.5 percent; it has averaged 0.5 percent annually over the past three calendar years. The average expense ratio for the 1,150 funds in this category is 1.3 percent. This fund's turnover rate over the past year has been 21 percent, while its peer group average has been 98 percent.

Summary

Dodge & Cox Balanced is a fund that has appeared in numerous past editions of this book. The Dodge & Cox small family of funds is considered excellent across the board. This particular offering beats out all of the competition when it comes to keeping costs low and turnover at a minimum.

Profile

minimum initial investment $2,500	*IRA accounts available* .... yes
subsequent minimum investment .. $100	*IRA minimum investment* $1,000
available in all 50 states.......... yes	*date of inception* .... Jun. 1931
telephone exchanges .... yes	*dividend/income paid* .... quarterly
number of funds in family 3	*average credit quality*........... AA

First Eagle Global A
1345 Avenue of the Americas
New York, NY 10105
(800) 334-2143
www.firsteaglefunds.com

total return	★★★★
risk reduction	★★★
management	★★★★
current income	★★
expense control	★★★★
symbol SGENX	17 points
up-market performance	fair
down-market performance	excellent
predictability of returns	very good

Total Return   ★★★★

Over the past five years, First Eagle Global A has taken $10,000 and turned it into $15,890 ($13,330 over three years and $29,220 over the past 10 years). This translates into an annualized return of 10 percent over the past five years, 10 percent over the past three years, and 11 percent for the decade. Over the past five years, this fund has outperformed 97 percent of all mutual funds; within its general category it has done better than 99 percent of its peers. Balanced funds have averaged 2 percent annually over these same five years.

During the past five years, a $10,000 initial investment grew to $13,120 after taxes, assuming a 40 percent income tax bracket (state and federal combined) and a capital gains rate of 20 percent. This means that investors in this fund were able to preserve 53 percent of their total returns. Compared to other funds in its category, this fund's tax savings are considered to be good.

Risk/Volatility   ★★★

Over the past five years, First Eagle Global A has experienced average risk for its category. Over the past decade, the fund has had one negative year, while the S&P 500 has had three (off 9 percent in 2000, 12 percent in 2001, and 22 percent in 2002); the Lehman Brothers Aggregate Bond Index fell twice (off 3 percent in 1994 and 1 percent in 1999). The fund has underperformed the S&P 500 five times and the Lehman Brothers Aggregate Bond Index five times in the past 10 years. Consistency of *overperformance* for this fund has been very good.

	last 5 years		last 10 years	
worst year	-0.3%	1998	-0.3%	1998
best year	19.6%	1999	26.2%	1993

During the past five years, the fund's three worst months have been December 2000 (-13 percent), August 1998 (-9 percent), and July 1998 (-9 percent). During the same period, the three best months have been April 1999 (7 percent), April 2001 (5 percent), and March 2000 (4 percent). In the past, First Eagle

Global A has done better than 30 percent of its peer group during the most recent bull market and outperformed 98 percent of its peer group during the most recent bear market. Consistency, or predictability, of returns for First Eagle Global A can be described as very good. This fund's risk-adjusted return over the past three/five years ranks in the top quintile.

Management   ★★★★

There are 135 stocks and 55 fixed-income securities in this $2 billion portfolio. The average balanced fund today is $270 million in size. Close to 70 percent of this fund's holdings are in stocks and 16 percent in bonds. The stocks in this portfolio have an average p/e ratio of 22 and a median market capitalization of $2 billion. The portfolio's equity holdings can be categorized as mid-cap and value-oriented issues.

Jean-Marie Eveillard and Charles de Vaulx have managed this fund for the past 24 years. Management has a long-term view of their portfolio, as evidenced by the fund's low turnover rate. The managers are known to be contrarians, often buying issues that their peers are shunning; more often than not, the strategy pays off. They are open to buying stocks of any size. There are four funds besides Global within the First Eagle family. Overall, the fund family's risk adjusted performance can be described as excellent.

Current Income   ★★

Over the past year, First Eagle Global A had a 12-month yield of 1.9 percent. During this same 12-month period, the typical balanced fund had a yield that averaged 2.2 percent.

Expenses   ★★★★

First Eagle Global A's expense ratio is 1.4 percent; it has averaged 1.4 percent annually over the past three calendar years. The average expense ratio for the 1,150 funds in this category is 1.3 percent. This fund's turnover rate over the past year has been 29 percent, while its peer group average has been 98 percent.

Summary

First Eagle Global A is run by a couple of managers who have stood their ground over the past. Their consistent, cautious management style has paid off, time and time again. Lead manager Eveillard is viewed as one of the very best in the entire industry. He has kept a level head, even during the go-go years of the 1990s. This defensive play has smoked its category averages over the past three and five years while maintaining an average level of risk.

Profile

minimum initial investment $2,500	*IRA accounts available* .... yes
subsequent minimum investment .. $100	*IRA minimum investment* $1,000
available in all 50 states .... yes	*date of inception* .... Apr. 1970
telephone exchanges .... yes	*dividend/income paid* .... annually
number of funds in family 5	*average credit quality* .... N/A

FPA Crescent Institutional

11400 West Olympic Boulevard, Suite 1200
Los Angeles, CA 90064
(800) 982-4372
www.fpafunds.com

total return	★★★
risk reduction	★
management	★★★
current income	★★★
expense control	★★★
symbol FPACX	13 points
up-market performance	poor
down-market performance	excellent
predictability of returns	poor

Total Return   ★★★

Over the past five years, FPA Crescent Institutional has taken $10,000 and turned it into $14,090 ($14,630 over three years). This translates into an annualized return of 7 percent over the past five years and 14 percent over the past three years. Over the past five years, this fund has outperformed 94 percent of all mutual funds; within its general category it has done better than 97 percent of its peers. Balanced funds have averaged 2 percent annually over these same five years.

During the past five years, a $10,000 initial investment grew to $13,150 after taxes, assuming a 40 percent income tax bracket (state and federal combined) and a capital gains rate of 20 percent. This means that investors in this fund were able to preserve 77 percent of their total returns. Compared to other funds in its category, this fund's tax savings are considered to be excellent.

Risk/Volatility   ★

Over the past five years, FPA Crescent Institutional has experienced above average risk for its category. Over the past decade, the fund has had one negative year, while the S&P 500 has had three (off 9 percent in 2000, 12 percent in 2001, and 22 percent in 2002); the Lehman Brothers Aggregate Bond Index fell twice (off 3 percent in 1994 and 1 percent in 1999). The fund has underperformed the S&P 500 six times and the Lehman Brothers Aggregate Bond Index five times in the past 10 years. Consistency of *overperformance* for this fund has been good.

	last 5 years		last 10 years	
worst year	-6.3%	1999	-6.3%	1999
best year	36.1%	2001	36.1%	2001

In the past, FPA Crescent Institutional has only done better than 8 percent of its peer group during the most recent bull market but outperformed 98 percent of its peer group during the most recent bear market. Consistency, or predictability, of returns for FPA Crescent Institutional can be described as poor. This fund's risk-adjusted return over the past three/five years ranks in the top quintile.

Management   ★★★
There are 30 stocks and 25 fixed-income securities in this $190 million portfolio. The average balanced fund today is $270 million in size. Close to 40 percent of this fund's holdings are in stocks and 30 percent in bonds. The stocks in this portfolio have an average p/e ratio of 29 and a median market capitalization of $1 billion. The bonds in the portfolio have an average coupon rate of 6 percent. The portfolio's equity holdings can be categorized as small-cap and a blend of growth and value stocks.

Steven T. Romick has managed this fund for the past 10 years. Management is known for its iconoclastic approach, often avoiding what its peers are favoring. There are three funds besides Crescent Institutional within the FPA family. Overall, the fund family's risk adjusted performance can be described as between good and very good.

Current Income   ★★★
Over the past year, FPA Crescent Institutional had a 12-month yield of 2.5 percent. During this same 12-month period, the typical balanced fund had a yield that averaged 2.2 percent.

Expenses   ★★★
FPA Crescent Institutional's expense ratio is 1.5 percent; it has averaged 1.6 percent annually over the past three calendar years. The average expense ratio for the 1,150 funds in this category is 1.3 percent. This fund's turnover rate over the past year has been 34 percent, while its peer group average has been 98 percent.

Summary
FPA Crescent Institutional has the best three-year track record of any of its peer group in the book by a wide margin. The fund's five-year record is better than its category average by a ratio of over four-to-one. The fund's volatility and risk level are fairly high, but not when compared to equity categories. This is the kind of portfolio you want to own during uncertain or negative market periods.

Profile
minimum initial investment $1,500	*IRA accounts available* .... yes
subsequent minimum investment .. $100	*IRA minimum investment* $1,000
available in all 50 states .... yes	*date of inception* .... Jun. 1993
telephone exchanges .... yes	*dividend/income paid* .... semiannually
number of funds in family 4	*average credit quality* .... N/A

Franklin Income A

One Franklin Parkway
San Mateo, CA 94403
(800) 342-5236
www.franklintempleton.com

total return	★★★
risk reduction	★★★★
management	★★★★
current income	★★★★★
expense control	★★★★★
symbol FKINX	21 points
up-market performance	poor
down-market performance	excellent
predictability of returns	very good

Total Return   ★★★

Over the past five years, Franklin Income A has taken $10,000 and turned it into $12,030 ($12,010 over three years and $21,430 over the past 10 years). This translates into an annualized return of 4 percent over the past five years, 6 percent over the past three years, and 8 percent for the decade. Over the past five years, this fund has outperformed 60 percent of all mutual funds; within its general category it has done better than 76 percent of its peers. Balanced funds have averaged 2 percent annually over these same five years.

During the past five years, a $10,000 initial investment grew to $10,930 after taxes, assuming a 40 percent income tax bracket (state and federal combined) and a capital gains rate of 20 percent. This means that investors in this fund were able to preserve 46 percent of their total returns. Compared to other funds in its category, this fund's tax savings are considered to be good.

Risk/Volatility   ★★★★

Over the past five years, Franklin Income A has experienced below average risk for its category. Over the past decade, the fund has had three negative years, while the S&P 500 has had three (off 9 percent in 2000, 12 percent in 2001, and 22 percent in 2002); the Lehman Brothers Aggregate Bond Index fell twice (off 3 percent in 1994 and 1 percent in 1999). The fund has underperformed the S&P 500 six times and the Lehman Brothers Aggregate Bond Index four times in the past 10 years. Consistency of *overperformance* for this fund has been good.

	last 5 years		last 10 years	
worst year	-1.1%	2002	-6.4%	1994
best year	20.6%	2000	21.5%	1993

During the past five years, the fund's three worst months have been August 1998 (-7 percent), September 2001 (-5 percent), and February 1999 (-3 percent). During the same period, the three best months have been August 2000 (5 percent), September 1998 (4 percent), and April 1999 (4 percent). In the past, Franklin

Income A has only done better than 9 percent of its peer group during the most recent bull market but outperformed 95 percent of its peer group during the most recent bear market. Consistency, or predictability, of returns for Franklin Income A can be described as very good. This fund's risk-adjusted return over the past three/five years ranks in the top-two quintiles.

Management   ★★★★

There are 55 stocks and 465 fixed-income securities in this $7 billion portfolio. The average balanced fund today is $270 million in size. Close to 30 percent of this fund's holdings are in stocks and 55 percent in bonds. The stocks in this portfolio have an average p/e ratio of 17 and a median market capitalization of $9 billion. The bonds in the portfolio have an average coupon rate of 7 percent. The portfolio's equity holdings can be categorized as large-cap and value-oriented issues.

Charles B. Johnson and Edward D. Perks have managed this fund for the past forty-six years. There are few, if any, funds that have this kind of management tenure. Unlike their competitors, the managers favor utility stocks, high-yield bonds, as well as other income-producing securities. There are 92 funds besides Income within the Franklin Templeton family. Overall, the fund family's risk adjusted performance can be described as very good.

Current Income   ★★★★★

Over the past year, Franklin Income A had a 12-month yield of 8.1 percent. During this same 12-month period, the typical balanced fund had a yield that averaged 2.2 percent.

Expenses   ★★★★★

Franklin Income A's expense ratio is 0.7 percent; it has averaged 0.7 percent annually over the past three calendar years. The average expense ratio for the 1,150 funds in this category is 1.3 percent. This fund's turnover rate over the past year has been 51 percent, while its peer group average has been 98 percent.

Summary

Franklin Income A is the leader when it comes to current income; no other balanced fund in the book even comes close. Part of the reason for such high yields has been Franklin's ability to keep overhead costs very low and turnover modest. On a total point score basis, there is only one other fund that receives a higher score. This defensive play has served investors well over the short and long haul.

Profile

minimum initial investment $1,000	*IRA accounts available* .... yes
subsequent minimum investment ... $50	*IRA minimum investment* $250
available in all 50 states .... yes	*date of inception* .... Aug. 1948
telephone exchanges .... yes	*dividend/income paid* .... monthly
number of funds in family 93	*average credit quality* .... N/A

MFS Total Return A
P.O. Box 2281
Boston, MA 02107
(800) 637-2929
www.mfs.com

total return	★★★
risk reduction	★★★★
management	★★★★
current income	★★★★
expense control	★★★★
symbol MSFRX	19 points
up-market performance	fair
down-market performance	excellent
predictability of returns	very good

Total Return   ★★★
Over the past five years, MFS Total Return A has taken $10,000 and turned it into $12,790 ($11,170 over three years and $24,290 over the past 10 years). This translates into an annualized return of 5 percent over the past five years, 4 percent over the past three years, and 9 percent for the decade. Over the past five years, this fund has outperformed 85 percent of all mutual funds; within its general category it has done better than 91 percent of its peers. Balanced funds have averaged 2 percent annually over these same five years.

During the past five years, a $10,000 initial investment grew to $11,340 after taxes, assuming a 40 percent income tax bracket (state and federal combined) and a capital gains rate of 20 percent. This means that investors in this fund were able to preserve 48 percent of their total returns. Compared to other funds in its category, this fund's tax savings are considered to be good.

Risk/Volatility   ★★★★
Over the past five years, MFS Total Return A has experienced below average risk for its category. Over the past decade, the fund has had three negative years, while the S&P 500 has had three (off 9 percent in 2000, 12 percent in 2001, and 22 percent in 2002); the Lehman Brothers Aggregate Bond Index fell twice (off 3 percent in 1994 and 1 percent in 1999). The fund has underperformed the S&P 500 six times and the Lehman Brothers Aggregate Bond Index twice in the past 10 years. Consistency of *overperformance* for this fund has been very good.

	last 5 years		last 10 years	
worst year	-5.6%	2002	-5.6%	2002
best year	19.0%	2000	26.9%	1995

During the past five years, the fund's three worst months have been December 1998 (-11 percent), August 1998 (-7 percent), and December 1999 (-6 percent). During the same period, the three best months have been March 2000 (8 percent), August 2000 (5 percent), and April 1999 (4 percent). In the past, MFS

Total Return A has only done better than 35 percent of its peer group during the most recent bull market but outperformed 85 percent of its peer group during the most recent bear market. Consistency, or predictability, of returns for MFS Total Return A can be described as very good. This fund's risk-adjusted return over the past three/five years ranks in the top-two quintiles.

Management   ★★★★
There are 220 stocks and 335 fixed-income securities in this $5 billion portfolio. The average balanced fund today is $270 million in size. Close to 50 percent of this fund's holdings are in stocks and 35 percent in bonds. The stocks in this portfolio have an average p/e ratio of 24 and a median market capitalization of $17 billion. The average maturity of the bonds in this account is 13 years. The portfolio's equity holdings can be categorized as large-cap and value-oriented issues. The portfolio's fixed-income holdings can be categorized as intermediate-term, high-quality debt.

A team has managed this fund for the past eight years. Lead manager Dave Calabro employs a strategy that eschews price risk by favoring corporations with superior earnings growth potential that trade at a discount to their benchmark. Management is equally cautious when it comes to the fixed-income portion of their holdings. There are 60 funds besides Total Return within the MFS family. Overall, the fund family's risk adjusted performance can be described as between good and very good.

Current Income   ★★★★
Over the past year, MFS Total Return A had a 12-month yield of 3.1 percent. During this same 12-month period, the typical balanced fund had a yield that averaged 2.2 percent.

Expenses   ★★★★
MFS Total Return A's expense ratio is 0.9 percent; it has averaged 0.9 percent annually over the past three calendar years. The average expense ratio for the 1,150 funds in this category is 1.3 percent. This fund's turnover rate over the past year has been 86 percent, while its peer group average has been 98 percent.

Summary
MFS Total Return A has done a very good job across the board. This fund ranks highly in every category measured. The portfolio has beaten out 85 percent of all mutual funds and more than 90 percent of its peers. Overall risk and volatility have been low while predictability of returns has been on the high side.

Profile
minimum initial investment $1,000	*IRA accounts available* .... yes
subsequent minimum investment ... $50	*IRA minimum investment* $250
available in all 50 states .... yes	*date of inception* .... Oct. 1970
telephone exchanges .... yes	*dividend/income paid* .... monthly
number of funds in family 61	*average credit quality* .... N/A

Oakmark Equity & Income I
Two North LaSalle Street
Chicago, IL 60602
(800) 625-6275
www.oakmark.com

total return	★★★★★
risk reduction	★★★
management	★★★★
current income	★
expense control	★★★
symbol OAKBX	16 points
up-market performance	fair
down-market performance	excellent
predictability of returns	very good

Total Return   ★★★★★
Over the past five years, Oakmark Equity & Income I has taken $10,000 and turned it into $16,790 ($13,850 over three years). This translates into an annualized return of 11 percent over the past five years and 11 percent over the past three years. Over the past five years, this fund has outperformed 99 percent of all mutual funds; within its general category it has also done better than 99 percent of its peers. Balanced funds have averaged 2 percent annually over these same five years.

During the past five years, a $10,000 initial investment grew to $15,910 after taxes, assuming a 40 percent income tax bracket (state and federal combined) and a capital gains rate of 20 percent. This means that investors in this fund were able to preserve 87 percent of their total returns. Compared to other funds in its category, this fund's tax savings are considered to be excellent.

Risk/Volatility   ★★★
Over the past five years, Oakmark Equity & Income I has experienced average risk for its category. Over the past decade, the fund has had one negative year, while the S&P 500 has had three (off 9 percent in 2000, 12 percent in 2001, and 22 percent in 2002); the Lehman Brothers Aggregate Bond Index fell twice (off 3 percent in 1994 and 1 percent in 1999). The fund has underperformed the S&P 500 seven times and the Lehman Brothers Aggregate Bond Index three times in the past 10 years. Consistency of *overperformance* for this fund has been very good.

	last 5 years		last 10 years	
worst year	-2.1%	2002	-2.1%	2002
best year	19.9%	2000	26.6%	1997

During the past five years, the fund's three worst months have been November 1999 (-11 percent), August 1998 (-9 percent), and November 2000 (-7 percent). During the same period, the three best months have been September 1998 (6 percent), April 1999 (5 percent), and December 1998 (5 percent). In the past, Oakmark Equity & Income I has done better than 45 percent of its peer group during the most recent bull market and outperformed 90 percent of its peer group during the most recent bear market. Consistency, or predictability, of returns for Oakmark Equity & Income I can be described as very good. This fund's risk-adjusted return over the past three/five years ranks in the top quintile.

Management   ★★★★

There are 50 stocks and 35 fixed-income securities in this $3 billion portfolio. The average balanced fund today is $270 million in size. Close to 55 percent of this fund's holdings are in stocks and 45 percent in bonds. The stocks in this portfolio have an average p/e ratio of 21 and a median market capitalization of $4 billion. The bonds in the portfolio have an average coupon rate of 4 percent. The portfolio's equity holdings can be categorized as mid-cap and a blend of growth and value stocks.

Clyde S. McGregor and Edward Studzinski have managed this fund for the past seven years. Management invests quite of bit of its own money in this fund. The managers' overall philosophy is to buy stocks of companies they would personally like to own for a long time. There are five funds besides Equity & Income within the Oakmark family. Overall, the fund family's risk adjusted performance can be described as very good.

Current Income   ★

Over the past year, Oakmark Equity & Income I had a 12-month yield of 1.3 percent. During this same 12-month period, the typical balanced fund had a yield that averaged 2.2 percent.

Expenses   ★★★

Oakmark Equity & Income I's expense ratio is 1.1 percent; it has averaged 1.1 percent annually over the past three calendar years. The average expense ratio for the 1,150 funds in this category is 1.3 percent. This fund's turnover rate over the past year has been 124 percent, while its peer group average has been 98 percent.

Summary

Oakmark Equity & Income I sports the best combined three- and five-year track record. Oakmark is a name that has been in past editions of this book repeatedly. The fund has turned in extremely good results during bear markets while posting respectable results during bull market periods. Risk-adjusted returns are tops.

Profile

minimum initial investment $1,000	*IRA accounts available* .... yes
subsequent minimum investment .. $100	*IRA minimum investment* $1,000
available in all 50 states .... yes	*date of inception* .... Nov. 1995
telephone exchanges .... yes	*dividend/income paid* .... annually
number of funds in family 6	*average credit quality* .... N/A

Vanguard Wellesley Income
Vanguard Financial Center
P.O. Box 2600
Valley Forge, PA 19482
(800) 662-7447
www.vanguard.com

total return	★★★
risk reduction	★★★★★
management	★★★★★
current income	★★★★★
expense control	★★★★★
symbol VWINX	23 points
up-market performance	poor
down-market performance	excellent
predictability of returns	excellent

Total Return   ★★★

Over the past five years, Vanguard Wellesley Income has taken $10,000 and turned it into $14,000 ($13,050 over three years and $26,010 over the past 10 years). This translates into an annualized return of 7 percent over the past five years, 9 percent over the past three years, and 10 percent for the decade. Over the past five years, this fund has outperformed 94 percent of all mutual funds; within its general category it has done better than 96 percent of its peers. Balanced funds have averaged 2 percent annually over these same five years.

During the past five years, a $10,000 initial investment grew to $12,240 after taxes, assuming a 40 percent income tax bracket (state and federal combined) and a capital gains rate of 20 percent. This means that investors in this fund were able to preserve 56 percent of their total returns. Compared to other funds in its category, this fund's tax savings are considered to be good.

Risk/Volatility   ★★★★★

Over the past five years, Vanguard Wellesley Income has experienced low risk for its category. Over the past decade, the fund has had two negative years, while the S&P 500 has had three (off 9 percent in 2000, 12 percent in 2001, and 22 percent in 2002); the Lehman Brothers Aggregate Bond Index fell twice (off 3 percent in 1994 and 1 percent in 1999). The fund has underperformed the S&P 500 six times and the Lehman Brothers Aggregate Bond Index four times in the past 10 years. Consistency of *overperformance* for this fund has been very good.

	last 5 years		last 10 years	
worst year	-4.1%	1999	-4.4%	1994
best year	16.2%	2000	28.9%	1995

During the past five years, the fund's three worst months have been December 1999 (-8 percent), December 1998 (-5 percent), and December 2001 (-4 percent). During the same period, the three best months have been September

1998 (4 percent), March 2000 (4 percent), and April 1999 (3 percent). In the past, Vanguard Wellesley Income has only done better than 20 percent of its peer group during the most recent bull market and outperformed 96 percent of its peer group during the most recent bear market. Consistency, or predictability, of returns for Vanguard Wellesley Income can be described as excellent. This fund's risk-adjusted return over the past three/five years ranks in the top quintile.

Management   ★★★★★

There are 55 stocks and 230 fixed-income securities in this $7 billion portfolio. The average balanced fund today is $270 million in size. Close to 35 percent of this fund's holdings are in stocks and 65 percent in bonds. The stocks in this portfolio have an average p/e ratio of 22 and a median market capitalization of $22 billion. The average maturity of the bonds in this account is nine years; the weighted coupon rate averages 6 percent. The portfolio's equity holdings can be categorized as large-cap and value-oriented issues. The portfolio's fixed-income holdings can be categorized as intermediate-term, medium-quality debt.

Earl E. McEvoy and John R. Ryan have managed this fund for the past 20 years. Management favors dividend-rich companies and sticks to quality when it comes to the fixed-income portion of the portfolio. There are 78 funds besides Wellesley Income within the Vanguard family. Overall, the fund family's risk adjusted performance can be described as between good and very good.

Current Income   ★★★★★

Over the past year, Vanguard Wellesley Income had a 12-month yield of 4.6 percent. During this same 12-month period, the typical balanced fund had a yield that averaged 2.2 percent.

Expenses   ★★★★★

Vanguard Wellesley Income's expense ratio is 0.3 percent; it has averaged 0.3 percent annually over the past three calendar years. The average expense ratio for the 1,150 funds in this category is 1.3 percent. This fund's turnover rate over the past year has been 24 percent, while its peer group average has been 98 percent.

Summary

Vanguard Wellesley Income ranks number one when it comes to low risk, consistency of returns, low turnover, and expense control. None of its competitors even come close. It is no wonder that this balanced portfolio has outperformed 94 percent of all funds along with 96 percent of its peers.

Profile

minimum initial investment $3,000	*IRA accounts available* .... yes
subsequent minimum investment .. $100	*IRA minimum investment* $1,000
available in all 50 states .... yes	*date of inception* .... Jul. 1970
telephone exchanges .... yes	*dividend/income paid* .... quarterly
number of funds in family 79	*average credit quality* .... A

Corporate Bond Funds

Traditionally, bond funds are held by investors who require high current income and low risk. Interest income is normally paid on a monthly basis. Corporate bond funds are made up primarily of bonds issued by domestic corporations; government securities often represent a moderate part of these funds. Portfolio composition is almost always exclusively U.S. issues.

Bonds are normally purchased because of their income stream; the principal in a bond fund fluctuates. The major influence on bond prices, and therefore on the value of the fund's shares, is interest rates. There is an inverse relationship between interest rates and bond values; whatever one does, the other does the opposite. If interest rates rise, the price per share of a bond fund will fall, and vice versa.

The amount of appreciation or loss of a corporate bond fund depends primarily on the average maturity of the bonds in the portfolio. The cumulative amount of interest-rate movement and the typical yield of the bonds in the fund's portfolio are distant secondary concerns. *Short-term* bond funds, made up of debt instruments with an average maturity of five years or less, are subject to very little interest-rate risk or reward. *Medium-term* bond funds, with maturities averaging between six and 10 years, are subject to one-third to one-half the risk level of long-term funds. A long-term corporate bond fund will average an 8 percent increase or decrease in share price for every cumulative 1 percent change in interest rates.

Often investors can tell what kind of corporate bond fund they are purchasing by its name. Unless the fund includes the term *short* in its title, chances are that it is a medium- or long-term bond fund. Investors would be wise to contact the fund or meet with an investment advisor to learn more about the portfolio's average maturity; most bond funds will dramatically reduce their portfolio's average maturity during periods of interest-rate uncertainty.

The average weighted maturity for the bonds in these funds is just over seven years, the average coupon rate is 6 percent, and the average weighted price is $1,040 (meaning that the bonds are worth $40 more than face value, on average). A price, or value, of par ($1,000 per bond) means that the bonds in a portfolio are worth face value and are not currently being traded at a discount (a price less than $1,000 per bond) or at a premium (some figure above $1,000). The portfolio of the average corporate bond fund is made up of securities purchased at a $40-per-bond discount ($1,040 versus $1,000 for bonds bought at face value). A portfolio manager purchases bonds at a premium for one of two reasons: to increase the portfolio's current income, or to slightly decrease the fund's volatility (the lower the coupon rate, the more susceptible a bond is to the effects of interest-rate changes).

During the past 10 years, corporate bond funds have underperformed the Lehman Brothers Aggregate Bond Index by a little more than 1 percent per year. Over the past three and five years, the gap widens to roughly 2 percent. Average turnover during the past three years has been 185 percent, a surprisingly high figure given the general belief that stocks are traded (turned over) much more frequently than bonds. (The typical growth fund has a turnover rate of 110 percent annually.) The average corporate bond fund throws off an annual income stream of about 4.4 percent. The typical annual expense ratio for this group is just under 1 percent.

Over the past 15 years (ending December 31, 2002), individual corporate bonds have underperformed common stocks by just 0.5 percent per year. From 1988 through 2002, long-term corporate bonds averaged 8.8 percent compounded per year, compared to 9.3 percent for common stocks and 12.3 percent for small stocks. A $10,000 investment in corporate bonds grew to $41,710 over the past 15 years; a similar initial investment in common stocks grew to $51,020 and $56,660 for small stocks.

Over the past half-century, corporate bonds have only outpaced inflation on a pretax basis. A dollar invested in corporate bonds at the beginning of 1953 grew to $25.60 by the end of 2002. This translates into an average compound return of 6.7 percent per year. During this same period, $1 inflated to $6.80; this translates into an average annual inflation rate of 3.9 percent. This creates an inflation-adjusted rate of return of just 2.8 percent for corporate bonds. Factoring in taxes that would have been paid on the interest as it was received year by year lowers the real rate of return. This often results in flat and even negative real rates of return to the investor, especially for those in higher tax brackets.

Over the past 50 years, the worst year for long-term corporate bonds, on a total return basis (yield plus or minus principal appreciation or loss), was 1969, when a loss of 8 percent was suffered. The best year so far has been 1982, when corporate bonds posted a gain of 43 percent.

More than 1,030 funds make up the corporate bonds category. Over the past three and five years, corporate bond funds have had an average compound return of 7.6 percent and 5.8 percent per year, respectively. For the decade, corporate bond funds have averaged 6.4 percent per year and 7.7 percent per annum for the past 15 years (all periods ending December 31, 2002). All of these figures represent total returns. This means that bond appreciation (or depreciation) was added (or subtracted) from current yield.

The standard deviation for corporate bond funds has been 3.7 percent over the past three years. As you may recall, a low standard deviation means a greater predictability of returns (fewer surprises—for better or worse). If a fund, or fund category, such as corporate bonds, has an average annual return of 7 percent and a standard deviation of 3.7 percent, this means that returns for every two out of three years should be roughly 7 percent, plus or minus 3.7 percent (one standard deviation). If you want to increase certainty of returns, then you must look at two standard deviations. This means that returns, for about 95 percent of the time, would be 7 percent plus or minus 7.4 percent (or -0.4 percent to +14.4 percent). These funds have been less volatile than any equity fund and have shown similar return variances (volatility) as government bond funds.

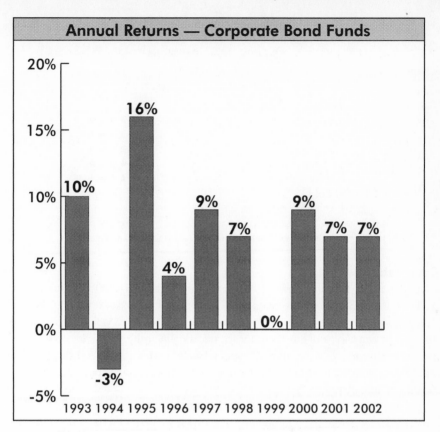

Dodge & Cox Income
One Sansome Street, 35th Floor
San Francisco, CA 94104
(800) 621-3979
www.dodgeandcox.com

total return	★★★★★
risk reduction	★★★★★
management	★★★★★
current income	★★★★★
expense control	★★★★★
symbol DODIX	25 points
up-market performance	good
down-market performance	excellent
predictability of returns	very good

Total Return   ★★★★★

Over the past five years, Dodge & Cox Income has taken $10,000 and turned it into $14,500 ($13,530 over three years and $21,490 over the past 10 years). This translates into an annualized return of 8 percent over the past five years, 11 percent over the past three years, and 8 percent for the decade. Over the past five years, this fund has outperformed 95 percent of all mutual funds; within its general category it has also done better than 95 percent of its peers. Corporate bond funds have averaged 6 percent annually over these same five years.

During the past five years, a $10,000 initial investment grew to $11,200 after taxes, assuming a 40 percent income tax bracket (state and federal combined) and a capital gains rate of 20 percent. This means that investors in this fund were able to preserve 68 percent of their total returns. Compared to other funds in its category, this fund's tax savings are considered to be excellent.

Risk/Volatility   ★★★★★

Over the past five years, Dodge & Cox Income has experienced below average risk for its category. Over the past decade, the fund has had two negative years, while the Lehman Brothers Aggregate Bond Index has had two (off 3 percent in 1994 and 1 percent in 1999). The fund has underperformed the Lehman Brothers Aggregate Bond Index twice in the past 10 years. Consistency of *overperformance* for this fund has been excellent.

	last 5 years		last 10 years	
worst year	-0.8%	1999	-2.9%	1994
best year	10.8%	2002	20.2%	1995

During the past five years, the fund's three worst months have been December 2001 (-2 percent), June 1999 (-2 percent), and December 1999 (-2 percent). During the same period, the three best months have been January 2001 (2 percent), July 2001 (2 percent), and October 2001 (2 percent). In the past, Dodge & Cox Income has done better than 60 percent of its peer group during the most recent bull market and outperformed 90 percent of its peer group during the most recent bear market. Consistency, or predictability, of returns for Dodge & Cox Income can be described as very good. This fund's risk-adjusted return over the past three/five years ranks in the top quintile.

Management   ★★★★★
There are 175 fixed-income securities in this $2 billion portfolio. The average corporate bond fund today is $355 million in size. Close to 90 percent of the fund's holdings are in bonds. The average maturity of the bonds in this account is seven years; the weighted coupon rate averages 7 percent. The portfolio's fixed-income holdings can be categorized as intermediate-term, high-quality debt.

A team has managed this fund for the past 14 years. Management performs rigorous credit research and spends quite a bit of time selecting each security. The managers favor mortgage-backed securities that have stable cash values as well as mid- and high-quality corporate issues. The fund's price movement is strongly correlated to that of the Lehman Brothers Aggregate Bond Index. There are two funds besides Income within the Dodge & Cox family. Overall, the fund family's risk adjusted performance can be described as excellent.

Current Income   ★★★★★
Over the past year, Dodge & Cox Income had a 12-month yield of 5.1 percent. During this same 12-month period, the typical corporate bond fund had a yield that averaged 4.4 percent.

Expenses   ★★★★★
Dodge & Cox Income's expense ratio is 0.5 percent; it has averaged 0.5 percent annually over the past three calendar years. The average expense ratio for the 1,030 funds in this category is 1.0 percent. This fund's turnover rate over the past year has been 40 percent, while its peer group average has been 184 percent.

Summary
Dodge & Cox Income has some of the best returns in its category for the past three and five years, yet the fund ties for number one as having the lowest risk. Expenses and turnover are also quite low. Overall, this corporate bond fund has outperformed 95 percent of the entire fund industry as well as 95 percent of its class. Investors would be wise to include other Dodge & Cox offerings in their portfolio as well. Its overall point score is perfect. A record only a couple of funds in the entire book can match.

Profile
minimum initial investment $2,500	*IRA accounts available* . . . . yes
subsequent minimum investment . . $100	*IRA minimum investment* $1,000
available in all 50 states . . . . yes	*date of inception* . . . . Jan. 1989
telephone exchanges . . . . yes	*dividend/income paid* . . . . quarterly
number of funds in family 3	*average credit quality* . . . . AA

Fidelity Short-Term Bond
82 Devonshire Street
Boston, MA 02109
(800) 544-8888
www.fidelity.com

total return	★★★★
risk reduction	★★★★
management	★★★★
current income	★★★★
expense control	★★★★
symbol FSHBX	20 points
up-market performance	very good
down-market performance	fair
predictability of returns	excellent

Total Return   ★★★★

Over the past five years, Fidelity Short-Term Bond has taken $10,000 and turned it into $13,580 ($12,380 over three years and $17,380 over the past 10 years). This translates into an annualized return of 6 percent over the past five years, 7 percent over the past three years, and 6 percent for the decade. Over the past five years, this fund has outperformed 87 percent of all mutual funds; within its general category it has done better than 80 percent of its peers. Corporate bond funds have averaged 6 percent annually over these same five years.

During the past five years, a $10,000 initial investment grew to $11,200 after taxes, assuming a 40 percent income tax bracket (state and federal combined) and a capital gains rate of 20 percent. This means that investors in this fund were able to preserve 65 percent of their total returns. Compared to other funds in its category, this fund's tax savings are considered to be excellent.

Risk/Volatility   ★★★★

Over the past five years, Fidelity Short-Term Bond has experienced below average risk for its category. Over the past decade, the fund has had one negative year, while the Lehman Brothers Aggregate Bond Index has had two (off 3 percent in 1994 and 1 percent in 1999). The fund has underperformed the Lehman Brothers Aggregate Bond Index eight times in the past 10 years. Consistency of *overperformance* for this fund has been fair.

	last 5 years		last 10 years	
worst year	3.3%	1999	-4.1%	1994
best year	7.9%	2000	9.8%	1995

During the past five years, the fund's three worst months have been November 2001 (-1 percent), May 1999 (-1 percent), and February 1999 (-1 percent). During the same period, the three best months have been January 2001 (1 percent), July 2001 (1 percent), and September 1998 (1 percent). In the past, Fidelity Short-Term Bond has done better than 75 percent of its peer group during the most recent bull market and outperformed 40 percent of its peer group during the most recent bear market. Consistency, or predictability, of returns for Fidelity Short-Term Bond can be described as excellent. This fund's risk-adjusted return over the past three/five years ranks in the top-two quintiles.

Management   ★★★★
There are 520 fixed-income securities in this $5 billion portfolio. The average corporate bond fund today is $355 million in size. Close to 95 percent of the fund's holdings are in bonds. The average maturity of the bonds in this account is two years. The portfolio's fixed-income holdings can be categorized as short-term, medium-quality debt.

Andrew J. Dudley has managed this fund for the past six years. Management prefers to keep the portfolio's overall interest-rate risk close to that of the Lehman Brothers 1-3 Government/Corporate Bond Index. Because of the large number of holdings, issue-specific problems have virtually no impact on performance. The fund's price movement is highly correlated to that of the Lehman Brothers Aggregate Bond Index. There are 76 funds besides Short-Term Bond within the Fidelity family. Overall, the fund family's risk adjusted performance can be described as very good.

Current Income   ★★★★
Over the past year, Fidelity Short-Term Bond had a 12-month yield of 4.3 percent. During this same 12-month period, the typical corporate bond fund had a yield that averaged 4.4 percent.

Expenses   ★★★★
Fidelity Short-Term Bond's expense ratio is 0.6 percent; it has averaged 0.6 percent annually over the past three calendar years. The average expense ratio for the 1,030 funds in this category is 1.0 percent. This fund's turnover rate over the past year has been 145 percent, while its peer group average has been 184 percent.

Summary
Fidelity Short-Term Bond is one of the most consistent offerings in its field. The risk of this fund is quite low; two year bonds have very little volatility. It is one of the very few funds in the entire book that scores very well in every single category. There are certainly more exciting funds out there, but few with this kind of predictability.

Profile
minimum initial investment $2,500	*IRA accounts available* . . . . yes
subsequent minimum investment . . $250	*IRA minimum investment* $500
available in all 50 states . . . . yes	*date of inception* . . . . Sept. 1986
telephone exchanges . . . . yes	*dividend/income paid*. . . . . monthly
number of funds in family 77	*average credit quality* . . . . A

Fremont Bond
50 Beale Street, Suite 100
San Francisco, CA 94105
(800) 548-4539
www.fremontinstitutional.com

total return	★★★★★
risk reduction	★★
management	★★★★
current income	★★★
expense control	★★★★
symbol FBDFX	18 points
up-market performance	very good
down-market performance	very good
predictability of returns	good

Total Return   ★★★★★
Over the past five years, Fremont Bond has taken $10,000 and turned it into
$14,760 ($13,590 over three years). This translates into an annualized return of
8 percent over the past five years and 11 percent over the past three years. Over the
past five years, this fund has outperformed 96 percent of all mutual funds; within
its general category it has done better than 98 percent of its peers. Corporate bond
funds have averaged 6 percent annually over these same five years.

During the past five years, a $10,000 initial investment grew to $11,200 after
taxes, assuming a 40 percent income tax bracket (state and federal combined) and
a capital gains rate of 20 percent. This means that investors in this fund were able
to preserve 68 percent of their total returns. Compared to other funds in its category, this fund's tax savings are considered to be excellent.

Risk/Volatility   ★★
Over the past five years, Fremont Bond has experienced above average risk for its
category. Over the past decade, the fund has had two negative years, while the
Lehman Brothers Aggregate Bond Index has had two (off 3 percent in 1994 and
1 percent in 1999). The fund has underperformed the Lehman Brothers Aggregate
Bond Index four times in the past 10 years. Consistency of *overperformance* for
this fund has been excellent.

	last 5 years		last 10 years	
worst year	-1.2%	1999	-4.0%	1994
best year	12.8%	2000	21.2%	1995

During the past five years, the fund's three worst months have been
December 2001 (-2 percent), February 1999 (-2 percent), and November 2001 (-2
percent). During the same period, the three best months have been September 1998
(2 percent), July 2001 (2 percent), and June 2000 (1 percent). In the past, Fremont
Bond has done better than 77 percent of its peer group during the most recent bull
market and outperformed 75 percent of its peer group during the most recent bear

market. Consistency, or predictability, of returns for Fremont Bond can be described as good. This fund's risk-adjusted return over the past three/five years ranks in the top quintile.

Management   ★★★★

There are 360 fixed-income securities in this $1 billion portfolio. The average corporate bond fund today is $355 million in size. Close to 65 percent of the fund's holdings are in bonds. The average maturity of the bonds in this account is seven years; the weighted coupon rate averages 6 percent. The portfolio's fixed-income holdings can be categorized as intermediate-term, high-quality debt.

   William H. Gross has managed this fund for the past nine years. Management relies on macroeconomic analysis to help set the portfolio's interest-rate sensitivity. Gross is quick to take advantage of price inefficiencies. He is particularly deft at sector rotation and the direction of interest rates. The fund's price movement is strongly correlated to that of the Lehman Brothers Aggregate Bond Index. There are six funds besides Bond within the Fremont Investment Advisors family. Overall, the fund family's risk adjusted performance can be described as very good.

Current Income   ★★★

Over the past year, Fremont Bond had a 12-month yield of 3.6 percent. During this same 12-month period, the typical corporate bond fund had a yield that averaged 4.4 percent.

Expenses   ★★★★

Fremont Bond's expense ratio is 0.6 percent; it has averaged 0.6 percent annually over the past three calendar years. The average expense ratio for the 1,030 funds in this category is 1.0 percent. This fund's turnover rate over the past year has been 160 percent, while its peer group average has been 184 percent.

Summary

Fremont Bond has the best five-year track record plus the second best three-year record in its class. Risk level is a little higher than average, but quite low when compared to virtually any other mutual fund category. The portfolio is overseen by legendary fixed-income manager Bill Gross. He has an almost uncanny ability when it comes to the bond marketplace. Even though this is a corporate bond fund, it has managed to turn in better results than 96 percent of the mutual fund universe.

Profile

minimum initial investment $2,000	*IRA accounts available* . . . . yes
subsequent minimum investment . . $100	*IRA minimum investment* $1,000
available in all 50 states . . . . yes	*date of inception* . . . . Apr. 1993
telephone exchanges . . . . yes	*dividend/income paid* . . . . monthly
number of funds in family 7	*average credit quality* . . . . AA

Janus Short-Term Bond

100 Fillmore Street, Suite 300
Denver, CO 80206
(800) 525-8983
www.janus.com

total return	★★★★
risk reduction	★★★★★
management	★★★★
current income	★★★
expense control	★★★
symbol JASBX	19 points
up-market performance	very good
down-market performance	poor
predictability of returns	excellent

Total Return   ★★★★

Over the past five years, Janus Short-Term Bond has taken $10,000 and turned it into $13,090 ($11,920 over three years and $17,050 over the past 10 years). This translates into an annualized return of 6 percent over the past five years, 6 percent over the past three years, and 5 percent for the decade. Over the past five years, this fund has outperformed 80 percent of all mutual funds; within its general category it has done better than 35 percent of its peers. Corporate bond funds have averaged 6 percent annually over these same five years.

During the past five years, a $10,000 initial investment grew to $11,200 after taxes, assuming a 40 percent income tax bracket (state and federal combined) and a capital gains rate of 20 percent. This means that investors in this fund were able to preserve 63 percent of their total returns. Compared to other funds in its category, this fund's tax savings are considered to be excellent.

Risk/Volatility   ★★★★★

Over the past five years, Janus Short-Term Bond has experienced below average risk for its category. Over the past decade, the fund has had no negative years, while the Lehman Brothers Aggregate Bond Index has had two (off 3 percent in 1994 and 1 percent in 1999). The fund has underperformed the Lehman Brothers Aggregate Bond Index seven times in the past 10 years. Consistency of *overperformance* for this fund has been poor.

	last 5 years		last 10 years	
worst year	2.9%	1999	0.4%	1994
best year	7.7%	2000	7.9%	1995

During the past five years, the fund's three worst months have been April 2000 (-1 percent), February 1999 (-1 percent), and May 1999 (-1 percent). During the same period, the three best months have been September 1998 (1 percent), June 2000 (1 percent), and January 1998 (1 percent). In the past, Janus Short-Term Bond has done better than 77 percent of its peer group during the most recent bull market but outperformed just 15 percent of its peer group during the most recent bear market. Consistency, or predictability, of returns for Janus Short-Term Bond can be described as excellent. This fund's risk-adjusted return over the past three/five years ranks in the top-three quintiles.

Management   ★★★★

There are 65 fixed-income securities in this $480 million portfolio. The average corporate bond fund today is $355 million in size. Close to 90 percent of the fund's holdings are in bonds. The average maturity of the bonds in this account is three years; the weighted coupon rate averages 4 percent. The portfolio's fixed-income holdings can be categorized as short-term, high-quality debt.

Sandy R. Rufenacht has managed this fund for the past seven years. Management keeps the vast majority of the portfolio in investment-grade issues. Rufenacht makes sure the fund stays broadly diversified across the corporate, government, and mortgage-backed bond landscape. Hedging helps reduce potential problems with any interest rate increases. The fund's price movement is only modestly correlated to that of the Lehman Brothers Aggregate Bond Index. There are 30 funds besides Short-Term Bond within the Janus family. Overall, the fund family's risk adjusted performance can be described as good.

Current Income   ★★★

Over the past year, Janus Short-Term Bond had a 12-month yield of 3.5 percent. During this same 12-month period, the typical corporate bond fund had a yield that averaged 4.4 percent.

Expenses   ★★★

Janus Short-Term Bond's expense ratio is 0.7 percent; it has averaged 0.7 percent annually over the past three calendar years. The average expense ratio for the 1,030 funds in this category is 1.0 percent. This fund's turnover rate over the past year has been 201 percent, while its peer group average has been 184 percent.

Summary

Janus Short-Term Bond ties for first place when it comes to risk reduction. It takes first place honors when it comes to consistency of returns. By keeping average maturities in the three-year range, Janus is able to offer investors a fund that will never disappoint investors.

Profile

minimum initial investment $2,500	*IRA accounts available* . . . . yes
subsequent minimum investment . . $100	*IRA minimum investment* $500
available in all 50 states . . . . yes	*date of inception* . . . . Sept. 1992
telephone exchanges . . . . yes	*dividend/income paid*. . . . . monthly
number of funds in family 31	*average credit quality*. . . . . AA

TIAA-CREF Bond Plus
c/o State Street Bank
P.O. Box 8009
Boston, MA 02266
(800) 223-1200
www.tiaa-cref.org

total return	★★★★★
risk reduction	★★★
management	★★★★★
current income	★★★★★
expense control	★★★★
symbol TIPBX	22 points
up-market performance	fair
down-market performance	excellent
predictability of returns	good

Total Return   ★★★★★

Over the past five years, TIAA-CREF Bond Plus has taken $10,000 and turned it into $14,390 ($13,340 over three years). This translates into an annualized return of 8 percent over the past five years and 10 percent over the past three years. Over the past five years, this fund has outperformed 95 percent of all mutual funds; within its general category it has done better than 92 percent of its peers. Corporate bond funds have averaged 6 percent annually over these same five years.

During the past five years, a $10,000 initial investment grew to $11,200 after taxes, assuming a 40 percent income tax bracket (state and federal combined) and a capital gains rate of 20 percent. This means that investors in this fund were able to preserve 64 percent of their total returns. Compared to other funds in its category, this fund's tax savings are considered to be excellent.

Risk/Volatility   ★★★

Over the past five years, TIAA-CREF Bond Plus has experienced average risk for its category. Over the past decade, the fund has had one negative year, while the Lehman Brothers Aggregate Bond Index has had two (off 3 percent in 1994 and 1 percent in 1999). The fund has underperformed the Lehman Brothers Aggregate Bond Index six times in the past 10 years. Consistency of *overperformance* for this fund has been excellent.

	last 5 years		last 10 years	
worst year	-1.0%	1999	-1.0%	1999
best year	11.7%	2000	11.7%	2000

During the past five years, the fund's three worst months have been December 2001 (-2 percent), February 1999 (-2 percent), and November 2001 (-2 percent). During the same period, the three best months have been September 1998 (2 percent), July 2001 (2 percent), and June 2000 (1 percent). In the past, TIAA-CREF Bond Plus has only done better than 25 percent of its peer group during the most recent bull market and outperformed 95 percent of its peer group during the most recent bear market. Consistency, or predictability, of returns for TIAA-CREF Bond Plus can be described as good. This fund's risk-adjusted return over the past three/five years ranks in the top quintile.

Management   ★★★★★
There are 210 fixed-income securities in this $330 million portfolio. The average corporate bond fund today is $355 million in size. Close to 80 percent of the fund's holdings are in bonds. The average maturity of the bonds in this account is eight years; the weighted coupon rate averages 6 percent. The portfolio's fixed-income holdings can be categorized as intermediate-term, high-quality debt.

A team has managed this fund for the past five years. Management is able to keep risk to a minimum by making sure the portfolio stays broadly diversified. Lead manager Lisa Black minimizes any kind of interest rate risk, focusing instead on investment grade issues. The fund's price movement is close to 100 percent correlated to that of the Lehman Brothers Aggregate Bond Index. There are 15 funds besides Bond Plus within the TIAA-CREF Mutual Funds family. Overall, the fund family's risk adjusted performance can be described as good.

Current Income   ★★★★★
Over the past year, TIAA-CREF Bond Plus had a 12-month yield of 4.9 percent. During this same 12-month period, the typical corporate bond fund had a yield that averaged 4.4 percent.

Expenses   ★★★★
TIAA-CREF Bond Plus's expense ratio is 0.3 percent; it has averaged 0.3 percent annually over the past three calendar years. The average expense ratio for the 1,030 funds in this category is 1.0 percent. This fund's turnover rate over the past year has been 234 percent, while its peer group average has been 184 percent.

Summary
TIAA-CREF Bond Plus turns in a near-perfect score of 22 out of 25. Only one other corporate bond fund has a better overall score. Performance over the past three and five years has been outstanding while risk level has been average. The TIAA-CREF group is just beginning to make a name for itself outside the educational marketplace. All investors should welcome this addition.

Profile

minimum initial investment $2,500	*IRA accounts available* . . . . yes
subsequent minimum investment . . . $50	*IRA minimum investment* $2,000
available in all 50 states . . . . yes	*date of inception* . . . . Sept. 1997
telephone exchanges . . . . yes	*dividend/income paid* . . . . monthly
number of funds in family 16	*average credit quality* . . . . AA

Vanguard Intermediate-Term Bond Index

Vanguard Financial Center
P.O. Box 2600
Valley Forge, PA 19482
(800) 662-7447
www.vanguard.com

total return	★★★★★
risk reduction	★
management	★★★★
current income	★★★★★
expense control	★★★★★
symbol VBIIX	20 points
up-market performance	poor
down-market performance	excellent
predictability of returns	fair

Total Return   ★★★★★

Over the past five years, Vanguard Intermediate-Term Bond Index has taken $10,000 and turned it into $14,590 ($13,660 over three years). This translates into an annualized return of 8 percent over the past five years and 11 percent over the past three years. Over the past five years, this fund has outperformed 95 percent of all mutual funds; within its general category it has done better than 94 percent of its peers. Corporate bond funds have averaged 6 percent annually over these same five years.

During the past five years, a $10,000 initial investment grew to $11,200 after taxes, assuming a 40 percent income tax bracket (state and federal combined) and a capital gains rate of 20 percent. This means that investors in this fund were able to preserve 63 percent of their total returns. Compared to other funds in its category, this fund's tax savings are considered to be excellent.

Risk/Volatility   ★

Over the past five years, Vanguard Intermediate-Term Bond Index has experienced high risk for its category. Over the past decade, the fund has had one negative year, while the Lehman Brothers Aggregate Bond Index has had two (off 3 percent in 1994 and 1 percent in 1999). The fund has underperformed the Lehman Brothers Aggregate Bond Index four times in the past 10 years. Consistency of *overperformance* for this fund has been very good.

	last 5 years		last 10 years	
worst year	-3.0%	1999	-3.0%	1999
best year	12.8%	2000	21.0%	1995

During the past five years, the fund's three worst months have been February 1999 (-3 percent), November 2000 (-2 percent), and April 2001 (-1 percent). During the same period, the three best months have been September 1998 (3 percent), July 2001 (2 percent), and June 2000 (2 percent). In the past, Vanguard

Intermediate-Term Bond Index has only done better than 10 percent of its peer group during the most recent bull market but outperformed 95 percent of its peer group during the most recent bear market. Consistency, or predictability, of returns for Vanguard Intermediate-Term Bond Index can be described as fair. This fund's risk-adjusted return over the past three/five years ranks in the top quintile.

Management   ★★★★

There are 295 fixed-income securities in this $2 billion portfolio. The average corporate bond fund today is $355 million in size. Close to 100 percent of the fund's holdings are in bonds. The average maturity of the bonds in this account is eight years; the weighted coupon rate averages 7 percent. The portfolio's fixed-income holdings can be categorized as intermediate-term, high-quality debt.

Ian A. MacKinnon and Kenneth Volpert have managed this fund for the past nine years. Management's goal is to approximate the performance and risk level of the Lehman Brothers 5-10 Government/Credit Index. Manager Volpert seeks higher-yielding corporates over Treasuries in an effort to boost overall returns. The fund's price movement is very highly correlated to that of the Lehman Brothers Aggregate Bond Index. There are 78 funds besides Intermediate-Term Bond Index within the Vanguard family. Overall, the fund family's risk adjusted performance can be described as between good and very good.

Current Income   ★★★★★

Over the past year, Vanguard Intermediate-Term Bond Index had a 12-month yield of 5.6 percent. During this same 12-month period, the typical corporate bond fund had a yield that averaged 4.4 percent.

Expenses   ★★★★★

Vanguard Intermediate-Term Bond Index's expense ratio is 0.2 percent; it has averaged 0.2 percent annually over the past three calendar years. The average expense ratio for the 1,030 funds in this category is 1.0 percent. This fund's turnover rate over the past year has been 135 percent, while its peer group average has been 184 percent.

Summary

Vanguard Intermediate-Term Bond Index ranks as the number one performer for the past three years and number two for the last five years. Current income is also higher than any of its peers. Part of the fund's success is due to its low expenses; known to be the lowest in the industry. The fund's risk level is high, but not when compared to other mutual fund categories.

Profile

minimum initial investment $3,000	*IRA accounts available* . . . . yes
subsequent minimum investment . . $100	*IRA minimum investment* $1,000
available in all 50 states . . . . yes	*date of inception*. . . . . Mar. 1994
telephone exchanges . . . . yes	*dividend/income paid*. . . . . monthly
number of funds in family 79	*average credit quality* . . . . AA

Financial Funds

A potential problem with including sector funds is that investors may be tempted to get away from diversification and go right into one or more specialized plays. Indeed, the following bar chart makes a convincing case for the financial stocks.

Over the past 15 years (ending December 31, 2002), financial funds have outperformed common stocks by 4.5 percent per year, as measured by the S&P 500. From 1988–2002, financial funds averaged 16.0 percent, while common stocks averaged 11.5 percent compounded per year. A $10,000 investment in financial funds grew to $92,700 over the past 15 years; while $10,000 invested in the S&P 500 grew to $51,020.

During the past three years, financial funds have outperformed the S&P 500 by 18.3 percent per year. Over the past five and 10 years, this fund category has outperformed the S&P 500 by an average of 3.5 percent and 3.2 percent per year, respectively. Average turnover during the past three years has been 140 percent.

The p/e ratio is 18 for the typical financial fund, versus 25 for the S&P 500. The typical stock in these portfolios is only 42 percent the size of the average stock in the S&P 500. The average beta is 0.7, which means the group has a market-related risk that is 30 percent lower than the S&P 500. The average financial fund throws off a 0.7 percent annual income stream. The typical annual expense ratio for this group is 1.7 percent.

Over the past three years, financial funds have averaged a compound return of 3.7 percent per year. The annual return has been 2.9 percent for the past five years, 12.6 percent for the past decade, and 16.0 percent for the past 15 years. The standard deviation has been 22 percent over the past three years, versus 16 percent for the S&P 500.

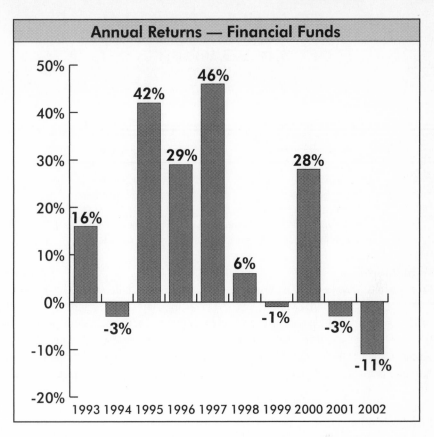

FBR Small Cap Financial A

4922 Fairmont Avenue
Bethesda, MD 20814
(888) 888-0025
www.fbrfunds.com

total return	★★★★★
risk reduction	★★★★★
management	★★★★★
tax minimization	★★★★★
expense control	★★★★★
symbol FBRSX	25 points
up-market performance	fair
down-market performance	excellent
predictability of returns	excellent

Total Return   ★★★★★

Over the past five years, FBR Small Cap Financial A has taken $10,000 and turned it into $15,900 ($19,470 over three years). This translates into an annualized return of 10 percent over the past five years and 25 percent over the past three years. Over the past five years, this fund has outperformed 98 percent of all mutual funds; within its general category it has done better than 97 percent of its narrow peer group. Financial funds have averaged 3 percent annually over these same five years.

Risk/Volatility   ★★★★★

Over the past five years, FBR Small Cap Financial A has experienced low risk for its category. Over the past decade, the fund has had two negative years, while the S&P 500 has had three (off 9 percent in 2000, 12 percent in 2001, and 22 percent in 2002); the Wilshire 5000 fell four times (off less than 1 percent in 1994, 11 percent in 2000, 11 percent in 2001, and 21 percent in 2002). The fund has underperformed the S&P 500 six times and the Wilshire 5000 five times in the past 10 years. Consistency of *overperformance* for this fund has been good.

	last 5 years		last 10 years	
worst year	-13.6%	1998	-13.6%	1998
best year	32.4%	2000	58.4%	1997

During the past five years, the fund's three worst months have been August 1998 (-20 percent), December 1998 (-14 percent), and January 2000 (-6 percent). During the same period, the three best months have been December 2000 (10 percent), August 2000 (8 percent), and September 1998 (7 percent). In the past, FBR Small Cap Financial A has only done better than 20 percent of its peer group during the most recent bull market but outperformed 99 percent of its peer group during the most recent bear market. Consistency, or predictability, of returns for FBR Small Cap Financial A can be described as excellent. This fund's risk-adjusted return over the past three/five years ranks in the top quintile.

Management   ★★★★★

There are 50 stocks in this $360 million portfolio. The average financial fund today is $110 million in size. Close to 85 percent of the fund's holdings are in stocks. The stocks in this portfolio have an average p/e ratio of 15 and a median market capitalization of $220 million. The 10 largest holdings compose 34 percent of the fund's total assets. The portfolio's equity holdings can be categorized as small-cap and a blend of growth and value stocks.

David Ellison has managed this fund for the past six years. Management invests in small banks and thrifts with basic and transparent business models. Ellison emphasizes holdings that are trading at low p/e and price/book ratios. The fund's price movement is not correlated to that of the S&P 500. There are two funds besides Small Cap Financial within the FBR family. Overall, the fund family's risk adjusted performance can be described as between good and very good.

Tax Minimization   ★★★★★

During the past five years, a $10,000 initial investment grew to $13,990 after taxes, assuming a 40 percent income tax bracket (state and federal combined) and a capital gains rate of 20 percent. This means that investors in this fund were able to preserve 92 percent of their total returns. Compared to other funds in its category, this fund's tax savings are considered to be excellent.

Expenses   ★★★★★

FBR Small Cap Financial A's expense ratio is 1.5 percent; it has averaged 1.7 percent annually over the past three calendar years. The average expense ratio for the 105 funds in this category is 1.7 percent. This fund's turnover rate over the past year has been 68 percent, while its peer group average has been 140 percent.

Summary

FBR Small Cap Financial A is only one of two funds in the financial sector to make this book. It also happens to be the number one performer in its category. Returns have been outrageously high, yet risk has been quite low. Predictability of returns has also been outstanding when measured against its peer group. This is one of the few funds in the entire book to receive a perfect score.

Profile

minimum initial investment $2,000	*IRA accounts available* . . . . yes
subsequent minimum investment . . $100	*IRA minimum investment* $1,000
available in all 50 states . . . . yes	*date of inception*. . . . . Dec. 1996
telephone exchanges . . . . yes	*dividend/income paid* . . . . annually
number of funds in family 3	*largest sector weighting* . . . . financials

Hancock Regional Bank B
101 Huntington Avenue
Boston, MA 02199
(800) 225-5291
www.jhancock.com

total return	★★★
risk reduction	★★★
management	★★★
tax minimization	★★★★
expense control	★★★★
symbol FRBFX	17 points
up-market performance	poor
down-market performance	excellent
predictability of returns	good

Total Return   ★★★
Over the past five years, Hancock Regional Bank B has taken $10,000 and turned it into $9,980 ($11,850 over three years and $34,770 over the past 10 years). This translates into an annualized return of 0 percent over the past five years, 6 percent over the past three years, and 13 percent for the decade. Over the past five years, this fund has outperformed 45 percent of all mutual funds; within its general category it has done better than 25 percent of its narrow peer group. Financial funds have averaged 3 percent annually over these same five years.

Risk/Volatility   ★★★
Over the past five years, Hancock Regional Bank B has experienced average risk for its category. Over the past decade, the fund has had three negative years, while the S&P 500 has had three (off 9 percent in 2000, 12 percent in 2001, and 22 percent in 2002); the Wilshire 5000 fell four times (off less than 1 percent in 1994, 11 percent in 2000, 11 percent in 2001, and 21 percent in 2002). The fund has underperformed the S&P 500 three times and the Wilshire 5000 three times in the past 10 years. Consistency of *overperformance* for this fund has been good.

	last 5 years		last 10 years	
worst year	-16.4%	1999	-16.4%	1999
best year	21%	2000	52.8%	1997

During the past five years, the fund's three worst months have been August 1998 (-21 percent), December 1999 (-18 percent), and February 2000 (-13 percent). During the same period, the three best months have been March 2000 (14 percent), December 2000 (13 percent), and October 1999 (12 percent). In the past, Hancock Regional Bank B has only done better than 15 percent of its peer group during the most recent bull market and outperformed 87 percent of its peer group during the most recent bear market. Consistency, or predictability, of returns for Hancock Regional Bank B can be described as good. This fund's risk-adjusted return over the past three/five years ranks in the top-three quintiles.

Management   ★★★

There are 85 stocks in this $1 billion portfolio. The average financial fund today is $110 million in size. Close to 100 percent of the fund's holdings are in stocks. The stocks in this portfolio have an average p/e ratio of 15 and a median market capitalization of $8 billion. The 10 largest holdings compose 25 percent of the fund's total assets. The portfolio's equity holdings can be categorized as large-cap and value-oriented issues.

A team has managed this fund for the past 17 years. Management primarily looks for banks that are takeover candidates. Thrift institutions in the portfolio are those that are well managed with defensible market niches along with stable deposits. The fund's price movement is not correlated to that of the S&P 500. There are 38 funds besides Regional Bank within the John Hancock family. Overall, the fund family's risk adjusted performance can be described as good.

Tax Minimization   ★★★★

During the past five years, a $10,000 initial investment grew to $13,990 after taxes, assuming a 40 percent income tax bracket (state and federal combined) and a capital gains rate of 20 percent. This means that investors in this fund were able to preserve 85 percent of their total returns. Compared to other funds in its category, this fund's tax savings are considered to be very good.

Expenses   ★★★★

Hancock Regional Bank B's expense ratio is 2 percent; it has averaged 2 percent annually over the past three calendar years. The average expense ratio for the 105 funds in this category is 1.7 percent. This fund's turnover rate over the past year has been 23 percent, while its peer group average has been 140 percent.

Summary

Hancock Regional Bank B is just one of two financial sector funds to appear in the book. This fund has outperformed its peer group over the past three and five years. Risk levels have been average and consistency has been good. Turnover is quite low. For a niche play, this is one of the very best.

Profile

minimum initial investment $1,000	*IRA accounts available* . . . . yes
subsequent minimum investment . . . $25	*IRA minimum investment* $250
available in all 50 states . . . . yes	*date of inception* . . . . Oct. 1985
telephone exchanges . . . . yes	*dividend/income paid* . . . . quarterly
number of funds in family 39	*largest sector weighting* . . . . financials

Global Equity (Stock) Funds

International, also known as "foreign," funds invest only in stocks of foreign companies, while global funds invest in both foreign and U.S. stocks. For the purposes of this book, the universe of global equity funds shown encompasses both foreign (international) and world (global) portfolios.

The economic outlook of foreign countries is the major factor in mutual fund management's decision about which nations and industries are to be favored. A secondary concern is the future anticipated value of the U.S. dollar relative to foreign currencies. A strong or weak dollar can detract or add to an international fund's overall performance. A strong dollar will lower a foreign portfolio's return; a weak dollar will enhance international performance. Trying to gauge the direction of any currency is as difficult as trying to figure out what the U.S. stock market will do tomorrow, next week, or the following year.

Investors who do not wish to be subjected to currency swings may wish to use a fund family that practices currency hedging for their foreign holdings. Currency hedging means that management is buying a kind of insurance policy that pays off in the event of a strong U.S. dollar. Basically, the foreign or international fund that is being hurt by the dollar is making a killing in currency futures contracts. When done properly, the gains in the futures contracts, the insurance policy, offset some, most, or all security losses attributable to a strong dollar. Some people may feel that buying currency contracts is risky business for the fund; it is not.

Like automobile insurance, currency hedging only pays off if there is an accident; that is, if the U.S. dollar increases in value against the currencies represented by the portfolio's securities. If the dollar remains level or decreases in value, so much the better; the foreign securities increase in value and the currency contracts become virtually worthless. The price of these contracts becomes a cost of doing business; as with car insurance, the protection is simply renewed. In the case of a currency contract, the contract expires and a new one is purchased, covering another period.

It is wise to consider investing abroad, since different economies experience prosperity and recession at different times. During the 1980s, foreign stocks were the number-one performing investment, averaging a compound return of more than 22 percent per year, compared to 18 percent for U.S. stocks and 5 percent for residential real estate. But during the past 10 years (ending December 31, 2002), U.S. stocks, as measured by S&P 500, have outperformed foreign stocks, as measured by the MSCI EAFE index, 9.3 percent versus 4.0 percent (compounded annual rates of return). Over the past 15 years (ending December 31, 2002), U.S. stocks have had an average compound annual return of 11.5 percent versus 3.1 percent for foreign stocks. To give you a broader perspective, take a look at how U.S. securities have fared against their foreign counterparts over each of the past 31 years.

Why Global Stocks and Bonds Deserve a Place in Every Investor's Portfolio
The following table shows the total return for each investment category in each of the past 31 years.

Year	U.S. Stocks	U.S. Gov. Bonds	Non-U.S. Stocks	Non-U.S. Bonds
1972	+19.0	+7.3	+37.4	+4.4
1973	-14.6	+2.3	-14.2	+6.3
1974	-26.5	+0.2	-22.1	+5.3
1975	+37.2	+12.3	+37.0	+8.8
1976	+24.0	+15.6	+3.8	+10.5
1977	-7.2	+3.0	+19.4	+38.9
1978	+6.5	+1.2	+34.3	+18.5
1979	+18.6	+2.3	+6.2	-5.0
1980	+32.3	+3.1	+24.4	+13.7
1981	-5.0	+7.3	-1.0	-4.6
1982	+21.5	+31.1	-0.9	+11.9
1983	+22.6	+8.0	+24.6	+4.3
1984	+6.3	+15.0	+7.9	-2.0
1985	+31.7	+21.3	+56.7	+37.2
1986	+18.6	+15.6	+67.9	+33.9
1987	+5.3	+2.3	+24.9	+36.1
1988	+16.6	+7.6	+28.6	+3.0
1989	+31.6	+14.2	+10.8	-4.5
1990	-3.1	+8.3	-14.9	+14.1
1991	+30.4	+16.1	+12.5	+17.9
1992	+7.7	+8.1	-12.2	+7.1
1993	+10.1	+18.2	+32.6	+15.1
1994	+1.3	-7.8	+7.8	+6.7
1995	+37.4	+31.7	+11.2	+19.6
1996	+23.1	-0.9	+6.1	+4.1
1997	+33.3	+16.0	+1.8	-4.3
1998	+28.6	+13.1	+20.0	+17.8
1999	+21.0	-9.0	+27.0	-5.1
2000	-9.1	+21.5	-14.2	-2.6
2001	-11.9	+3.7	-21.4	-3.5
2002	-22.1	+17.8	-16.0	+19.5

Number of years this category achieved the best results

U.S. Stocks	U.S. Gov. Bonds	Non-U.S. Stocks	Non-U.S. Bonds
10	6	9	6

Increasing your investment returns and reducing portfolio risk are two reasons to consider adding global/foreign funds to your portfolio. Global investing allows you to maximize your returns by investing in some of the world's best-managed and most profitable companies. Japan, for example, is the world's leading producer of sophisticated electronics goods; Germany is the leading producer of heavy machinery; the United States is the leading producer of biotechnology; and Southeast Asia is the leading producer of commodity-manufactured goods.

Diversification reduces investment risk. Recent studies have once again proved this most basic investment principle. A 1996 study showed that the least volatile investment portfolio over the 25-year period (1972–1996) would have been composed of 60 percent U.S. equities and 40 percent foreign equities. These results reflect the importance of balancing a portfolio between U.S. and foreign equities.

Japan, the most economically mature country in the Pacific Basin, has become the dominant force behind the development of the newly industrialized countries (NICs) of Hong Kong, Korea, Thailand, Singapore, Malaysia, and Taiwan. As demand for Japanese products has grown and costs in Japan have risen, the search for affordable production of goods has caused Japanese investment to flow into neighboring countries, fostering their development as economically independent and prosperous nations.

The NICs, with some of the cheapest labor forces and richest untapped natural resources in the world, have recently experienced an enormous influx of international investment capital and today represent the world's fastest growing source of low-cost manufacturing. The Pacific Region (which includes Japan, Hong Kong, Korea, Taiwan, Thailand, Singapore, Malaysia, and Australia) has experienced outstanding economic growth and today represents 25 percent of the world's stock market capital—nearly double what it was 15 years ago.

The newly industrialized countries are favored locations for the manufacture and assembly of consumer electronics products. Displaced from high-cost countries such as the United States and Japan, electronics factories in these developing countries significantly benefit from reduced labor costs. Today, in fact, Korea is the world's third-largest manufacturer of semiconductors.

The Pacific Region yields yet another country with strong economic growth: China. Opportunities to benefit from the industrialization of China come from firms listed on the Hong Kong Stock Exchange, in such basic areas as electricity, construction materials, public transportation, and fundamental telecommunications. Indeed, these low-tech and essential industries, once growth industries in the United States, are now the foundation of a natural growth progression occurring in the NICs of Southeast Asia.

Companies such as China Light and Power (Hong Kong), Siam Cement (Thailand), and Hyundai (Korea) offer much the same profit potential today as their northern European counterparts did 100 years ago, their U.S. counterparts 40 years ago, and their Japanese counterparts as recently as 20 years ago.

Investors have long been familiar with the names of many of Europe's major producers: Nestlé, Olivetti, Shell, Bayer, Volkswagen, and Perrier, to name just a few. Europe's impressive manufacturing capacity, diverse industrial base, quality labor pools, and many leading, multinational, blue-chip corporations make it an environment for growth, accessible to you through foreign funds.

With economic deregulation and the elimination of international trade barriers, many European companies are, for the first time in history, investing in and competing for exposure to the whole European market. Companies formerly restricted to manufacturing and distributing within their national boundaries are now able to locate facilities anywhere in Europe, maximizing the efficient employment of labor, capital, and raw materials.

The global stock category is made up of 1,640 funds (360 "World," 930 "Foreign," 170 "European," and 180 "Pacific"). These funds typically throw off a dividend of 0.5 percent and have an expense ratio of 1.9 percent. The price-earnings (p/e) ratio is 21, versus a p/e ratio of 25 for the typical stock in the S&P 500.

Over the past three years, global equity funds have had an average compound return of *negative* 17.0 percent per year. The annual return for the past five years has been -1.7 percent, 4.9 percent for the past 10 years, and 6.8 percent for the past 15 years. The standard deviation for global equity funds has been 16.8 percent over the past three years. This means that global equity funds have experienced about 20 percent less volatility than growth funds.

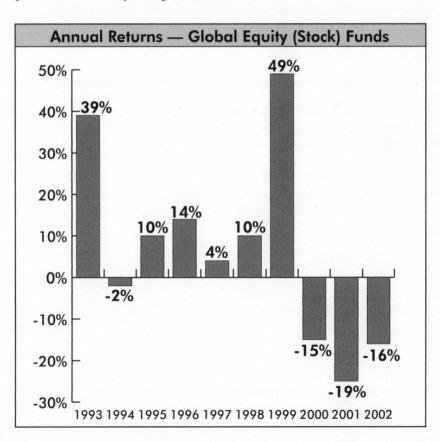

Annual Returns — Global Equity (Stock) Funds

American Funds Capital World Growth & Income A

333 South Hope Street
Los Angeles, CA 90071
(800) 421-4120
www.americanfunds.com

total return	★★★
risk reduction	★★★★
management	★★★★
tax minimization	★★★★
expense control	★★★★★
symbol CWGIX	20 points
up-market performance	very good
down-market performance	very good
predictability of returns	very good

Total Return   ★★★

Over the past five years, American Funds Capital World Growth & Income A has taken $10,000 and turned it into $13,230 ($8,950 over three years). This translates into an annualized return of 6 percent over the past five years and -4 percent over the past three years. Over the past five years, this fund has outperformed 91 percent of all mutual funds; within its general category it has done better than 96 percent of its peers. Global equity funds have averaged 2 percent annually over these same five years.

Risk/Volatility   ★★★★

Over the past five years, American Funds Capital World Growth & Income A has experienced below average risk for its category. Over the past decade, the fund has had two negative years, while the S&P 500 has had three (off 9 percent in 2000, 12 percent in 2001, and 22 percent in 2002); the EAFE also fell three times (off 14 percent in 2000, 21 percent in 2001, and 16 percent in 2002). The fund has underperformed the S&P 500 six times and the EAFE Index three times in the past 10 years. Consistency of *overperformance* for this fund has been very good.

	last 5 years		last 10 years	
worst year	-7.2%	2002	-7.2%	2002
best year	27.3%	1999	27.3%	1999

During the past five years, the fund's three worst months have been August 1998 (-13 percent), September 2001 (-8 percent), and December 2000 (-6 percent). During the same period, the three best months have been October 1998 (7 percent), February 1998 (6 percent), and April 1999 (6 percent). In the past, American Funds Capital World Growth & Income A has done better than 75 percent of its peer group during the most recent bull market and outperformed 72 percent of its peer group during the most recent bear market. Consistency, or predictability, of returns for American Funds Capital World Growth & Income A can be described as very good. This fund's risk-adjusted return over the past three/five years ranks in the top quintile.

Management   ★★★★

There are 315 stocks in this $9 billion portfolio. The average global equity fund today is $190 million in size. Close to 80 percent of the fund's holdings are in stocks. The stocks in this portfolio have an average p/e ratio of 20 and a median market capitalization of $10 billion. The 10 largest holdings compose 15 percent of the fund's total assets. The three largest sector weightings are industrial cyclicals (50 percent), financials (25 percent), and consumer staples (20 percent). The portfolio's equity holdings can be categorized as large-cap and a blend of growth and value stocks.

A team has managed this fund for the past 10 years. Management focuses on yield. Quite a bit of the portfolio is in blue-chip stocks that have a healthy dividend stream. Cash equivalents are used to keep volatility in check. The managers' conservative bent has served shareholders well. The fund's price movement is highly correlated to that of the S&P 500. There are 27 funds besides Capital World Growth & Income within the American Funds family. Overall, the fund family's risk adjusted performance can be described as very good.

Tax Minimization   ★★★★

During the past five years, a $10,000 initial investment grew to $13,990 after taxes, assuming a 40 percent income tax bracket (state and federal combined) and a capital gains rate of 20 percent. This means that investors in this fund were able to preserve 83 percent of their total returns. Compared to other funds in its category, this fund's tax savings are considered to be very good.

Expenses   ★★★★★

American Funds Capital World Growth & Income A's expense ratio is 0.8 percent; it has averaged 0.8 percent annually over the past three calendar years. The average expense ratio for the 1,610 funds in this category is 1.9 percent. This fund's turnover rate over the past year has been 45 percent, while its peer group average has been 105 percent.

Summary

American Funds Capital World Growth & Income A rates number one when it comes to keeping costs down. When it comes to returns, the fund has outperformed 96 percent of its peers. This is just one of several American Funds offerings to make this and previous editions of the book. The fund family is one of the most respected in the industry and continues to keep shareholder interests at the forefront.

Profile

minimum initial investment $250
subsequent minimum investment . . . $50
available in all 50 states . . . . yes
telephone exchanges . . . . yes
number of funds in family 28

IRA accounts available . . . . yes
IRA minimum investment $250
date of inception . . . . Mar. 1993
dividend/income paid . . . . quarterly
largest sector weighting . . . . . industrial cyclicals

American Funds New Perspective A
333 South Hope Street
Los Angeles, CA 90071
(800) 421-4120
www.americanfunds.com

total return	★★
risk reduction	★★★
management	★★★
tax minimization	★★★★
expense control	★★★★★
symbol ANWPX	17 points
up-market performance	excellent
down-market performance	fair
predictability of returns	excellent

Total Return   ★★
Over the past five years, American Funds New Perspective A has taken $10,000 and turned it into $12,850 ($7,140 over three years and $27,290 over the past 10 years). This translates into an annualized return of 5 percent over the past five years, -11 percent over the past three years, and 11 percent for the decade. Over the past five years, this fund has outperformed 90 percent of all mutual funds; within its general category it has done better than 93 percent of its peers. Global equity funds have averaged 2 percent annually over these same five years.

Risk/Volatility   ★★★
Over the past five years, American Funds New Perspective A has experienced average risk for its category. Over the past decade, the fund has had three negative years, while the S&P 500 has had three (off 9 percent in 2000, 12 percent in 2001, and 22 percent in 2002); the EAFE also fell three times (off 14 percent in 2000, 21 percent in 2001, and 16 percent in 2002). The fund has underperformed the S&P 500 four times and the EAFE Index three times in the past 10 years. Consistency of *overperformance* for this fund has been excellent.

	last 5 years		last 10 years	
worst year	-16.1%	2002	-16.1%	2002
best year	40.1%	1999	40.1%	1999

During the past five years, the fund's three worst months have been August 1998 (-14 percent), September 2001 (-10 percent), and December 2000 (-9 percent). During the same period, the three best months have been October 1998 (8 percent), April 2001 (7 percent), and February 1998 (6 percent). In the past, American Funds New Perspective A has done better than 93 percent of its peer group during the most recent bull market but outperformed just 35 percent of its peer group during the most recent bear market. Consistency, or predictability, of returns for American Funds New Perspective A can be described as excellent. This fund's risk-adjusted return over the past three/five years ranks in the top-two quintiles.

Management   ★★★

There are 280 stocks in this $22 billion portfolio. The average global equity fund today is $190 million in size. Close to 90 percent of the fund's holdings are in stocks. The stocks in this portfolio have an average p/e ratio of 24 and a median market capitalization of $26 billion. The 10 largest holdings compose 20 percent of the fund's total assets. The three largest sector weightings are industrial cyclicals (45 percent), consumer durables (26 percent), and consumer staples (20 percent). The portfolio's equity holdings can be categorized as large-cap and growth-oriented issues.

A team has managed this fund for the past 11 years. Management frequently buys out-of-favor companies and then holds these positions for a number of years. Speculative stocks are never chased. The management team is constantly looking for corporations around the world that are taking advantage of international trade patterns as well as economic and political policies. The fund's price movement is highly correlated to that of the S&P 500. There are 27 funds besides New Perspective within the American Funds family. Overall, the fund family's risk adjusted performance can be described as very good.

Tax Minimization   ★★★★

During the past five years, a $10,000 initial investment grew to $13,990 after taxes, assuming a 40 percent income tax bracket (state and federal combined) and a capital gains rate of 20 percent. This means that investors in this fund were able to preserve 85 percent of their total returns. Compared to other funds in its category, this fund's tax savings are considered to be very good.

Expenses   ★★★★★

American Funds New Perspective A's expense ratio is 0.8 percent; it has averaged 0.8 percent annually over the past three calendar years. The average expense ratio for the 1,610 funds in this category is 1.9 percent. This fund's turnover rate over the past year has been 26 percent, while its peer group average has been 105 percent.

Summary

American Funds New Perspective A ties for number one as the most frugally run operation within its broad category. The fund does an excellent job during bull markets, plus it receives the highest marks possible when it comes to predictability of returns. This is certainly not a defensive fund but it is a portfolio with which medium- and long-term investors will be quite pleased. This is just one of several great offerings from American Funds.

Profile

minimum initial investment $250	*IRA accounts available* . . . . yes
subsequent minimum investment . . . $50	*IRA minimum investment* $250
available in all 50 states . . . . yes	*date of inception* . . . . Mar. 1973
telephone exchanges . . . . yes	*dividend/income paid* . . . . annually
number of funds in family 28	*largest sector weighting*. . . . . industrial cyclicals

First Eagle Overseas A

1345 Avenue of the Americas
New York, NY 10105
(800) 334-2143
www.firsteaglefunds.com

total return	★★★★★
risk reduction	★★★★★
management	★★★★★
tax minimization	★★★
expense control	★★★★
symbol SGOVX	22 points
up-market performance	fair
down-market performance	excellent
predictability of returns	very good

Total Return ★★★★★

Over the past five years, First Eagle Overseas A has taken $10,000 and turned it into $17,110 ($12,530 over three years). This translates into an annualized return of 11 percent over the past five years and 8 percent over the past three years. Over the past five years, this fund has outperformed 98 percent of all mutual funds; within its general category it has also done better than 98 percent of its peers. Global equity funds have averaged 2 percent annually over these same five years.

Risk/Volatility ★★★★★

Over the past five years, First Eagle Overseas A has experienced low risk for its category. Over the past decade, the fund has had no negative years, while the S&P 500 has had three (off 9 percent in 2000, 12 percent in 2001, and 22 percent in 2002); the EAFE also fell three times (off 14 percent in 2000, 21 percent in 2001, and 16 percent in 2002). The fund has underperformed the S&P 500 five times and the EAFE Index twice in the past 10 years. Consistency of *overperformance* for this fund has been very good.

	last 5 years		last 10 years	
worst year	2.5%	1998	2.5%	1993
best year	33.2%	1999	33.2%	1999

During the past five years, the fund's three worst months have been December 2000 (-21 percent), August 1998 (-11 percent), and September 2001 (-9 percent). During the same period, the three best months have been April 1999 (10 percent), June 2000 (6 percent), and April 2001 (5 percent). In the past, First Eagle Overseas A has only done better than 30 percent of its peer group during the most recent bull market but outperformed 99 percent of its peer group during the most recent bear market. Consistency, or predictability, of returns for First Eagle Overseas A can be described as very good. This fund's risk-adjusted return over the past three/five years ranks in the top quintile.

Management   ★★★★★
There are 175 stocks in this $910 million portfolio. The average global equity fund today is $190 million in size. Close to 75 percent of the fund's holdings are in stocks. The stocks in this portfolio have an average p/e ratio of 22 and a median market capitalization of $1 billion. The 10 largest holdings compose 25 percent of the fund's total assets. The three largest sector weightings are industrial cyclicals (50 percent), consumer durables (35 percent), and services (20 percent). The port- folio's equity holdings can be categorized as mid-cap and value-oriented issues.

Jean-Marie Eveillard and Charles de Vaulx have managed this fund for the past nine years. Management steers clear of most well-known stocks, preferring relatively unknown and/or unpopular small- and mid-cap firms. The managers are long-term players and have little interest in short-term trends. The fund's price movement is only modestly correlated to that of the S&P 500. There are four funds besides Overseas within the First Eagle family. Overall, the fund family's risk adjusted performance can be described as excellent.

Tax Minimization   ★★★
During the past five years, a $10,000 initial investment grew to $10,100 after taxes, assuming a 40 percent income tax bracket (state and federal combined) and a cap- ital gains rate of 20 percent. This means that investors in this fund were able to pre- serve 59 percent of their total returns. Compared to other funds in its category, this fund's tax savings are considered to be good.

Expenses   ★★★★
First Eagle Overseas A's expense ratio is 1.5 percent; it has averaged 1.5 percent annually over the past three calendar years. The average expense ratio for the 1,610 funds in this category is 1.9 percent. This fund's turnover rate over the past year has been 17 percent, while its peer group average has been 105 percent.

Summary
First Eagle Overseas A ranks as the number two best performer in its category over the past five years. It also ties for first place when it comes to risk reduction. There may not exist a better defensive equity play—the fund has topped 99 per- cent of its 1,600+ peers during the most recent bear market. First Eagle is a small fund family, but one of the very best. Overseas has appeared frequently in past editions of this book.

Profile
minimum initial investment $2,500	*IRA accounts available* . . . . yes
subsequent minimum investment . . $100	*IRA minimum investment* $1,000
available in all 50 states . . . . yes	*date of inception* . . . . Aug. 1993
telephone exchanges . . . . yes	*dividend/income paid* . . . . annually
number of funds in family 5	*largest sector weighting*. . . . . industrial cyclicals

Julius Baer International Equity A
431 North Pennsylvania Street
Indianapolis, IN 46204
(800) 435-4659
www.us-funds.juliusbaer.com

total return	★★★★
risk reduction	★★★
management	★★★★
tax minimization	★★★★★
expense control	★★★★
symbol BJBIX	20 points
up-market performance	fair
down-market performance	excellent
predictability of returns	very good

Total Return   ★★★★

Over the past five years, Julius Baer International Equity A has taken $10,000 and turned it into $16,130 ($7,190 over three years). This translates into an annualized return of 10 percent over the past five years and -10 percent over the past three years. Over the past five years, this fund has outperformed 98 percent of all mutual funds; within its general category it has also done better than 98 percent of its peers. Global equity funds have averaged 2 percent annually over these same five years.

Risk/Volatility   ★★★

Over the past five years, Julius Baer International Equity A has experienced above average risk for its category. Over the past decade, the fund has had five negative years, while the S&P 500 has had three (off 9 percent in 2000, 12 percent in 2001, and 22 percent in 2002); the EAFE also fell three times (off 14 percent in 2000, 21 percent in 2001, and 16 percent in 2002). The fund has underperformed the S&P 500 seven times and the EAFE Index three times in the past 10 years. Consistency of *overperformance* for this fund has been excellent.

	last 5 years		last 10 years	
worst year	-18.9%	2001	-33.6%	1994
best year	76.6%	1999	76.6%	1999

During the past five years, the fund's three worst months have been August 1998 (-16 percent), April 2000 (-8 percent), and September 2001 (-7 percent). During the same period, the three best months have been December 1999 (18 percent), February 2000 (18 percent), and February 1998 (10 percent). In the past, Julius Baer International Equity A has only done better than 25 percent of its peer group during the most recent bull market but outperformed 91 percent of its peer group during the most recent bear market. Consistency, or predictability, of returns for Julius Baer International Equity A can be described as very good. This fund's risk-adjusted return over the past three/five years ranks in the top quintile.

Management   ★★★★

There are 165 stocks in this $500 million portfolio. The average global equity fund today is $190 million in size. Close to 75 percent of the fund's holdings are in stocks. The 10 largest holdings compose 25 percent of the fund's total assets. The three largest sector weightings are industrial cyclicals (55 percent), consumer staples (25 percent), and consumer durables (20 percent). The portfolio's equity holdings can be categorized as large-cap and a blend of growth and value stocks.

Rudolph-Riad Younes and Richard C. Pell have managed this fund for the past eight years. Management emphasizes sector selection more than most of its competitors. Once favored industry groups have been chosen, intensive individual issue research begins. The managers are not afraid to be contrarians, sometimes making huge plays in areas others would avoid. The boldness frequently pays off. The fund's price movement is not correlated to that of the S&P 500. There is one other fund besides International Equity within the Julius Baer Investment "family." Overall, the fund family's risk adjusted performance can be described as between good and very good.

Tax Minimization   ★★★★★

During the past five years, a $10,000 initial investment grew to $15,000 after taxes, assuming a 40 percent income tax bracket (state and federal combined) and a capital gains rate of 20 percent. This means that investors in this fund were able to preserve 92 percent of their total returns. Compared to other funds in its category, this fund's tax savings are considered to be excellent.

Expenses   ★★★★

Julius Baer International Equity A's expense ratio is 1.4 percent; it has averaged 1.4 percent annually over the past three calendar years. The average expense ratio for the 1,610 funds in this category is 1.9 percent. This fund's turnover rate over the past year has been 89 percent, while its peer group average has been 105 percent.

Summary

Julius Baer International Equity A receives between good and excellent marks across the board. Its strong suits are total return, management, expense control, and tax minimization. This offering is a solid choice for the cautious investor who wants global equity exposure but wants protection during negative market cycles. This portfolio has outperformed 98 percent of the entire mutual fund universe as well as 98 percent of its rather large peer group.

Profile

minimum initial investment $2,500
subsequent minimum investment . $1,000
available in all 50 states . . . . yes
telephone exchanges . . . . yes
number of funds in family 2

IRA accounts available . . . . yes
IRA minimum investment $100
date of inception . . . . Oct. 1993
dividend/income paid . . . . annually
largest sector weighting . . . . . industrial
cyclicals

Matthews Asian Growth & Income

456 Montgomery Street, Suite 1200
San Francisco, CA 94104
(800) 789-2742
www.matthewsfunds.com

total return	★★★★★
risk reduction	★★★★★
management	★★★★★
tax minimization	★★★★
expense control	★★★
symbol MACSX	22 points
up-market performance	poor
down-market performance	excellent
predictability of returns	excellent

Total Return   ★★★★★

Over the past five years, Matthews Asian Growth & Income has taken $10,000 and turned it into $19,480 ($12,930 over three years). This translates into an annualized return of 14 percent over the past five years and 9 percent over the past three years. Over the past five years, this fund has outperformed 99 percent of all mutual funds; within its general category it has done better than 95 percent of its peers. Global equity funds have averaged 2 percent annually over these same five years.

Risk/Volatility   ★★★★★

Over the past five years, Matthews Asian Growth & Income has experienced low risk for its category. Over the past decade, the fund has had one negative year, while the S&P 500 has had three (off 9 percent in 2000, 12 percent in 2001, and 22 percent in 2002); the EAFE also fell three times (off 14 percent in 2000, 21 percent in 2001, and 16 percent in 2002). The fund has underperformed the S&P 500 six times and the EAFE Index five times in the past 10 years. Consistency of *overperformance* for this fund has been very good.

	last 5 years		last 10 years	
worst year	1.2%	1998	-23.2%	1997
best year	48.9%	1999	48.9%	1999

During the past five years, the fund's three worst months have been June 1998 (-13 percent), December 2000 (-9 percent), and August 1998 (-8 percent). During the same period, the three best months have been February 1998 (13 percent), April 1999 (12 percent), and November 1998 (9 percent). In the past, Matthews Asian Growth & Income has only done better than 11 percent of its peer group during the most recent bull market but outperformed 99 percent of its peer group during the most recent bear market. Consistency, or predictability, of returns for Matthews Asian Growth & Income can be described as excellent. This fund's risk-adjusted return over the past three/five years ranks in the top quintile.

Management

There are 55 stocks in this $180 million portfolio. The average global equity fund today is $190 million in size. Close to 60 percent of the fund's holdings are in stocks. The stocks in this portfolio have an average p/e ratio of 14 and a median market capitalization of $5 billion. The 10 largest holdings compose 35 percent of the fund's total assets. The three largest sector weightings are industrial cyclicals (50 percent), utilities (30 percent), and financials (30 percent). The portfolio's equity holdings can be categorized as mid-cap and value-oriented issues.

G. Paul Matthews has managed this fund for the past eight years. Management favors foreign convertibles, a strategy not used by any of its competitors. Matthews has a strong bias toward value plays. This form of conservatism has well served the fund. The fund's price movement is only modestly correlated to that of the S&P 500. There are five funds besides Asian Growth & Income within the Matthews family. Overall, the fund family's risk adjusted performance can be described as between good and very good.

Tax Minimization   ★★★★

During the past five years, a $10,000 initial investment grew to $14,810 after taxes, assuming a 40 percent income tax bracket (state and federal combined) and a capital gains rate of 20 percent. This means that investors in this fund were able to preserve 71 percent of their total returns. Compared to other funds in its category, this fund's tax savings are considered to be very good.

Expenses   ★★★

Matthews Asian Growth & Income's expense ratio is 1.9 percent; it has averaged 1.9 percent annually over the past three calendar years. The average expense ratio for the 1,610 funds in this category is 1.9 percent. This fund's turnover rate over the past year has been 34 percent, while its peer group average has been 105 percent.

Summary

Matthews Asian Growth & Income rates as the highest overall point score. This sector play has the best three- and five-year track record of any global fund in the book. The surprisingly high returns are amazing when you consider that this portfolio ties for number one as the least risky in its broad category of 1,600+ funds. The expense ratio is just average, but an often more important figure, turnover rate, is one of the lowest in the industry. Given the fund's name, it would not seem likely that performance would be so good during a bear market. Yet, this Matthews offering outperformed 99 percent of all other funds during the most recent extended market downturn.

Profile

minimum initial investment $2,500	*IRA accounts available* . . . . yes
subsequent minimum investment . . $250	*IRA minimum investment* $500
available in all 50 states . . . . yes	*date of inception* . . . . Sept. 1994
telephone exchanges . . . . yes	*dividend/income paid*. . . . semiannually
number of funds in family 6	*largest sector weighting*. . . . . industrial cyclicals

Matthews Pacific Tiger
456 Montgomery Street, Suite 1200
San Francisco, CA 94104
(800) 789-2742
www.matthewsfunds.com

total return	★★★★
risk reduction	★★
management	★★★
tax minimization	★★★★
expense control	★★★
symbol MAPTX	16 points
up-market performance	fair
down-market performance	fair
predictability of returns	excellent

Total Return   ★★★★
Over the past five years, Matthews Pacific Tiger has taken $10,000 and turned it into $13,770 ($7,750 over three years). This translates into an annualized return of 7 percent over the past five years and -8 percent over the past three years. Over the past five years, this fund has outperformed 73 percent of all mutual funds; within its general category it has done better than 93 percent of its peers. Global equity funds have averaged 2 percent annually over these same five years.

Risk/Volatility   ★★
Over the past five years, Matthews Pacific Tiger has experienced above average risk for its category. Over the past decade, the fund has had four negative years, while the S&P 500 has had three (off 9 percent in 2000, 12 percent in 2001, and 22 percent in 2002); the EAFE also fell three times (off 14 percent in 2000, 21 percent in 2001, and 16 percent in 2002). The fund has underperformed the S&P 500 six times and the EAFE Index six times in the past 10 years. Consistency of *overperformance* for this fund has been excellent.

	last 5 years		last 10 years	
worst year	-23.3%	2000	-40.9%	1997
best year	83.0%	1999	83.0%	1999

During the past five years, the fund's three worst months have been August 1998 (-17 percent), May 1998 (-15 percent), and June 1998 (-15 percent). During the same period, the three best months have been April 1999 (25 percent), June 1999 (23 percent), and October 1998 (21 percent). In the past, Matthews Pacific Tiger has done better than 70 percent of its peer group during the most recent bull market and outperformed 85 percent of its peer group during the most recent bear market. Consistency, or predictability, of returns for Matthews Pacific Tiger can be described as excellent. This fund's risk-adjusted return over the past three/five years ranks in the top-two quintiles.

Management   ★★★

There are 35 stocks in this $110 million portfolio. The average global equity fund today is $190 million in size. Close to 100 percent of the fund's holdings are in stocks. The stocks in this portfolio have an average p/e ratio of 18 and a median market capitalization of $2 billion. The 10 largest holdings compose 45 percent of the fund's total assets. The three largest sector weightings are services (25 percent), industrial cyclicals (25 percent), and financials (20 percent). The portfolio's equity holdings can be categorized as mid-cap and a blend of growth and value stocks.

G. Paul Matthews and Mark W. Headley have managed this fund for the past eight years. Management likes companies with robust long-term earnings expectations and moderate valuations. The managers' bias toward growth issues has proven to be quite a positive for the overall portfolio. The fund's price movement is only modestly correlated to that of the S&P 500. There are five funds besides Pacific Tiger within the Matthews family. Overall, the fund family's risk adjusted performance can be described as between good and very good.

Tax Minimization   ★★★★

During the past five years, a $10,000 initial investment grew to $11,020 after taxes, assuming a 40 percent income tax bracket (state and federal combined) and a capital gains rate of 20 percent. This means that investors in this fund were able to preserve 80 percent of their total returns. Compared to other funds in its category, this fund's tax savings are considered to be very good.

Expenses   ★★★

Matthews Pacific Tiger's expense ratio is 1.9 percent; it has averaged 1.9 percent annually over the past three calendar years. The average expense ratio for the 1,610 funds in this category is 1.9 percent. This fund's turnover rate over the past year has been 64 percent, while its peer group average has been 105 percent.

Summary

Matthews Pacific Tiger is one of two funds from the same group that appears in the book (Matthews Asian Growth & Income is the other). This is a much more aggressive play and returns have not been as stable or predictable. Still, the fund's three-year performance record is leaps and bounds ahead of its peer group average. And even though its three-year numbers do not initially appear good, they are still over twice as good as its category.

Profile

minimum initial investment $2,500	*IRA accounts available* . . . . yes
subsequent minimum investment . . $250	*IRA minimum investment* $500
available in all 50 states . . . . yes	*date of inception* . . . . Sept. 1994
telephone exchanges . . . . yes	*dividend/income paid* . . . . annually
number of funds in family 6	*largest sector weighting* . . . . . . services

Tweedy, Browne Global Value
350 Park Avenue
New York, NY 10022
(800) 432-4789
www.tweedy.com

total return	★★★
risk reduction	★★★★★
management	★★★★
tax minimization	★★★
expense control	★★★★
symbol TBGVX	19 points
up-market performance	poor
down-market performance	very good
predictability of returns	excellent

Total Return   ★★★

Over the past five years, Tweedy, Browne Global Value has taken $10,000 and turned it into $13,090 ($9,410 over three years). This translates into an annualized return of 6 percent over the past five years and -2 percent over the past three years. Over the past five years, this fund has outperformed 87 percent of all mutual funds; within its general category it has done better than 94 percent of its peers. Global equity funds have averaged 2 percent annually over these same five years.

Risk/Volatility   ★★★★★

Over the past five years, Tweedy, Browne Global Value has experienced low risk for its category. Over the past decade, the fund has had two negative years, while the S&P 500 has had three (off 9 percent in 2000, 12 percent in 2001, and 22 percent in 2002); the EAFE also fell three times (off 14 percent in 2000, 21 percent in 2001, and 16 percent in 2002). The fund has underperformed the S&P 500 five times and the EAFE Index five times in the past 10 years. Consistency of *overperformance* for this fund has been good.

	last 5 years		last 10 years	
worst year	-12.1%	2002	-12.1%	2002
best year	25.3%	1999	25.3%	1999

During the past five years, the fund's three worst months have been August 1998 (-13 percent), December 2000 (-11 percent), and September 2001 (-9 percent). During the same period, the three best months have been April 1999 (9 percent), October 1998 (8 percent), and November 1998 (7 percent). In the past, Tweedy, Browne Global Value has only done better than 15 percent of its peer group during the most recent bull market but outperformed 71 percent of its peer group during the most recent bear market. Consistency, or predictability, of returns for Tweedy, Browne Global Value can be described as excellent. This fund's risk-adjusted return over the past three/five years ranks in the top quintile.

Management   ★★★★

There are 215 stocks in this $4 billion portfolio. The average global equity fund today is $190 million in size. Close to 85 percent of the fund's holdings are in stocks. The stocks in this portfolio have an average p/e ratio of 19 and a median market capitalization of $3 billion. The 10 largest holdings compose 25 percent of the fund's total assets. The three largest sector weightings are industrial cyclicals (35 percent), services (25 percent), and financials (25 percent). The portfolio's equity holdings can be categorized as mid-cap and a blend of growth and value stocks.

A team has managed this fund for the past 10 years. Management often ends up favoring financials, industrial cyclicals, and a wide range of service-oriented issues. The managers are known for their conservative stock-picking. Price movement is only modestly correlated to that of the S&P 500. There is one other fund besides Global Value within the Tweedy, Browne "family." Overall, the fund family's risk adjusted performance can be described as between very good and excellent.

Tax Minimization   ★★★

During the past five years, a $10,000 initial investment grew to $13,990 after taxes, assuming a 40 percent income tax bracket (state and federal combined) and a capital gains rate of 20 percent. This means that investors in this fund were able to preserve 54 percent of their total returns. Compared to other funds in its category, this fund's tax savings are considered to be good.

Expenses   ★★★★

Tweedy, Browne Global Value's expense ratio is 1.4 percent; it has averaged 1.4 percent annually over the past three calendar years. The average expense ratio for the 1,610 funds in this category is 1.9 percent. This fund's turnover rate over the past year has been 7 percent, while its peer group average has been 105 percent.

Summary

Tweedy, Browne Global Value ties for first place as the lowest risk fund in its category. Return figures have radically beaten its benchmark averages over the past three and five years. Predictability of returns is also greater with this fund than any of its group. Another positive: The portfolio has one of the lowest turnover rates in the industry. As you might suspect by the fund's name, this is a defensive play for the equity investor.

Profile

minimum initial investment $2,500
subsequent minimum investment . . $250
available in all 50 states . . . . yes
telephone exchanges . . . . yes
number of funds in family 2

IRA accounts available . . . . yes
IRA minimum investment $500
date of inception . . . . Jun. 1993
dividend/income paid . . . . annually
largest sector weighting. . . . . industrial
cyclicals

Government Bond Funds

These funds invest in direct and indirect U.S. government obligations. Government bond funds are made up of one or more of the following: T-bills, T-notes, T-bonds, and mortgage-backed securities such as GNMAs (Government National Mortgage Association) and FNMAs (Federal National Mortgage Association). Treasury bills, notes, and bonds make up the entire marketable debt of the U.S. government. Such instruments are exempt from state income taxes.

Although GNMAs are considered an indirect obligation of the government, they are still backed by the full faith and credit of the United States. FNMAs are not issued by the government but are considered virtually identical in safety to GNMAs. Both instruments are subject to state and local income taxes. All of the securities in a government bond fund are subject to federal income taxes.

The average maturity of securities found in government bond funds varies broadly depending on the type of fund as well as on management's perception of risk and the future direction of interest rates. A more thorough discussion of interest rates and the volatility of bond fund prices can be found in the introduction to the corporate bond section, beginning on page 91.

Over the past 15 years (1988–2002), government bonds have returned an average compound return of 10.5 percent—versus 10.0 percent for corporate bonds. A $10,000 investment in U.S. government bonds grew to $44,640 over the past 15 years; a similar initial investment in corporate bonds grew to $41,710.

Over the past 50 years, the worst year for government bonds was 1967, when a loss of 9 percent was suffered. The second worst year was 1999, when the bonds suffered a loss of just less than 9 percent. The best year so far has been 1982, when government bonds posted a gain of 40 percent. All of these figures are based on total return (current yield plus or minus any appreciation or loss of principal). The second best year was 1995, when these debt instruments had a total return of just less than 32 percent.

Over the past 50 years, there have been 46 five-year periods (1953–1957, 1954–1958, etc.). On a pretax basis, government bonds have outperformed inflation during 28 of the 46 five-year periods (61 percent of the time). The last five-year period in which inflation outperformed long-term government bonds was 1979–1983 (8.4 percent versus 6.4 percent for bonds). Over the past 50 years, there have been 41 10-year periods (1953–1962, 1954–1963, etc.). On a pretax basis, government bonds have outperformed inflation during 23 of the 41 10-year periods, including the past 18 in a row. The last 10-year period in which inflation outperformed long-term government bonds was 1975–1984 (7.3 percent versus 7.0 percent for bonds). Over the past half-century, there have been 31 20-year periods (1952–1971, 1953–1972, etc.). On a pretax basis, government bonds have outperformed inflation during the past 17 consecutive 20-year periods (out of the possible 31 20-year periods starting in 1953). Inflation outperformed long-term government bonds every 20-year period starting with 1952–1971 through 1966–1985.

More than 610 funds make up the government bonds category. Over the past three and five years (all periods ending December 31, 2002), government funds have had an average compound annual return of 8.8 percent and 6.4 percent, respectively. For the decade, these funds have averaged 6.3 percent per year; over the past 15 years, 7.4 percent a year. The average yield is 3.9 percent. The standard deviation for government bond funds has been 3.7 percent over the past three years. This means that these funds have been less volatile than any other category except money market funds.

Government bond funds are the perfect choice for the conservative investor who wants to avoid any possibility of default. However, these securities should be avoided by even conservative investors who are in a high tax bracket or who are unable to shelter such an investment in a retirement plan or annuity. Such investors should first look at the advantages of municipal bond funds that pay interest that is generally non-taxable. Over the past 50 years, government bonds have had a compound average rate of return of 6.5 percent, with inflation running 3.9 percent over the same period. Always remember that government and corporate bonds are generally not a good investment once inflation and taxes are factored in. The investor who appreciates the cumulative effects of even low levels of inflation should probably avoid government and corporate bonds except as part of a retirement plan when nearing retirement.

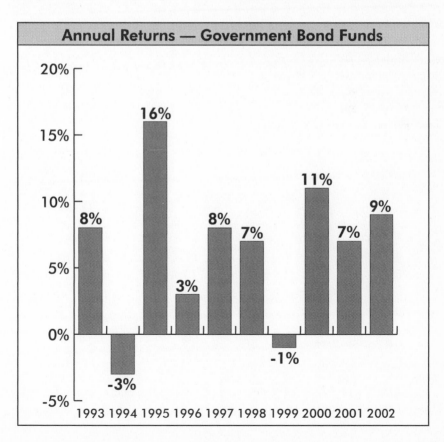

American Century Ginnie Mae Investor
4500 Main Street
P.O. Box 419200
Kansas City, MO 64141
(800) 345-2021
www.americancentury.com

total return	★★★★
risk reduction	★★★★★
management	★★★★★
current income	★★★★★
expense control	★★★★★
symbol BGNMX	24 points
up-market performance	very good
down-market performance	good
predictability of returns	very good

Total Return   ★★★★
Over the past five years, American Century Ginnie Mae Investor has taken $10,000 and turned it into $13,780 ($12,840 over three years and $19,160 over the past 10 years). This translates into an annualized return of 7 percent over the past five years, 9 percent over the past three years, and 7 percent for the decade. Over the past five years, this fund has outperformed 90 percent of all mutual funds; within its general category it has done better than 55 percent of its peers. Government bond funds have averaged 6 percent annually over these same five years.

During the past five years, a $10,000 initial investment grew to $11,580 after taxes, assuming a 40 percent income tax bracket (state and federal combined) and a capital gains rate of 20 percent. This means that investors in this fund were able to preserve 63 percent of their total returns. Compared to other funds in its category, this fund's tax savings are considered to be excellent.

Risk/Volatility   ★★★★★
Over the past five years, American Century Ginnie Mae Investor has experienced low risk for its category. Over the past decade, the fund has had one negative year, while the Lehman Brothers Aggregate Bond Index had two (off 3 percent in 1994 and 1 percent in 1999); the Lehman Brothers Government Bond Index also fell twice (off 3 percent in 1994 and 2 percent in 1999). The fund has underperformed the Lehman Brothers Aggregate Bond Index seven times and the Lehman Brothers Government Bond Index six times in the past 10 years. Consistency of *overperformance* for this fund has been fair.

	last 5 years		last 10 years	
worst year	1.0%	1999	-1.7%	1994
best year	10.4%	2000	15.9%	1995

During the past five years, the fund's three worst months have been January 2000 (-1 percent), November 2001 (-1 percent), and May 1999 (-1 percent). During the same period, the three best months have been January 2001 (1 percent), July 2001 (1 percent), and June 2000 (1 percent). In the past, American Century Ginnie Mae Investor has done better than 71 percent of its peer group during the most recent bull market and outperformed 42 percent of its peer group during the most recent bear market. Consistency, or predictability, of returns for American Century Ginnie Mae Investor can be described as very good. This fund's risk-adjusted return over the past three/five years ranks in the top-three quintiles.

Management   ★★★★★
There are 2,910 fixed-income securities in this $2 billion portfolio. The average government bond fund today is $300 million in size. Close to 85 percent of the fund's holdings are in bonds. The average maturity of the bonds in this account is six years; the weighted coupon rate averages 6 percent. The portfolio's fixed-income holdings can be categorized as short-term, high-quality debt.

C. Casey Colton has managed this fund for the past nine years. Management concentrates almost exclusively on GNMAs and issues backed by the U.S. Government. Management adds value by trading among various coupons. Colton is considered a cautious money manager. The fund's price movement is highly correlated to the Lehman Brothers Aggregate Bond Index. There are 50 funds besides Ginnie Mae Investor within the American Century Investments family. Overall, the fund family's risk adjusted performance can be described as between good and very good.

Current Income   ★★★★★
Over the past year, American Century Ginnie Mae Investor had a 12-month yield of 5.3 percent. During this same 12-month period, the typical government bond fund had a yield that averaged 3.9 percent.

Expenses   ★★★★★
American Century Ginnie Mae Investor's expense ratio is 0.6 percent; it has averaged 0.6 percent annually over the past three calendar years. The average expense ratio for the 605 funds in this category is 1.1 percent. This fund's turnover rate over the past year has been 218 percent, while its peer group average has been 204 percent.

Summary
American Century Ginnie Mae Investor has outperformed 90 percent of all mutual funds during the past five years. This is quite an accomplishment since this is a government securities fund. The portfolio ties for number one as the overall top point earner. It is number one when it comes to current income. Few funds ever receive 24 out of 25 possible points in this, or any other, edition of the book.

Profile

minimum initial investment $2,500	*IRA accounts available* . . . . yes
subsequent minimum investment . . . $50	*IRA minimum investment* $2,500
available in all 50 states . . . . yes	*date of inception* . . . . Sept. 1985
telephone exchanges . . . . yes	*dividend/income paid*. . . . . monthly
number of funds in family 51	*average credit quality* . . . . AAA

ING GNMA Income A

7337 East Doubletree Ranch Road
Scottsdale, AZ 85258
(800) 334-3444
www.ingfunds.com

total return	★★★★★
risk reduction	★★★
management	★★★★
current income	★★★★★
expense control	★★★★
symbol LEXNX	21 points
up-market performance	fair
down-market performance	excellent
predictability of returns	good

Total Return   ★★★★★

Over the past five years, ING GNMA Income A has taken $10,000 and turned it
into $14,260 ($13,190 over three years and $20,360 over the past 10 years). This
translates into an annualized return of 7 percent over the past five years, 10 percent
over the past three years, and 7 percent for the decade. Over the past five years, this
fund has outperformed 94 percent of all mutual funds; within its general category
it has done better than 96 percent of its peers. Government bond funds have averaged 6 percent annually over these same five years.

During the past five years, a $10,000 initial investment grew to $11,580 after
taxes, assuming a 40 percent income tax bracket (state and federal combined) and
a capital gains rate of 20 percent. This means that investors in this fund were able
to preserve 65 percent of their total returns. Compared to other funds in its category, this fund's tax savings are considered to be excellent.

Risk/Volatility   ★★★

Over the past five years, ING GNMA Income A has experienced average risk for
its category. Over the past decade, the fund has had one negative year, while the
Lehman Brothers Aggregate Bond Index had two (off 3 percent in 1994 and 1 percent
in 1999); the Lehman Brothers Government Bond Index also fell twice (off 3 percent
in 1994 and 2 percent in 1999). The fund has underperformed the Lehman Brothers
Aggregate Bond Index five times and the Lehman Brothers Government Bond
Index five times in the past 10 years. Consistency of *overperformance* for this fund
has been fair.

	last 5 years		last 10 years	
worst year	0.6%	1999	-2.1%	1994
best year	10.4%	2000	15.9%	1995

In the past, ING GNMA Income A has only done better than 31 percent of its
peer group during the most recent bull market but outperformed 85 percent of its
peer group during the most recent bear market. Consistency, or predictability, of

returns for ING GNMA Income A can be described as good. This fund's risk-adjusted return over the past three/five years ranks in the top-three quintiles.

Management   ★★★★
There are 265 fixed-income securities in this $640 million portfolio. The average government bond fund today is $300 million in size. Close to 100 percent of the fund's holdings are in bonds. The average maturity of the bonds in this account is six years; the weighted coupon rate averages 6 percent. The portfolio's fixed-income holdings can be categorized as short-term, high-quality debt.

Denis P. Jamison has managed this fund for the past 22 years. Management favors GNMAs. By holding an eclectic mix of mortgage-backed issues, Jamison is able to temper interest-rate risk. The fund's price movement is highly correlated to the Lehman Brothers Aggregate Bond Index. There are forty-four funds besides GNMA Income within the ING Funds family. Overall, the fund family's risk adjusted performance can be described as good.

Current Income   ★★★★★
Over the past year, ING GNMA Income A had a 12-month yield of 4.9 percent. During this same 12-month period, the typical government bond fund had a yield that averaged 3.9 percent.

Expenses   ★★★★
ING GNMA Income A's expense ratio is 1.2 percent; it has averaged 1.2 percent annually over the past three calendar years. The average expense ratio for the 605 funds in this category is 1.1 percent. This fund's turnover rate over the past year has been 76 percent, while its peer group average has been 204 percent.

Summary
ING GNMA Income A rates as the second-best overall performer in its entire category; quite an accomplishment when you consider it competed against 600+ other government bond funds. The fund ranks number one when it comes to performance. Current income is also quite high. As a side note, ING is a leader in the area of insurance products and offers some of the very best fixed and variable annuities. The group also offers some of the most attractive money market and checking accounts.

Profile
minimum initial investment $1,000	*IRA accounts available* . . . . yes
subsequent minimum investment . . $100	*IRA minimum investment* $250
available in all 50 states . . . . yes	*date of inception* . . . . Oct. 1973
telephone exchanges . . . . yes	*dividend/income paid* . . . . monthly
number of funds in family 45	*average credit quality* . . . . AAA

Sit U.S. Government Securities
4600 Norwest Center
90 South 7th Street
Minneapolis, MN 55402
(800) 332-5580
www.sitfunds.com

total return	★★★★
risk reduction	★★★
management	★★★★
current income	★★★★
expense control	★★★★★
symbol SNGVX	20 points
up-market performance	very good
down-market performance	poor
predictability of returns	excellent

Total Return   ★★★★
Over the past five years, Sit U.S. Government Securities has taken $10,000 and
turned it into $13,480 ($12,500 over three years and $18,670 over the past 10
years). This translates into an annualized return of 6 percent over the past five
years, 8 percent over the past three years, and 6 percent for the decade. Over the
past five years, this fund has outperformed 87 percent of all mutual funds; within
its general category it has done better than 70 percent of its peers. Government
bond funds have averaged 6 percent annually over these same five years.

During the past five years, a $10,000 initial investment grew to $11,580 after
taxes, assuming a 40 percent income tax bracket (state and federal combined) and
a capital gains rate of 20 percent. This means that investors in this fund were able
to preserve 65 percent of their total returns. Compared to other funds in its category, this fund's tax savings are considered to be excellent.

Risk/Volatility   ★★★
Over the past five years, Sit U.S. Government Securities has experienced average
risk for its category. Over the past decade, the fund has had no negative years,
while the Lehman Brothers Aggregate Bond Index had two (off 3 percent in 1994
and 1 percent in 1999); the Lehman Brothers Government Bond Index also fell
twice (off 3 percent in 1994 and 2 percent in 1999). The fund has underperformed
the Lehman Brothers Aggregate Bond Index six times and the Lehman Brothers
Government Bond Index six times in the past 10 years. Consistency of *overperformance* for this fund has been very good.

	last 5 years		last 10 years	
worst year	1.3%	1999	1.3%	1999
best year	9.1%	2000	11.5%	1995

During the past five years, the fund's three worst months have been January
2000 (-4 percent), February 1999 (-1 percent), and December 1998 (-1 percent).

During the same period, the three best months have been October 2001 (1 percent), December 2000 (1 percent), and July 2001 (1 percent). In the past, Sit U.S. Government Securities has done better than 70 percent of its peer group during the most recent bull market but only outperformed 16 percent of its peer group during the most recent bear market. Consistency, or predictability, of returns for Sit U.S. Government Securities can be described as excellent. This fund's risk-adjusted return over the past three/five years ranks in the top-two quintiles.

Management ★★★★

There are 675 fixed-income securities in this $390 million portfolio. The average government bond fund today is $300 million in size. Close to 95 percent of the fund's holdings are in bonds. The average maturity of the bonds in this account is 18 years; the weighted coupon rate averages 8 percent. The portfolio's fixed-income holdings can be categorized as long-term, high-quality debt.

Michael C. Brilley and Bryce Doty have managed this fund for the past 16 years. Management is not afraid to load up on lesser-known fixed-income securities. Interest rate risk is kept to a minimum. Virtually every one of the almost 700 issues in the portfolio has its own unique characteristic. The fund's price movement is highly correlated to the Lehman Brothers Aggregate Bond Index. There are 10 funds besides U.S. Government Securities within the Sit family. Overall, the fund family's risk adjusted performance can be described as between good and very good.

Current Income ★★★★

Over the past year, Sit U.S. Government Securities had a 12-month yield of 4.5 percent. During this same 12-month period, the typical government bond fund had a yield that averaged 3.9 percent.

Expenses ★★★★★

Sit U.S. Government Securities's expense ratio is 0.8 percent; it has averaged 0.8 percent annually over the past three calendar years. The average expense ratio for the 605 funds in this category is 1.1 percent. This fund's turnover rate over the past year has been 55 percent, while its peer group average has been 204 percent.

Summary

Sit U.S. Government Securities has one of the lowest expense ratios and turnover rates in its group. The fund's overall score is quite high. Predictability, or consistency of returns, is better than any other offering in its category. Sit is a well-known name to readers of previous editions of this book. In the past, the fund has done best during bull markets.

Profile

minimum initial investment $5,000	*IRA accounts available* . . . . yes
subsequent minimum investment . . $100	*IRA minimum investment* $2,000
available in all 50 states . . . . yes	*date of inception* . . . . Jun. 1987
telephone exchanges . . . . yes	*dividend/income paid* . . . . monthly
number of funds in family 11	*average credit quality* . . . . AAA

Vanguard GNMA
Vanguard Financial Center
P.O. Box 2600
Valley Forge, PA 19482
(800) 662-7447
www.vanguard.com

total return	★★★★★
risk reduction	★★★★
management	★★★★★
current income	★★★★★
expense control	★★★★★
symbol VFIIX	24 points
up-market performance	excellent
down-market performance	very good
predictability of returns	very good

Total Return   ★★★★★

Over the past five years, Vanguard GNMA has taken $10,000 and turned it into $14,180 ($13,140 over three years and $20,060 over the past 10 years). This translates into an annualized return of 7 percent over the past five years, 10 percent over the past three years, and 7 percent for the decade. Over the past five years, this fund has outperformed 94 percent of all mutual funds; within its general category it has also done better than 94 percent of its peers. Government bond funds have averaged 6 percent annually over these same five years.

During the past five years, a $10,000 initial investment grew to $11,580 after taxes, assuming a 40 percent income tax bracket (state and federal combined) and a capital gains rate of 20 percent. This means that investors in this fund were able to preserve 65 percent of their total returns. Compared to other funds in its category, this fund's tax savings are considered to be excellent.

Risk/Volatility   ★★★★

Over the past five years, Vanguard GNMA has experienced below average risk for its category. Over the past decade, the fund has had one negative year, while the Lehman Brothers Aggregate Bond Index had two (off 3 percent in 1994 and 1 percent in 1999); the Lehman Brothers Government Bond Index also fell twice (off 3 percent in 1994 and 2 percent in 1999). The fund has underperformed the Lehman Brothers Aggregate Bond Index seven times and the Lehman Brothers Government Bond Index six times in the past 10 years. Consistency of *overperformance* for this fund has been fair.

	last 5 years		last 10 years	
worst year	0.8%	1999	-1.0%	1994
best year	11.2%	2000	17.0%	1995

During the past five years, the fund's three worst months have been January 2000 (-2 percent), November 2001 (-2 percent), and May 1999 (-1 percent). During the same period, the three best months have been July 2001 (1 percent), September 1999 (1 percent), and March 2000 (1 percent). In the past, Vanguard GNMA has done better than 85 percent of its peer group during the most recent bull market and outperformed 65 percent of its peer group during the most recent bear market. Consistency, or predictability, of returns for Vanguard GNMA can be described as very good. This fund's risk-adjusted return over the past three/five years ranks in the top quintile.

Management ★★★★★

There are 31,900 fixed-income securities in this $21 billion portfolio. The average government bond fund today is $300 million in size. Close to 90 percent of the fund's holdings are in bonds. The average maturity of the bonds in this account is six years; the weighted coupon rate averages 7 percent. The portfolio's fixed-income holdings can be categorized as intermediate-term, high-quality debt.

Paul D. Kaplan has managed this fund for the past nine years. Management's track record is quite enviable due to its philosophy of avoiding the fancy and esoteric while embracing ordinary GNMAs. Kaplan favors a buy-and-hold strategy. He constantly looks for ways to minimize prepayments that are typically a concern of mortgage-backed securities. The fund's price movement is highly correlated to the Lehman Brothers Aggregate Bond Index. There are 78 funds besides GNMA within the Vanguard family. Overall, the fund family's risk adjusted performance can be described as between good and very good.

Current Income ★★★★★

Over the past year, Vanguard GNMA had a 12-month yield of 5.2 percent. During this same 12-month period, the typical government bond fund had a yield that averaged 3.9 percent.

Expenses ★★★★★

Vanguard GNMA's expense ratio is 0.3 percent; it has averaged 0.3 percent annually over the past three calendar years. The average expense ratio for the 605 funds in this category is 1.1 percent. This fund's turnover rate over the past year has been 8 percent, while its peer group average has been 204 percent.

Summary

Vanguard GNMA ties for first place as the best performer in its category of 600+ entries. Current income is about 25 percent higher than its category average. Despite the portfolio's low level of risk, it has still managed to outperform 94 percent of all mutual funds over the past five years. Expenses and turnover are low. This is just one of many Vanguard offerings to appear in this, and previous, editions of the book.

Profile

minimum initial investment $3,000	*IRA accounts available* . . . . yes
subsequent minimum investment . . $100	*IRA minimum investment* $1,000
available in all 50 states . . . . yes	*date of inception* . . . . Jun. 1980
telephone exchanges . . . . yes	*dividend/income paid* . . . . monthly
number of funds in family 79	*average credit quality* . . . . AAA

Vanguard Short-Term Federal
Vanguard Financial Center
P.O. Box 2600
Valley Forge, PA 19482
(800) 662-7447
www.vanguard.com

total return	★★★★★
risk reduction	★★★★
management	★★★★★
current income	★★★★★
expense control	★★★★★
symbol VSGBX	24 points
up-market performance	good
down-market performance	fair
predictability of returns	very good

Total Return   ★★★★★
Over the past five years, Vanguard Short-Term Federal has taken $10,000 and turned it into $14,090 ($12,880 over three years and $18,700 over the past 10 years). This translates into an annualized return of 7 percent over the past five years, 9 percent over the past three years, and 6 percent for the decade. Over the past five years, this fund has outperformed 92 percent of all mutual funds; within its general category it has also done better than 92 percent of its peers. Government bond funds have averaged 6 percent annually over these same five years.

During the past five years, a $10,000 initial investment grew to $11,580 after taxes, assuming a 40 percent income tax bracket (state and federal combined) and a capital gains rate of 20 percent. This means that investors in this fund were able to preserve 69 percent of their total returns. Compared to other funds in its category, this fund's tax savings are considered to be excellent.

Risk/Volatility   ★★★★
Over the past five years, Vanguard Short-Term Federal has experienced average risk for its category. Over the past decade, the fund has had one negative year, while the Lehman Brothers Aggregate Bond Index had two (off 3 percent in 1994 and 1 percent in 1999); the Lehman Brothers Government Bond Index also fell twice (off 3 percent in 1994 and 2 percent in 1999). The fund has underperformed the Lehman Brothers Aggregate Bond Index six times and the Lehman Brothers Government Bond Index six times in the past 10 years. Consistency of *overperformance* for this fund has been excellent.

	last 5 years		last 10 years	
worst year	2.1%	1999	-0.9%	1994
best year	9.2%	2000	12.3%	1995

During the past five years, the fund's three worst months have been February 1999 (-1 percent), November 2001 (-1 percent), and May 1999 (-0.8 percent).

During the same period, the three best months have been September 2001 (1 percent), September 1998 (1 percent), and January 2001 (1 percent). In the past, Vanguard Short-Term Federal has done better than 60 percent of its peer group during the most recent bull market and outperformed 40 percent of its peer group during the most recent bear market. Consistency, or predictability, of returns for Vanguard Short-Term Federal can be described as very good. This fund's risk-adjusted return over the past three/five years ranks in the top quintile.

Management   ★★★★★
There are 75 fixed-income securities in this $3 billion portfolio. The average government bond fund today is $300 million in size. Close to 80 percent of the fund's holdings are in bonds. The average maturity of the bonds in this account is 3 years; the weighted coupon rate averages 6 percent. The portfolio's fixed-income holdings can be categorized as short-term, high-quality debt.

Ian A. MacKinnon and John Hollyer have managed this fund for the past seven years. Management prefers agency bonds and mortgages instead of Treasuries, a contrarian view when compared to the competition. By clever sector rotation, the managers have been able to beat their peers while minimizing overall volatility. Interest rate risk is kept low. The fund's price movement is highly correlated to the Lehman Brothers Aggregate Bond Index. There are 78 funds besides Short-Term Federal within the Vanguard family. Overall, the fund family's risk adjusted performance can be described as between good and very good.

Current Income   ★★★★★
Over the past year, Vanguard Short-Term Federal had a 12-month yield of 4.9 percent. During this same 12-month period, the typical government bond fund had a yield that averaged 3.9 percent.

Expenses   ★★★★★
Vanguard Short-Term Federal's expense ratio is 0.3 percent; it has averaged 0.3 percent annually over the past three calendar years. The average expense ratio for the 605 funds in this category is 1.1 percent. This fund's turnover rate over the past year has been 80 percent, while its peer group average has been 204 percent.

Summary
Vanguard Short-Term Federal ties for first place within its category as the overall best choice for a government securities fund. This is surprising because the portfolio's maturity is so low. It is difficult for any money manager to have such an overall short maturity but such high returns.

Profile

minimum initial investment $3,000	*IRA accounts available* . . . . yes
subsequent minimum investment . . $100	*IRA minimum investment* $1,000
available in all 50 states . . . . yes	*date of inception*. . . . . Dec. 1987
telephone exchanges . . . . yes	*dividend/income paid* . . . . monthly
number of funds in family 79	*average credit quality* . . . . AAA

Growth Funds

These funds generally seek capital appreciation, with current income as a distant secondary concern. Growth funds typically invest in U.S. common stocks, while avoiding speculative issues and aggressive trading techniques. The goal of most of these funds is long-term growth. The approaches used to attain this appreciation can vary significantly among growth funds.

Over the past 15 years, U.S. stocks have outperformed both corporate and government bonds. From 1988 through 2002, common stocks have averaged 11.5 percent compounded per year, compared to 10.0 percent for corporate bonds and 10.5 percent for government bonds. A $10,000 investment in stocks, as measured by the S&P 500, grew to over $51,020 over the past 15 years; a similar initial investment in corporate bonds grew to only $41,710.

Looking at a longer time frame, you do even better: $10,000 invested in stocks at the beginning of 1953 would have grown to $1,901,610 by the end of 2002 (versus $256,070 for long-term corporate bonds). This translates into an average compound return of 11.1 percent per year. Over the past 50 years, the worst year for common stocks was 1974, when a loss of 26 percent was suffered. One year later, these same stocks posted a gain of 37 percent. The second worst year was 2002, when stocks dropped just over 22 percent. The best year so far has been 1954, when growth stocks posted a gain of 53 percent.

Growth stocks have outperformed bonds in every single decade. If George Washington had invested $1 in common stocks with an average return of 12 percent, his investment would be worth over $455 billion today. If he had averaged 14 percent, his portfolio would be large enough to pay our national debt five times over!

The following table covers 129 years and shows the odds of making money (a positive return) over each of several different time periods.

Standard & Poor's Composite 500 Stock Index
Various periods, 1871–1977 (dividends not included)

length of period	total number of periods	number of periods in which stock prices			percentage opportunity for profit (not including dividends)
		rose	declined	unchanged	
1 year	129	84	45	65	65
5 years	125	100	25	80	80
10 years	120	108	12	90	90
15 years	116	107	9	92	92
20 years	110	107	3	97	97
25 years	105	104	1	99	99
30 years	100	100	0	100	100

More than 3,600 funds make up the growth category. The standard deviation is 20.9 percent; beta (stock market-related risk) is 1.0, the same as the overall market, as measured by the S&P 500. The typical portfolio is divided into 88 percent U.S. stocks, 3 percent foreign stocks, and the balance in money market instruments. The average turnover rate for all growth funds is 110 percent per year. The yield on growth funds averages just 0.2 percent annually. Fund expenses average 1.5 percent per year.

Volatility (standard deviation) in today's markets is unprecedented. As this chart shows, nearly half of the past year's 105 trading days (through May 31, 2000) saw changes of 1 percent. Nearly one-quarter saw changes greater than 2 percent. Finally, all but six days experienced at least a 1 percent change between the intraday low and high.

Percentage of Time S&P 500
Had 1–2% Daily Changes (1990–2000)
Percentage of trading days with changes of positive or negative

Year	S&P 500	1%	2%	1% intraday	2% intraday
1990	-3.2%	29.6	5.1	60.1	14.7
1991	30.6%	23.3	3.6	50.2	7.1
1992	7.7%	11.0	0.0	28.0	0.8
1993	10.0%	6.7	0.4	14.6	1.6
1994	1.3%	10.7	0.8	27.0	1.6
1995	37.4%	5.2	0.0	17.9	1.2
1996	23.1%	15.0	1.2	39.4	4.4
1997	33.4%	32.0	5.9	70.8	15.1
1998	28.6%	31.4	9.1	69.1	22.2
1999	21.1%	36.5	9.1	77.0	21.0
2000 *	-2.8%	48.1	22.1	94.2	44.2

* through May 31, 2000

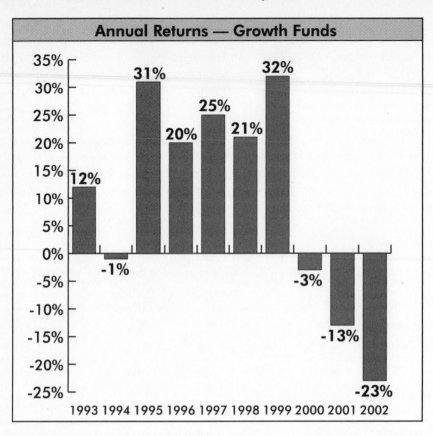

Historical returns over the past three, five, ten, and 15 years for growth funds are shown here. All the figures shown are *compound annual* rates of return (all periods ending December 31, 2002).

3 years	5 years	10 years	15 years
-13.8%	-0.8%	7.4%	10.1%

Calamos Growth A
1111 East Warrenville Road
Naperville, IL 60563
(800) 823-7386
www.calamos.com

total return	★★★★★
risk reduction	★★★
management	★★★★
tax minimization	★★★★★
expense control	★★
symbol CVGRX	19 points
up-market performance	poor
down-market performance	excellent
predictability of returns	poor

Total Return   ★★★★★
Over the past five years, Calamos Growth A has taken $10,000 and turned it into
$22,240 ($9,830 over three years and $48,150 over the past 10 years). This trans-
lates into an annualized return of 17 percent over the past five years, -1 percent
over the past three years, and 17 percent for the decade. Over the past five years,
this fund has outperformed 99 percent of all mutual funds; within its general category it has also done better than 99 percent of its peers. Growth funds have averaged less than 1 percent annually over these same five years.

Risk/Volatility   ★★★
Over the past five years, Calamos Growth A has experienced average risk for its
category. Over the past decade, the fund has had three negative years, while the
S&P 500 has had three (off 9 percent in 2000, 12 percent in 2001, and 22 percent
in 2002). The fund has underperformed the S&P 500 five times in the past 10 years.
Consistency of *overperformance* for this fund has been very good.

	last 5 years		last 10 years	
worst year	-15.9%	2002	-15.9%	2002
best year	77.7%	1999	77.7%	1999

During the past five years, the fund's three worst months have been
November 2000 (-23 percent), August 1998 (-21 percent), and July 2000 (-11 percent). During the same period, the three best months have been February 2000
(41 percent), August 2000 (18 percent), and June 2000 (17 percent). In the past,
Calamos Growth A has only done better than 10 percent of its peer group during
the most recent bull market but outperformed 95 percent of its peer group during
the most recent bear market. Consistency, or predictability, of returns for Calamos
Growth A can be described as poor. This fund's risk-adjusted return over the past
three/five years ranks in the top quintile.

Management   ★★★★

There are 110 stocks in this $2 billion portfolio. The average growth fund today is $260 million in size. Close to 95 percent of the fund's holdings are in stocks. The stocks in this portfolio have an average p/e ratio of 25 and a median market capitalization of $3 billion. The 10 largest holdings compose 20 percent of the fund's total assets. The three largest sector weightings are services (60 percent), health (15 percent), and industrial cyclicals (15 percent). The portfolio's equity holdings can be categorized as mid-cap and growth-oriented issues.

A team has managed this fund for the past 12 years. Management uses a quantitative method for searching out corporations that surpass analyst expectations. Free cash flow is an important measurement tool for the managers. Stocks are dumped once they hit fair valuation or when the company's outlook weakens. The fund's price movement is not correlated to that of the S&P 500. There are six funds besides Growth within the Calamos family. Overall, the fund family's risk adjusted performance can be described as excellent.

Tax Minimization   ★★★★★

During the past five years, a $10,000 initial investment grew to $17,340 after taxes, assuming a 40 percent income tax bracket (state and federal combined) and a capital gains rate of 20 percent. This means that investors in this fund were able to preserve 92 percent of their total returns. Compared to other funds in its category, this fund's tax savings are considered to be excellent.

Expenses   ★★

Calamos Growth A's expense ratio is 1.5 percent; it has averaged 1.7 percent annually over the past three calendar years. The average expense ratio for the 3,515 funds in this category is 1.5 percent. This fund's turnover rate over the past year has been 91 percent, while its peer group average has been 112 percent.

Summary

Calamos Growth A has outperformed 99 percent of all mutual funds as well as 99 percent of its peer group. Tax efficiency is an astounding 92 percent, making it a great choice for the tax-conscious investor. Even though three-year return figures are barely negative, the fund's returns were still more than thirtyfold greater than growth funds in general. On a five-year basis, performance ranks number one. This is just one of several Calamos funds you should check out.

Profile

minimum initial investment $1,000	*IRA accounts available* . . . . yes
subsequent minimum investment . . . $50	*IRA minimum investment* $500
available in all 50 states . . . . yes	*date of inception* . . . . Sept. 1990
telephone exchanges . . . . yes	*dividend/income paid* . . . . annually
number of funds in family 7	*largest sector weighting* . . . . . . services

Clipper
9601 Wilshire Boulevard, Suite 828
Beverly Hills, CA 90210
(800) 776-5033
www.clipperfund.com

total return	★★★★
risk reduction	★★★
management	★★★★
tax minimization	★★★★
expense control	★★★★
symbol CFIMX	19 points
up-market performance	good
down-market performance	excellent
predictability of returns	very good

Total Return   ★★★★
Over the past five years, Clipper has taken $10,000 and turned it into $16,710 ($14,310 over three years and $41,020 over the past 10 years). This translates into an annualized return of 11 percent over the past five years, 13 percent over the past three years, and 15 percent for the decade. Over the past five years, this fund has outperformed 99 percent of all mutual funds; within its general category it has also done better than 99 percent of its peers. Growth funds have averaged less than 1 percent annually over these same five years.

Risk/Volatility   ★★★
Over the past five years, Clipper has experienced below average risk for its category. Over the past decade, the fund has had three negative years, while the S&P 500 has had three (off 9 percent in 2000, 12 percent in 2001, and 22 percent in 2002). The fund has underperformed the S&P 500 five times in the past 10 years. Consistency of *overperformance* for this fund has been very good.

	last 5 years		last 10 years	
worst year	-5.5%	2002	-5.5%	2002
best year	37.4%	2000	45.2%	1995

During the past five years, the fund's three worst months have been August 1998 (-21 percent), December 1999 (-12 percent), and February 2000 (-8 percent). During the same period, the three best months have been October 1998 (11 percent), March 2000 (8 percent), and April 1999 (6 percent). In the past, Clipper has done better than 45 percent of its peer group during the most recent bull market and outperformed 97 percent of its peer group during the most recent bear market. Consistency, or predictability, of returns for Clipper can be described as very good. This fund's risk-adjusted return over the past three/five years ranks in the top quintile.

Management   ★★★★

There are 35 stocks in this $4 billion portfolio. The average growth fund today is $260 million in size. Close to 90 percent of the fund's holdings are in stocks. The stocks in this portfolio have an average p/e ratio of 16 and a median market capitalization of $28 billion. The 10 largest holdings compose 50 percent of the fund's total assets. The three largest sector weightings are financials (35 percent), industrial cyclicals (35 percent), and services (25 percent). The portfolio's equity holdings can be categorized as large-cap and value-oriented issues.

A team has managed this fund for the past 19 years. Management looks for established corporations that have dominant franchises and whose stock is trading at a discount. Holdings are concentrated and the managers are not afraid to keep a substantial portion of the portfolio in fixed-income during periods when few bargains can be found. The fund's price movement is only vaguely correlated to that of the S&P 500. Clipper is the only fund within the Clipper "family." Overall, the fund family's risk adjusted performance can be described as excellent.

Tax Minimization   ★★★★

During the past five years, a $10,000 initial investment grew to $11,870 after taxes, assuming a 40 percent income tax bracket (state and federal combined) and a capital gains rate of 20 percent. This means that investors in this fund were able to preserve 77 percent of their total returns. Compared to other funds in its category, this fund's tax savings are considered to be very good.

Expenses   ★★★★

Clipper's expense ratio is 1.1 percent; it has averaged 1.1 percent annually over the past three calendar years. The average expense ratio for the 3,515 funds in this category is 1.5 percent. This fund's turnover rate over the past year has been 23 percent, while its peer group average has been 112 percent.

Summary

Clipper has the best three- and five-year combined performance record. The fund scores well in every single category. The portfolio does a good job during up markets but a superb showing during bear markets. With more than 3,500 growth funds to choose, this is one of the best choices. Hopefully, the parent company will add more funds to its "orphan" family. The Clipper fund has appeared in past editions of this book.

Profile

minimum initial investment $25,000	*IRA accounts available* .... yes
subsequent minimum investment . $1,000	*IRA minimum investment* $3,000
available in all 50 states .... yes	*date of inception* .... Feb. 1984
telephone exchanges .... yes	*dividend/income paid* .... annually
number of funds in family 1	*largest sector weighting* .... financials

Hartford Midcap A
P.O. Box 64387
St. Paul, MN 55164
888-843-7824
www.thehartford.com

total return	★★★★★
risk reduction	★★★★
management	★★★★
tax minimization	★★★★
expense control	★★★
symbol HFMCX	20 points
up-market performance	very good
down-market performance	excellent
predictability of returns	good

Total Return   ★★★★★
Over the past five years, Hartford Midcap A has taken $10,000 and turned it into $18,710 ($10,120 over three years). This translates into an annualized return of 13 percent over the past five years and 0 percent over the past three years. Over the past five years, this fund has outperformed 90 percent of all mutual funds; within its general category it has done better than 98 percent of its peers. Growth funds have averaged less than 1 percent annually over these same five years.

Risk/Volatility   ★★★★
Over the past five years, Hartford Midcap A has experienced below average risk for its category. Over the past decade, the fund has had two negative years, while the S&P 500 has had three (off 9 percent in 2000, 12 percent in 2001, and 22 percent in 2002). The fund has underperformed the S&P 500 six times in the past 10 years. Consistency of *overperformance* for this fund has been very good.

	last 5 years		last 10 years	
worst year	-15.0%	2002	-15.0%	2002
best year	50.2%	1999	50.2%	1999

During the past five years, the fund's three worst months have been August 1998 (-20 percent), November 2000 (-19 percent), and September 2001 (-12 percent). During the same period, the three best months have been December 1999 (16 percent), February 2000 (16 percent), and December 1998 (11 percent). In the past, Hartford Midcap A has done better than 75 percent of its peer group during the most recent bull market and outperformed 85 percent of its peer group during the most recent bear market. Consistency, or predictability, of returns for Hartford Midcap A can be described as good. This fund's risk-adjusted return over the past three/five years ranks in the top quintile.

Management   ★★★★

There are 90 stocks in this $760 million portfolio. The average growth fund today is $260 million in size. Close to 95 percent of the fund's holdings are in stocks. The stocks in this portfolio have an average p/e ratio of 27 and a median market capitalization of $4 billion. The 10 largest holdings compose 20 percent of the fund's total assets. The three largest sector weightings are industrial cyclicals (25 percent), financials (25 percent), and services (20 percent). The portfolio's equity holdings can be categorized as mid-cap and a blend of growth and value stocks.

Phillip H. Perelmuter has managed this fund for the past five years. Management leans toward mid-cap growth issues that represent industry leadership. Perelmuter has been far more successful than his peers when it comes to playing it defensively. The fund's price movement is fairly correlated to that of the S&P 500. There are 31 funds besides Midcap within the Hartford Mutual Funds family. Overall, the fund family's risk adjusted performance can be described as good.

Tax Minimization   ★★★★

During the past five years, a $10,000 initial investment grew to $18,710 after taxes, assuming a 40 percent income tax bracket (state and federal combined) and a capital gains rate of 20 percent. This means that investors in this fund were able to preserve 84 percent of their total returns. Compared to other funds in its category, this fund's tax savings are considered to be very good.

Expenses   ★★★

Hartford Midcap A's expense ratio is 1.4 percent; it has averaged 1.4 percent annually over the past three calendar years. The average expense ratio for the 3,515 funds in this category is 1.5 percent. This fund's turnover rate over the past year has been 116 percent, while its peer group average has been 112 percent.

Summary

Hartford Midcap A does a fine job across the board. In fact, it is this consistency that earns it an overall score that is the second best in its rather huge category. The portfolio exhibits below average risk, yet returns have been quite compelling. The fund's three-year record is slightly positive, versus an annualized loss of about 14 percent per year for the growth fund category. Similarly, five-year return figures for growth funds in general have been negative while this offering turned in annualized returns of more than 13 percent.

Profile

minimum initial investment $500	*IRA accounts available* .... yes
subsequent minimum investment ... $25	*IRA minimum investment* $250
available in all 50 states .... yes	*date of inception* .... Dec. 1997
telephone exchanges .... yes	*dividend/income paid* .... annually
number of funds in family 32	*largest sector weighting* ..... industrial cyclicals

Longleaf Partners
6410 Poplar Avenue, Suite 900
Memphis, TN 38119
(800) 445-9469
www.longleafpartners.com

total return	★★★★
risk reduction	★★★
management	★★★★
tax minimization	★★★
expense control	★★★★★
symbol LLPFX	19 points
up-market performance	good
down-market performance	excellent
predictability of returns	very good

Total Return   ★★★★
Over the past five years, Longleaf Partners has taken $10,000 and turned it into $14,240 ($12,200 over three years and $37,530 over the past 10 years). This translates into an annualized return of 7 percent over the past five years, 7 percent over the past three years, and 14 percent for the decade. Over the past five years, this fund has outperformed 97 percent of all mutual funds; within its general category it has done better than 86 percent of its peers. Growth funds have averaged less than 1 percent annually over these same five years.

Risk/Volatility   ★★★
Over the past five years, Longleaf Partners has experienced average risk for its category. Over the past decade, the fund has had one negative year, while the S&P 500 has had three (off 9 percent in 2000, 12 percent in 2001, and 22 percent in 2002). The fund has underperformed the S&P 500 five times in the past 10 years. Consistency of *overperformance* for this fund has been good.

	last 5 years		last 10 years	
worst year	-8.3%	2002	-8.3%	2002
best year	20.6%	2000	28.3%	1997

During the past five years, the fund's three worst months have been November 1999 (-18 percent), August 1998 (-14 percent), and September 2001 (-13 percent). During the same period, the three best months have been April 1999 (14 percent), October 1998 (9 percent), and March 2000 (8 percent). In the past, Longleaf Partners has done better than 47 percent of its peer group during the most recent bull market and outperformed 97 percent of its peer group during the most recent bear market. Consistency, or predictability, of returns for Longleaf Partners can be described as very good. This fund's risk-adjusted return over the past three/five years ranks in the top-two quintiles.

Management   ★★★★
There are 25 stocks in this $5 billion portfolio. The average growth fund today is $260 million in size. Close to 90 percent of the fund's holdings are in stocks. The stocks in this portfolio have an average p/e ratio of 18 and a median market capitalization of $9 billion. The 10 largest holdings compose 55 percent of the fund's total assets. The three largest sector weightings are services (55 percent), industrial cyclicals (20 percent), and financials (15 percent). The portfolio's equity holdings can be categorized as large-cap and a blend of growth and value stocks.

A team has managed this fund for the past 16 years. Management takes a value approach as it tries to find stocks trading at a 40 percent-plus discount. The managers use a discounted cash-flow model that includes asset valuation and sales of comparable companies. The fund's price movement is moderately correlated to that of the S&P 500. There are two funds besides Partners Fund within the Longleaf Partners family. Overall, the fund family's risk adjusted performance can be described as between very good and excellent.

Tax Minimization   ★★★
During the past five years, a $10,000 initial investment grew to $11,580 after taxes, assuming a 40 percent income tax bracket (state and federal combined) and a capital gains rate of 20 percent. This means that investors in this fund were able to preserve 71 percent of their total returns. Compared to other funds in its category, this fund's tax savings are considered to be good.

Expenses   ★★★★★
Longleaf Partners's expense ratio is 0.9 percent; it has averaged 0.9 percent annually over the past three calendar years. The average expense ratio for the 3,515 funds in this category is 1.5 percent. This fund's turnover rate over the past year has been 18 percent, while its peer group average has been 112 percent.

Summary
Longleaf Partners boasts some of the lowest overhead costs and turnover rates in its category. Return figures are equally impressive: It has outperformed 97 percent of all funds along with 86 percent of its peers. The fund has done a good job during bull markets but has had excellent results during bear periods. Although this is only a three-fund family, check out other members of the Longleaf group.

Profile
minimum initial investment .... $10,000   *IRA accounts available* .... yes
subsequent minimum investment .... $1   *IRA minimum investment* $10,000
available in all 50 states .... yes   *date of inception* .... Apr. 1987
telephone exchanges .... yes   *dividend/income paid* .... annually
number of funds in family 3   *largest sector weighting* ...... services

Lord Abbett Mid-Cap Value A
90 Hudson Street
Jersey City, NJ 07302
(800) 201-6984
www.lordabbett.com

total return	★★★★
risk reduction	★★★
management	★★★★
tax minimization	★★★★
expense control	★★★★
symbol LAVLX	19 points
up-market performance	fair
down-market performance	excellent
predictability of returns	very good

Total Return ★★★★
Over the past five years, Lord Abbett Mid-Cap Value A has taken $10,000 and turned it into $15,510 ($14,940 over three years and $34,370 over the past 10 years). This translates into an annualized return of 9 percent over the past five years, 14 percent over the past three years, and 13 percent for the decade. Over the past five years, this fund has outperformed 98 percent of all mutual funds; within its general category it has done better than 95 percent of its peers. Growth funds have averaged less than 1 percent annually over these same five years.

Risk/Volatility ★★★
Over the past five years, Lord Abbett Mid-Cap Value A has experienced average risk for its category. Over the past decade, the fund has had three negative years, while the S&P 500 has had three (off 9 percent in 2000, 12 percent in 2001, and 22 percent in 2002). The fund has underperformed the S&P 500 six times in the past 10 years. Consistency of *overperformance* for this fund has been good.

	last 5 years		last 10 years	
worst year	-9.8%	2002	-9.8%	2002
best year	53.3%	2000	53.3%	2000

During the past five years, the fund's three worst months have been August 1998 (-16 percent), January 2000 (-11 percent), and January 1999 (-10 percent). During the same period, the three best months have been March 2000 (14 percent), February 1998 (9 percent), and April 1999 (8 percent). In the past, Lord Abbett Mid-Cap Value A has only done better than 35 percent of its peer group during the most recent bull market but outperformed 95 percent of its peer group during the most recent bear market. Consistency, or predictability, of returns for Lord Abbett Mid-Cap Value A can be described as very good. This fund's risk-adjusted return over the past three/five years ranks in the top quintile.

Management   ★★★★

There are 55 stocks in this $2 billion portfolio. The average growth fund today is $260 million in size. Close to 100 percent of the fund's holdings are in stocks. The stocks in this portfolio have an average p/e ratio of 27 and a median market capitalization of $3 billion. The 10 largest holdings compose 25 percent of the fund's total assets. The three largest sector weightings are industrial cyclicals (55 percent), consumer durables (25 percent), and services (20 percent). The portfolio's equity holdings can be categorized as mid-cap and value-oriented issues.

Edward von der Linde and Howard E. Hansen have managed this fund for the past 15 years. Management continues to follow the same strategy it has used for the past 20 years: Use a quantitative model to isolate the top performers as ranked by past revenue growth. The next step is to pare down the list even further by looking for at least two catalysts that might lead to strong performance moving forward. The fund's price movement is only modestly correlated to that of the S&P 500. There are 34 funds besides Mid-Cap Value within the Lord Abbett family. Overall, the fund family's risk adjusted performance can be described as good.

Tax Minimization   ★★★★

During the past five years, a $10,000 initial investment grew to $10,230 after taxes, assuming a 40 percent income tax bracket (state and federal combined) and a capital gains rate of 20 percent. This means that investors in this fund were able to preserve 84 percent of their total returns. Compared to other funds in its category, this fund's tax savings are considered to be very good.

Expenses   ★★★★

Lord Abbett Mid-Cap Value A's expense ratio is 1.2 percent; it has averaged 1.3 percent annually over the past three calendar years. The average expense ratio for the 3,515 funds in this category is 1.5 percent. This fund's turnover rate over the past year has been 32 percent, while its peer group average has been 112 percent.

Summary

Lord Abbett Mid-Cap Value A has one of the best three- and five-year combined performance records. Over the past three years it is only slightly below the number one performer. Tax efficiency, turnover, and expense minimization have all also been very good. The fund really shines during bear markets.

Profile

minimum initial investment $1,000	*IRA accounts available* . . . . yes
subsequent minimum investment $1	*IRA minimum investment* $250
available in all 50 states. . . . . yes	*date of inception* . . . . Jun. 1983
telephone exchanges. . . . . yes	*dividend/income paid* . . . . annually
number of funds in family 35	*largest sector weighting*. . . . . industrial cyclicals

Mairs & Power Growth
W-1420 First National Bank Building
St. Paul, MN 55101
(651) 222-8478
800-304-7404

total return	★★★★
risk reduction	★★★★
management	★★★★★
tax minimization	★★★★
expense control	★★★★★
symbol MPGFX	22 points
up-market performance	good
down-market performance	excellent
predictability of returns	very good

Total Return   ★★★★
Over the past five years, Mairs & Power Growth has taken $10,000 and turned it into $14,500 ($12,370 over three years and $41,960 over the past 10 years). This translates into an annualized return of 8 percent over the past five years, 7 percent over the past three years, and 15 percent for the decade. Over the past five years, this fund has outperformed 97 percent of all mutual funds; within its general category it has done better than 99 percent of its peers. Growth funds have averaged less than 1 percent annually over these same five years.

Risk/Volatility   ★★★★
Over the past five years, Mairs & Power Growth has experienced below average risk for its category. Over the past decade, the fund has had one negative year, while the S&P 500 has had three (off 9 percent in 2000, 12 percent in 2001, and 22 percent in 2002). The fund has underperformed the S&P 500 three times in the past 10 years. Consistency of *overperformance* for this fund has been good.

	last 5 years		last 10 years	
worst year	-8.1%	2002	-8.1%	2002
best year	26.5%	2000	47.7%	1995

During the past five years, the fund's three worst months have been August 1998 (-15 percent), December 1999 (-6 percent), and September 2001 (-6 percent). During the same period, the three best months have been March 2000 (11 percent), April 1999 (9 percent), and November 2001 (8 percent). In the past, Mairs & Power Growth has done better than 40 percent of its peer group during the most recent bull market and outperformed 95 percent of its peer group during the most recent bear market. Consistency, or predictability, of returns for Mairs & Power Growth can be described as very good. This fund's risk-adjusted return over the past three/five years ranks in the top quintile.

Management   ★★★★★
There are 35 stocks in this $850 million portfolio. The average growth fund today is $260 million in size. Close to 100 percent of the fund's holdings are in stocks. The stocks in this portfolio have an average p/e ratio of 24 and a median market capitalization of $14 billion. The 10 largest holdings compose 40 percent of the fund's total assets. The three largest sector weightings are industrial cyclicals (40 percent), consumer durables (30 percent), and health (20 percent). The portfolio's equity holdings can be categorized as large-cap and a blend of growth and value stocks.

George A. Mairs III and William B. Frels have managed this fund for the past 23 years. Management seeks out companies with strong management and a strong market presence. Most of the stocks in the portfolio are from companies located in Mairs's home state, Minnesota. The fund's price movement is only modestly correlated to that of the S&P 500. There is one other fund besides Growth within the Mairs & Power "family." Overall, the fund family's risk adjusted performance can be described as excellent.

Tax Minimization   ★★★★
During the past five years, a $10,000 initial investment grew to $12,320 after taxes, assuming a 40 percent income tax bracket (state and federal combined) and a capital gains rate of 20 percent. This means that investors in this fund were able to preserve 83 percent of their total returns. Compared to other funds in its category, this fund's tax savings are considered to be very good.

Expenses   ★★★★★
Mairs & Power Growth's expense ratio is 0.8 percent; it has averaged 0.8 percent annually over the past three calendar years. The average expense ratio for the 3,515 funds in this category is 1.5 percent. This fund's turnover rate over the past year has been 8 percent, while its peer group average has been 112 percent.

Summary
Mairs & Power Growth ties for number one as the overall top point earner. Part of the fund's success is due to its very low overhead and extremely low turnover rate. Over the past three and five years, the portfolio has radically outperformed its peer group while having below average risk. This is only a two-fund family, but its other sibling should be considered as well. For the investor who is looking for a management style that combines value and growth, this is as good as it gets.

Profile

minimum initial investment $2,500	*IRA accounts available* . . . . yes
subsequent minimum investment . . $100	*IRA minimum investment* $1,000
available in all 50 states . . . . yes	*date of inception* . . . . Nov. 1958
telephone exchanges . . . . yes	*dividend/income paid*. . . . semiannually
number of funds in family 2	*largest sector weighting*. . . . . industrial cyclicals

Merger
100 Summit Lake Drive
Valhalla, NY 10595
(800) 343-8959

total return	★★★★
risk reduction	★★★★★
management	★★★★
tax minimization	★★★★
expense control	★★
symbol MERFX	19 points
up-market performance	n/a
down-market performance	n/a
predictability of returns	excellent

Total Return   ★★★★

Over the past five years, Merger has taken $10,000 and turned it into $13,990 ($11,310 over three years and $24,710 over the past 10 years). This translates into an annualized return of 7 percent over the past five years, 4 percent over the past three years, and 9 percent for the decade. Over the past five years, this fund has outperformed 94 percent of all mutual funds; within its general category it has done better than 96 percent of its peers. Growth funds have averaged less than 1 percent annually over these same five years.

Risk/Volatility   ★★★★★

Over the past five years, Merger has experienced low risk for its category. Over the past decade, the fund has had one negative year, while the S&P 500 has had three (off 9 percent in 2000, 12 percent in 2001, and 22 percent in 2002). The fund has underperformed the S&P 500 five times in the past 10 years. Consistency of *over-performance* for this fund has been good.

	last 5 years		last 10 years	
worst year	-5.7%	2002	-5.7%	2002
best year	17.6%	2000	17.7%	1993

During the past five years, the fund's three worst months have been December 2000 (-10 percent), December 1999 (-8 percent), and December 2001 (-7 percent). During the same period, the three best months have been November 1999 (3 percent), June 1999 (3 percent), and November 1998 (2 percent). Consistency, or predictability, of returns for Merger can be described as excellent. This fund's risk-adjusted return over the past three/five years ranks in the top quintile.

Management   ★★★★

There are 65 stocks in this $820 million portfolio. The average growth fund today is $260 million in size. Close to 60 percent of the fund's holdings are in stocks. The stocks in this portfolio have an average p/e ratio of 18 and a median market capitalization of $6 billion. The 10 largest holdings compose 45 percent of the fund's total assets. The three largest sector weightings are industrial cyclicals (40 percent), technology (20 percent), and consumer staples (20 percent). The portfolio's equity holdings can be categorized as mid-cap and a blend of growth and value stocks.

Frederick W. Green and Bonnie L. Smith have managed this fund for the past 14 years. Management buys companies that are the announced targets of acquisitions. Sometimes the managers will short the acquirer's stock. The fund's price movement is not correlated to that of the S&P 500. Merger is the only fund within the Merger "family." Overall, the fund family's risk adjusted performance can be described as excellent.

Tax Minimization ★★★★
During the past five years, a $10,000 initial investment grew to $11,580 after taxes, assuming a 40 percent income tax bracket (state and federal combined) and a capital gains rate of 20 percent. This means that investors in this fund were able to preserve 86 percent of their total returns. Compared to other funds in its category, this fund's tax savings are considered to be very good.

Expenses ★★
Merger's expense ratio is 1.3 percent; it has averaged 1.3 percent annually over the past three calendar years. The average expense ratio for the 3,515 funds in this category is 1.5 percent. This fund's turnover rate over the past year has been 384 percent, while its peer group average has been 112 percent.

Summary
Merger has outshined 94 percent of all funds along with 96 percent of its peers when it comes to raw performance. Expenses are lower than average but turnover has been amazingly high. According to traditional views, a high turnover rate translates into an inefficiently tax-managed portfolio, but this has not been the case. Investors have been able to preserve 86 percent of their gains. With such an overall record, one would hope that the parent company would add a couple more funds to its group.

Profile
minimum initial investment $2,000
subsequent minimum investment $1
available in all 50 states . . . . yes
telephone exchanges . . . . yes
number of funds in family 1

IRA accounts available . . . . yes
IRA minimum investment $2,000
date of inception . . . . Jan. 1989
dividend/income paid . . . . annually
largest sector weighting . . . . . industrial
cyclicals

Meridian Value

60 East Sir Francis Drake Boulevard, Suite 306
Larkspur, CA 94939
(800) 446-6662
www.meridianfund.com

total return	★★★★★
risk reduction	★★★★
management	★★★★
tax minimization	★★★★★
expense control	★★★★
symbol MVALX	22 points
up-market performance	fair
down-market performance	excellent
predictability of returns	very good

Total Return   ★★★★★

Over the past five years, Meridian Value has taken $10,000 and turned it into $21,830 ($13,270 over three years). This translates into an annualized return of 17 percent over the past five years and 10 percent over the past three years. Over the past five years, this fund has outperformed 99 percent of all mutual funds; within its general category it has also done better than 99 percent of its peers. Growth funds have averaged less than 1 percent annually over these same five years.

Risk/Volatility   ★★★★

Over the past five years, Meridian Value has experienced average risk for its category. Over the past decade, the fund has had one negative year, while the S&P 500 has had three (off 9 percent in 2000, 12 percent in 2001, and 22 percent in 2002). The fund has underperformed the S&P 500 five times in the past 10 years. Consistency of *overperformance* for this fund has been very good.

	last 5 years		last 10 years	
worst year	-13.4%	2002	-13.4%	2002
best year	38.3%	1999	38.3%	1999

During the past five years, the fund's three worst months have been August 1998 (-17 percent), September 2001 (-10 percent), and September 1999 (-9 percent). During the same period, the three best months have been December 2000 (10 percent), February 2000 (10 percent), and April 1999 (9 percent). In the past, Meridian Value has done better than 40 percent of its peer group during the most recent bull market and outperformed 85 percent of its peer group during the most recent bear market. Consistency, or predictability, of returns for Meridian Value can be described as very good. This fund's risk-adjusted return over the past three/five years ranks in the top quintile.

Management   ★★★★

There are 75 stocks in this $1 billion portfolio. The average growth fund today is $260 million in size. Close to 100 percent of the fund's holdings are in stocks. The stocks in this portfolio have an average p/e ratio of 25 and a median market capitalization of $3 billion. The 10 largest holdings compose 30 percent of the fund's total assets. The three largest sector weightings are services (30 percent), industrial cyclicals (25 percent), and health (20 percent). The portfolio's equity holdings can be categorized as mid-cap and a blend of growth and value stocks.

Kevin C. O'Boyle and Richard F. Aster Jr. have managed this fund for the past nine years. Management looks for companies that have had two or more disappointing consecutive quarters of performance. By picking up stocks of companies that have been overly punished while sticking with market leaders has paid off. O'Boyle favors small- and mid-cap issues but has no problem owning a multi-cap portfolio. The fund's price movement is only modestly correlated to that of the S&P 500. There is one other fund besides Value within the Meridian "family." Overall, the fund family's risk adjusted performance can be described as between very good and excellent.

Tax Minimization   ★★★★★

During the past five years, a $10,000 initial investment grew to $19,210 after taxes, assuming a 40 percent income tax bracket (state and federal combined) and a capital gains rate of 20 percent. This means that investors in this fund were able to preserve 93 percent of their total returns. Compared to other funds in its category, this fund's tax savings are considered to be excellent.

Expenses   ★★★★

Meridian Value's expense ratio is 1.1 percent; it has averaged 1.2 percent annually over the past three calendar years. The average expense ratio for the 3,515 funds in this category is 1.5 percent. This fund's turnover rate over the past year has been 54 percent, while its peer group average has been 112 percent.

Summary

Meridian Value ties for first place as the overall winner in its category of 3,500+ funds. The portfolio scores either very well or excellent in every category measured. The fund's combined performance score for the past three and five years is unmatched. Tax efficiency has been an astounding 93 percent; again the best in its category. Risk over the last three years has been below average.

Profile

minimum initial investment $1,000	*IRA accounts available* . . . . yes
subsequent minimum investment . . . $50	*IRA minimum investment* $1,000
available in all 50 states . . . . yes	*date of inception* . . . . Feb. 1994
telephone exchanges . . . . yes	*dividend/income paid* . . . . annually
number of funds in family 2	*largest sector weighting* . . . . . . services

Yacktman

1110 Lake Cook Road, Suite 385
Buffalo Grove, IL 60089
(800) 525-8258
www.yacktman.com

total return	★★★
risk reduction	★★★
management	★★★★
tax minimization	★★★★
expense control	★★★★
symbol YACKX	18 points
up-market performance	excellent
down-market performance	excellent
predictability of returns	very good

Total Return   ★★★

Over the past five years, Yacktman has taken $10,000 and turned it into $12,630 ($15,100 over three years and $24,940 over the past 10 years). This translates into an annualized return of 5 percent over the past five years, 15 percent over the past three years, and 10 percent for the decade. Over the past five years, this fund has outperformed 80 percent of all mutual funds; within its general category it has done better than 60 percent of its peers. Growth funds have averaged less than 1 percent annually over these same five years.

Risk/Volatility   ★★★

Over the past five years, Yacktman has experienced average risk for its category. Over the past decade, the fund has had two negative years, while the S&P 500 has had three (off 9 percent in 2000, 12 percent in 2001, and 22 percent in 2002). The fund has underperformed the S&P 500 five times in the past 10 years. Consistency of *overperformance* for this fund has been good.

	last 5 years		last 10 years	
worst year	-16.9%	1999	-16.9%	1999
best year	19.5%	2001	30.4%	1995

During the past five years, the fund's three worst months have been August 1998 (-16 percent), December 1998 (-15 percent), and September 2001 (-8 percent). During the same period, the three best months have been November 2001 (11 percent), February 1998 (10 percent), and October 1998 (10 percent). In the past, Yacktman has done better than 85 percent of its peer group during the most recent bull market and outperformed 98 percent of its peer group during the most recent bear market. Consistency, or predictability, of returns for Yacktman can be described as very good. This fund's risk-adjusted return over the past three/five years ranks in the top-two quintiles.

Management   ★★★★

There are 70 stocks in this $170 million portfolio. The average growth fund today is $260 million in size. Close to 70 percent of the fund's holdings are in stocks. The stocks in this portfolio have an average p/e ratio of 17 and a median market capitalization of $24 billion. The 10 largest holdings compose 40 percent of the fund's total assets. The three largest sector weightings are industrial cyclicals (45 percent), services (30 percent), and consumer staples (25 percent). The portfolio's equity holdings can be categorized as large-cap and a blend of growth and value stocks.

Donald A. Yacktman has managed this fund for the past 11 years. Management takes a somewhat old-fashioned approach to stock ownership: Stick with those corporations that generate cash, have little or no debt, and are selling at a discount. The fund is fairly concentrated. Yacktman emphasizes a buy-and-hold approach when looking for shareholder-friendly companies that pay dividends and buy back their own stock. The fund's price movement is only somewhat correlated to that of the S&P 500. There is one other fund besides Yacktman within the Yacktman Fund "family." Overall, the fund family's risk adjusted performance can be described as between very good and excellent.

Tax Minimization   ★★★★

During the past five years, a $10,000 initial investment grew to $19,210 after taxes, assuming a 40 percent income tax bracket (state and federal combined) and a capital gains rate of 20 percent. This means that investors in this fund were able to preserve 83 percent of their total returns. Compared to other funds in its category, this fund's tax savings are considered to be very good.

Expenses   ★★★★

Yacktman's expense ratio is 1.2 percent; it has averaged 1.2 percent annually over the past three calendar years. The average expense ratio for the 3,515 funds in this category is 1.5 percent. This fund's turnover rate over the past year has been 43 percent, while its peer group average has been 112 percent.

Summary

Yacktman enjoys the number one position when it comes to three-year returns, an eye-popping annualized average 14.7 percent (vs. -13.8 percent for its colleagues). Despite these high returns, predictability of returns has been quite appealing while risk has been average. The portfolio is one of the very few that has done a tremendous job in both up and down markets.

Profile

minimum initial investment $2,500	*IRA accounts available* . . . . yes
subsequent minimum investment . . $100	*IRA minimum investment* $500
available in all 50 states . . . . yes	*date of inception* . . . . Jul. 1992
telephone exchanges . . . . yes	*dividend/income paid* . . . . annually
number of funds in family 2	*largest sector weighting* . . . . . industrial cyclicals

Growth and Income Funds

These funds attempt to produce both capital appreciation and current income, giving priority to the appreciation potential in the stocks purchased. Growth and income fund portfolios include seasoned, well-established firms that pay comparatively high cash dividends. But do not let this category's name mislead you. The average growth and "income" fund has an annual yield of just 0.7 percent. The goal of these funds is to provide long-term growth without excessive volatility in share price. Portfolios are almost always composed exclusively of U.S. stocks.

Over the past 50 years (ending December 31, 2002), common stocks have outperformed inflation, on average, 66 percent of the time over one-year periods, 83 percent of the time over five-year periods, 86 percent of the time over 10-year periods, 92 percent of the time over 15-year periods, and 100 percent of the time over any given 20-year period. Over the same period, high-quality, long-term corporate bonds have outperformed inflation, on average, 62 percent of the time over one-year periods, 66 percent of the time over five-year periods, 70 percent of the time over 10-year periods, 78 percent of the time over 15-year periods, and 82 percent over any given 20-year period.

More than 1,100 funds make up the growth and income category. Another category, equity-income (280 funds), has been combined with growth and income. Equity-income funds have had a standard deviation of 15.1 percent, an average annual dividend yield of 2.2 percent, a 65 percent turnover rate, and an average annual expense ratio of 1.4 percent. Over the past three years, equity-income funds have had a compounded annualized return of -5.0 percent, 0.3 percent over the past five years, 3.5 percent for 10 years, and 10.3 percent for the past 15 years.

Over the past three and five years, growth and income funds have had an average compound return of -10.2 and -0.6 percent per year, respectively. These funds have averaged 8.6 percent annually over the past 10 years and 10.3 percent annually for the past 15 years. The standard deviation for growth and income funds has been 16.8 percent over the past three years (compared to 15.1 for equity-income and 20.8 percent for growth funds). This means that growth and income funds have been 27 percent more predictable than growth funds but have been about 10 percent less predictable than pure equity-income funds.

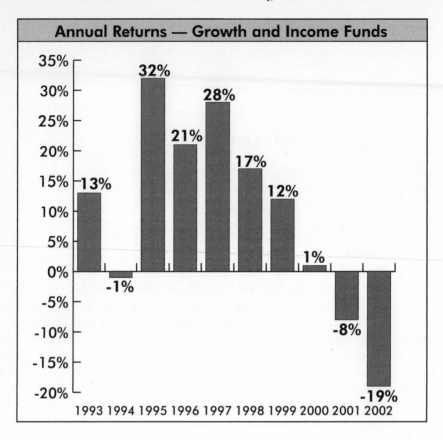

Annual Returns — Growth and Income Funds

American Century Equity Income
4500 Main Street
P.O. Box 419200
Kansas City, MO 64141
(800) 345-2021
www.americancentury.com

total return	★★★★★
risk reduction	★★★★★
management	★★★★★
tax minimization	★★★★
expense control	★★★★
symbol TWEIX	23 points
up-market performance	fair
down-market performance	excellent
predictability of returns	very good

Total Return   ★★★★★
Over the past five years, American Century Equity Income has taken $10,000 and turned it into $14,540 ($12,890 over three years). This translates into an annualized return of 8 percent over the past five years and 9 percent over the past three years. Over the past five years, this fund has outperformed 97 percent of all mutual funds; within its general category it has done better than 87 percent of its peers. Growth and income funds have averaged less than 1 percent annually over these same five years.

Risk/Volatility   ★★★★★
Over the past five years, American Century Equity Income has experienced low risk for its category. Over the past decade, the fund has had two negative years, while the S&P 500 has had three (off 9 percent in 2000, 12 percent in 2001, and 22 percent in 2002). The fund has underperformed the S&P 500 six times in the past 10 years. Consistency of *overperformance* for this fund has been good.

	last 5 years		last 10 years	
worst year	-5.0%	2002	-5.0%	2002
best year	21.9%	2000	29.6%	1995

During the past five years, the fund's three worst months have been December 1998 (-13 percent), December 1999 (-10 percent), and August 1998 (-8 percent). During the same period, the three best months have been March 2000 (9 percent), April 1999 (8 percent), and October 1998 (7 percent). In the past, American Century Equity Income has only done better than 30 percent of its peer group during the most recent bull market but outperformed 92 percent of its peer group during the most recent bear market. Consistency, or predictability, of returns for American Century Equity Income can be described as very good. This fund's risk-adjusted return over the past three/five years ranks in the top quintile.

Management   ★★★★★

There are 85 stocks in this $1 billion portfolio. The average growth and income fund today is $560 million in size. Close to 70 percent of the fund's holdings are in stocks. The stocks in this portfolio have an average p/e ratio of 24 and a median market capitalization of $8 billion. The 10 largest holdings compose 30 percent of the fund's total assets. The three largest sector weightings are industrial cyclicals (65 percent), consumer durables (25 percent), and financials (20 percent). The portfolio's equity holdings can be categorized as mid-cap and value-oriented issues.

Phillip N. Davidson and Scott A. Moore have managed this fund for the past eight years. Management employs an all-cap approach when searching for companies that are considered inexpensive, as measured by price/dividend yield or price/cash flow. Yield is comparatively high due to the fund's convertible holdings. The managers are quick to sell positions they believe have gotten too pricey. The fund's price movement is only moderately correlated to that of the S&P 500. There are 50 funds besides Equity Income within the American Century Investments family. Overall, the fund family's risk adjusted performance can be described as between good and very good.

Tax Minimization   ★★★★

During the past five years, a $10,000 initial investment grew to $19,210 after taxes, assuming a 40 percent income tax bracket (state and federal combined) and a capital gains rate of 20 percent. This means that investors in this fund were able to preserve 71 percent of their total returns. Compared to other funds in its category, this fund's tax savings are considered to be very good.

Expenses   ★★★★

American Century Equity Income's expense ratio is 1 percent; it has averaged 1 percent annually over the past three calendar years. The average expense ratio for the 1,340 funds in this category is 1.3 percent. This fund's turnover rate over the past year has been 169 percent, while its peer group average has been 74 percent.

Summary

American Century Equity Income turns in the best overall score, a near-perfect 23 out of 25 possible points. Not only is this the best fund in its large category of 1,340 funds, it also has the best combined three- and five-year performance record. Equally amazing, the fund's risk level has been lower than any of its contemporaries over the same periods. What a great choice for any growth and income equity investor.

Profile

minimum initial investment $2,500	*IRA accounts available* . . . . yes
subsequent minimum investment . . . $50	*IRA minimum investment* $2,500
available in all 50 states . . . . yes	*date of inception* . . . . Aug. 1994
telephone exchanges . . . . yes	*dividend/income paid* . . . . quarterly
number of funds in family 51	*largest sector weighting*. . . . . industrial cyclicals

American Funds Capital Income Builder A

333 South Hope Street
Los Angeles, CA 90071
(800) 421-4120
www.americanfunds.com

total return	★★★
risk reduction	★★★★
management	★★★★
tax minimization	★★★★
expense control	★★★★★
symbol CAIBX	20 points
up-market performance	poor
down-market performance	excellent
predictability of returns	excellent

Total Return   ★★★

Over the past five years, American Funds Capital Income Builder A has taken $10,000 and turned it into $12,890 ($11,860 over three years and $26,340 over the past 10 years). This translates into an annualized return of 5 percent over the past five years, 6 percent over the past three years, and 10 percent for the decade. Over the past five years, this fund has outperformed 85 percent of all mutual funds; within its general category it has done better than 87 percent of its peers. Growth and income funds have averaged less than 1 percent annually over these same five years.

Risk/Volatility   ★★★★

Over the past five years, American Funds Capital Income Builder A has experienced below average risk for its category. Over the past decade, the fund has had two negative years, while the S&P 500 has had three (off 9 percent in 2000, 12 percent in 2001, and 22 percent in 2002). The fund has underperformed the S&P 500 six times in the past 10 years. Consistency of *overperformance* for this fund has been good.

	last 5 years		last 10 years	
worst year	-2.8%	1999	-2.8%	1999
best year	12.5%	2000	25.1%	1995

During the past five years, the fund's three worst months have been August 1998 (-8 percent), December 1998 (-4 percent), and September 2001 (-4 percent). During the same period, the three best months have been March 2000 (4 percent), September 1998 (4 percent), and March 1998 (3 percent). In the past, American Funds Capital Income Builder A has only done better than 5 percent of its peer group during the most recent bull market but outperformed 98 percent of its peer group during the most recent bear market. Consistency, or predictability, of returns for American Funds Capital Income Builder A can be described as excellent. This fund's risk-adjusted return over the past three/five years ranks in the top-two quintiles.

Management   ★★★★
There are 430 stocks in this $10 billion portfolio. The average growth and income fund today is $560 million in size. Close to 50 percent of the fund's holdings are in stocks. The stocks in this portfolio have an average p/e ratio of 20 and a median market capitalization of $8 billion. The 10 largest holdings compose 15 percent of the fund's total assets. The three largest sector weightings are industrial cyclicals (40 percent), financials (40 percent), and consumer staples (15 percent). The portfolio's equity holdings can be categorized as large-cap and a blend of growth and value stocks.

A team has managed this fund for the past 16 years. Management focuses on income. The fund contains a number of dividend-rich industry groups such as REITs, utilities, and banking. Management has a conservative bent. The fund's price movement is not correlated to that of the S&P 500. There are 27 funds besides Income Builder within the American Funds family. Overall, the fund family's risk adjusted performance can be described as very good.

Tax Minimization   ★★★★
During the past five years, a $10,000 initial investment grew to $19,210 after taxes, assuming a 40 percent income tax bracket (state and federal combined) and a capital gains rate of 20 percent. This means that investors in this fund were able to preserve 75 percent of their total returns. Compared to other funds in its category, this fund's tax savings are considered to be very good.

Expenses   ★★★★★
American Funds Capital Income Builder A's expense ratio is 0.7 percent; it has averaged 0.7 percent annually over the past three calendar years. The average expense ratio for the 1,340 funds in this category is 1.3 percent. This fund's turnover rate over the past year has been 37 percent, while its peer group average has been 74 percent.

Summary
American Funds Capital Income Builder A has the lowest expense ratio in its category and one of the smallest turnover rates. Risk has been below average while returns have been quite high when compared to its colleagues (who have averaged negative returns over the last three and five years). This is just one of a number of offerings from the American Funds group that has been in this and previous editions of the book.

Profile

minimum initial investment $250	*IRA accounts available* . . . . yes
subsequent minimum investment . . . $50	*IRA minimum investment* $250
available in all 50 states . . . . yes	*date of inception* . . . . Jul. 1987
telephone exchanges . . . . yes	*dividend/income paid* . . . . quarterly
number of funds in family 28	*largest sector weighting* . . . . . industrial cyclicals

Ameristock
1301 East Ninth Street, 36th Floor
Cleveland, OH 44114
(800) 394-5064
www.ameristock.com

total return	★★★★
risk reduction	★★
management	★★★★
tax minimization	★★★★★
expense control	★★★★★
symbol AMSTX	20 points
up-market performance	excellent
down-market performance	good
predictability of returns	good

Total Return   ★★★★
Over the past five years, Ameristock has taken $10,000 and turned it into $13,920 ($10,270 over three years). This translates into an annualized return of 7 percent over the past five years and 1 percent over the past three years. Over the past five years, this fund has outperformed 97 percent of all mutual funds; within its general category it has done better than 99 percent of its peers. Growth and income funds have averaged less than 1 percent annually over these same five years.

Risk/Volatility   ★★
Over the past five years, Ameristock has experienced average risk for its category. Over the past decade, the fund has had one negative year, while the S&P 500 has had three (off 9 percent in 2000, 12 percent in 2001, and 22 percent in 2002). The fund has underperformed the S&P 500 five times in the past 10 years. Consistency of *overperformance* for this fund has been very good.

	last 5 years		last 10 years	
worst year	-16.0%	2002	-16.0%	2002
best year	32.0%	1998	32.9%	1997

During the past five years, the fund's three worst months have been August 1998 (-11 percent), February 2000 (-9 percent), and September 2001 (-7 percent). During the same period, the three best months have been March 2000 (13 percent), October 1998 (8 percent), and April 1999 (7 percent). In the past, Ameristock has done better than 95 percent of its peer group during the most recent bull market and outperformed 56 percent of its peer group during the most recent bear market. Consistency, or predictability, of returns for Ameristock can be described as good. This fund's risk-adjusted return over the past three/five years ranks in the top quintile.

Management   ★★★★
There are 55 stocks in this $1 billion portfolio. The average growth and income fund today is $560 million in size. Close to 95 percent of the fund's holdings are in stocks. The stocks in this portfolio have an average p/e ratio of 21 and a median market capitalization of $53 billion. The 10 largest holdings compose 40 percent of the fund's total assets. The three largest sector weightings are industrial cyclicals (30 percent), financials (25 percent), and consumer durables (20 percent). The portfolio's equity holdings can be categorized as large-cap and value-oriented issues.

Nicholas D. Gerber and Andrew Ngim have managed this fund for the past seven years. Management sticks with $15 billion-plus companies whose stock is inexpensively priced. Management leans towards issues that pay high dividends or are not currently doing well from a growth perspective but have bright outlooks. The fund's price movement is moderately correlated to that of the S&P 500. There is one other fund besides Ameristock within the Ameristock "family." Overall, the fund family's risk adjusted performance can be described as very good.

Tax Minimization   ★★★★★
During the past five years, a $10,000 initial investment grew to $12,810 after taxes, assuming a 40 percent income tax bracket (state and federal combined) and a capital gains rate of 20 percent. This means that investors in this fund were able to preserve 86 percent of their total returns. Compared to other funds in its category, this fund's tax savings are considered to be excellent.

Expenses   ★★★★★
Ameristock's expense ratio is 0.8 percent; it has averaged 0.9 percent annually over the past three calendar years. The average expense ratio for the 1,340 funds in this category is 1.3 percent. This fund's turnover rate over the past year has been 6 percent, while its peer group average has been 74 percent.

Summary
Ameristock ties for number two as the overall best fund in the growth and income category. Performance has been better than 99 percent of its contemporaries while risk levels have been decent. The portfolio does a decent job during down periods but really excels during bull markets. For the value investor this is a smart choice.

Profile
minimum initial investment $1,000	*IRA accounts available* . . . . yes
subsequent minimum investment . . $100	*IRA minimum investment* $1,000
available in all 50 states . . . . yes	*date of inception* . . . . Aug. 1985
telephone exchanges . . . . yes	*dividend/income paid* . . . . semiannually
number of funds in family 2	*largest sector weighting* . . . . . industrial cyclicals

Dodge & Cox Stock
One Sansome Street, 35th Floor
San Francisco, CA 94104
(800) 621-3979
www.dodgeandcox.com

total return	★★★★★
risk reduction	★★★
management	★★★★
tax minimization	★★★★
expense control	★★★★★
symbol DODGX	21 points
up-market performance	good
down-market performance	excellent
predictability of returns	good

Total Return   ★★★★★
Over the past five years, Dodge & Cox Stock has taken $10,000 and turned it into $14,420 ($11,380 over three years and $37,560 over the past 10 years). This translates into an annualized return of 8 percent over the past five years, 4 percent over the past three years, and 14 percent for the decade. Over the past five years, this fund has outperformed 97 percent of all mutual funds; within its general category it has done better than 99 percent of its peers. Growth and income funds have averaged less than 1 percent annually over these same five years.

Risk/Volatility   ★★★
Over the past five years, Dodge & Cox Stock has experienced average risk for its category. Over the past decade, the fund has had one negative year, while the S&P 500 has had three (off 9 percent in 2000, 12 percent in 2001, and 22 percent in 2002). The fund has underperformed the S&P 500 five times in the past 10 years. Consistency of *overperformance* for this fund has been very good.

	last 5 years		last 10 years	
worst year	-10.5%	2002	-10.5%	2002
best year	20.2%	1999	33.4%	1995

During the past five years, the fund's three worst months have been August 1998 (-14 percent), September 2001 (-8 percent), and June 2000 (-7 percent). During the same period, the three best months have been April 1999 (12 percent), November 2001 (8 percent), and October 1998 (8 percent). In the past, Dodge & Cox Stock has done better than 45 percent of its peer group during the most recent bull market and outperformed 85 percent of its peer group during the most recent bear market. Consistency, or predictability, of returns for Dodge & Cox Stock can be described as good. This fund's risk-adjusted return over the past three/five years ranks in the top quintile.

Management   ★★★★
There are 85 stocks in this $12 billion portfolio. The average growth and income fund today is $560 million in size. Close to 95 percent of the fund's holdings are in stocks. The stocks in this portfolio have an average p/e ratio of 26 and a median market capitalization of $10 billion. The 10 largest holdings compose 25 percent of the fund's total assets. The three largest sector weightings are industrial cyclicals (45 percent), consumer durables (25 percent), and financials (20 percent). The portfolio's equity holdings can be categorized as large-cap and value-oriented issues.

A team has managed this fund for the past 36 years. Management favors mid- and large-cap stocks that look inexpensive by a number of measurements. Corporations with dominant market positions and good management are also strongly considered. The fund's price movement is only moderately correlated to that of the S&P 500. There are two funds besides Stock within the Dodge & Cox family. Overall, the fund family's risk adjusted performance can be described as excellent.

Tax Minimization   ★★★★
During the past five years, a $10,000 initial investment grew to $10,240 after taxes, assuming a 40 percent income tax bracket (state and federal combined) and a capital gains rate of 20 percent. This means that investors in this fund were able to preserve 67 percent of their total returns. Compared to other funds in its category, this fund's tax savings are considered to be very good.

Expenses   ★★★★★
Dodge & Cox Stock's expense ratio is 0.5 percent; it has averaged 0.5 percent annually over the past three calendar years. The average expense ratio for the 1,340 funds in this category is 1.3 percent. This fund's turnover rate over the past year has been 10 percent, while its peer group average has been 74 percent.

Summary
Dodge & Cox Stock has lower expenses than any of its peers plus one of the best turnover rates. The fund's performance puts it in the top 1 percent of its category. This growth and income fund is part of a small fund family that has one of the best short-, medium-, and long-term records in the industry. It does not get much better than a Dodge & Cox fund.

Profile
minimum initial investment $2,500
subsequent minimum investment . . $100
available in all 50 states . . . . yes
telephone exchanges . . . . yes
number of funds in family 3

IRA accounts available . . . . yes
IRA minimum investment $1,000
date of inception . . . . Jan. 1965
dividend/income paid . . . . quarterly
largest sector weighting . . . . . industrial
                                        cyclicals

FPA Perennial

11400 West Olympic Boulevard, Suite 1200
Los Angeles, CA 90064
(800) 982-4372
www.fpafunds.com

total return	★★★★★
risk reduction	★★★
management	★★★★
tax minimization	★★★★
expense control	★★★★
symbol FPPFX	20 points
up-market performance	very good
down-market performance	excellent
predictability of returns	fair

Total Return   ★★★★★

Over the past five years, FPA Perennial has taken $10,000 and turned it into $15,880 ($12,090 over three years and $29,140 over the past 10 years). This translates into an annualized return of 10 percent over the past five years, 7 percent over the past three years, and 11 percent for the decade. Over the past five years, this fund has outperformed 99 percent of all mutual funds; within its general category it has done better than 97 percent of its peers. Growth and income funds have averaged less than 1 percent annually over these same five years.

Risk/Volatility   ★★★

Over the past five years, FPA Perennial has experienced average risk for its category. Over the past decade, the fund has had two negative years, while the S&P 500 has had three (off 9 percent in 2000, 12 percent in 2001, and 22 percent in 2002). The fund has underperformed the S&P 500 six times in the past 10 years. Consistency of *overperformance* for this fund has been very good.

	last 5 years		last 10 years	
worst year	-10.6%	2002	-10.6%	2002
best year	25.3%	1999	25.3%	1999

During the past five years, the fund's three worst months have been August 1998 (-21 percent), December 1999 (-14 percent), and September 2001 (-12 percent). During the same period, the three best months have been April 1999 (13 percent), April 2001 (12 percent), and November 1999 (8 percent). In the past, FPA Perennial has done better than 65 percent of its peer group during the most recent bull market and outperformed 95 percent of its peer group during the most recent bear market. Consistency, or predictability, of returns for FPA Perennial can be described as fair. This fund's risk-adjusted return over the past three/five years ranks in the top quintile.

Management   ★★★★

There are 40 stocks in this $70 million portfolio. The average growth and income fund today is $560 million in size. Close to 85 percent of the fund's holdings are in stocks. The stocks in this portfolio have an average p/e ratio of 23 and a median market capitalization of $1 billion. The 10 largest holdings compose 35 percent of the fund's total assets. The three largest sector weightings are consumer durables (45 percent), industrial cyclicals (35 percent), and services (25 percent). The portfolio's equity holdings can be categorized as mid-cap and growth-oriented issues.

Eric S. Ende and Steven R. Geist have managed this fund for the past seven years. Management looks for companies that have clean balance sheets, post above-average returns, and are trading at historical discounts. The fund's price movement is only moderately correlated to that of the S&P 500. There are three funds besides Perennial within the FPA family. Overall, the fund family's risk adjusted performance can be described as between good and very good.

Tax Minimization   ★★★★

During the past five years, a $10,000 initial investment grew to $10,800 after taxes, assuming a 40 percent income tax bracket (state and federal combined) and a capital gains rate of 20 percent. This means that investors in this fund were able to preserve 70 percent of their total returns. Compared to other funds in its category, this fund's tax savings are considered to be very good.

Expenses   ★★★★

FPA Perennial's expense ratio is 1.2 percent; it has averaged 1.2 percent annually over the past three calendar years. The average expense ratio for the 1,340 funds in this category is 1.3 percent. This fund's turnover rate over the past year has been 25 percent, while its peer group average has been 74 percent.

Summary

FPA Perennial has done a good job during bull markets and made an excellent showing during bear periods. The portfolio's returns rank number one over the last five years and at the top for the most recent three years. Risk-adjusted return measurements have also been quite appealing. For an overall score, the fund ties for second place in a field of more than 1,300 challengers.

Profile

minimum initial investment $1,500	*IRA accounts available* . . . . yes
subsequent minimum investment . . $100	*IRA minimum investment* $100
available in all 50 states . . . . yes	*date of inception* . . . . Apr. 1984
telephone exchanges . . . . yes	*dividend/income paid* . . . . semiannually
number of funds in family 4	*largest sector weighting* . . . . consumer durables

Franklin Rising Dividends A
One Franklin Parkway
San Mateo, CA 94403
(800) 342-5236
www.franklintempleton.com

total return	★★★
risk reduction	★★★★
management	★★★★
tax minimization	★★★
expense control	★★★★
symbol FRDPX	18 points
up-market performance	poor
down-market performance	excellent
predictability of returns	very good

Total Return ★★★
Over the past five years, Franklin Rising Dividends A has taken $10,000 and turned it into $12,580 ($13,220 over three years and $24,490 over the past 10 years). This translates into an annualized return of 5 percent over the past five years, 10 percent over the past three years, and 9 percent for the decade. Over the past five years, this fund has outperformed 80 percent of all mutual funds; within its general category it has done better than 60 percent of its peers. Growth and income funds have averaged less than 1 percent annually over these same five years.

Risk/Volatility ★★★★
Over the past five years, Franklin Rising Dividends A has experienced below average risk for its category. Over the past decade, the fund has had four negative years, while the S&P 500 has had three (off 9 percent in 2000, 12 percent in 2001, and 22 percent in 2002). The fund has underperformed the S&P 500 six times in the past 10 years. Consistency of *overperformance* for this fund has been good.

	last 5 years		last 10 years	
worst year	-10.3%	1999	-10.3%	1999
best year	19.0%	2000	32.4%	1997

During the past five years, the fund's three worst months have been August 1998 (-16 percent), December 1999 (-9 percent), and September 2001 (-9 percent). During the same period, the three best months have been October 1998 (11 percent), December 2000 (9 percent), and March 2000 (8 percent). In the past, Franklin Rising Dividends A has only done better than 20 percent of its peer group during the most recent bull market but outperformed 96 percent of its peer group during the most recent bear market. Consistency, or predictability, of returns for Franklin Rising Dividends A can be described as very good. This fund's risk-adjusted return over the past three/five years ranks in the top-two quintiles.

Management   ★★★★

There are 50 stocks in this $570 million portfolio. The average growth and income fund today is $560 million in size. Close to 100 percent of the fund's holdings are in stocks. The stocks in this portfolio have an average p/e ratio of 19 and a median market capitalization of $3 billion. The 10 largest holdings compose 40 percent of the fund's total assets. The three largest sector weightings are industrial cyclicals (45 percent), financials (30 percent), and consumer durables (30 percent). The portfolio's equity holdings can be categorized as mid-cap and a blend of growth and value stocks.

A team has managed this fund for the past 16 years. Management buys stocks of companies that have long histories of increasing dividends and are trading in the lower half of their 10-year p/e range. The managers like industrial and financial stocks and are not afraid to own unloved stocks. The fund's price movement is only modestly correlated to that of the S&P 500. There are 92 funds besides Rising Dividends within the Franklin Templeton family. Overall, the fund family's risk adjusted performance can be described as very good.

Tax Minimization   ★★★

During the past five years, a $10,000 initial investment grew to $19,210 after taxes, assuming a 40 percent income tax bracket (state and federal combined) and a capital gains rate of 20 percent. This means that investors in this fund were able to preserve 55 percent of their total returns. Compared to other funds in its category, this fund's tax savings are considered to be very good.

Expenses   ★★★★

Franklin Rising Dividends A's expense ratio is 1.5 percent; it has averaged 1.5 percent annually over the past three calendar years. The average expense ratio for the 1,340 funds in this category is 1.3 percent. This fund's turnover rate over the past year has been 19 percent, while its peer group average has been 74 percent.

Summary

Franklin Rising Dividends A is part of one of the largest and oldest mutual fund companies in the country. The company's acquisition of the Templeton group and Mutual Shares several years ago has only enhanced its reputation. This particular Franklin offering has the best three-year performance record in its class. Five-year returns may not appear to be that special but are when compared to its category average (which was negative). Stability has been quite high and turnover quite low.

Profile

minimum initial investment $1,000	*IRA accounts available* . . . . yes
subsequent minimum investment . . . $50	*IRA minimum investment* $250
available in all 50 states . . . . yes	*date of inception* . . . . Jan. 1987
telephone exchanges . . . . yes	*dividend/income paid* . . . . quarterly
number of funds in family 93	*largest sector weighting* . . . . . industrial cyclicals

Prudential Jennison Equity Opportunities A

One Seaport Plaza
New York, NY 10292
(800) 225-1852
www.prudential.com

total return	★★★★★
risk reduction	★★
management	★★★
tax minimization	★★★★
expense control	★★
symbol PJIAX	16 points
up-market performance	very good
down-market performance	very good
predictability of returns	excellent

Total Return   ★★★★★

Over the past five years, Prudential Jennison Equity Opportunities A has taken $10,000 and turned it into $15,150 ($11,690 over three years). This translates into an annualized return of 9 percent over the past five years and 5 percent over the past three years. Over the past five years, this fund has outperformed 98 percent of all mutual funds; within its general category it has done better than 92 percent of its peers. Growth and income funds have averaged less than 1 percent annually over these same five years.

Risk/Volatility   ★★

Over the past five years, Prudential Jennison Equity Opportunities A has experienced average risk for its category. Over the past decade, the fund has had one negative year, while the S&P 500 has had three (off 9 percent in 2000, 12 percent in 2001, and 22 percent in 2002). The fund has underperformed the S&P 500 seven times in the past 10 years. Consistency of *overperformance* for this fund has been good.

	last 5 years		last 10 years	
worst year	-20.6%	2002	-20.6%	2002
best year	32.3%	2000	32.3%	2000

During the past five years, the fund's three worst months have been November 2000 (-16 percent), August 1998 (-13 percent), and September 2001 (-10 percent). During the same period, the three best months have been March 2000 (14 percent), December 2000 (12 percent), and April 1999 (12 percent). In the past, Prudential Jennison Equity Opportunities A has done better than 75 percent of its peer group during the most recent bull market and outperformed 65 percent of its peer group during the most recent bear market. Consistency, or predictability, of returns for Prudential Jennison Equity Opportunities A can be described as excellent. This fund's risk-adjusted return over the past three/five years ranks in the top-two quintiles.

Management   ★★★

There are 70 stocks in this $240 million portfolio. The average growth and income fund today is $560 million in size. Close to 100 percent of the fund's holdings are in stocks. The stocks in this portfolio have an average p/e ratio of 27 and a median market capitalization of $3 billion. The 10 largest holdings compose 25 percent of the fund's total assets. The three largest sector weightings are industrial cyclicals (25 percent), consumer durables (25 percent), and services (20 percent). The portfolio's equity holdings can be categorized as mid-cap and a blend of growth and value stocks.

A team has managed this fund for the past six years. Management looks for companies that have three times more upside potential than downside risk. The managers are able to buy stocks of any size. The fund's price movement is moderately correlated to that of the S&P 500. There are 36 funds besides Jennison Equity Opportunities within the Prudential family. Overall, the fund family's risk adjusted performance can be described as good.

Tax Minimization   ★★★★

During the past five years, a $10,000 initial investment grew to $19,210 after taxes, assuming a 40 percent income tax bracket (state and federal combined) and a capital gains rate of 20 percent. This means that investors in this fund were able to preserve 75 percent of their total returns. Compared to other funds in its category, this fund's tax savings are considered to be very good.

Expenses   ★★

Prudential Jennison Equity Opportunities A's expense ratio is 1.1 percent; it has averaged 1.4 percent annually over the past three calendar years. The average expense ratio for the 1,340 funds in this category is 1.3 percent. This fund's turnover rate over the past year has been 144 percent, while its peer group average has been 74 percent.

Summary

Prudential Jennison Equity Opportunities A rates number two for five-year returns and tax efficiency has been quite high. Since the fund's consistency of returns has been so good, this would be an excellent choice for the nervous investor who longs for predictability. The portfolio has done quite well during bull and bear markets alike.

Profile

minimum initial investment $1,000	*IRA accounts available* . . . . yes
subsequent minimum investment . . $100	*IRA minimum investment* $100
available in all 50 states . . . . yes	*date of inception* . . . . Nov. 1996
telephone exchanges . . . . yes	*dividend/income paid* . . . . semiannually
number of funds in family 37	*largest sector weighting* . . . . . industrial
	cyclicals

Scudder Dreman High Return Equity A

Two International Place
Boston, MA 02110
(800) 621-1048
www.scudder.com

total return	★★★
risk reduction	★
management	★★
tax minimization	★★★★
expense control	★★★
symbol KDHAX	13 points
up-market performance	fair
down-market performance	good
predictability of returns	fair

Total Return   ★★★

Over the past five years, Scudder Dreman High Return Equity A has taken
$10,000 and turned it into $11,330 ($11,660 over three years and $30,560 over
the past 10 years). This translates into an annualized return of 3 percent over the
past five years, 5 percent over the past three years, and 12 percent for the decade.
Over the past five years, this fund has outperformed 52 percent of all mutual
funds; within its general category it has done better than 85 percent of its peers.
Growth and income funds have averaged less than 1 percent annually over these
same five years.

Risk/Volatility   ★

Over the past five years, Scudder Dreman High Return Equity A has experienced
above average risk for its category. Over the past decade, the fund has had three
negative years, while the S&P 500 has had three (off 9 percent in 2000, 12 percent in 2001, and 22 percent in 2002). The fund has underperformed the S&P 500
five times in the past 10 years. Consistency of *overperformance* for this fund has
been good.

	last 5 years		last 10 years	
worst year	-18.5%	2002	-18.5%	2002
best year	41.3%	2000	46.9%	1995

During the past five years, the fund's three worst months have been August
1998 (-15 percent), December 1999 (-12 percent), and February 2000 (-8 percent).
During the same period, the three best months have been March 2000 (12 percent),
August 2000 (11 percent), and September 1998 (9 percent). In the past, Scudder
Dreman High Return Equity A has only done better than 35 percent of its peer
group during the most recent bull market but outperformed 55 percent of its peer
group during the most recent bear market. Consistency, or predictability, of returns
for Scudder Dreman High Return Equity A can be described as fair. This fund's
risk-adjusted return over the past three/five years ranks in the top-two quintiles.

Management ★★

There are 55 stocks in this $2 billion portfolio. The average growth and income fund today is $560 million in size. Close to 95 percent of the fund's holdings are in stocks. The stocks in this portfolio have an average p/e ratio of 19 and a median market capitalization of $34 billion. The 10 largest holdings compose 55 percent of the fund's total assets. The three largest sector weightings are industrial cyclicals (40 percent), financials (30 percent), and consumer staples (25 percent). The portfolio's equity holdings can be categorized as large-cap and value-oriented issues.

David N. Dreman has managed this fund for the past 15 years. Management is contrarian in its approach to stock selection. Dreman seeks out-of-favor companies and is not afraid to take large positions. He tends toward companies with solid balance sheets with a record of increasing sales and profits. The fund's price movement is only modestly correlated to that of the S&P 500. There are 89 funds besides High Return Equity within the Scudder family. Overall, the fund family's risk adjusted performance can be described as between good and very good.

Tax Minimization ★★★★

During the past five years, a $10,000 initial investment grew to $19,210 after taxes, assuming a 40 percent income tax bracket (state and federal combined) and a capital gains rate of 20 percent. This means that investors in this fund were able to preserve 77 percent of their total returns. Compared to other funds in its category, this fund's tax savings are considered to be very good.

Expenses ★★★

Scudder Dreman High Return Equity A's expense ratio is 1.3 percent; it has averaged 1.3 percent annually over the past three calendar years. The average expense ratio for the 1,340 funds in this category is 1.3 percent. This fund's turnover rate over the past year has been 29 percent, while its peer group average has been 74 percent.

Summary

Scudder Dreman High Return Equity A has demonstrated more risk than its peers, but the volatility has paid off; the portfolio has outperformed 85 percent of its colleagues. The fund will also appeal to non-sheltered accounts because of its high tax efficiency. Both Scudder and Dreman are highly regarded names in the financial services community.

Profile

minimum initial investment $1,000	IRA accounts available . . . . yes
subsequent minimum investment . . $100	IRA minimum investment $250
available in all 50 states . . . . yes	date of inception . . . . Mar. 1988
telephone exchanges . . . . yes	dividend/income paid . . . . quarterly
number of funds in family 90	largest sector weighting. . . . . industrial cyclicals

Van Kampen Equity and Income A

One Parkview Plaza
Oakbrook Terrace, IL 60181
(800) 421-5666
www.vankampen.com

total return	★★★★
risk reduction	★★★
management	★★★★
tax minimization	★★★
expense control	★★★★★
symbol ACEIX	19 points
up-market performance	poor
down-market performance	excellent
predictability of returns	excellent

Total Return   ★★★★

Over the past five years, Van Kampen Equity and Income A has taken $10,000 and turned it into $13,860 ($10,780 over three years and $29,970 over the past 10 years). This translates into an annualized return of 7 percent over the past five years, 3 percent over the past three years, and 12 percent for the decade. Over the past five years, this fund has outperformed 95 percent of all mutual funds; within its general category it has done better than 97 percent of its peers. Growth and income funds have averaged less than 1 percent annually over these same five years.

Risk/Volatility   ★★★

Over the past five years, Van Kampen Equity and Income A has experienced average risk for its category. Over the past decade, the fund has had three negative years, while the S&P 500 has had three (off 9 percent in 2000, 12 percent in 2001, and 22 percent in 2002). The fund has underperformed the S&P 500 six times in the past 10 years. Consistency of *overperformance* for this fund has been good.

	last 5 years		last 10 years	
worst year	-8.3%	2002	-8.3%	2002
best year	20.2%	2000	32.6%	1995

During the past five years, the fund's three worst months have been August 1998 (-9 percent), December 1999 (-7 percent), and September 2001 (-6 percent). During the same period, the three best months have been August 2000 (7 percent), February 1998 (5 percent), and October 1999 (5 percent). In the past, Van Kampen Equity and Income A has only done better than 15 percent of its peer group during the most recent bull market but outperformed 90 percent of its peer group during the most recent bear market. Consistency, or predictability, of returns for Van Kampen Equity and Income A can be described as excellent. This fund's risk-adjusted return over the past three/five years ranks in the top-two quintiles.

Management   ★★★★

There are 250 stocks in this $3 billion portfolio. The average growth and income fund today is $560 million in size. Close to 55 percent of the fund's holdings are in stocks. The stocks in this portfolio have an average p/e ratio of 26 and a median market capitalization of $20 billion. The 10 largest holdings compose 15 percent of the fund's total assets. The three largest sector weightings are industrial cyclicals (40 percent), financials (25 percent), and energy (15 percent). The portfolio's equity holdings can be categorized as large-cap and value-oriented issues.

A team has managed this fund for the past 13 years. Management is frequently overweighted in equities and convertibles as compared to its peers. The managers employ a mix of momentum- and value-investing styles when selecting equities. The fund's price movement is highly correlated to that of the S&P 500. There are 47 funds besides Equity and Income within the Van Kampen family. Overall, the fund family's risk adjusted performance can be described as good.

Tax Minimization   ★★★

During the past five years, a $10,000 initial investment grew to $19,210 after taxes, assuming a 40 percent income tax bracket (state and federal combined) and a capital gains rate of 20 percent. This means that investors in this fund were able to preserve 51 percent of their total returns. Compared to other funds in its category, this fund's tax savings are considered to be good.

Expenses   ★★★★★

Van Kampen Equity and Income A's expense ratio is 0.8 percent; it has averaged 0.8 percent annually over the past three calendar years. The average expense ratio for the 1,340 funds in this category is 1.3 percent. This fund's turnover rate over the past year has been 92 percent, while its peer group average has been 74 percent.

Summary

Van Kampen Equity and Income A ties for second place as the most predictable of its group. Management's ability to keep expenses low is another plus. Returns for the last half decade are better than 95 percent of the mutual fund universe and 97 percent of its contemporaries. Van Kampen is a large fund family that offers a number of solid choices.

Profile

minimum initial investment $1,000	*IRA accounts available* . . . . yes
subsequent minimum investment . . . $25	*IRA minimum investment* $500
available in all 50 states . . . . yes	*date of inception* . . . . Aug. 1960
telephone exchanges . . . . yes	*dividend/income paid* . . . . quarterly
number of funds in family 48	*largest sector weighting* . . . . . industrial cyclicals

Health Care Funds

Sector funds, such as health care, technology, and utilities, allow investors the opportunity to invest in a particular area of the market without exposing their portfolios to the same risk as investing in just a few individual stocks. The health care sector includes pharmaceuticals, medical products, medical services, and biotechnology.

People spend money on health care even in a slowing economy, and the segment of the population that spends the most on health care has grown every year since 1929. According to Pharmaceutical Research and Manufacturers of America, those age 65 and older spend nearly four times more on health care than those younger than 65. In the United States, 35 million people are 65 or older; that number is expected to increase to 40 million by 2010, 46 million by 2015, and 54 million by 2020.

These companies that make up this broad sector offer attractive revenue and earnings visibility that is generally immune to economic cycles. At the same time, the sector is benefiting from an overwhelming demographic shift.

Across the United States, Europe, and Asia, the sizable baby-boom generation is aging and demanding more treatments to improve their lifestyles. This trend could drive tremendous industry demand growth over the next several decades. At the same time, groundbreaking discoveries in the biotechnology area are creating a multitude of exciting products to meet the demands of this aging population.

Biotechnology companies are developing advancements for medical, agricultural, and industrial application. A number of biotechnology companies have shown progressive leadership, but few have successfully marketed drugs or generated earnings. As a result, stocks in this area can be very volatile and highly sensitive to adverse news. It is for this reason that those health-care mutual funds that have exposure to this subsector and are concerned with risk have only modest exposure to biotechnology. Research companies in areas such as genomics represent the ultimate in risk and reward potential.

Over the past couple of years, mutual fund managers have been more selective, focusing on profitable biotechnology companies that have products in the pipeline or currently on the market. In response to this, these companies have forged alliances with drug firms to expand their product portfolio and enhance profitability.

The medical supplies subsector remains strong. Increased demand for defibrillators, pacemakers, and cancer treatments such as radioactive seed implants, coupled with new-product approvals at the federal level, have kept this area's growth vigorous.

On the positive side, it is expected that the Bush administration will encourage and embrace market-driven policies. On the negative side, looming patent expirations and rising competition from generic drug companies continue to plague brand-dependent firms. The rising costs of brand-name drugs have prompted health maintenance organizations (HMOs) and preferred provider organizations (PPOs) to provide incentives for members to use generic drugs. In response, brand-dependent firms have beefed up their research and development efforts by merging with other drug firms.

The long-term growth prospects for health care are attractive and are largely based on three factors: People are living longer, products are coming to market faster, and the industry is benefiting from technological advances.

According to Data Resources, roughly 26 percent of the U.S. population is over 50. By the year 2006, that number is expected to be 30 percent and close to 35 percent by the year 2015. Product approval cycles are shorter. According to the FDA, the mean number of approved products from 1989–1993 was 25, with a mean approval time of 29 months. Over the 1994–1998 period, the mean number increased to 34 and approval time dropped to 17 months. Technological advances can also enhance profit potential.

There are more than 180 funds that make up the health-care category. Over the past three years, the average turnover rate has been a rather high 145 percent. The price-earnings (p/e) ratio for health care funds is 28. Dividend yield is close to zero. Over the past three years, these funds have averaged a -0.3 percent annualized gain per year with a standard deviation of 29.4 percent. For the past five and 10 years, average annualized returns have been 4.8 percent and 10.0 percent, respectively; for the past 15 years, annual returns have averaged 15.3 percent. The category has underperformed the S&P 500 in six of the past 10 years; yet for the entire 10-year period, average returns have been higher by 0.7 percent per year.

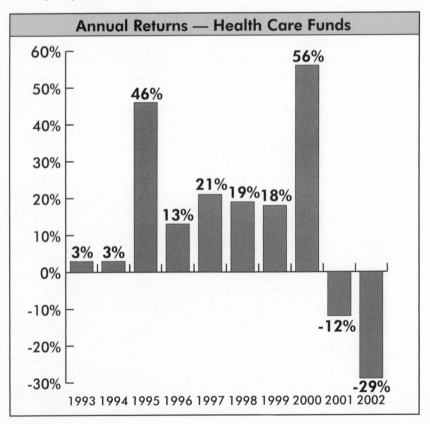

Annual Returns — Health Care Funds

Eaton Vance World Health A

255 State Street
Boston, MA 02109
(617) 482-8260
www.eatonvance.com

total return	★★★★★
risk reduction	★★★
management	★★★★
tax minimization	★★★★★
expense control	★★★★
symbol ETHSX	21 points
up-market performance	excellent
down-market performance	fair
predictability of returns	good

Total Return   ★★★★★

Over the past five years, Eaton Vance World Health A has taken $10,000 and turned it into $19,230 ($12,560 over three years and $47,950 over the past 10 years). This translates into an annualized return of 14 percent over the past five years, 8 percent over the past three years, and 17 percent for the decade. Over the past five years, this fund has outperformed 99 percent of all mutual funds; within its general category it has done better than 97 percent of its peers. Health funds have averaged 5 percent annually over these same five years.

Risk/Volatility   ★★★

Over the past five years, Eaton Vance World Health A has experienced average risk for its category. Over the past decade, the fund has had three negative years, while the S&P 500 has had three (off 9 percent in 2000, 12 percent in 2001, and 22 percent in 2002); the Wilshire 5000 fell four times (off less than 1 percent in 1994, 11 percent in 2000, 11 percent in 2001, and 21 percent in 2002). The fund has underperformed the S&P 500 five times and the Wilshire 5000 four times in the past 10 years. Consistency of *overperformance* for this fund has been good.

	last 5 years		last 10 years	
worst year	-25.9%	2002	-25.9%	2002
best year	81.6%	2000	81.6%	2000

During the past five years, the fund's three worst months have been August 1998 (-14 percent), March 2001 (-11 percent), and September 2001 (-9 percent). During the same period, the three best months have been February 2000 (29 percent), June 2000 (6 percent), and September 1998 (14 percent). In the past, Eaton Vance World Health A has done better than 85 percent of its peer group during the most recent bull market but outperformed just 37 percent of its peer group during the most recent bear market. Consistency, or predictability, of returns for Eaton Vance World Health A can be described as good. This fund's risk-adjusted return over the past three/five years ranks in the top quintile.

Management   ★★★★

There are 50 stocks in this $760 million portfolio. The average health fund today is $200 million in size. Close to 90 percent of the fund's holdings are in stocks. The stocks in this portfolio have an average p/e ratio of 32 and a median market capitalization of $8 billion. The 10 largest holdings compose 50 percent of the fund's total assets. The portfolio's equity holdings can be categorized as large-cap and growth-oriented issues.

Samuel D. Isaly has managed this fund for the past 13 years. Management looks for companies around the world. Isaly divides the fund portfolio into two parts: drug discovery and drug distribution stocks. Management is considered aggressive in its approach. The fund's price movement is not correlated to that of the S&P 500. There are 72 funds besides World Health within the Eaton Vance family. Overall, the fund family's risk adjusted performance can be described as good.

Tax Minimization   ★★★★★

During the past five years, a $10,000 initial investment grew to $16,150 after taxes, assuming a 40 percent income tax bracket (state and federal combined) and a capital gains rate of 20 percent. This means that investors in this fund were able to preserve 91 percent of their total returns. Compared to other funds in its category, this fund's tax savings are considered to be excellent.

Expenses   ★★★★

Eaton Vance World Health A's expense ratio is 1.7 percent; it has averaged 1.7 percent annually over the past three calendar years. The average expense ratio for the 175 funds in this category is 1.8 percent. This fund's turnover rate over the past year has been 24 percent, while its peer group average has been 146 percent.

Summary

Eaton Vance World Health A receives five stars for performance while demonstrating only average risk. Tax efficiency has been an amazing 90 percent, making this a top choice for the sector fund investor who is concerned with after-tax results. The fund's turnover rate is a fraction of its peer group. The portfolio does best during bull markets. Only two out of 175 health care funds are in the book and this is one of them.

Profile

minimum initial investment $1,000	*IRA accounts available* . . . . yes
subsequent minimum investment . . . $50	*IRA minimum investment* $50
available in all 50 states . . . . yes	*date of inception* . . . . Jul. 1985
telephone exchanges . . . . yes	*dividend/income paid* . . . . annually
number of funds in family 73	*largest sector weighting* . . . . health

Vanguard Health Care

Vanguard Financial Center
P.O. Box 2600
Valley Forge, PA 19482
(800) 662-7447
www.vanguard.com

total return	★★★★★
risk reduction	★★★★★
management	★★★★★
tax minimization	★★★★
expense control	★★★★★
symbol VGHCX	24 points
up-market performance	good
down-market performance	excellent
predictability of returns	excellent

Total Return   ★★★★★

Over the past five years, Vanguard Health Care has taken $10,000 and turned it into $19,970 ($13,250 over three years and $54,880 over the past 10 years). This translates into an annualized return of 15 percent over the past five years, 10 percent over the past three years, and 19 percent for the decade. Over the past five years, this fund has outperformed 99 percent of all mutual funds; within its general category it has also done better than 99 percent of its peers. Health funds have averaged 5 percent annually over these same five years.

Risk/Volatility   ★★★★★

Over the past five years, Vanguard Health Care has experienced low risk for its category. Over the past decade, the fund has had two negative years, while the S&P 500 has had three (off 9 percent in 2000, 12 percent in 2001, and 22 percent in 2002); the Wilshire 5000 fell four times (off less than 1 percent in 1994, 11 percent in 2000, 11 percent in 2001, and 21 percent in 2002). The fund has underperformed the S&P 500 three times and the Wilshire 5000 twice in the past 10 years. Consistency of *overperformance* for this fund has been very good.

	last 5 years		last 10 years	
worst year	-11.4%	2002	-11.4%	2002
best year	60.6%	2000	60.6%	2000

During the past five years, the fund's three worst months have been August 1998 (-10 percent), March 2001 (-8 percent), and January 2001 (-7 percent). During the same period, the three best months have been June 2000 (10 percent), September 1998 (10 percent), and February 1998 (7 percent). In the past, Vanguard Health Care has done better than 70 percent of its peer group during the most recent bull market and outperformed 98 percent of its peer group during the most recent bear market. Consistency, or predictability, of returns for Vanguard Health Care can be described as excellent. This fund's risk-adjusted return over the past three/five years ranks in the top quintile.

Management ★★★★★

There are 130 stocks in this $14 billion portfolio. The average health fund today is $200 million in size. Close to 90 percent of the fund's holdings are in stocks. The stocks in this portfolio have an average p/e ratio of 27 and a median market capitalization of $21 billion. The 10 largest holdings compose 35 percent of the fund's total assets. The portfolio's equity holdings can be categorized as large-cap and growth-oriented issues.

Edward P. Owens has managed this fund for the past 19 years. Management is interested in five areas of the health care market: foreign companies, pharmaceuticals, services, devices, and biotech. Because of the fund's large size, Owens is frequently forced to concentrate on large-cap issues. The fund's price movement is only slightly correlated to that of the S&P 500. There are 78 funds besides Health Care within the Vanguard family. Overall, the fund family's risk adjusted performance can be described as between good and very good.

Tax Minimization ★★★★

During the past five years, a $10,000 initial investment grew to $17,380 after taxes, assuming a 40 percent income tax bracket (state and federal combined) and a capital gains rate of 20 percent. This means that investors in this fund were able to preserve 83 percent of their total returns. Compared to other funds in its category, this fund's tax savings are considered to be very good.

Expenses ★★★★★

Vanguard Health Care's expense ratio is 0.3 percent; it has averaged 0.3 percent annually over the past three calendar years. The average expense ratio for the 175 funds in this category is 1.8 percent. This fund's turnover rate over the past year has been 13 percent, while its peer group average has been 146 percent.

Summary

Vanguard Health Care turns in a near-perfect score of 24 out of 25 points, making it one of the best funds, regardless of category. It just so happens that this is also the number one choice for its sector. The fund's risk level is incredibly low, and so are its operating costs and turnover rate. This fund is frequently cited as "the" choice for anyone interested in owning health care stocks.

Profile

minimum initial investment $25,000	IRA accounts available . . . . yes
subsequent minimum investment . . $100	IRA minimum investment $25,000
available in all 50 states . . . . yes	date of inception . . . . May 1984
telephone exchanges . . . . yes	dividend/income paid . . . . annually
number of funds in family 79	largest sector weighting . . . . health

High-Yield Corporate Bond Funds

Sometimes referred to as "junk bond" funds, high-yield bond funds invest in corporate bonds rated lower than BBB or BAA. The world of bonds is divided into two general categories: investment grade and high-yield. Investment grade, sometimes referred to as "bank quality," means that the bond issue has been rated AAA, AA, A, or BAA (or BBB if the rating service is Standard & Poor's instead of Moody's). Certain institutions and fiduciaries are forbidden to invest their clients' monies in anything less than investment grade. Everything less than bank quality is considered junk.

Yet the world of bonds is not black and white. There are several categories of high-yield bonds. Junk bond funds contain issues that range from BB to C; a rating less than C means that the bond is in default, and payment of interest and/or principal is in arrears. High-yield bond funds perform best during good economic times. Traditional investors should avoid such issues during recessionary periods, since the underlying corporations may have difficulty making interest and principal payments when business slows down. However, these bonds, like common stocks, can perform very well during the second half of a recession.

Although junk bonds may exhibit greater volatility than their investment-grade peers, they are safer when it comes to interest-rate risk. Since junk issues have higher-yielding coupons and often shorter maturities than quality corporate bond funds, they fluctuate less in value when interest rates change. Thus, during expansionary periods in the economy when interest rates are rising, high-yield funds will generally drop less in value than high-quality corporate or government bond funds. Conversely, when interest rates are falling, government and corporate bonds will appreciate more in value than junk funds. High-yield bonds resemble equities at least as much as they do traditional bonds when it comes to economic cycles and certain important technical factors. Studies show that only 19 percent of the average junk fund's total return is explained by the up or down movement of the Lehman Brothers Government/Corporate Bond Index. To give an idea of how low this number is, 94 percent of a typical high-quality corporate bond fund's performance is explainable by movement in the same index. Indeed, even international bond funds have a higher correlation coefficient than junk, with 25 percent of their performance explained by the Lehman index.

The following table covers the three-, five-, 10-, and 15-year periods ending December 31, 2002, and compares the total return of the Wilshire REIT index and five well-known bond indexes: Credit Suisse High Yield Index (bonds rated BBB or lower), the Lehman Brothers Aggregate Bond Index (securities from the Lehman Government/Corporate, Mortgage-Backed Securities, and Asset-Backed

Indexes), the Lehman Brothers Government Bond Index (all publicly traded domestic debt of the U.S. government), the Lehman Brothers Municipal Bond Index, and the Salomon Brothers World Government Bond Index.

Bond & REIT indices: average annual returns (all periods ending 12/31/02)

Index	3 years	5 years	10 years	15 years
High Yield	1.1%	1.4%	6.5%	8.4%
Aggregate Bond	10.1%	7.5%	7.5%	8.6%
U.S. Government Bond	10.6%	7.8%	7.6%	8.5%
Municipal Bond	8.8%	6.1%	6.7%	7.7%
World Government Bond	6.6%	6.0%	6.7%	7.2%
Wilshire REIT	15.1%	5.3%	10.4%	8.8%

The high end of the junk bond market, those debentures rated BA and BB, have been able to withstand the general beating the junk bond market incurred during the late 1980s and early 1990s. Moderate and conservative investors who want high-yield bonds as part of their portfolio should focus on funds that have a high percentage of their assets in higher-rated bonds, BB or better.

Over the past three and five years, high-yield corporate bond funds have had an average compound total return of *negative* 2.7 percent and 1.3 percent, respectively. The annual return for the past 10 years has been 4.7 percent, and 6.2 percent for the past 15 years (all figures as of December 31, 2002). These funds throw off about 9.3 percent in annual income, making them the dividend and/or interest income kings. The standard deviation for high-yield bond funds has been 9.4 percent over the past three years. This means that these funds have been less volatile than any equity fund category but have experienced over twice the return variances of other types of domestic bond funds. Turnover has averaged 100 percent. More than 400 funds make up the high-yield category.

The majority of investors believe that the track record of high-yield bonds has been mixed, particularly in recent years. There was a crash in this market in 1990, but the overall track record has been quite good. These bond funds were up 13.4 percent in 1987, the year of the stock market crash. As the junk bond scare started in 1989, the fund category was still able to show a 12.8 percent return for the calendar year. The following year the group showed a negative return of 9.5 percent.

The 1990 loss was caused by regulatory agencies putting pressure on the insurance industry, formerly the largest owner of this investment category. This, together with the demise of Drexel Burnham, the largest issuer of junk bonds, caused high-yield bonds to suffer their biggest loss in recent memory. And yet the very next year, 1991, high-yield bond funds did better than ever before, up over 36.3 percent. The following two years were also quite good—up 17.0 percent in 1992 and up 18.9 percent in 1993. The following year, 1994, these funds fell -3.0 percent, followed by gains of 16.7, 13.5, and 13.0 percent the next 3 years; then flat in 1998; a gain of 4.7 percent in 1999; a loss of 7.8 percent in 2000; a small gain of 1.9 percent in 2001, followed by a loss of 2.0 percent in 2002.

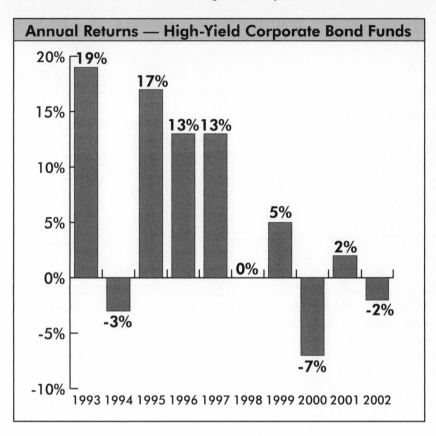

Janus High-Yield
100 Fillmore Street, Suite 300
Denver, CO 80206
(800) 525-8983
www.janus.com

total return	★★★★★
risk reduction	★★★★★
management	★★★★★
current income	★★
expense control	★★★
symbol JAHYX	20 points
up-market performance	poor
down-market performance	excellent
predictability of returns	excellent

Total Return   ★★★★★
Over the past five years, Janus High-Yield has taken $10,000 and turned it into $11,720 ($10,990 over three years). This translates into an annualized return of 3 percent over the past five years and 3 percent over the past three years. Over the past five years, this fund has outperformed 52 percent of all mutual funds; within its general category it has done better than 96 percent of its peers. High-yield bond funds have averaged -1 percent annually over these same five years.

During the past five years, a $10,000 initial investment grew to $19,210 after taxes, assuming a 40 percent income tax bracket (state and federal combined) and a capital gains rate of 20 percent. This means that investors in this fund were able to preserve 76 percent of their total returns. Compared to other funds in its category, this fund's tax savings are considered to be excellent.

Risk/Volatility   ★★★★★
Over the past five years, Janus High-Yield has experienced low risk for its category. Over the past decade, the fund has had no negative years, while the Lehman Brothers Aggregate Bond Index has had two (off 3 percent in 1994 and 1 percent in 1999); the Credit Suisse High-Yield Bond Index also fell twice (off 1 percent in 1994 and 5 percent in 2000). The fund has underperformed the Lehman Brothers Aggregate Bond Index six times and the Credit Suisse High-Yield Bond Index four times in the past 10 years. Consistency of *overperformance* for this fund has been good.

	last 5 years		last 10 years	
worst year	1.0%	1998	1.0%	1998
best year	5.5%	1999	24%	1996

During the past five years, the fund's three worst months have been September 2001 (-5 percent), August 1998 (-5 percent), and October 1998 (-4 percent). During the same period, the three best months have been November 1998 (4 percent), January 2001 (3 percent), and October 2001 (2 percent). In the past, Janus High-Yield has only done better than 10 percent of its peer group during the most recent bull market but outperformed 95 percent of its peer group during the most recent bear market. Consistency, or predictability, of returns for Janus High-Yield can be described as excellent. This fund's risk-adjusted return over the past three/five years ranks in the top quintile.

Management ★★★★★
There are 155 fixed-income securities in this $670 million portfolio. The average high-yield bond fund today is $225 million in size. Close to 75 percent of the fund's holdings are in bonds. The average maturity of the bonds in this account is five years. The portfolio's fixed-income holdings can be categorized as short-term, low-quality debt.

Sandy R. Rufenacht has managed this fund for the past seven years. Management looks for companies that want to pay off their debt, a good method for reducing portfolio risk. Rufenacht focuses on corporations that have steady and reliable cash flows—another risk-reduction tool. The fund's price movement is very highly correlated to that of the CSFB Global High-Yield Bond Index, but has zero correlation to the Lehman Brothers Aggregate Bond Index. There are 30 funds besides High-Yield within the Janus family. Overall, the fund family's risk adjusted performance can be described as good.

Current Income ★★
Over the past year, Janus High-Yield had a 12-month yield of 7.0 percent. During this same 12-month period, the typical high-yield bond fund had a yield that averaged 9.3 percent.

Expenses ★★★
Janus High-Yield's expense ratio is 1 percent; it has averaged 1 percent annually over the past three calendar years. The average expense ratio for the 385 funds in this category is 1.3 percent. This fund's turnover rate over the past year has been 358 percent, while its peer group average has been 100 percent.

Summary
Janus High-Yield is the choice for the sophisticated bond investor who understands that total return is much more important than current yield. The portfolio ties for number one when it comes to risk reduction; predictability of returns has also been outstanding. Tax efficiency has also been tops.

Profile

minimum initial investment $2,500	*IRA accounts available* . . . . yes
subsequent minimum investment . . $100	*IRA minimum investment* $500
available in all 50 states . . . . yes	*date of inception* . . . . Dec. 1995
telephone exchanges . . . . yes	*dividend/income paid* . . . . monthly
number of funds in family 31	*average credit quality* . . . . BB

Lord Abbett Bond-Debenture A
90 Hudson Street
Jersey City, NJ 07302
(800) 201-6984
www.lordabbett.com

total return	★★★★★
risk reduction	★★★★
management	★★★★
current income	★★★
expense control	★★★★
symbol LBNDX	20 points
up-market performance	good
down-market performance	very good
predictability of returns	very good

Total Return   ★★★★★

Over the past five years, Lord Abbett Bond-Debenture A has taken $10,000 and turned it into $11,190 ($10,280 over three years and $18,370 over the past 10 years). This translates into an annualized return of 2 percent over the past five years, 1 percent over the past three years, and 6 percent for the decade. Over the past five years, this fund has outperformed 50 percent of all mutual funds; within its general category it has done better than 95 percent of its peers. High-yield bond funds have averaged -1 percent annually over these same five years.

During the past five years, a $10,000 initial investment grew to $19,210 after taxes, assuming a 40 percent income tax bracket (state and federal combined) and a capital gains rate of 20 percent. This means that investors in this fund were able to preserve 73 percent of their total returns. Compared to other funds in its category, this fund's tax savings are considered to be excellent.

Risk/Volatility   ★★★★

Over the past five years, Lord Abbett Bond-Debenture A has experienced below average risk for its category. Over the past decade, the fund has had three negative years, while the Lehman Brothers Aggregate Bond Index has had two (off 3 percent in 1994 and 1 percent in 1999); the Credit Suisse High-Yield Bond Index also fell twice (off 1 percent in 1994 and 5 percent in 2000). The fund has underperformed the Lehman Brothers Aggregate Bond Index six times and the Credit Suisse High-Yield Bond Index five times in the past 10 years. Consistency of *overperformance* for this fund has been very good.

	last 5 years		last 10 years	
worst year	-1.1%	2002	-3.9%	1994
best year	4.9%	2001	17.5%	1995

During the past five years, the fund's three worst months have been August 1998 (-7 percent), September 2001 (-6 percent), and November 2000 (-4 percent). During the same period, the three best months have been January 2001 (5 percent),

November 1998 (4 percent), and October 2001 (2 percent). In the past, Lord Abbett Bond-Debenture A has done better than 45 percent of its peer group during the most recent bull market and outperformed 65 percent of its peer group during the most recent bear market. Consistency, or predictability, of returns for Lord Abbett Bond-Debenture A can be described as very good. This fund's risk-adjusted return over the past three/five years ranks in the top-two quintiles.

Management   ★★★★
There are 385 fixed-income securities in this $3 billion portfolio. The average high-yield bond fund today is $225 million in size. Close to 85 percent of the fund's holdings are in bonds. The average maturity of the bonds in this account is eight years; the weighted coupon rate averages 8 percent. The portfolio's fixed-income holdings can be categorized as intermediate-term, low-quality debt.

A team has managed this fund for the past 15 years. Management likes to keep anywhere from 20 to 35 percent in investment-grade bonds. The managers seek out companies that are low-cost producers and industry market-share leaders. The fund's price movement is very extremely correlated to that of the CSFB Global High-Yield Bond Index, but has virtually zero correlation to the Lehman Brothers Aggregate Bond Index. There are 34 funds besides Bond-Debenture within the Lord Abbett family. Overall, the fund family's risk adjusted performance can be described as good.

Current Income   ★★★
Over the past year, Lord Abbett Bond-Debenture A had a 12-month yield of 8.7 percent. During this same 12-month period, the typical high-yield bond fund had a yield that averaged 9.3 percent.

Expenses   ★★★★
Lord Abbett Bond-Debenture A's expense ratio is 1 percent; it has averaged 1 percent annually over the past three calendar years. The average expense ratio for the 385 funds in this category is 1.3 percent. This fund's turnover rate over the past year has been 55 percent, while its peer group average has been 100 percent.

Summary
Lord Abbett Bond-Debenture A does a good job across the board. The fund really shines in the area of performance, beating out 95 percent of its category. Tax efficiency has also been superb. The fund's risk level is below average and expense control is commendable. Turnover is among the lowest in its field. This would be a good addition to the fixed-income investor who wants to venture beyond government securities and money market accounts.

Profile

minimum initial investment $1,000	*IRA accounts available* . . . . yes
subsequent minimum investment $1	*IRA minimum investment* $250
available in all 50 states . . . . yes	*date of inception* . . . . Apr. 1971
telephone exchanges . . . . yes	*dividend/income paid* . . . . monthly
number of funds in family 35	*average credit quality* . . . . BB

T. Rowe Price High-Yield
100 East Pratt Street
Baltimore, MD 21202
(800) 638-5660
www.troweprice.com

total return	★★★★★
risk reduction	★★★★
management	★★★★★
current income	★★★★
expense control	★★★★★
symbol PRHYX	23 points
up-market performance	fair
down-market performance	excellent
predictability of returns	very good

Total Return   ★★★★★
Over the past five years, T. Rowe Price High-Yield has taken $10,000 and turned it into $11,510 ($10,580 over three years and $19,090 over the past 10 years). This translates into an annualized return of 3 percent over the past five years, 2 percent over the past three years, and 7 percent for the decade. Over the past five years, this fund has outperformed 50 percent of all mutual funds; within its general category it has done better than 95 percent of its peers. High-yield bond funds have averaged -1 percent annually over these same five years.

During the past five years, a $10,000 initial investment grew to $19,210 after taxes, assuming a 40 percent income tax bracket (state and federal combined) and a capital gains rate of 20 percent. This means that investors in this fund were able to preserve 79 percent of their total returns. Compared to other funds in its category, this fund's tax savings are considered to be excellent.

Risk/Volatility   ★★★★
Over the past five years, T. Rowe Price High-Yield has experienced below average risk for its category. Over the past decade, the fund has had two negative years, while the Lehman Brothers Aggregate Bond Index has had two (off 3 percent in 1994 and 1 percent in 1999); the Credit Suisse High-Yield Bond Index also fell twice (off 1 percent in 1994 and 5 percent in 2000). The fund has underperformed the Lehman Brothers Aggregate Bond Index six times and the Credit Suisse High-Yield Bond Index four times in the past 10 years. Consistency of *overperformance* for this fund has been excellent.

	last 5 years		last 10 years	
worst year	-3.3%	2000	-8.0%	1994
best year	6.1%	2001	21.8%	1993

During the past five years, the fund's three worst months have been September 2001 (-6 percent), August 1998 (-6 percent), and November 2000 (-4 percent). During the same period, the three best months have been January 2001 (5 percent), November 1998 (22 percent), and October 2001 (2 percent). In the past, T. Rowe Price High-Yield has only done better than 30 percent of its peer group during the most recent bull market but outperformed 90 percent of its peer group during the most recent bear market. Consistency, or predictability, of returns for T. Rowe Price High-Yield can be described as very good. This fund's risk-adjusted return over the past three/five years ranks in the top two quintiles.

Management   ★★★★★
There are 360 fixed-income securities in this $2 billion portfolio. The average high-yield bond fund today is $225 million in size. Close to 90 percent of the fund's holdings are in bonds. The average maturity of the bonds in this account is seven years; the weighted coupon rate averages 10 percent. The portfolio's fixed-income holdings can be categorized as intermediate-term, low-quality debt.

Mark Vaselkiv has managed this fund for the past seven years. Management reduces specific-issue risk by owning a large number of securities. Vaselkiv likes the more established sectors of the marketplace. The fund's price movement is almost perfectly correlated to that of the CSFB Global High-Yield Bond Index, but has zero correlation to the Lehman Brothers Aggregate Bond Index. There are 85 funds besides High-Yield within the T. Rowe Price family. Overall, the fund family's risk adjusted performance can be described as between good and very good.

Current Income   ★★★★
Over the past year, T. Rowe Price High-Yield had a 12-month yield of 9.4 percent. During this same 12-month period, the typical high-yield bond fund had a yield that averaged 9.3 percent.

Expenses   ★★★★★
T. Rowe Price High-Yield's expense ratio is 0.8 percent; it has averaged 0.8 percent annually over the past three calendar years. The average expense ratio for the 385 funds in this category is 1.3 percent. This fund's turnover rate over the past year has been 71 percent, while its peer group average has been 100 percent.

Summary
T. Rowe Price High-Yield turns in the best overall score in its category. Scoring 23 out of 25 possible points, the fund's rankings are high, regardless of category. Returns have been positive over the past three and five years, versus negative results over the same period for its peer group. Risk has been below average while predictability of returns has been quite high. This is part of a very large mutual fund family that offers a number of fine selections.

Profile
minimum initial investment $2,500	*IRA accounts available* . . . . yes
subsequent minimum investment . . $100	*IRA minimum investment* $1,000
available in all 50 states . . . . yes	*date of inception* . . . . Dec. 1984
telephone exchanges . . . . yes	*dividend/income paid* . . . . monthly
number of funds in family 86	*average credit quality* . . . . B

Vanguard High-Yield Corporate
Vanguard Financial Center
P.O. Box 2600
Valley Forge, PA 19482
(800) 662-7447
www.vanguard.com

total return	★★★★★
risk reduction	★★★★
management	★★★★★
current income	★★★
expense control	★★★★★
symbol VWEHX	22 points
up-market performance	good
down-market performance	fair
predictability of returns	very good

Total Return   ★★★★★
Over the past five years, Vanguard High-Yield Corporate has taken $10,000 and turned it into $11,230 ($10,380 over three years and $19,070 over the past 10 years). This translates into an annualized return of 2 percent over the past five years, 1 percent over the past three years, and 7 percent for the decade. Over the past five years, this fund has outperformed 50 percent of all mutual funds; within its general category it has done better than 92 percent of its peers. High-yield bond funds have averaged -1 percent annually over these same five years.

During the past five years, a $10,000 initial investment grew to $19,210 after taxes, assuming a 40 percent income tax bracket (state and federal combined) and a capital gains rate of 20 percent. This means that investors in this fund were able to preserve 75 percent of their total returns. Compared to other funds in its category, this fund's tax savings are considered to be excellent.

Risk/Volatility   ★★★★
Over the past five years, Vanguard High-Yield Corporate has experienced below average risk for its category. Over the past decade, the fund has had two negative years, while the Lehman Brothers Aggregate Bond Index has had two (off 3 percent in 1994 and 1 percent in 1999); the Credit Suisse High-Yield Bond Index also fell twice (off 1 percent in 1994 and 5 percent in 2000). The fund has underperformed the Lehman Brothers Aggregate Bond Index four times and the Credit Suisse High-Yield Bond Index seven times in the past 10 years. Consistency of *overperformance* for this fund has been good.

	last 5 years		last 10 years	
worst year	-0.9%	2000	-1.7%	1994
best year	5.6%	1998	19.2%	1995

During the past five years, the fund's three worst months have been September 2001 (-5 percent), August 1998 (-5 percent), and November 2000

(-4 percent). During the same period, the three best months have been January 2001 (4 percent), November 1998 (4 percent), and November 2001 (2 percent). In the past, Vanguard High-Yield Corporate has done better than 50 percent of its peer group during the most recent bull market and outperformed 76 percent of its peer group during the most recent bear market. Consistency, or predictability, of returns for Vanguard High-Yield Corporate can be described as very good. This fund's risk-adjusted return over the past three/five years ranks in the top-two quintiles.

Management   ★★★★★
There are 250 fixed-income securities in this $5 billion portfolio. The average high-yield bond fund today is $225 million in size. Close to 95 percent of the fund's holdings are in bonds. The average maturity of the bonds in this account is seven years; the weighted coupon rate averages 9 percent. The portfolio's fixed-income holdings can be categorized as intermediate-term, low-quality debt.

Earl E. McEvoy has managed this fund for the past 19 years. Management definitely favors the higher-end of the junk bond market. Risk is further reduced by rarely allowing any one issuer's bonds to make up more than 2 percent of the fund's portfolio. McEvoy is the steward of one of the most stable funds in the high-yield category. There are 78 funds besides High-Yield Corporate within the Vanguard family. Overall, the fund family's risk adjusted performance can be described as between good and very good.

Current Income   ★★★
Over the past year, Vanguard High-Yield Corporate had a 12-month yield of 8.6 percent. During this same 12-month period, the typical high-yield bond fund had a yield that averaged 9.3 percent.

Expenses   ★★★★★
Vanguard High-Yield Corporate's expense ratio is 0.3 percent; it has averaged 0.3 percent annually over the past three calendar years. The average expense ratio for the 385 funds in this category is 1.3 percent. This fund's turnover rate over the past year has been 29 percent, while its peer group average has been 100 percent.

Summary
Vanguard High-Yield Corporate rates overall as the second-best choice for its entire category. The junk bond category includes more than 380 choices. Expenses are lower than any of its competitors and so is turnover. Risk minimization has been quite low while tax efficiency has been outstanding. Vanguard offers a large number of exceptional fixed-income funds. This is just one of them.

Profile

minimum initial investment $3,000	*IRA accounts available* . . . . yes
subsequent minimum investment . . $100	*IRA minimum investment* $1,000
available in all 50 states . . . . yes	*date of inception* . . . . Dec. 1978
telephone exchanges . . . . yes	*dividend/income paid* . . . . monthly
number of funds in family 79	*average credit quality* . . . . BB

Waddell & Reed Advisor High-Income A

6300 Lamar Avenue
P.O. Box 29217
Shawnee Mission, KS 66201
(800) 366-5465
www.waddell.com

total return	★★★★
risk reduction	★★★★★
management	★★★★
current income	★★
expense control	★★★★
symbol UNHIX	19 points
up-market performance	poor
down-market performance	excellent
predictability of returns	excellent

Total Return ★★★★

Over the past five years, Waddell & Reed Advisor High-Income A has taken $10,000 and turned it into $10,730 ($10,040 over three years and $18,340 over the past 10 years). This translates into an annualized return of 1 percent over the past five years, 0 percent over the past three years, and 6 percent for the decade. Over the past five years, this fund has outperformed 40 percent of all mutual funds; within its general category it has done better than 85 percent of its peers. High-yield bond funds have averaged -1 percent annually over these same five years.

During the past five years, a $10,000 initial investment grew to $19,210 after taxes, assuming a 40 percent income tax bracket (state and federal combined) and a capital gains rate of 20 percent. This means that investors in this fund were able to preserve 74 percent of their total returns. Compared to other funds in its category, this fund's tax savings are considered to be excellent.

Risk/Volatility ★★★★★

Over the past five years, Waddell & Reed Advisor High-Income A has experienced low risk for its category. Over the past decade, the fund has had two negative years, while the Lehman Brothers Aggregate Bond Index has had two (off 3 percent in 1994 and 1 percent in 1999); the Credit Suisse High-Yield Bond Index also fell twice (off 1 percent in 1994 and 5 percent in 2000). The fund has underperformed the Lehman Brothers Aggregate Bond Index six times and the Credit Suisse High-Yield Bond Index six times in the past 10 years. Consistency of *overperformance* for this fund has been good.

	last 5 years		last 10 years	
worst year	-6.5%	2000	-6.5%	2000
best year	6.7%	2001	17.8%	1995

During the past five years, the fund's three worst months have been August 1998 (-6 percent), January 2000 (-6 percent), and September 2001 (-5 percent).

During the same period, the three best months have been January 2001 (5 percent), November 1998 (4 percent), and October 2001 (2 percent). In the past, Waddell & Reed Advisor High-Income A has only done better than 10 percent of its peer group during the most recent bull market but outperformed 80 percent of its peer group during the most recent bear market. Consistency, or predictability, of returns for Waddell & Reed Advisor High-Income A can be described as excellent. This fund's risk-adjusted return over the past three/five years ranks in the top-two quintiles.

Management   ★★★★
There are 160 fixed-income securities in this $770 million portfolio. The average high-yield bond fund today is $225 million in size. Close to 85 percent of the fund's holdings are in bonds. The average maturity of the bonds in this account is seven years; the weighted coupon rate averages 9 percent. The portfolio's fixed-income holdings can be categorized as intermediate-term, low-quality debt.

Louise D. Rieke has managed this fund for the past 13 years. Management is more concerned with avoiding mistakes than trying to hit a home run. Consistency has been Rieke's mantra. The fund's price movement is extremely correlated to that of the CSFB Global High-Yield Bond Index, but has zero correlation to the Lehman Brothers Aggregate Bond Index. There are 29 funds besides High-Income within the Waddell & Reed Advisors family. Overall, the fund family's risk adjusted performance can be described as good.

Current Income   ★★
Over the past year, Waddell & Reed Advisor High-Income A had a 12-month yield of 7.7 percent. During this same 12-month period, the typical high-yield bond fund had a yield that averaged 9.3 percent.

Expenses   ★★★★
Waddell & Reed Advisor High-Income A's expense ratio is 1.1 percent; it has averaged 1.1 percent annually over the past three calendar years. The average expense ratio for the 385 funds in this category is 1.3 percent. This fund's turnover rate over the past year has been 74 percent, while its peer group average has been 100 percent.

Summary
Waddell & Reed Advisor High-Income A has the lowest risk of any of its peers. Three- and five-year return figures may not appear to be that good, but even these slightly positive figures are impressive. The junk bond fund category has experienced negative returns over both of these periods. Tax minimization has been excellent while cost containment is commendable.

Profile

minimum initial investment $500	*IRA accounts available* . . . . yes
subsequent minimum investment . . . $50	*IRA minimum investment* $50
available in all 50 states . . . . yes	*date of inception* . . . . Jul. 1979
telephone exchanges . . . . yes	*dividend/income paid* . . . . monthly
number of funds in family 30	*average credit quality* . . . . BB

Metals and Natural Resources Funds

As their name implies, metals funds purchase precious metals in one or more of the following forms: bullion, South African gold stocks, and non-South African mining stocks. The United States, Canada, and Australia are the three major stock-issuing producers of metals outside South Africa. Metals funds, also referred to as gold funds, often own minor positions in other precious metals stocks, such as silver and platinum.

The proportion and type of metal held by a fund can have a great impact on its performance and volatility. Outright ownership of gold bullion is almost always less volatile than owning stock in a gold mining company. Thus, much greater gains or losses occur in metals funds that purchase only gold stocks, compared to funds that hold high levels of bullion, coins, and stock. Silver, incidentally, has nearly twice the volatility of gold, yet has not enjoyed any greater returns over the long term.

Gold, or metals, funds can do well during periods of political uncertainty and inflationary concerns. Over the past several hundred years, gold and silver have served as hedges against inflation. Most readers will be surprised to learn that, historically, both metals have outperformed inflation by less than 1 percent annually.

Metals funds are the riskiest category of mutual funds described in this book with a standard deviation of 40.3 (followed by technology stocks, with a standard deviation of 37.4, and natural resources, with a standard deviation of 27.1). And yet, although this is certainly a high-risk investment when viewed on its own, ownership of a metals fund can sometimes reduce a portfolio's overall risk level. Why? Because gold usually has a negative correlation to other investments.

There are 45 metals funds. Turnover has averaged 80 percent annually over the past three years. The price-earnings (p/e) ratio for metals funds is 18, while dividend yield is 3.7 percent. Over the past three years, these funds have averaged 17.2 percent per year, 7.6 percent for the past five years, 3.0 percent for the past decade, and *negative* 0.8 percent for the past 15 years.

Natural resources funds invest in the stocks of companies that deal in the ownership, production, transmission, transportation, refinement, and/or storage of oil, natural gas, and timber. These funds also invest in companies that either own or are involved in real estate.

There are 75 natural resources funds. This group has had a standard deviation of 27.1 percent over the past three years. Beta, or market-related risk, is 0.7, but do not let this low number fool you. As you can see by the standard deviation, few equity categories are as risky. Annual turnover has averaged an amazingly high

225 percent. The p/e ratio for natural resources funds is 30; dividend yield is 0.5 percent. Over the past three years, these funds have averaged 4.2 percent, 2.1 percent for the past five years, 9.1 percent for the past 10 years, and 7.9 percent for the past 15 years.

Metals and natural resources funds should be avoided by anyone who cannot tolerate wide price swings in any single part of the portfolio. These funds are designed as an integral part of a diversified portfolio, for investors who look at the overall return of their holdings. Despite the potential benefits of diversification, metals funds are still not recommended for the vast majority of investors. The track record for metals funds is simply terrible except for an occasional great year (for example, +81 percent in 1993, +19 percent in 2001, and +63 percent in 2002) and variations of return are frequently wild.

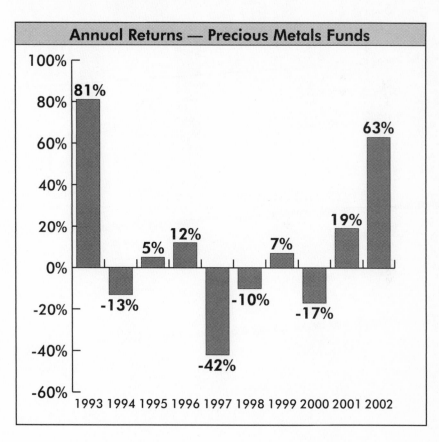

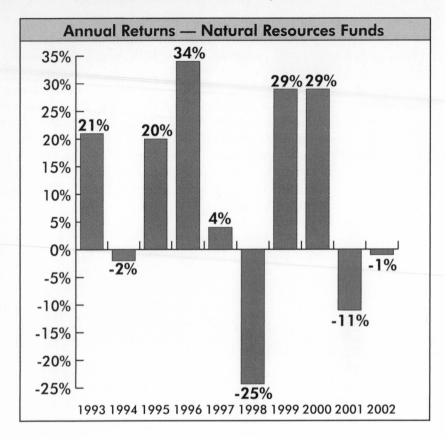

Annual Returns — Natural Resources Funds

American Century Global Gold Investments
4500 Main Street
P.O. Box 419200
Kansas City, MO 64141
(800) 345-2021
www.americancentury.com

total return	★★★★
risk reduction	★★
management	★★★★
tax minimization	★★★★
expense control	★★★★★
symbol BGEIX	19 points
up-market performance	poor
down-market performance	excellent
predictability of returns	fair

Total Return   ★★★★

Over the past five years, American Century Global Gold has taken $10,000 and turned it into $15,000 ($17,640 over three years and $14,080 over the past 10 years). This translates into an annualized return of 8 percent over the past five years, 21 percent over the past three years, and 3 percent for the decade. Over the past five years, this fund has outperformed 71 percent of all mutual funds; within its general category it has done better than 40 percent of its peers. Metals and natural resources funds have averaged 4 percent annually over these same five years.

Risk/Volatility   ★★

Over the past five years, American Century Global Gold has experienced above average risk for its category. Over the past decade, the fund has had six negative years, while the S&P 500 has had three (off 9 percent in 2000, 12 percent in 2001, and 22 percent in 2002). The fund has underperformed the S&P 500 seven times in the past 10 years. Consistency of *overperformance* for this fund has been fair.

	last 5 years		last 10 years	
worst year	-24.0%	2000	-41.5%	1997
best year	73.0%	2002	81.2%	1993

During the past five years, the fund's three worst months have been August 1998 (-23 percent), May 1999 (-17 percent), and May 1998 (-16 percent). During the same period, the three best months have been September 1998 (53 percent), September 1999 (28 percent), and April 1999 (15 percent). In the past, American Century Global Gold has only done better than 5 percent of its peer group during the most recent bull market but outperformed 95 percent of its peer group during the most recent bear market. Consistency, or predictability, of returns for American Century Global Gold can be described as fair. This fund's risk-adjusted return over the past three/five years ranks in the top-three quintiles.

Management   ★★★★
There are 50 stocks in this $320 million portfolio. The average metals and natural resources fund today is $70 million in size. Close to 100 percent of the fund's holdings are in stocks. The stocks in this portfolio have a median market capitalization of $2 billion. The 10 largest holdings compose 65 percent of the fund's total assets. The portfolio's equity holdings can be categorized as mid-cap and a blend of growth and value stocks.

A team has managed this fund for the past 11 years. Management is only interested in gold and no other metal. Lead manager Bill Martin prefers to own stocks from around the globe, North America, Australia, and South Africa. The managers are not allowed to let any one stock comprise more than 10 percent of the portfolio. Martin tends to favor the larger gold producing companies. The fund's price movement is not correlated to that of the S&P 500. There are 50 funds besides Global Gold within the American Century Investments family. Overall, the fund family's risk adjusted performance can be described as between good and very good.

Tax Minimization   ★★★★
During the past five years, a $10,000 initial investment grew to $13,350 after taxes, assuming a 40 percent income tax bracket (state and federal combined) and a capital gains rate of 20 percent. This means that investors in this fund were able to preserve 87 percent of their total returns. Compared to other funds in its category, this fund's tax savings are considered to be very good.

Expenses   ★★★★★
American Century Global Gold expense ratio is 0.7 percent; it has averaged 0.7 percent annually over the past three calendar years. The average expense ratio for the 120 funds in this category is 2.0 percent. This fund's turnover rate over the past year has been 14 percent, while its peer group average has been 173 percent.

Summary
American Century Global Gold has done a phenomenal job during bear markets, making this an excellent portfolio reduction tool. The fund's expenses are the lowest of its group. The same thing is true with its turnover rate. Metals funds often react differently to traditional equity funds; when one zigs, the other frequently zags.

Profile
minimum initial investment $2,500
subsequent minimum investment . . . $50
available in all 50 states . . . . yes
telephone exchanges . . . . yes
number of funds in family 51

IRA accounts available . . . . yes
IRA minimum investment $2,500
date of inception . . . . Aug. 1988
dividend/income paid . . . . semiannually
largest sector weighting . . . . consumer
durables

First Eagle Gold

1345 Avenue of the Americas
New York, NY 10105
(800) 334-2143
www.firsteaglefunds.com

total return	★★★★★
risk reduction	★★★★
management	★★★★
tax minimization	★★★★★
expense control	★★★
symbol SGGDX	21 points
up-market performance	fair
down-market performance	excellent
predictability of returns	fair

Total Return   ★★★★★

Over the past five years, First Eagle Gold has taken $10,000 and turned it into
$20,560 ($23,330 over three years). This translates into an annualized return of 16
percent over the past five years and 33 percent over the past three years. Over the
past five years, this fund has outperformed 98 percent of all mutual funds; within
its general category it has done better than 90 percent of its peers. Metals and natural resources funds have averaged 4 percent annually over these same five years.

Risk/Volatility   ★★★★

Over the past five years, First Eagle Gold has experienced low risk for its category.
Over the past decade, the fund has had four negative years, while the S&P 500 has
had three (off 9 percent in 2000, 12 percent in 2001, and 22 percent in 2002). The
fund has underperformed the S&P 500 eight times in the past 10 years. Consistency
of *overperformance* for this fund has been fair.

	last 5 years		last 10 years	
worst year	-18.4%	1998	-29.8%	1997
best year	107.0%	2002	107.0%	2002

During the past five years, the fund's three worst months have been August
1998 (-18 percent), May 1999 (-13 percent), and October 2000 (-13 percent).
During the same period, the three best months have been September 1998 (23 percent), September 1999 (22 percent), and April 1999 (11 percent). In the past, First
Eagle Gold has only done better than 25 percent of its peer group during the most
recent bull market but outperformed 99 percent of its peer group during the most
recent bear market. Consistency, or predictability, of returns for First Eagle Gold
can be described as fair. This fund's risk-adjusted return over the past three/five
years ranks in the top quintile.

Management   ★★★★
There are 50 stocks in this $100 million portfolio. The average metals and natural resources fund today is $70 million in size. Close to 70 percent of the fund's holdings are in stocks. The stocks in this portfolio have an average p/e ratio of 40 and a median market capitalization of $820 million. The 10 largest holdings compose 46 percent of the fund's total assets. The portfolio's equity holdings can be categorized as small-cap and growth-oriented issues.

Jean-Marie Eveillard and Charles de Vaulx have managed this fund for the past nine years. Management has a strong taste for indirect gold plays. Eveillard and de Vaulx are value players, but the fund's style is categorized as "growth" due to the portfolio's leveraged plays. The fund's price movement is not correlated to that of the S&P 500. There are four funds besides Gold within the First Eagle family. Overall, the fund family's risk adjusted performance can be described as excellent.

Tax Minimization   ★★★★★
During the past five years, a $10,000 initial investment grew to $15,630 after taxes, assuming a 40 percent income tax bracket (state and federal combined) and a capital gains rate of 20 percent. This means that investors in this fund were able to preserve 96 percent of their total returns. Compared to other funds in its category, this fund's tax savings are considered to be excellent.

Expenses   ★★★
First Eagle Gold's expense ratio is 2.7 percent; it has averaged 2.7 percent annually over the past three calendar years. The average expense ratio for the 120 funds in this category is 2.0 percent. This fund's turnover rate over the past year has been 29 percent, while its peer group average has been 173 percent.

Summary
First Eagle Gold is one of several other members of the same fund family to appear in this book. Legendary manager Eveillard helps oversee this portfolio and he has done a great job; the fund has outperformed 98 percent of all other funds. Within its category it rates as the number one performer by a wide margin for the last three and five years. The portfolio's risk characteristics are also the best of its group.

Profile

minimum initial investment $1,000	*IRA accounts available* . . . . yes
subsequent minimum investment . . $100	*IRA minimum investment* $1,000
available in all 50 states . . . . yes	*date of inception* . . . . Aug. 1993
telephone exchanges . . . . yes	*dividend/income paid* . . . . annually
number of funds in family 5	*largest sector weighting* . . . . . industrial cyclicals

Oppenheimer Gold & Special Minerals A

P.O. Box 5270
Denver, CO 80217
(800) 525-7048
www.oppenheimerfunds.com

total return	★★★★
risk reduction	★★★★
management	★★★★★
tax minimization	★★★★★
expense control	★★★★
symbol OPGSX	22 points
up-market performance	fair
down-market performance	very good
predictability of returns	good

Total Return ★★★★

Over the past five years, Oppenheimer Gold & Special Minerals A has taken $10,000 and turned it into $16,500 ($14,480 over three years and $17,860 over the past 10 years). This translates into an annualized return of 11 percent over the past five years, 13 percent over the past three years, and 6 percent for the decade. Over the past five years, this fund has outperformed 95 percent of all mutual funds; within its general category it has done better than 65 percent of its peers. Metals and natural resources funds have averaged 4 percent annually over these same five years.

Risk/Volatility ★★★★

Over the past five years, Oppenheimer Gold & Special Minerals A has experienced average risk for its category. Over the past decade, the fund has had five negative years, while the S&P 500 has had three (off 9 percent in 2000, 12 percent in 2001, and 22 percent in 2002). The fund has underperformed the S&P 500 seven times in the past 10 years. Consistency of *overperformance* for this fund has been fair.

	last 5 years		last 10 years	
worst year	-15.1%	2000	-31.9%	1997
best year	42.5%	2002	61.8%	1993

During the past five years, the fund's three worst months have been August 1998 (-22 percent), May 1999 (-13 percent), and May 1998 (-14 percent). During the same period, the three best months have been September 1998 (47 percent), September 1999 (20 percent), and April 1999 (17 percent). In the past, Oppenheimer Gold & Special Minerals A has only done better than 20 percent of its peer group during the most recent bull market but outperformed 75 percent of its peer group during the most recent bear market. Consistency, or predictability, of returns for Oppenheimer Gold & Special Minerals A can be described as good. This fund's risk-adjusted return over the past three/five years ranks in the top-three quintiles.

Management   ★★★★★

There are 55 stocks in this $120 million portfolio. The average metals and natural resources fund today is $70 million in size. Close to 100 percent of the fund's holdings are in stocks. The stocks in this portfolio have an average p/e ratio of 43 and a median market capitalization of $2 billion. The 10 largest holdings compose 50 percent of the fund's total assets. The portfolio's equity holdings can be categorized as mid-cap and growth-oriented issues.

Shanquan Li has managed this fund for the past five years. Management seeks out large, low-cost mining operations. A fairly significant portion of the portfolio is devoted to palladium and platinum miners. Part of the reason the fund is viewed as conservative is because no single issuer can represent more than 5 percent of the overall portfolio. The fund's price movement is not correlated to that of the S&P 500. There are 50 funds besides Gold & Special Minerals within the Oppenheimer family. Overall, the fund family's risk adjusted performance can be described as good.

Tax Minimization   ★★★★★

During the past five years, a $10,000 initial investment grew to $11,550 after taxes, assuming a 40 percent income tax bracket (state and federal combined) and a capital gains rate of 20 percent. This means that investors in this fund were able to preserve 70 percent of their total returns. Compared to other funds in its category, this fund's tax savings are considered to be fair.

Expenses   ★★★★

Oppenheimer Gold & Special Minerals A's expense ratio is 1.5 percent; it has averaged 1.4 percent annually over the past three calendar years. The average expense ratio for the 120 funds in this category is 2.0 percent. This fund's turnover rate over the past year has been 60 percent, while its peer group average has been 173 percent.

Summary

Oppenheimer Gold & Special Minerals A rates as the number one choice for its category on an overall basis. The fund racks up 22 out of 25 possible points. Expenses are about 30 percent less than its colleagues, while turnover has been about 70 percent less. Like other metals funds, this one performs best during bear markets. This fund is one of several dozen offerings from Oppenheimer, a well-known mutual fund powerhouse.

Profile

minimum initial investment . . . . . $1,000   *IRA accounts available* . . . . yes

subsequent minimum investment . . . $50   *IRA minimum investment* $500

available in all 50 states . . . . yes   *date of inception* . . . . Jul. 1983

telephone exchanges . . . . yes   *dividend/income paid* . . . . annually

number of funds in family 51   *largest sector weighting* . . . . . industrial cyclicals

State Street Research Global Resources A

One Financial Center
Boston, MA 02111
(800) 882-0052
www.ssrfunds.com

total return	★★★★
risk reduction	★
management	★★
tax minimization	★★★★★
expense control	★★★★
symbol SSGRX	16 points
up-market performance	good
down-market performance	good
predictability of returns	fair

Total Return   ★★★★

Over the past five years, State Street Research Global Resources A has taken $10,000 and turned it into $11,180 ($18,790 over three years and $30,050 over the past 10 years). This translates into an annualized return of 2 percent over the past five years, 23 percent over the past three years, and 12 percent for the decade. Over the past five years, this fund has outperformed 30 percent of all mutual funds; within its general category it has done better than 35 percent of its peers. Metals and natural resources funds have averaged 4 percent annually over these same five years.

Risk/Volatility   ★

Over the past five years, State Street Research Global Resources A has experienced high risk for its category. Over the past decade, the fund has had three negative years, while the S&P 500 has had three (off 9 percent in 2000, 12 percent in 2001, and 22 percent in 2002). The fund has underperformed the S&P 500 five times in the past 10 years. Consistency of *overperformance* for this fund has been good.

	last 5 years		last 10 years	
worst year	-48.5%	1998	-48.5%	1998
best year	84.1%	2000	84.1%	2000

During the past five years, the fund's three worst months have been August 1998 (-28 percent), July 1998 (-18 percent), and December 1998 (-13 percent). During the same period, the three best months have been March 1999 (29 percent), December 2000 (27 percent), and September 1998 (23 percent). In the past, State Street Research Global Resources A has done better than 55 percent of its peer group during the most recent bull market and outperformed 50 percent of its peer group during the most recent bear market. Consistency, or predictability, of returns for State Street Research Global Resources A can be described as fair. This fund's risk-adjusted return over the past three/five years ranks in the top-three quintiles.

Management   ★★

There are 70 stocks in this $80 million portfolio. The average metals and natural resources fund today is $70 million in size. Close to 95 percent of the fund's holdings are in stocks. The stocks in this portfolio have an average p/e ratio of 12 and a median market capitalization of $630 million. The 10 largest holdings compose 45 percent of the fund's total assets. The portfolio's equity holdings can be categorized as small-cap and a blend of growth and value stocks.

Daniel J. Rice III has managed this fund for the past 13 years. Management finds the kind of companies that are very sensitive to energy prices. Rice likes corporations that are increasing production and cash flow. The fund's price movement is not correlated to that of the S&P 500. There are 15 funds besides Global Resources within the State Street Research family. Overall, the fund family's risk adjusted performance can be described as good.

Tax Minimization   ★★★★★

During the past five years, a $10,000 initial investment grew to $72,980 after taxes, assuming a 40 percent income tax bracket (state and federal combined) and a capital gains rate of 20 percent. This means that investors in this fund were able to preserve 93 percent of their total returns. Compared to other funds in its category, this fund's tax savings are considered to be excellent.

Expenses   ★★★★

State Street Research Global Resources A's expense ratio is 1.7 percent; it has averaged 1.7 percent annually over the past three calendar years. The average expense ratio for the 120 funds in this category is 2.0 percent. This fund's turnover rate over the past year has been 38 percent, while its peer group average has been 173 percent.

Summary

State Street Research Global Resources A has exhibited higher risk than any of its contemporaries, but the risk has been worth the ride. Annualized returns over the past three years have averaged more than 23 percent. Overhead costs are lower than average, while turnover rates have been quite small.

Profile

minimum initial investment $2,500	*IRA accounts available* . . . . yes
subsequent minimum investment . . . $50	*IRA minimum investment* $2,000
available in all 50 states . . . . yes	*date of inception* . . . . Mar. 1990
telephone exchanges . . . . yes	*dividend/income paid* . . . . annually
number of funds in family 16	*largest sector weighting* . . . . . industrial cyclicals

Money Market Funds

Money market funds invest in securities that mature in less than one year. They are made up of one or more of the following instruments: Treasury bills, certificates of deposit, commercial paper, repurchase agreements, Eurodollar CDs, and notes. There are four different categories of money market funds: all-purpose, government-backed, federally tax-free, and double tax-exempt.

All-purpose funds are the most popular and make up the bulk of the money market universe. Fully taxable, they are composed of securities such as CDs, commercial paper, and T-bills.

Government-backed money funds invest only in short-term paper, directly or indirectly backed by the U.S. government. These funds are technically safer than the all-purpose variety, but only one money market fund has ever defaulted (a fund set up by a bank for banks). The yield on government-backed funds is somewhat lower than that of its all-purpose peers.

Federally tax-free funds are made up of municipal notes. Investors in these funds do not have to pay federal income taxes on the interest earned. The before-tax yield on federally tax-free funds is certainly lower than that of all-purpose and government-backed funds, but the after-tax return can be greater for the moderate- or high-tax-bracket investor.

Double tax-exempt funds invest in the municipal obligations of a specific state. To avoid paying state income taxes on any interest earned, you must be a resident of that state. Nonresident investors will still receive a federal tax exemption.

All money market funds are safer than any other mutual fund or category of funds in this book. They have a perfect track record (if you exclude the one money market fund set up for banks)—investors can only make money in these interest-bearing accounts. The rate of return earned in a money market depends on the average maturity of the fund's paper, the kinds of securities held, the quality rating of that paper, and how efficiently the fund is operated. A lean fund will almost always outperform a similar fund with high operating costs.

Investments such as U.S. Treasury bills and, for all practical purposes, money market funds, are often referred to as "risk-free." These kinds of investments are free from price swings and default risk because of their composition. However, as we have come to learn, there is more than one form of risk. Money market funds should never be considered as a medium- or long-term investment. The *real return* on this investment is poor. An investment's real return takes into account the effects of inflation and income taxes. During virtually every period of time, the after-tax, after-inflation return on all money market funds has been near zero or even negative.

Over the past 50 years, Treasury bills—an index often used as a substitute for money market funds—have outperformed inflation on average 80 percent of the time over one-, five-, and 10-year periods and 100 percent over any given 20-year period of time. These figures are not adjusted for income taxes. Money market funds have rarely, if ever, outperformed inflation on an *after-tax* basis when looking at three-, five-, 10-, 15-, or 20-year holding positions.

Investors often look back to the good old days of the early 1980s, when money market funds briefly averaged 18 percent, and wish such times would come again. Well, those were not good times. During the early 1980s the top tax bracket, state and federal combined, was 55 percent. If you began with an 18-percent return and deducted taxes, many taxpayers saw their 18-percent return knocked down to about 9 percent. This may look great, especially for a "risk-free" investment, but we are not through yet. During the partial year in which money market accounts paid 18 percent, inflation was 12 percent. Now, if you take the 9-percent return and subtract 12 percent for inflation; the real return was actually minus 3 percent for the year—so much for the good old days.

Money market funds and ultra-short-term bond funds are the best places to park your money while you are looking at other investment alternatives or if you will be using the money during the next year. These funds can provide the convenience of check writing and a yield that is highly competitive with interest rates in general. These incredibly safe funds should only be considered for short-term periods or for regular expenditures, the way you would use a savings or checking account.

Since money market funds only came into existence for the general public in the mid-1970s, those who wish to analyze the performance of these funds over a long period often use Treasury bills as a substitute. The results are instructive. Over the past half-century (1953–2002), a dollar invested in T-bills grew to $13.16 by the end of 2002. By the beginning of 2003, you would have needed $6.77 to equal the purchasing power of a dollar at the beginning of 1953. This means that T-bills have outperformed inflation by roughly a two-to-one margin on a pretax basis over the past 50 years. If income taxes were factored in, using the then highest marginal rates, an investor would not have kept pace with inflation over the last half-century.

To give you a better sense of the cumulative effects of inflation, consider what a $100,000 investment in a money market fund would have to yield at the beginning of 2003 to equal the same purchasing power as the interest (or yield) from a $100,000 investment in a money market fund 20 years ago (1983). At the beginning of 2003, for instance, a $100,000 account held since 1983 would need to generate $11,250, or 11.2 percent, to equal the same purchasing power as a $100,000 account yielding approximately 6.3 percent in 1983 (the average interest rate for money market accounts that year). The reality, however, is that at the beginning of 2003, money market funds were yielding less than 2 percent (less than $2,000 a year versus the $11,250 that would be required to maintain 1983 purchasing power).

You may have avoided stock investing in the past because "stocks are too risky." Yet, it all depends on how you define risk. As an example, in 1969 a $100,000 CD generated enough interest ($7,900) to buy a new, fully loaded

Cadillac ($5,936) and take a week's cruise. As of the beginning of 1997, that same $100,000 CD would not generate enough income (CD rates were 4.95 percent) to buy an eighth of the Cadillac ($4,950 versus $43,000 for the cost of a 1997 Cadillac Hardtop Sedan De Ville).

Over the past one, three, five, and 10 years, ending December 31, 2002, money market funds have averaged 1.2 percent, 3.5 percent, 4.1 percent, and 4.3 percent, respectively. The standard deviation for money market funds is roughly a quarter of 1 percent, a figure much lower than any other mutual fund category. This means that these funds have had fewer return variances than any other group. Close to 1,300 funds make up the money market category. Total market capitalization of this category is over $2.3 trillion, making this the largest fund category by a wide margin.

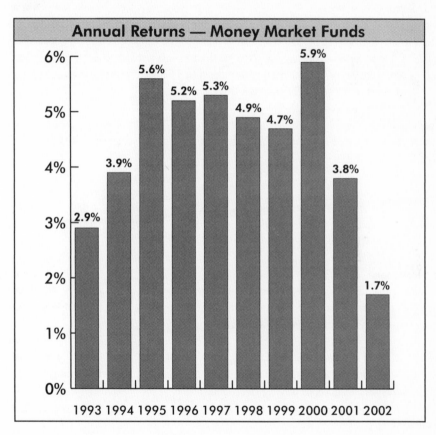

Dreyfus Basic Money Market

200 Park Avenue, 7th Floor
New York, NY 10166
(800) 645-6561
www.dreyfus.com

total return	★★★★★
risk reduction	★★★★★
management	★★★★★
expense control	★★★★★
symbol DBAXX	20 points

Total Return   ★★★★★

Over the past five years, Dreyfus Basic Money Market has taken $10,000 and turned it into $12,400 ($11,250 over three years). This translates into an annualized return of 4.4 percent over the past five years and 4.0 percent over the past three years. This is the number four performing taxable money market fund over the past five years and number two for the past three years.

Risk/Volatility   ★★★★★

During the past three and five years, the fund's standard deviation has been 0.2 percent.

	last 5 years		last 10 years	
worst year	1.7%	2002	1.7%	2002
best year	6.1%	2000	6.1%	2000

Management   ★★★★★

The average maturity of the paper in the portfolio is approximately 65 days. Patricia Larkin has managed the fund since May 1994. The fund has outperformed its peer group over the past one, three, five, and 10 years.

Expenses   ★★★★★

The expense ratio for this $1.5 billion fund is 0.5 percent. This means that for every $1,000 invested, $5 goes to paying overhead.

Summary

Dreyfus Basic Money Market is highly recommended.

Profile

minimum initial investment $25,000
subsequent minimum investment . $1,000
available in all 50 states . . . . yes
telephone exchanges . . . . yes
number of funds in family 125

IRA accounts available . . . . yes
IRA minimum investment $750
date of inception 1992
dividend/income paid . . . . daily

Federated Liquid Cash Trust
1001 Liberty Avenue
Pittsburgh, PA 15222
(800) 341-7400
www.federatedinvestors.com

total return	★★★★★
risk reduction	★★★★★
management	★★★★★
expense control	★★★★★
symbol LCTXX	20 points

Total Return   ★★★★★
Over the past five years, Federated Liquid Cash Trust has taken $10,000 and turned it into $12,420 ($11,220 over three years). This translates into an annualized return of 4.4 percent over the past five years and 3.9 percent over the past three years. This is the number four performing taxable money market fund over the past five years and number four for the past three years.

Risk/Volatility   ★★★★★
During the past three and five years, the fund's standard deviation has been 0.2 percent.

	last 5 years		last 10 years	
worst year	1.6%	2002	1.6%	2002
best year	6.3%	2000	6.3%	2000

Management   ★★★★★
The average maturity of the paper in the portfolio is approximately 3 days. Susan Hill has managed the fund since July 1993. The fund has outperformed its peer group over the past one, three, five, and 10 years.

Expenses   ★★★★★
The expense ratio for this $255 million fund is 0.2 percent. This means that for every $1,000 invested, $2 goes to paying overhead.

Summary
Federated Liquid Cash Trust is highly recommended.

Profile

minimum initial investment $25,000	*IRA accounts available* .... yes
subsequent minimum investment ... $10	*IRA minimum investment* $250
available in all 50 states .... yes	*date of inception* 1983
telephone exchanges .... yes	*dividend/income paid* .... daily
number of funds in family 73	

Federated Short-Term Government Trust

1001 Liberty Avenue
Pittsburgh, PA 15222
(800) 341-7400
www.federatedinvestors.com

total return	★★★★★
risk reduction	★★★★★
management	★★★★★
expense control	★★★★★
symbol FSUXX	20 points

Total Return   ★★★★★

Over the past five years, Federated Short-Term Government Trust has taken $10,000 and turned it into $12,300 ($11,160 over three years). This translates into an annualized return of 4.2 percent over the past five years and 3.7 percent over the past three years. This is the number two performing government money market fund over the past five years and also the number two for the past three years.

Risk/Volatility   ★★★★★

During the past three and five years, the fund's standard deviation has been 0.2 percent.

	last 5 years		last 10 years	
worst year	1.4%	2002	1.4%	2002
best year	6.0%	2000	6.0%	2000

Management   ★★★★★

The average maturity of the paper in the portfolio is approximately 44 days. Susan Hill has managed the fund since July 1993. The fund has outperformed its peer group over the past one, three, five, and 10 years.

Expenses   ★★★★★

The expense ratio for this $210 million fund is 0.5 percent. This means that for every $1,000 invested, $5 goes to paying overhead.

Summary

Federated Short-Term Government Trust is highly recommended.

Profile

minimum initial investment $25,000
subsequent minimum investment $1
available in all 50 states . . . . yes
telephone exchanges . . . . yes
number of funds in family 73

IRA accounts available . . . . yes
IRA minimum investment $250
date of inception 1987
dividend/income paid . . . . daily

Strong Municipal Money Market
100 Heritage Reserve
Menomonee Falls, WI 53051
(800) 368-3863
www.estrong.com

total return	★★★★★
risk reduction	★★★★★
management	★★★★★
expense control	★★★★★
symbol SXFXX	20 points

Total Return   ★★★★★
Over the past five years, Strong Municipal Money Market has taken $10,000 and turned it into $11,620 ($10,860 over three years). This translates into an annualized return of 3.1 percent over the past five years and 2.8 percent over the past three years. This is the number one performing tax-free money market fund over the past five years and also the number one for the past three years.

Risk/Volatility   ★★★★★
During the past three and five years, the fund's standard deviation has been 0.3 percent.

	last 5 years		last 10 years	
worst year	1.3%	2002	1.3%	2002
best year	4.2%	2000	4.2%	2000

Management   ★★★★★
The average maturity of the paper in the portfolio is approximately 37 days. John Bonnell has managed the fund since March 2000. The fund has outperformed its peer group over the past one, three, five, and 10 years.

Expenses   ★★★★★
The expense ratio for this $2.1 billion fund is 0.6 percent. This means that for every $1,000 invested, $6 goes to paying overhead.

Summary
Strong Municipal Money Market is highly recommended.

Profile

minimum initial investment $2,500	*IRA accounts available* . . . . yes
subsequent minimum investment . . $100	*IRA minimum investment* $250
available in all 50 states . . . . yes	*date of inception* 1986
telephone exchanges . . . . yes	*dividend/income paid* . . . . daily
number of funds in family 90	

Scudder Tax Exempt Money
Two International Place
Boston, MA 02110
(800) 621-1048
www.scudder.com

total return	★★★★★
risk reduction	★★★★★
management	★★★★★
expense control	★★★★★
symbol KXMXX	20 points

Total Return   ★★★★★
Over the past five years, Scudder Tax Exempt Money has taken $10,000 and turned it into $11,470 ($10,780 over three years). This translates into an annualized return of 2.8 percent over the past five years and 2.5 percent over the past three years. This is the number four performing tax-free money market fund over the past five years and also the number four for the past three years.

Risk/Volatility   ★★★★★
During the past three and five years, the fund's standard deviation has been 0.3 percent.

	last 5 years		last 10 years	
worst year	1.1%	2002	1.1%	2002
best year	3.9%	2000	3.9%	2000

Management   ★★★★★
The average maturity of the paper in the portfolio is approximately 21 days. Frank Rachwalski has managed the fund since September 1987. The fund has outperformed its peer group over the past one, three, five, and 10 years.

Expenses   ★★★★★
The expense ratio for this $680 million fund is 0.4 percent. This means that for every $1,000 invested, $4 goes to paying overhead.

Summary
Scudder Tax Exempt Money is highly recommended.

Profile

minimum initial investment $1,000	*IRA accounts available* . . . . yes
subsequent minimum investment . . $100	*IRA minimum investment* $500
available in all 50 states . . . . yes	*date of inception*. 1987
telephone exchanges . . . . yes	*dividend/income paid* . . . . daily
number of funds in family 90	

Scudder Yieldwise Money

Two International Place
Boston, MA 02110
(800) 621-1048
www.scudder.com

total return	★★★★★
risk reduction	★★★★★
management	★★★★★
expense control	★★★★★
symbol SYWXX	20 points

Total Return   ★★★★★
Over the past five years, Scudder Yieldwise Money has taken $10,000 and turned it into $12,440 ($11,240 over three years). This translates into an annualized return of 4.5 percent over the past five years and 4.0 percent over the past three years. This is the number two performing taxable money market fund over the past five years and number three for the past three years.

Risk/Volatility   ★★★★★
During the past three and five years, the fund's standard deviation has been 0.2 percent.

	last 5 years		last 10 years	
worst year	1.6%	2002	1.6%	2002
best year	6.4%	2000	6.4%	2000

Management   ★★★★★
The average maturity of the paper in the portfolio is approximately 32 days. Frank Rachwalski Jr. has managed the fund since April 1997. The fund has outperformed its peer group over the past one, three, five, and 10 years.

Expenses   ★★★★★
The expense ratio for this $630 million fund is 0.3 percent. This means that for every $1,000 invested, $3 goes to paying overhead.

Summary
Scudder Yieldwise Money is highly recommended.

Profile

minimum initial investment $25,000	*IRA accounts available* . . . . yes
subsequent minimum investment . $1,000	*IRA minimum investment* $250
available in all 50 states . . . . yes	*date of inception* 1997
telephone exchanges . . . . yes	*dividend/income paid* . . . . daily
number of funds in family 90	

TIAA-CREF Money Market
730 3rd Avenue
New York, NY 10017
(800) 223-1200
www.tiaa-cref.org

total return	★★★★★
risk reduction	★★★★★
management	★★★★★
expense control	★★★★★
symbol TIAXX	20 points

Total Return   ★★★★★
Over the past five years, TIAA-CREF Money Market has taken $10,000 and turned it into $12,430 ($11,240 over three years). This translates into an annualized return of 4.5 percent over the past five years and 4.0 percent over the past three years. This is the number three performing taxable money market fund over the past five years and number four for the past three years.

Risk/Volatility   ★★★★★
During the past three and five years, the fund's standard deviation has been 0.2 percent.

	last 5 years		last 10 years	
worst year	1.6%	2002	1.6%	2002
best year	6.3%	2000	6.3%	2000

Management   ★★★★★
The average maturity of the paper in the portfolio is approximately 47 days. Steven Traum has managed the fund since September 1997. The fund has outperformed its peer group over the past one, three, and five years.

Expenses   ★★★★★
The expense ratio for this $695 million fund is 0.3 percent. This means that for every $1,000 invested, $3 goes to paying overhead.

Summary
TIAA-CREF Money Market is highly recommended.

Profile

minimum initial investment $1,500	*IRA accounts available* . . . . yes
subsequent minimum investment . . . $50	*IRA minimum investment* $500
available in all 50 states . . . . yes	*date of inception* 1997
telephone exchanges . . . . yes	*dividend/income paid* . . . . daily
number of funds in family 16	

USAA Tax-Exempt Money Market
9800 Fredericksburg Road
San Antonio, TX 78288
(800) 531-8722
www.usaa.com

total return	★★★★★
risk reduction	★★★★★
management	★★★★★
expense control	★★★★★
symbol USEXX	20 points

Total Return ★★★★★
Over the past five years, USAA Tax-Exempt Money Market has taken $10,000 and turned it into $11,500 ($10,790 over three years). This translates into an annualized return of 2.8 percent over the past five years and 2.6 percent over the past three years. This is the number three performing tax-free money market fund over the past five years and also the number three for the past three years.

Risk/Volatility ★★★★★
During the past three and five years, the fund's standard deviation has been 0.3 percent.

	last 5 years		last 10 years	
worst year	1.2%	2002	1.2%	2002
best year	3.9%	2000	3.9%	2000

Management ★★★★★
The average maturity of the paper in the portfolio is approximately 37 days. Anthony Era has managed the fund since February 2000. The fund has outperformed its peer group over the past one, three, five, and 10 years.

Expenses ★★★★★
The expense ratio for this $1.9 billion fund is 0.5 percent. This means that for every $1,000 invested, $5 goes to paying overhead.

Summary
USAA Tax-Exempt Money Market is highly recommended.

Profile
minimum initial investment $3,000	*IRA accounts available* . . . . yes
subsequent minimum investment . . . $50	*IRA minimum investment* $250
available in all 50 states . . . . yes	*date of inception* 1984
telephone exchanges . . . . yes	*dividend/income paid* . . . . daily
number of funds in family 29	

Vanguard Federal Money Market

P.O. Box 2600
Valley Forge, PA 19482
(800) 662-2739
www.vanguard.com

total return	★★★★★
risk reduction	★★★★★
management	★★★★★
expense control	★★★★★
symbol VMFXX	20 points

Total Return ★★★★★

Over the past five years, Vanguard Federal Money Market has taken $10,000 and turned it into $12,430 ($11,250 over three years). This translates into an annualized return of 4.5 percent over the past five years and 4.0 percent over the past three years. This is the number one performing government money market fund over the past five years and also the number one for the past three years.

Risk/Volatility ★★★★★

During the past three and five years, the fund's standard deviation has been 0.2 percent.

	last 5 years		last 10 years	
worst year	1.6%	2002	1.6%	2002
best year	6.2%	2000	6.2%	2000

Management ★★★★★

The average maturity of the paper in the portfolio is approximately 62 days. Robert Auwaerter has managed the fund since November 1981. The fund has outperformed its peer group over the past one, three, five, and 10 years.

Expenses ★★★★★

The expense ratio for this $6.9 billion fund is 0.3 percent. This means that for every $1,000 invested, $3 goes to paying overhead.

Summary

Vanguard Federal Money Market is highly recommended.

Profile

minimum initial investment $3,000
subsequent minimum investment . . $100
available in all 50 states . . . . yes
telephone exchanges . . . . yes
number of funds in family 79

IRA accounts available . . . . yes
IRA minimum investment $1,000
date of inception 1981
dividend/income paid . . . . daily

Vanguard Prime Money Market
P.O. Box 2600
Valley Forge, PA 19482
(800) 662-2739
www.vanguard.com

total return	★★★★★
risk reduction	★★★★★
management	★★★★★
expense control	★★★★★
symbol VMMXX	20 points

Total Return   ★★★★★
Over the past five years, Vanguard Prime Money Market has taken $10,000 and turned it into $12,450 ($11,250 over three years). This translates into an annualized return of 4.5 percent over the past five years and 4.0 percent over the past three years. This is the number one performing taxable money market fund over the past five years and also the number one for the past three years.

Risk/Volatility   ★★★★★
During the past three and five years, the fund's standard deviation has been 0.2 percent.

	last 5 years		last 10 years	
worst year	1.6%	2002	1.6%	2002
best year	6.3%	2000	6.3%	2000

Management   ★★★★★
The average maturity of the paper in the portfolio is approximately 56 days. MacKinnon and Hollyer have co-managed the fund since October 1989. The fund has outperformed its peer group over the past one, three, five, and 10 years.

Expenses   ★★★★★
The expense ratio for this $50 billion fund is 0.3 percent. This means that for every $1,000 invested, $3 goes to paying overhead.

Summary
Vanguard Prime Money Market is highly recommended.

Profile

minimum initial investment $3,000	IRA accounts available . . . . yes
subsequent minimum investment . . $100	IRA minimum investment $1,000
available in all 50 states . . . . yes	date of inception. 1989
telephone exchanges . . . . yes	dividend/income paid . . . . daily
number of funds in family 79	

Wells Fargo National Tax-Free Money Market Fund

525 Market Street, 12th Floor
San Francisco, CA 94105
(800) 222-8222
www.wellsfargo.com

total return	★★★★★
risk reduction	★★★★★
management	★★★★★
expense control	★★★★★
symbol NWMXX	20 points

Total Return   ★★★★★

Over the past five years, Wells Fargo National Tax-Free Money Market Fund has taken $10,000 and turned it into $11,540 ($10,840 over three years). This translates into an annualized return of 2.9 percent over the past five years and 2.7 percent over the past three years. This is the number two performing tax-free money market fund over the past five years and also the number two for the past three years.

Risk/Volatility   ★★★★★

During the past three and five years, the fund's standard deviation has been 0.3 percent.

	last 5 years		last 10 years	
worst year	1.4%	2002	1.4%	2002
best year	4.1%	2000	4.1%	2000

Management   ★★★★★

The average maturity of the paper in the portfolio is approximately 55 days. Kevin Shaughnessy has managed the fund since November 1997. The fund has outperformed its peer group over the past one, three, and five years.

Expenses   ★★★★★

The expense ratio for this $500 million fund is 0.2 percent. This means that for every $1,000 invested, $2 goes to paying overhead.

Summary

Wells Fargo National Tax-Free Money Market Fund is highly recommended.

Profile

minimum initial investment $1	*IRA accounts available* . . . . yes
subsequent minimum investment $1	*IRA minimum investment* $1,000
available in all 50 states . . . . yes	*date of inception* 1997
telephone exchanges . . . . yes	*dividend/income paid* . . . . daily
number of funds in family 79	

Municipal Bond Funds

Municipal bond funds invest in securities issued by municipalities, political subdivisions, and U.S. territories. The type of security issued is either a note or bond, both of which are interest-bearing instruments that are exempt from federal income taxes. There are three different categories of municipal bond funds: national, state-free, and high-yield.

National municipal bond funds are made up of debt instruments issued by a wide range of states. These funds are exempt from federal income taxes only. To determine what small percentage is also exempt from state income taxes, consult the fund's prospectus and look for the weighting of U.S. territory issues (U.S. Virgin Islands, Guam, Puerto Rico), District of Columbia items, and obligations from your state of residence.

State-free municipal bond funds, sometimes referred to as "double tax-free funds," invest only in bonds and notes issued in a particular state. To avoid paying state income taxes on the fund's return, you must be a legal resident of that state. For example, most California residents who are in a high tax bracket will only want to consider purchasing a municipal bond fund that has the name "California" in it. Residents of New York who purchase a California tax-free fund will escape federal income taxes but not state taxes.

High-yield tax-free funds invest in the same kinds of issues found in a national municipal bond fund but with one important difference. By seeking higher returns, high-yield funds look for lower-rated or nonrated notes and bonds. A municipality may decide not to obtain a rating for its issue because of the costs involved compared to the relatively small size of the bond or note being floated. Many nonrated issues are very safe. High-yield municipal bond funds are relatively new but should not be overlooked by the tax-conscious investor. These kinds of tax-free funds have demonstrated less volatility and higher return than their other tax-free counterparts.

Prospective investors need to compare tax-free bond yields to after-tax yields on corporate or government bond funds. To determine which of these three fund categories is best for you, use your marginal tax bracket, subtract this amount from 1, and multiply the resulting figure by the taxable investment. For instance, suppose you were in the 35 percent bracket, state and federal combined. By subtracting this figure from 1, you are left with 0.65. Multiply 0.65 by the fully taxable yield you could get; let us say, 9 percent—65 percent of 9 percent is 5.85 percent. The 5.85 percent represents what you get on a 9-percent investment after you have paid state and federal income taxes on it. This means that if you can get 5.85 percent or higher from a tax-free investment, take it.

Interest paid on tax-free investments is generally lower than interest paid on taxable investments like corporate bonds and bank CDs. But you should compare the yields on tax-free investments to taxable investments only after you have considered the municipal bond fund's tax-free advantage. The result will be the taxable equivalent yield—the yield you will have to get on a similar taxable investment to equal the tax-free yield.

Municipal bond funds are not for investors who are in a low tax bracket. If such investors want to be in bonds, they would be better off in corporate or government issues. Furthermore, municipals should never be used in a retirement plan. There is only one way to make tax-free income taxable and that is to put it into a traditional IRA, pension, or profit-sharing plan. Everything that comes out of these plans is fully taxable by the federal government.

Over the past three and five years, the typical municipal bond fund has had an average compounded annual return of 7.4 and 4.7 percent, respectively (all periods ending December 31, 2002). They have averaged a total annual return (current yield plus bond appreciation or minus bond depreciation) of 5.6 percent over the past 10 years and 6.8 percent annually for the past 15 years. Municipal bond fund returns have been fairly stable over the past three years, having a standard deviation of 4.4 percent.

Nearly 1,800 funds make up the municipal bond category. Close to 98 percent of a typical municipal bond fund's portfolio is in tax-free bonds, with the balance in tax-free money market instruments. Close to 1,200 of the 3,000 municipal bond funds offered are single-state funds.

The typical municipal bond fund yields 3.9 percent in tax-free income each year. The average weighted maturity is just under 13 years. Expenses for this category are 1.1 percent each year.

As you read through the descriptions of the municipal bond funds selected, you will notice a paragraph in each describing the tax efficiency of the portfolio. This may surprise you, because municipal bonds are supposed to be tax-free. Keep in mind that only the income (current yield) from these instruments is free from federal income taxes (and often state income taxes, depending on the fund in question and your state of residence). Since bond funds generally have a high turnover rate (which triggers a potential capital gain or loss upon each sale of a security by the portfolio manager), there are capital gains considerations with municipal bonds.

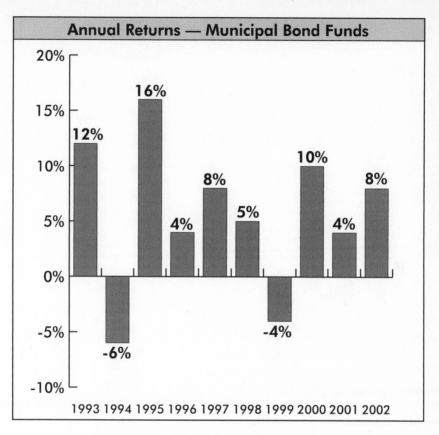

American Century California
High-Yield Municipal Investor

4500 Main Street
P.O. Box 419200
Kansas City, MO 64141
(800) 345-2021
www.americancentury.com

total return	★★★★★
risk reduction	★★★★
management	★★★★★
current income	★★★★★
expense control	★★★★
symbol BCHYX	23 points
up-market performance	fair
down-market performance	excellent
predictability of returns	good

Total Return   ★★★★★

Over the past five years, American Century California High-Yield Municipal Investor
has taken $10,000 and turned it into $13,260 ($12,850 over three years and $19,650
over the past 10 years). This translates into an annualized return of 6 percent over the
past five years, 9 percent over the past three years, and 7 percent for the decade. Over
the past five years, this fund has outperformed 85 percent of all mutual funds; within
its general category it has done better than 97 percent of its peers. Municipal bond
funds have averaged 5 percent annually over these same five years.

During the past five years, a $10,000 initial investment grew to $13,000 after
taxes, assuming a 40 percent income tax bracket (state and federal combined) and
a capital gains rate of 20 percent. This means that investors in this fund were able
to preserve 99 percent of their total returns. Compared to other funds in its category, this fund's tax savings are considered to be excellent.

Risk/Volatility   ★★★★

Over the past five years, American Century California High-Yield Municipal
Investor has experienced below average risk for its category. Over the past decade,
the fund has had two negative years, while the Lehman Brothers Aggregate Bond
Index has had two (off 3 percent in 1994 and 1 percent in 1999); the Lehman
Brothers Municipal Bond Index also fell twice (off 5 percent in 1994 and 2 percent
in 1999). The fund has underperformed the Lehman Brothers Aggregate Bond
Index six times and the Lehman Brothers Municipal Bond Index four times in the
past 10 years. Consistency of *overperformance* for this fund has been very good.

	last 5 years		last 10 years	
worst year	-3.3%	1999	-5.4%	1994
best year	12.5%	2000	18.3%	1995

During the past five years, the fund's three worst months have been October 1999 (-2 percent), April 2001 (-2 percent), and January 2000 (-2 percent). During the same period, the three best months have been March 2000 (2 percent), June 2000 (2 percent), and December 2000 (2 percent). In the past, American Century California High-Yield Municipal Investor has only done better than 25 percent of its peer group during the most recent bull market but outperformed 85 percent of its peer group during the most recent bear market. Consistency, or predictability, of returns for American Century California High-Yield Municipal Investor can be described as good. This fund's risk-adjusted return over the past three/five years ranks in the top quintile.

Management   ★★★★★
There are 155 fixed-income securities in this $370 million portfolio. The average municipal bond fund today is $185 million in size. Close to 95 percent of the fund's holdings are in bonds. The average maturity of the bonds in this account is 22 years; the weighted coupon rate averages 6 percent.

Steven Permut has managed this fund for the past 15 years. Roughly half of the portfolio is in nonrated bonds. Management balances the nonrated issues by having a large weighting of insured bonds. There are 50 funds besides California High-Yield Municipal Investor within the American Century Investments family. Overall, the fund family's risk adjusted performance can be described as between good and very good.

Current Income   ★★★★★
Over the past year, American Century California High-Yield Municipal Investor had a 12-month yield of 5.2 percent. During this same 12-month period, the typical municipal bond fund had a yield that averaged 4.0 percent.

Expenses   ★★★★
American Century California High-Yield Municipal Investor's expense ratio is 0.5 percent; it has averaged 0.5 percent annually over the past three calendar years. The average expense ratio for the 1,800 funds in this category is 1.1 percent. This fund's turnover rate over the past year has been 47 percent, while its peer group average has been 36 percent.

Summary
American Century California High-Yield Municipal Investor turns in a near perfect score: 23 out of 25 possible points. This tax-free fund overall ranks number two in its rather large category of 1,800 contenders. The portfolio really excels when it comes to total returns and low risk. When it comes to current income, it clearly leads the pack.

Profile
minimum initial investment $5,000	*IRA accounts available* . . . . yes
subsequent minimum investment . . . $50	*IRA minimum investment* $1,000
available in all 50 states . . . . yes	*date of inception*. . . . . Dec. 1986
telephone exchanges . . . . yes	*dividend/income paid* . . . . monthly
number of funds in family 51	*average credit quality* . . . . A

American Funds Limited-Term Tax-Exempt Bond Fund of America

333 South Hope Street
Los Angeles, CA 90071
(800) 421-4120
www.americanfunds.com

total return	★★★★★
risk reduction	★★★★★
management	★★★★★
current income	★★
expense control	★★★★
symbol LTEBX	21 points
up-market performance	very good
down-market performance	fair
predictability of returns	very good

Total Return   ★★★★★

Over the past five years, this fund has taken $10,000 and turned it into $12,790 ($12,190 over three years). This translates into an annualized return of 5 percent over the past five years and 7 percent over the past three years. Over the past five years, this fund has outperformed 70 percent of all mutual funds; within its general category it has done better than 50 percent of its peers. Municipal bond funds have averaged 5 percent annually over these same five years.

During the past five years, a $10,000 initial investment grew to $10,610 after taxes, assuming a 40 percent income tax bracket (state and federal combined) and a capital gains rate of 20 percent. This means that investors in this fund were able to preserve 99 percent of their total returns. Compared to other funds in its category, this fund's tax savings are considered to be excellent.

Risk/Volatility   ★★★★★

Over the past five years, American Funds Limited-Term Tax-Exempt Bond Fund of America has experienced low risk for its category. Over the past decade, the fund has had two negative years, while the Lehman Brothers Aggregate Bond Index has had two (off 3 percent in 1994 and 1 percent in 1999); the Lehman Brothers Municipal Bond Index also fell twice (off 5 percent in 1994 and 2 percent in 1999). The fund has underperformed the Lehman Brothers Aggregate Bond Index seven times and the Lehman Brothers Municipal Bond Index six times in the past 10 years. Consistency of *overperformance* for this fund has been good.

	last 5 years		last 10 years	
worst year	-0.6%	1999	-2.9%	1994
best year	7.8%	2002	12.4%	1995

During the past five years, the fund's three worst months have been June 1999 (-2 percent), November 2001 (-1 percent), and December 2001 (-1 percent). During the same period, the three best months have been December 2000 (1 percent), June 2000 (1 percent), and August 2001 (1 percent). In the past, it has done better than 77 percent of its peer group during the most recent bull market but outperformed just 30 percent of its peer group during the most recent bear market. Consistency, or predictability, of returns for this fund can be described as very good. This fund's risk-adjusted return over the past three/five years ranks in the bottom-two quintiles.

Management   ★★★★★
There are 370 fixed-income securities in this $590 million portfolio. The average municipal bond fund today is $185 million in size. Close to 95 percent of the fund's holdings are in bonds. The average weighted coupon rate is 5 percent. The portfolio's fixed-income holdings can be categorized as intermediate-term, high-quality debt.

Neil L. Langberg and Brenda S. Ellerin have managed this fund for the past nine years. Management likes the lower end of the investment-grade bond scale. Management has done a wonderful job of protecting its investors' underlying principal. Performance and price movement is extremely correlated to that of the Lehman Brothers Municipal Bond Index. There are 27 funds besides Limited-Term Tax-Exempt Bond Fund within the American Funds family. Overall, the fund family's risk adjusted performance can be described as very good.

Current Income   ★★
Over the past year, American Funds Limited-Term Tax-Exempt Bond Fund of America had a 12-month yield of 3.6 percent. During this same 12-month period, the typical municipal bond fund had a yield that averaged 4.0 percent.

Expenses   ★★★★
American Funds Limited-Term Tax-Exempt Bond Fund of America's expense ratio is 0.8 percent; it has averaged 0.8 percent annually over the past three calendar years. The average expense ratio for the 1,800 funds in this category is 1.1 percent. This fund's turnover rate over the past year has been 21 percent, while its peer group average has been 36 percent.

Summary
American Funds Limited-Term Tax-Exempt Bond Fund of America ties for first place when it comes to risk reduction. The fund scores well in virtually every category. As with most funds in its category, tax minimization is spectacular. This is just one of several offerings from American Funds to appear in the book. The fund family, along with Vanguard, clearly dominates the tax-free marketplace.

Profile
minimum initial investment $250	*IRA accounts available* . . . . yes
subsequent minimum investment . . . $50	*IRA minimum investment* $250
available in all 50 states . . . . yes	*date of inception* . . . . Oct. 1993
telephone exchanges . . . . yes	*dividend/income paid* . . . . monthly
number of funds in family 28	*average credit quality* . . . . AA

American Funds Tax-Exempt Bond A

333 South Hope Street
Los Angeles, CA 90071
(800) 421-4120
www.americanfunds.com

total return	★★★★★
risk reduction	★★★
management	★★★★
current income	★★★★
expense control	★★★★
symbol AFTEX	20 points
up-market performance	very good
down-market performance	good
predictability of returns	very good

Total Return   ★★★★★

Over the past five years, American Funds Tax-Exempt Bond A has taken $10,000 and turned it into $13,010 ($12,560 over three years and $18,490 over the past 10 years). This translates into an annualized return of 5 percent over the past five years, 8 percent over the past three years, and 6 percent for the decade. Over the past five years, this fund has outperformed 77 percent of all mutual funds; within its general category it has done better than 78 percent of its peers. Municipal bond funds have averaged 5 percent annually over these same five years.

During the past five years, a $10,000 initial investment grew to $10,800 after taxes, assuming a 40 percent income tax bracket (state and federal combined) and a capital gains rate of 20 percent. This means that investors in this fund were able to preserve 97 percent of their total returns. Compared to other funds in its category, this fund's tax savings are considered to be excellent.

Risk/Volatility   ★★★

Over the past five years, American Funds Tax-Exempt Bond A has experienced average risk for its category. Over the past decade, the fund has had two negative years, while the Lehman Brothers Aggregate Bond Index has had two (off 3 percent in 1994 and 1 percent in 1999); the Lehman Brothers Municipal Bond Index also fell twice (off 5 percent in 1994 and 2 percent in 1999). The fund has underperformed the Lehman Brothers Aggregate Bond Index eight times and the Lehman Brothers Municipal Bond Index seven times in the past 10 years. Consistency of *overperformance* for this fund has been good.

	last 5 years		last 10 years	
worst year	-2.3%	1999	-4.8%	1994
best year	9.7%	2000	17.3%	1995

During the past five years, the fund's three worst months have been June 1999 (-2 percent), November 2001 (-2 percent), and December 1998 (-1 percent). During the same period, the three best months have been December 2000 (2 percent),

March 2000 (1 percent), and August 2001 (1 percent). In the past, American Funds Tax-Exempt Bond A has done better than 65 percent of its peer group during the most recent bull market and outperformed 55 percent of its peer group during the most recent bear market. Consistency, or predictability, of returns for American Funds Tax-Exempt Bond A can be described as very good. This fund's risk-adjusted return over the past three/five years ranks in the top-three quintiles.

Management   ★★★★

There are 830 fixed-income securities in this $3 billion portfolio. The average municipal bond fund today is $185 million in size. Close to 95 percent of the fund's holdings are in bonds. The average maturity of the bonds in this account is eight years; the weighted coupon rate averages 5 percent. The portfolio's fixed-income holdings can be categorized as intermediate-term, high-quality debt.

A team has managed this fund for the past 23 years. Management focuses on noncallable issues. A good chunk of the portfolio is in bonds rated A or lower. Management has been quite successful in avoiding credit problems. Performance and price movement is extremely correlated to that of the Lehman Brothers Municipal Bond Index. There are 27 funds besides Tax-Exempt Bond within the American Funds family. Overall, the fund family's risk adjusted performance can be described as very good.

Current Income   ★★★★

Over the past year, American Funds Tax-Exempt Bond A had a 12-month yield of 4.5 percent. During this same 12-month period, the typical municipal bond fund had a yield that averaged 4.0 percent.

Expenses   ★★★★

American Funds Tax-Exempt Bond A's expense ratio is 0.7 percent; it has averaged 0.7 percent annually over the past three calendar years. The average expense ratio for the 1,800 funds in this category is 1.1 percent. This fund's turnover rate over the past year has been 22 percent, while its peer group average has been 36 percent.

Summary

American Funds Tax-Exempt Bond A is just one of two funds from the American Funds family to appear in this category. The fund's overhead costs are about 40 percent less than its peers. The portfolio's turnover rate is also on the low side. Risk has been average for its category, but very low when compared to any other fund group. Total return figures are considered to be excellent.

Profile

minimum initial investment $250	*IRA accounts available* . . . . yes
subsequent minimum investment . . . $50	*IRA minimum investment* $250
available in all 50 states . . . . yes	*date of inception* . . . . Oct. 1979
telephone exchanges . . . . yes	*dividend/income paid* . . . . monthly
number of funds in family 28	*average credit quality* . . . . AA

Fidelity Advisor Municipal Income T

82 Devonshire Street
Boston, MA 02109
(800) 522-7297
www.fidelity.com

total return	★★★★★
risk reduction	★★★
management	★★★★
current income	★★★
expense control	★★★★
symbol FAHIX	19 points
up-market performance	fair
down-market performance	excellent
predictability of returns	good

Total Return   ★★★★★

Over the past five years, Fidelity Advisor Municipal Income T has taken $10,000 and turned it into $13,280 ($12,850 over three years and $18,390 over the past 10 years). This translates into an annualized return of 6 percent over the past five years, 9 percent over the past three years, and 6 percent for the decade. Over the past five years, this fund has outperformed 85 percent of all mutual funds; within its general category it has done better than 95 percent of its peers. Municipal bond funds have averaged 5 percent annually over these same five years.

During the past five years, a $10,000 initial investment grew to $11,550 after taxes, assuming a 40 percent income tax bracket (state and federal combined) and a capital gains rate of 20 percent. This means that investors in this fund were able to preserve 100 percent of their total returns. Compared to other funds in its category, this fund's tax savings are considered to be excellent.

Risk/Volatility   ★★★

Over the past five years, Fidelity Advisor Municipal Income T has experienced below average risk for its category. Over the past decade, the fund has had two negative years, while the Lehman Brothers Aggregate Bond Index has had two (off 3 percent in 1994 and 1 percent in 1999); the Lehman Brothers Municipal Bond Index also fell twice (off 5 percent in 1994 and 2 percent in 1999). The fund has underperformed the Lehman Brothers Aggregate Bond Index seven times and the Lehman Brothers Municipal Bond Index seven times in the past 10 years. Consistency of *overperformance* for this fund has been excellent.

	last 5 years		last 10 years	
worst year	-2.7%	1999	-8.1%	1994
best year	11.7%	2000	16.7%	1995

During the past five years, the fund's three worst months have been June 1999 (-2 percent), December 2001 (-1 percent), and October 1999 (-1 percent). During the same period, the three best months have been December 2000 (2 percent), June

2000 (2 percent), and March 2000 (2 percent). In the past, Fidelity Advisor Municipal Income T has only done better than 35 percent of its peer group during the most recent bull market but outperformed 95 percent of its peer group during the most recent bear market. Consistency, or predictability, of returns for Fidelity Advisor Municipal Income T can be described as good. This fund's risk-adjusted return over the past three/five years ranks in the top-two quintiles.

Management   ★★★★
There are 270 fixed-income securities in this $350 million portfolio. The average municipal bond fund today is $185 million in size. Close to 100 percent of the fund's holdings are in bonds. The average maturity of the bonds in this account is 15 years. The portfolio's fixed-income holdings can be categorized as long-term, high-quality debt.

Christine Jones Thompson has managed this fund for the past five years. Management's strategy is to find the most attractive bonds by rotating among different coupon rates, maturities, sectors, and states. Jones has no desire to make bets on the direction of interest rates. Performance and price movement is extremely correlated to that of the Lehman Brothers Municipal Bond Index. There are 54 funds besides Municipal Income within the Fidelity Advisor family. Overall, the fund family's risk adjusted performance can be described as good.

Current Income   ★★★
Over the past year, Fidelity Advisor Municipal Income T had a 12-month yield of 4.2 percent. During this same 12-month period, the typical municipal bond fund had a yield that averaged 4.0 percent.

Expenses   ★★★★
Fidelity Advisor Municipal Income T's expense ratio is 0.7 percent; it has averaged 0.8 percent annually over the past three calendar years. The average expense ratio for the 1,800 funds in this category is 1.1 percent. This fund's turnover rate over the past year has been 16 percent, while its peer group average has been 36 percent.

Summary
Fidelity Advisor Municipal Income T has impressive return figures. Even though this is a tax-free offering, the fund has managed to beat out 85 percent of all mutual funds and 95 percent of its contemporaries. The fund's expenses are about 30 cheaper than its group while turnover has been less than half. This is not an overly exciting fund, but its consistency and good ratings in every category make this a solid choice for the tax-free investor.

Profile

minimum initial investment $2,500	*IRA accounts available* . . . . yes
subsequent minimum investment . . $100	*IRA minimum investment* $500
available in all 50 states . . . . yes	*date of inception* . . . . Sept. 1987
telephone exchanges . . . . yes	*dividend/income paid* . . . . monthly
number of funds in family 55	*average credit quality* . . . . AA

Franklin Federal Tax-Free Income A

One Franklin Parkway
San Mateo, CA 94403
(800) 342-5236
www.franklintempleton.com

total return	★★★★★
risk reduction	★★★★★
management	★★★★★
current income	★★★★★
expense control	★★★★
symbol FKTIX	24 points
up-market performance	very good
down-market performance	fair
predictability of returns	very good

Total Return   ★★★★★

Over the past five years, Franklin Federal Tax-Free Income A has taken $10,000 and turned it into $12,720 ($12,350 over three years and $17,890 over the past 10 years). This translates into an annualized return of 5 percent over the past five years, 7 percent over the past three years, and 6 percent for the decade. Over the past five years, this fund has outperformed 70 percent of all mutual funds; within its general category it has done better than 67 percent of its peers. Municipal bond funds have averaged 5 percent annually over these same five years.

During the past five years, a $10,000 initial investment grew to $10,300 after taxes, assuming a 40 percent income tax bracket (state and federal combined) and a capital gains rate of 20 percent. This means that investors in this fund were able to preserve 100 percent of their total returns. Compared to other funds in its category, this fund's tax savings are considered to be excellent.

Risk/Volatility   ★★★★★

Over the past five years, Franklin Federal Tax-Free Income A has experienced low risk for its category. Over the past decade, the fund has had two negative years, while the Lehman Brothers Aggregate Bond Index has had two (off 3 percent in 1994 and 1 percent in 1999); the Lehman Brothers Municipal Bond Index also fell twice (off 5 percent in 1994 and 2 percent in 1999). The fund has underperformed the Lehman Brothers Aggregate Bond Index eight times and the Lehman Brothers Municipal Bond Index eight times in the past 10 years. Consistency of *overperformance* for this fund has been good.

	last 5 years		last 10 years	
worst year	-2.8%	1999	-3.7%	1994
best year	10.1%	2000	15.1%	1995

During the past five years, the fund's three worst months have been June 1999 (-2 percent), October 1999 (-2 percent), and August 1999 (-1 percent). During the same period, the three best months have been June 2000 (2 percent), March 2000

(2 percent), and December 2000 (1 percent). In the past, Franklin Federal Tax-Free Income A has done better than 75 percent of its peer group during the most recent bull market but outperformed just 25 percent of its peer group during the most recent bear market. Consistency, or predictability, of returns for Franklin Federal Tax-Free Income A can be described as very good. This fund's risk-adjusted return over the past three/five years ranks in the top-three quintiles.

Management   ★★★★★
There are 995 fixed-income securities in this $7 billion portfolio. The average municipal bond fund today is $185 million in size. Close to 100 percent of the fund's holdings are in bonds. The average maturity of the bonds in this account is 20 years; the weighted coupon rate averages 6 percent. The portfolio's fixed-income holdings can be categorized as long-term, high-quality debt.

A team has managed this fund for the past 16 years. The bulk of the fund's performance is based on a buy-and-hold mentality. Performance and price movement is extremely correlated to that of the Lehman Brothers Municipal Bond Index. There are 92 funds besides Federal Tax-Free Income within the Franklin Templeton family. Overall, the fund family's risk adjusted performance can be described as very good.

Current Income   ★★★★★
Over the past year, Franklin Federal Tax-Free Income A had a 12-month yield of 5.0 percent. During this same 12-month period, the typical municipal bond fund had a yield that averaged 4.0 percent.

Expenses   ★★★★
Franklin Federal Tax-Free Income A's expense ratio is 0.6 percent; it has averaged 0.6 percent annually over the past three calendar years. The average expense ratio for the 1,800 funds in this category is 1.1 percent. This fund's turnover rate over the past year has been 10 percent, while its peer group average has been 36 percent.

Summary
Franklin Federal Tax-Free Income A ties for first place as the best overall municipal bond fund. Competing against close to 1,800 other funds, this portfolio has done a good job of keeping risk low while offering a very attractive income stream. The folks at Franklin are known for offering a wide range of tax-free funds. Whether you are interested in a single-state fund or a national offering, this will be one of the fund families you will want to check out first.

Profile
minimum initial investment $1,000	*IRA accounts available* . . . . yes
subsequent minimum investment . . . $50	*IRA minimum investment* $250
available in all 50 states . . . . yes	*date of inception* . . . . Oct. 1983
telephone exchanges . . . . yes	*dividend/income paid* . . . . monthly
number of funds in family 93	*average credit quality* . . . . AA

USAA Tax Exempt Intermediate-Term
USAA Building
San Antonio, TX 78288
(800) 382-8722
www.usaa.com

total return	★★★★★
risk reduction	★★★★
management	★★★★★
current income	★★★★★
expense control	★★★★★
symbol USATX	24 points
up-market performance	excellent
down-market performance	fair
predictability of returns	very good

Total Return   ★★★★★
Over the past five years, USAA Tax Exempt Intermediate-Term has taken $10,000 and turned it into $12,930 ($12,490 over three years and $18,200 over the past 10 years). This translates into an annualized return of 5 percent over the past five years, 8 percent over the past three years, and 6 percent for the decade. Over the past five years, this fund has outperformed 75 percent of all mutual funds; within its general category it has done better than 80 percent of its peers. Municipal bond funds have averaged 5 percent annually over these same five years.

During the past five years, a $10,000 initial investment grew to $12,930 after taxes, assuming a 40 percent income tax bracket (state and federal combined) and a capital gains rate of 20 percent. This means that investors in this fund were able to preserve 100 percent of their total returns. Compared to other funds in its category, this fund's tax savings are considered to be excellent.

Risk/Volatility   ★★★★
Over the past five years, USAA Tax Exempt Intermediate-Term has experienced below average risk for its category. Over the past decade, the fund has had two negative years, while the Lehman Brothers Aggregate Bond Index has had two (off 3 percent in 1994 and 1 percent in 1999); the Lehman Brothers Municipal Bond Index also fell twice (off 5 percent in 1994 and 2 percent in 1999). The fund has underperformed the Lehman Brothers Aggregate Bond Index eight times and the Lehman Brothers Municipal Bond Index six times in the past 10 years. Consistency of *overperformance* for this fund has been good.

	last 5 years		last 10 years	
worst year	-2.6%	1999	-4.0%	1994
best year	9.8%	2000	15.1%	1995

During the past five years, the fund's three worst months have been June 1999 (-2 percent), October 1999 (-1 percent), and April 2001 (-1 percent). During the same period, the three best months have been June 2000 (2 percent), December

2000 (2 percent), and March 2000 (1 percent). In the past, USAA Tax Exempt Intermediate-Term has done better than 88 percent of its peer group during the most recent bull market but outperformed just 25 percent of its peer group during the most recent bear market. Consistency, or predictability, of returns for USAA Tax Exempt Intermediate-Term can be described as very good. This fund's risk-adjusted return over the past three/five years ranks in the top quintile.

Management   ★★★★★
There are 415 fixed-income securities in this $3 billion portfolio. The average municipal bond fund today is $185 million in size. Close to 100 percent of the fund's holdings are in bonds. The average maturity of the bonds in this account is nine years; the weighted coupon rate averages 5 percent. The portfolio's fixed-income holdings can be categorized as short-term, high-quality debt.

Clifford A. Gladson has managed this fund for the past 10 years. Management prefers a buy-and-hold approach. Frequently, the fund ends up owning a number of older, comparatively higher-yielding bonds. Management is more interested in current income than anything else, as long as risk remains in check by largely avoiding long-term issues. Performance and price movement is extremely correlated to that of the Lehman Brothers Municipal Bond Index. There are 28 funds besides Tax Exempt Intermediate-Term within the USAA family. Overall, the fund family's risk adjusted performance can be described as good.

Current Income   ★★★★★
Over the past year, USAA Tax Exempt Intermediate-Term had a 12-month yield of 4.9 percent. During this same 12-month period, the typical municipal bond fund had a yield that averaged 4.0 percent.

Expenses   ★★★★★
USAA Tax Exempt Intermediate-Term's expense ratio is 0.5 percent; it has averaged 0.4 percent annually over the past three calendar years. The average expense ratio for the 1,800 funds in this category is 1.1 percent. This fund's turnover rate over the past year has been 13 percent, while its peer group average has been 36 percent.

Summary
USAA Tax Exempt Intermediate-Term ties for first place as the choice for municipal bond investors. Few funds in this, or any previous, edition of the book rack up a total point score of 24 points. Not much needs to be said about a portfolio that scores so highly in every single category measured.

Profile

minimum initial investment	$3,000	*IRA accounts available*	yes
subsequent minimum investment	$50	*IRA minimum investment*	$250
available in all 50 states	yes	*date of inception*	Mar. 1982
telephone exchanges	yes	*dividend/income paid*	monthly
number of funds in family	29	*average credit quality*	AA

Vanguard Intermediate-Term Tax-Exempt
Vanguard Financial Center
P.O. Box 2600
Valley Forge, PA 19482
(800) 662-7447
www.vanguard.com

total return	★★★★★
risk reduction	★★★★
management	★★★★★
current income	★★★
expense control	★★★★★
symbol VWITX	22 points
up-market performance	very good
down-market performance	fair
predictability of returns	very good

Total Return   ★★★★★
Over the past five years, Vanguard Intermediate-Term Tax-Exempt has taken $10,000 and turned it into $12,990 ($12,340 over three years and $17,980 over the past 10 years). This translates into an annualized return of 5 percent over the past five years, 7 percent over the past three years, and 6 percent for the decade. Over the past five years, this fund has outperformed 80 percent of all mutual funds; within its general category it has done better than 85 percent of its peers. Municipal bond funds have averaged 5 percent annually over these same five years.

During the past five years, a $10,000 initial investment grew to $12,860 after taxes, assuming a 40 percent income tax bracket (state and federal combined) and a capital gains rate of 20 percent. This means that investors in this fund were able to preserve 100 percent of their total returns. Compared to other funds in its category, this fund's tax savings are considered to be excellent.

Risk/Volatility   ★★★★
Over the past five years, Vanguard Intermediate-Term Tax-Exempt has experienced below average risk for its category. Over the past decade, the fund has had two negative years, while the Lehman Brothers Aggregate Bond Index has had two (off 3 percent in 1994 and 1 percent in 1999); the Lehman Brothers Municipal Bond Index also fell twice (off 5 percent in 1994 and 2 percent in 1999). The fund has underperformed the Lehman Brothers Aggregate Bond Index six times and the Lehman Brothers Municipal Bond Index eight times in the past 10 years. Consistency of *overperformance* for this fund has been good.

	last 5 years		last 10 years	
worst year	-0.5%	1999	-2.1%	1994
best year	9.2%	2000	13.6%	1995

During the past five years, the fund's three worst months have been June 1999 (-2 percent), April 2000 (-1 percent), and November 2001 (-1 percent). During the same period, the three best months have been August 2001 (2 percent), December 2000 (2 percent), and May 1998 (1 percent). In the past, Vanguard Intermediate-Term Tax-Exempt has done better than 67 percent of its peer group during the most recent bull market but outperformed just 35 percent of its peer group during the most recent bear market. Consistency, or predictability, of returns for Vanguard Intermediate-Term Tax-Exempt can be described as very good. This fund's risk-adjusted return over the past three/five years ranks in the top-two quintiles.

Management   ★★★★★

There are 1,205 fixed-income securities in this $7 billion portfolio. The average municipal bond fund today is $185 million in size. Close to 95 percent of the fund's holdings are in bonds. The average maturity of the bonds in this account is six years; the weighted coupon rate averages 5 percent. The portfolio's fixed-income holdings can be categorized as intermediate-term, high-quality debt.

Ian A. MacKinnon and Christopher M. Ryon have managed this fund for the past 21 years. Management is not afraid to own bonds from a large number of states. Performance and price movement is extremely correlated to that of the Lehman Brothers Municipal Bond Index. There are 78 funds besides Intermediate-Term Tax-Exempt within the Vanguard family. Overall, the fund family's risk adjusted performance can be described as between good and very good.

Current Income   ★★★

Over the past year, Vanguard Intermediate-Term Tax-Exempt had a 12-month yield of 4.1 percent. During this same 12-month period, the typical municipal bond fund had a yield that averaged 4.0 percent.

Expenses   ★★★★★

Vanguard Intermediate-Term Tax-Exempt's expense ratio is 0.2 percent; it has averaged 0.2 percent annually over the past three calendar years. The average expense ratio for the 1,800 funds in this category is 1.1 percent. This fund's turnover rate over the past year has been 13 percent, while its peer group average has been 36 percent.

Summary

Vanguard Intermediate-Term Tax-Exempt turns in the best three- and five-year return figures in its group. Part of the reason this fund does so well is management's continuing desire to keep costs and turnover rates low. What is somewhat surprising is the fund's low risk level. The fund's overall point score places it among its top competitors.

Profile

minimum initial investment $3,000	*IRA accounts available* . . . . yes
subsequent minimum investment . . $100	*IRA minimum investment* $1,000
available in all 50 states . . . . yes	*date of inception* . . . . Sept. 1977
telephone exchanges . . . . yes	*dividend/income paid* . . . . monthly
number of funds in family 79	*average credit quality* . . . . AA

Vanguard New York Long-Term Tax-Exempt Investor

Vanguard Financial Center
P.O. Box 2600
Valley Forge, PA 19482
(800) 662-7447
www.vanguard.com

total return	★★★★★
risk reduction	★★
management	★★★★
current income	★★★
expense control	★★★★★
symbol VNYTX	19 points
up-market performance	fair
down-market performance	excellent
predictability of returns	fair

Total Return   ★★★★★

Over the past five years, Vanguard New York Long-Term Tax-Exempt Investor has taken $10,000 and turned it into $13,400 ($13,050 over three years and $19,060 over the past 10 years). This translates into an annualized return of 6 percent over the past five years, 9 percent over the past three years, and 7 percent for the decade. Over the past five years, this fund has outperformed 85 percent of all mutual funds; within its general category it has done better than 98 percent of its peers. Municipal bond funds have averaged 5 percent annually over these same five years.

During the past five years, a $10,000 initial investment grew to $13,270 after taxes, assuming a 40 percent income tax bracket (state and federal combined) and a capital gains rate of 20 percent. This means that investors in this fund were able to preserve 99 percent of their total returns. Compared to other funds in its category, this fund's tax savings are considered to be excellent.

Risk/Volatility   ★★

Over the past five years, Vanguard New York Long-Term Tax-Exempt Investor has experienced above average risk for its category. Over the past decade, the fund has had two negative years, while the Lehman Brothers Aggregate Bond Index has had two (off 3 percent in 1994 and 1 percent in 1999); the Lehman Brothers Municipal Bond Index also fell twice (off 5 percent in 1994 and 2 percent in 1999). The fund has underperformed the Lehman Brothers Aggregate Bond Index six times and the Lehman Brothers Municipal Bond Index six times in the past 10 years. Consistency of *overperformance* for this fund has been good.

	last 5 years		last 10 years	
worst year	-3.4%	1999	-5.6%	1994
best year	13.8%	2000	17.7%	1995

During the past five years, the fund's three worst months have been October 1999 (-2 percent), December 2001 (-2 percent), and June 1999 (-2 percent). During the same period, the three best months have been December 2000 (3 percent), March 2000 (2 percent), and June 2000 (2 percent). In the past, Vanguard New York Long-Term Tax-Exempt Investor has only done better than 20 percent of its peer group during the most recent bull market but outperformed 95 percent of its peer group during the most recent bear market. Consistency, or predictability, of returns for Vanguard New York Long-Term Tax-Exempt Investor can be described as fair. This fund's risk-adjusted return over the past three/five years ranks in the top quintile.

Management ★★★★
There are 275 fixed-income securities in this $1 billion portfolio. The average municipal bond fund today is $185 million in size. Close to 100 percent of the fund's holdings are in bonds. The average maturity of the bonds in this account is nine years; the weighted coupon rate averages 5 percent. The portfolio's fixed-income holdings can be categorized as intermediate-term, high-quality debt.

Ian A. MacKinnon and Christopher M. Ryon have managed this fund for the past 17 years. Management has vowed to keep at least 75 percent of the fund's holdings in bonds rated A or higher. Modest interest rate bets are made, but always within a known range. Performance and price movement is extremely correlated to that of the Lehman Brothers Municipal Bond Index. There are 78 funds besides New York Long-Term Tax-Exempt Investor within the Vanguard family. Overall, the fund family's risk adjusted performance can be described as between good and very good.

Current Income ★★★
Over the past year, Vanguard New York Long-Term Tax-Exempt Investor had a 12-month yield of 4.0 percent. During this same 12-month period, the typical municipal bond fund had a yield that averaged 4.0 percent.

Expenses ★★★★★
Vanguard New York Long-Term Tax-Exempt Investor's expense ratio is 0.2 percent; it has averaged 0.2 percent annually over the past three calendar years. The average expense ratio for the 1,800 funds in this category is 1.1 percent. This fund's turnover rate over the past year has been 12 percent, while its peer group average has been 36 percent.

Summary
Vanguard New York Long-Term Tax-Exempt Investor is the only New York municipal bond fund in the book. The fund ranks as number one when it comes to three-year performance figures. The fund is also the number one performer for the past five years.

Profile
minimum initial investment $3,000	*IRA accounts available* . . . . yes
subsequent minimum investment . . $100	*IRA minimum investment* $1,000
available in all 50 states . . . . yes	*date of inception* . . . . Apr. 1986
telephone exchanges . . . . yes	*dividend/income paid* . . . . monthly
number of funds in family 79	*average credit quality* . . . . AAA

Vanguard Short-Term Tax-Exempt
Vanguard Financial Center
P.O. Box 2600
Valley Forge, PA 19482
(800) 662-7447
www.vanguard.com

total return	★★★★
risk reduction	★★★★★
management	★★★★★
current income	★
expense control	★★★★★
symbol VWSTX	20 points
up-market performance	excellent
down-market performance	poor
predictability of returns	excellent

Total Return   ★★★★
Over the past five years, Vanguard Short-Term Tax-Exempt has taken $10,000 and turned it into $12,170 ($11,370 over three years and $14,690 over the past 10 years). This translates into an annualized return of 4 percent over the past five years, 4 percent over the past three years, and 4 percent for the decade. Over the past five years, this fund has outperformed 60 percent of all mutual funds; within its general category it has done better than 30 percent of its peers. Municipal bond funds have averaged 5 percent annually over these same five years.

During the past five years, a $10,000 initial investment grew to $12,170 after taxes, assuming a 40 percent income tax bracket (state and federal combined) and a capital gains rate of 20 percent. This means that investors in this fund were able to preserve 100 percent of their total returns. Compared to other funds in its category, this fund's tax savings are considered to be excellent.

Risk/Volatility   ★★★★★
Over the past five years, Vanguard Short-Term Tax-Exempt has experienced low risk for its category. Over the past decade, the fund has had no negative years, while the Lehman Brothers Aggregate Bond Index has had two (off 3 percent in 1994 and 1 percent in 1999); the Lehman Brothers Municipal Bond Index also fell twice (off 5 percent in 1994 and 2 percent in 1999). The fund has underperformed the Lehman Brothers Aggregate Bond Index seven times and the Lehman Brothers Municipal Bond Index eight times in the past 10 years. Consistency of *overperformance* for this fund has been fair.

	last 5 years		last 10 years	
worst year	2.6%	1999	1.6%	1994
best year	4.9%	2000	6.0%	1995

During the past five years, the fund's three worst months have been June 1999 (-0.4 percent), November 2001 (-0.3 percent), and May 2001 (-0.3 percent). During the same period, the three best months have been January 2001 (1 percent), June 2000 (0.4 percent), and December 2000 (0.4 percent). In the past, Vanguard Short-Term Tax-Exempt has done better than 99 percent of its peer group during the most recent bull market but outperformed just 5 percent of its peer group during the most recent bear market. Consistency, or predictability, of returns for Vanguard Short-Term Tax-Exempt can be described as excellent. This fund's risk-adjusted return over the past three/five years ranks in the bottom-two quintiles.

Management   ★★★★★

There are 360 fixed-income securities in this $2 billion portfolio. The average municipal bond fund today is $185 million in size. Close to 85 percent of the fund's holdings are in bonds. The average maturity of the bonds in this account is 5 years; the weighted coupon rate averages 4 percent. The portfolio's fixed-income holdings can be categorized as short-term, high-quality debt.

Ian A. MacKinnon and Pam Wisehaupt-Tynan have managed this fund for the past 21 years. Management's desire to own short-term bonds along with variable-interest rate notes makes this Vanguard offering almost look like a tax-free money market account. More than 95 percent of the fund's holdings are in fixed-income instruments rated AAA or AA. There are 78 funds besides Short-Term Tax-Exempt within the Vanguard family. Overall, the fund family's risk adjusted performance can be described as between good and very good.

Current Income   ★

Over the past year, Vanguard Short-Term Tax-Exempt had a 12-month yield of 2.7 percent. During this same 12-month period, the typical municipal bond fund had a yield that averaged 4.0 percent.

Expenses   ★★★★★

Vanguard Short-Term Tax-Exempt's expense ratio is 0.2 percent; it has averaged 0.2 percent annually over the past three calendar years. The average expense ratio for the 1,800 funds in this category is 1.1 percent. This fund's turnover rate over the past year has been 47 percent, while its peer group average has been 36 percent.

Summary

Vanguard Short-Term Tax-Exempt has lower risk than any of its peer group by a wide margin. Predictability of returns is also quite high. The fund ties for first place as being the most frugal when it comes to expenses. This is just one of three Vanguard offerings that appear in this section. There is no other fund more highly recommended for the conservative tax-free investor.

Profile

minimum initial investment $3,000	*IRA accounts available* . . . . yes
subsequent minimum investment . . $100	*IRA minimum investment* $1,000
available in all 50 states . . . . yes	*date of inception* . . . . Sept. 1977
telephone exchanges . . . . yes	*dividend/income paid* . . . . monthly
number of funds in family 79	*average credit quality* . . . . AA

Real Estate Funds

Real estate, financial, health care, metals, natural resources, and technology represent some of the most popular sectors for investors. These industry-specific mutual funds hone in on a particular group of stocks and invest accordingly. Each sector has its pluses and minuses; certain sectors, such as technology and metals, are much more volatile than others, such as utilities and natural resources. In the case of real estate, a potential problem for prospective investors is overweighting; that is, committing too much of an overall portfolio to one particular asset group. With this particular sector, defining one's holdings can be difficult.

Securities investors who own residential property must ask themselves if they view their home as an investment, a place to live, or both. Since most people would describe their home as their largest or second-largest asset, the decision as to whether it is "an investment" becomes important. If you view your home as an investment, real estate funds are probably not for you. Similarly, if you own any vacant land or income-producing property, you may already have enough, or even too much, in this one category. However, the case could be made that a real estate fund would provide a homeowner with broad diversification within the category. Real estate funds invest in real estate investment trusts (REITs) that are diversified by category (shopping centers, medical buildings, apartment buildings, etc.) or location (the West, the South, etc.). In addition, if a portfolio were to be weighted too much in any category, real estate would be more desirable than most other sectors.

The risk level for REITs and real estate funds vary significantly. A fund that specializes in mortgages is usually going to be more stable than one that owns land that is yet to be developed. A portfolio comprised of properties from one geographical area is conceptually at greater risk than one that owns land across the country. A fund that owns triple net leased properties is more conservative than a portfolio of apartment buildings.

Over the past 15 years (ending December 31, 2002), real estate funds have underperformed common stocks by 4.1 percent per year, as measured by the Standard & Poor's 500 Stock Index. From 1988 through 2002, real estate funds averaged 10.1 percent, while common stocks averaged 11.5 percent compounded per year. A $10,000 investment in real estate funds grew to $42,400 over the past 15 years; a similar initial investment in the S&P 500 grew to $51,020.

During the past three years, real estate funds have outperformed the S&P 500 by an astounding 27.4 percent per year; the figured drops to 3.4 percent over the last five years. Over the past 10 years, this fund category has underperformed the S&P 500 by an average of 0.5 percent per year. Average turnover during the past three years has been 60 percent.

The price-earnings (p/e) ratio is 21 for the typical real estate fund, versus 25 for the S&P 500. The typical stock in these portfolios is only 5 percent the size of the average stock in the S&P 500. The average beta is 0.2, which means the group has a market-related risk that is 80 percent lower than the S&P 500. The average real estate fund has an amazingly high annual income stream of 3.9 percent. The typical annual expense ratio for this group is 1.6 percent.

Over the past three years, real estate funds have had an average compound return of 12.8 percent per year. The annual return has been 2.8 percent for the past five years, 8.9 percent for the past decade, and 10.1 percent per year for the past 15 years. The standard deviation for this category has been 14 percent over the past three years, versus 16 percent for the S&P 500.

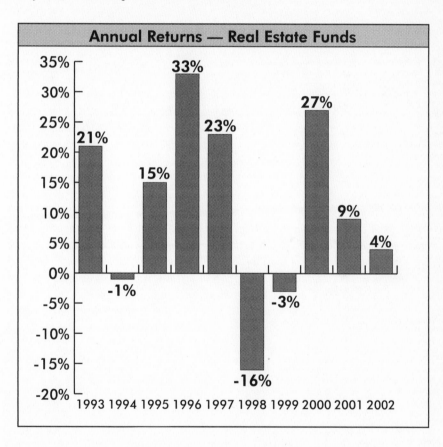

Security Capital U.S. Real Estate

11 South LaSalle Street, 2nd Floor
Chicago, IL 60603
(888) 732-8748
www.securitycapital.com

total return	★★★★★
risk reduction	★★
management	★★★
tax minimization	★★★★
expense control	★★★
symbol SUSIX	17 points
up-market performance	good
down-market performance	poor
predictability of returns	good

Total Return   ★★★★★

Over the past five years, Security Capital U.S. Real Estate has taken $10,000 and turned it into $12,820 ($14,480 over three years). This translates into an annualized return of 5 percent over the past five years and 13 percent over the past three years. Over the past five years, this fund has outperformed 80 percent of all mutual funds; within its general category it has done better than 90 percent of its peers. Real estate funds have averaged 3 percent annually over these same five years.

Risk/Volatility   ★★

Over the past five years, Security Capital U.S. Real Estate has experienced above average risk for its category. Over the past decade, the fund has had two negative years, while the S&P 500 has had three (off 9 percent in 2000, 12 percent in 2001, and 22 percent in 2002); the Wilshire REIT Index fell twice (off 17 percent in 1998 and 3 percent in 1999). The fund has underperformed the S&P 500 seven times and the Wilshire REIT Index six times in the past 10 years. Consistency of *overperformance* for this fund has been good.

	last 5 years		last 10 years	
worst year	-11.9%	1998	-11.9%	1998
best year	35.8%	2000	35.8%	2000

During the past five years, the fund's three worst months have been August 1998 (-10 percent), July 1998 (-7 percent), and September 2001 (-5 percent). During the same period, the three best months have been April 1999 (13 percent), July 2000 (8 percent), and April 2000 (7 percent). In the past, Security Capital U.S. Real Estate has done better than 50 percent of its peer group during the most recent bull market but outperformed just 15 percent of its peer group during the most recent bear market. Consistency, or predictability, of returns for Security Capital U.S. Real Estate can be described as good. This fund's risk-adjusted return over the past three/five years ranks in the top-two quintiles.

Management ★★★

There are 30 stocks in this $210 million portfolio. The average real estate fund today is $105 million in size. Close to 95 percent of the fund's holdings are in stocks. The stocks in this portfolio have an average p/e ratio of 20 and a median market capitalization of $2 billion. The 10 largest holdings compose 55 percent of the fund's total assets. The portfolio's equity holdings can be categorized as mid-cap and value-oriented issues.

A team has managed this fund for the past six years. Management uses a valuation matrix in order to establish guidelines for security price targets. Management is not shy about loading up the portfolio with a small number of sector groups. One of the managers' favorite models is to project cash flows five years into the future. They are particularly concerned with local real estate market conditions. The fund's share price movement has no correlation to that of the S&P 500. There are 16 other funds besides U.S. Real Estate within the Security Capital family. Overall, the fund family's risk adjusted performance can be described as between good and very good.

Tax Minimization ★★★★

During the past five years, a $10,000 initial investment grew to $13,200 after taxes, assuming a 40 percent income tax bracket (state and federal combined) and a capital gains rate of 20 percent. This means that investors in this fund were able to preserve 73 percent of their total returns. Compared to other funds in its category, this fund's tax savings are considered to be very good.

Expenses ★★★

Security Capital U.S. Real Estate's expense ratio is 1.2 percent; it has averaged 1.3 percent annually over the past three calendar years. The average expense ratio for the 150 funds in this category is 1.6 percent. This fund's turnover rate over the past year has been 91 percent, while its peer group average has been 61 percent.

Summary

Security Capital U.S. Real Estate is only one of two funds in its entire category to make the grade. The fund's five-year record is superior but risk has been a little on the high side. Still, consistency has been good and the portfolio has beat out 90 percent of its peers and 80 percent of all mutual funds. Moreover, this offering has only had two negative years over the last decade. Management has a good handle on the local real estate markets. Tax minimization has been quite good. The addition of this kind of real estate fund to your portfolio is a fine idea since real estate has virtually no correlation to common stocks.

Profile

minimum initial investment $1,000	*IRA accounts available* . . . . yes
subsequent minimum investment . . $100	*IRA minimum investment* $500
available in all 50 states . . . . yes	*date of inception* . . . . Dec. 1996
telephone exchanges . . . . yes	*dividend/income paid* . . . . quarterly
number of funds in family 17	*largest sector weighting* . . . . financials

Vanguard REIT Index
Vanguard Financial Center
P.O. Box 2600
Valley Forge, PA 19482
(800) 662-7447
www.vanguard.com

total return	★★★★
risk reduction	★★★
management	★★★★
tax minimization	★★★
expense control	★★★★★
symbol VGSIX	19 points
up-market performance	good
down-market performance	good
predictability of returns	good

Total Return   ★★★★
Over the past five years, Vanguard REIT Index has taken $10,000 and turned it into $11,830 ($14,730 over three years). This translates into an annualized return of 3 percent over the past five years and 14 percent over the past three years. Over the past five years, this fund has outperformed 55 percent of all mutual funds; within its general category it has also done better than 55 percent of its peers. Real estate funds have averaged 3 percent annually over these same five years.

Risk/Volatility   ★★★
Over the past five years, Vanguard REIT Index has experienced average risk for its category. Over the past decade, the fund has had two negative years, while the S&P 500 has had three (off 9 percent in 2000, 12 percent in 2001, and 22 percent in 2002); the Wilshire REIT Index fell twice (off 17 percent in 1998 and 3 percent in 1999). The fund has underperformed the S&P 500 seven times and the Wilshire REIT Index eight times in the past 10 years. Consistency of *overperformance* for this fund has been good.

	last 5 years		last 10 years	
worst year	-16.3%	1998	-16.3%	1998
best year	26.4%	2000	26.4%	2000

During the past five years, the fund's three worst months have been August 1998 (-9 percent), July 1998 (-7 percent), and September 1999 (-6 percent). During the same period, the three best months have been April 1999 (10 percent), July 2000 (9 percent), and April 2000 (7 percent). In the past, Vanguard REIT Index has done better than 45 percent of its peer group during the most recent bull market and outperformed 60 percent of its peer group during the most recent bear market. Consistency, or predictability, of returns for Vanguard REIT Index can be described as good. This fund's risk-adjusted return over the past three/five years ranks in the top-three quintiles.

Management   ★★★★
There are 115 stocks in this $2 billion portfolio. The average real estate fund today
is $105 million in size. Close to 98 percent of the fund's holdings are in stocks. The
stocks in this portfolio have an average p/e ratio of 21 and a median market capitalization of $2 billion. The 10 largest holdings compose 35 percent of the fund's
total assets. The portfolio's equity holdings can be categorized as mid-cap and
value-oriented issues.

George U. Sauter has managed this fund for the past seven years.
Management's goal is to track the performance of the Morgan Stanley REIT Index.
The managers are fairly passive in their approach to security selection. The fund's
share price movement has no correlation to that of the S&P 500. There are 78 funds
besides REIT Index within the Vanguard family. Overall, the fund family's risk
adjusted performance can be described as between good and very good.

Tax Minimization   ★★★
During the past five years, a $10,000 initial investment grew to $13,200 after taxes,
assuming a 40 percent income tax bracket (state and federal combined) and a capital gains rate of 20 percent. This means that investors in this fund were able to preserve 54 percent of their total returns. Compared to other funds in its category, this
fund's tax savings are considered to be good.

Expenses   ★★★★★
Vanguard REIT Index's expense ratio is 0.3 percent; it has averaged 0.3 percent
annually over the past three calendar years. The average expense ratio for the 150
funds in this category is 1.6 percent. This fund's turnover rate over the past year
has been 10 percent, while its peer group average has been 61 percent.

Summary
Vanguard REIT Index is one of only two real estate funds to appear in the book
and its overall ranking is the best. The fund's five-year track record is number one,
while risk-adjusted returns have been right in line with its category average.
Management's goal is to track a widely-based real estate index and by keeping
overhead costs down, investors will not be unpleasantly surprised with the results.
Adding a real estate fund to your portfolio is a good idea since there is little, if any,
correlation between its performance and that of the overall stock market.

Profile
minimum initial investment . . . . . $3,000   *IRA accounts available* . . . . yes
subsequent minimum investment . . $100   *IRA minimum investment* $1,000
available in all 50 states . . . . yes   *date of inception* . . . . May 1996
telephone exchanges . . . . yes   *dividend/income paid* . . . . quarterly
number of funds in family 79   *largest sector weighting* . . . . financials

Technology Funds

Consider the following statistics: The first desktop PC was introduced in 1981, the World Wide Web was invented in Switzerland in 1989, 46 million U.S. adults had Net access in 1997, 98 million U.S. adults had Net access in 1999, and the World Wide Web surpassed 1 billion unique pages in the year 2000. Just five years ago, it would have taken forty-seven minutes to download 1,000 pages; today this transmission takes just seconds.

Around the world, consumers who are rapidly embracing existing hardware and software in areas such as electronics, information technology, and cellular technology are driving the burgeoning need for technology. Technologies once considered highly advanced are now seen as household essentials—with progressively lower prices as a result of mass marketing. Because of intense global competition, lack of pricing flexibility, and tight labor markets, corporations seeking to maintain their profit margins are increasingly investing in technology to enhance productivity.

However, technology stocks are also inherently more volatile and, consequently, riskier than the broad market as well as most, if not all, industry sectors. To demonstrate, let us examine standard deviation, the most common measure of performance volatility, or its tendency to move up or down. The higher the fund's standard deviation, the greater the fund's swings in performance. The standard deviation of returns for technology funds typically is 2.3 times that of the S&P 500 Index (37 vs. 16).

Not all technology stocks are created equal. At the very basic level, Internet-related companies and general, non-Internet technology companies (those that make computers, chips, hard drives, or software) are at very different stages in their evolution. Internet companies are where regular technology companies were 10 to 15 years ago. The instability of Internet companies is what has made these stocks so volatile and so susceptible to momentum. As an example, Morgan Stanley's MOX Index of Internet stocks gained a staggering 514 percent between the end of 1998 and its peak on March 9, 2000, only to give up close to half of those gains over the next several weeks.

Technology stocks represent one of the fastest growing and largest contributors to the S&P 500 Index. At year-end 1999, technology stocks represented 30 percent of the S&P 500 Index and accounted for 80 percent of the Index's overall growth. Eight of the 10 largest contributors to the S&P 500's 1999 return were technology companies.

Technology fund investing can be quite complex. Not only are there more than 360 funds that are specifically in the technology sector, but hundreds more in other categories are also moderately technology oriented. And this may not be the whole story. Just defining technology can be a challenging endeavor.

Since 1986, the technology sector has underperformed the S&P 500 in the following years: 1986 by 11 percent, 1987 by 6 percent, 1988 by 10 percent, 1989 by 10 percent, 1996 by 3 percent, 1997 by 24 percent, by 22 percent in 2000, by 25 percent in 2001, and 21 percent in 2002. However, in 1999, technology funds outperformed the S&P 500 by 114 percent.

The typical price-earnings (p/e) ratio for stocks in this category is 38, a yield of zero, and a standard deviation of 37 percent.

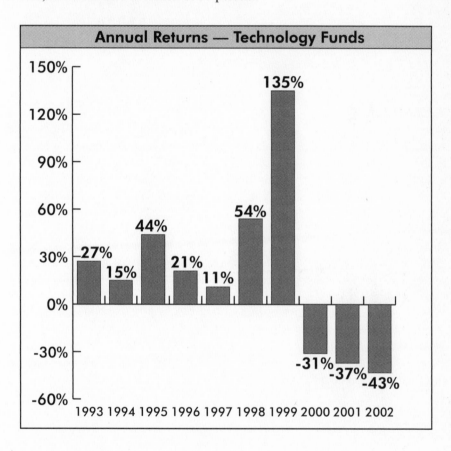

Icon Information Technology
12835 East Arapahoe Road, Tower II
Englewood, CO 80112
(800) 764-0442
www.iconfunds.com

total return	★★★★★
risk reduction	★★★★
management	★★★★★
tax minimization	★★★★
expense control	★★★★★
symbol ICTEX	23 points
up-market performance	poor
down-market performance	excellent
predictability of returns	very good

Total Return   ★★★★★
Over the past five years, Icon Information Technology has taken $10,000 and turned it into $16,440 ($5,820 over three years). This translates into an annualized return of 10 percent over the past five years and -17 percent over the past three years. Over the past five years, this fund has outperformed 99 percent of all mutual funds; within its general category it has done better than 95 percent of its peers. Technology funds have averaged -3 percent annually over these same five years.

Risk/Volatility   ★★★★
Over the past five years, Icon Information Technology has experienced below average risk for its category. Over the past decade, the fund has had two negative years, while the NASDAQ Index has had four (off 3 percent in 1994, 39 percent in 2000, 21 percent in 2001, and 32 percent in 2002); the Russell 2000 also fell four times (off 2 percent in 1994, 3 percent in 1998, 3 percent in 2000, and 20 percent in 2002). The fund has underperformed the NASDAQ Index six times and the Russell 2000 six times in the past 10 years. Consistency of *overperformance* for this fund has been poor.

	last 5 years		last 10 years	
worst year	-41.4%	2002	-41.4%	2002
best year	111%	1999	111%	1999

During the past five years, the fund's three worst months have been December 2000 (-44 percent), September 2001 (-23 percent), and August 1998 (-23 percent). During the same period, the three best months have been February 2000 (21 percent), January 1999 (21 percent), and October 2001 (17 percent). In the past, Icon Information Technology has only done better than 10 percent of its peer group during the most recent bull market but outperformed 91 percent of its peer group during the most recent bear market. Consistency, or predictability, of returns for Icon Information Technology can be described as very good. This fund's risk-adjusted return over the past three/five years ranks in the top quintile.

Management   ★★★★★

There are 55 stocks in this $90 million portfolio. The average technology fund today is $100 million in size. Close to 100 percent of the fund's holdings are in stocks. The stocks in this portfolio have an average p/e ratio of 19 and a median market capitalization of $2 billion. The 10 largest holdings compose 40 percent of the fund's total assets. The portfolio's equity holdings can be categorized as mid-cap and growth-oriented issues.

Craig T. Callahan has managed this fund for the past six years. Management utilizes an all-cap approach while rotating among the 12 industries that comprise the technology sector. When it comes to individual selection, Callahan looks for companies that demonstrate emerging leadership. Valuation calculations are based on current as well as future earnings expectations. The fund's share price movement is moderately correlated to that of the S&P 500. There are 12 funds besides Information Technology within the Icon family. Overall, the fund family's risk adjusted performance can be described as good.

Tax Minimization   ★★★★

During the past five years, a $10,000 initial investment grew to $13,200 after taxes, assuming a 40 percent income tax bracket (state and federal combined) and a capital gains rate of 20 percent. This means that investors in this fund were able to preserve 86 percent of their total returns. Compared to other funds in its category, this fund's tax savings are considered to be very good.

Expenses   ★★★★★

Icon Information Technology's expense ratio is 1.3 percent; it has averaged 1.3 percent annually over the past three calendar years. The average expense ratio for the 355 funds in this category is 2.0 percent. This fund's turnover rate over the past year has been 190 percent, while its peer group average has been 215 percent.

Summary

Icon Information Technology has trounced its colleagues when it comes to performance over the past half decade. The fund has averaged more than 10 percent a year over the last five years while its peers have averaged negative numbers. Investors who are concerned with keeping their profits will love this fund because of its high tax efficiency. Management clearly has the pulse of the marketplace; the portfolio has done a superb job during the most recent bear market. The fund's overall score makes it the best choice in its category of more than 350 possibilities.

Profile

minimum initial investment $1,000	*IRA accounts available* . . . . yes
subsequent minimum investment . . $100	*IRA minimum investment* $1,000
available in all 50 states . . . . yes	*date of inception* . . . . Feb. 1997
telephone exchanges . . . . yes	*dividend/income paid* . . . . annually
number of funds in family 13	*largest sector weighting* . . . . consumer durables

Seligman Communications & Information A

100 Park Avenue
New York, NY 10017
(800) 221-2783
www.seligman.com

total return	★★★★
risk reduction	★★★★
management	★★★★
tax minimization	★★★★★
expense control	★★★★★
symbol SLMCX	22 points
up-market performance	poor
down-market performance	excellent
predictability of returns	very good

Total Return   ★★★★

Over the past five years, Seligman Communications & Information A has taken $10,000 and turned it into $9,560 ($4,090 over three years and $34,490 over the past 10 years). This translates into an annualized return of -1 percent over the past five years, -26 percent over the past three years, and 13 percent for the decade. Over the past five years, this fund has outperformed 35 percent of all mutual funds; within its general category it has done better than 60 percent of its peers. Technology funds have averaged -3 percent annually over these same five years.

Risk/Volatility   ★★★★

Over the past five years, Seligman Communications & Information A has experienced below average risk for its category. Over the past decade, the fund has had two negative years, while the NASDAQ Index has had four (off 3 percent in 1994, 39 percent in 2000, 21 percent in 2001, and 32 percent in 2002); the Russell 2000 also fell four times (off 2 percent in 1994, 3 percent in 1998, 3 percent in 2000, and 20 percent in 2002). The fund has underperformed the NASDAQ Index four times and the Russell 2000 three times in the past 10 years. Consistency of *overperformance* for this fund has been very good.

	last 5 years		last 10 years	
worst year	-37.5%	2000	-37.5%	2000
best year	74.5%	1999	74.5%	1999

During the past five years, the fund's three worst months have been November 2000 (-30 percent), August 1998 (-22 percent), and February 2001 (-20 percent). During the same period, the three best months have been January 2001 (24 percent), April 2001 (24 percent), and February 2000 (17 percent). In the past, Seligman Communications & Information A has only done better than 20 percent of its peer group during the most recent bull market and outperformed 85 percent of its peer group during the most recent bear market. Consistency, or predictability, of returns for Seligman Communications & Information A can be described as very good.

This fund's risk-adjusted return over the past three/five years ranks in the top-two quintiles.

Management   ★★★★
There are 125 stocks in this $2 billion portfolio. The average technology fund today is $100 million in size. Close to 85 percent of the fund's holdings are in stocks. The stocks in this portfolio have an average p/e ratio of 28 and a median market capitalization of $3 billion. The 10 largest holdings compose 50 percent of the fund's total assets. The portfolio's equity holdings can be categorized as mid-cap and growth-oriented issues.

Paul H. Wick has managed this fund for the past 13 years. Management's two biggest criteria are decent valuations coupled with good growth prospects. Wick is hesitant to own companies that do not generate cash. The fund's share price movement is fairly correlated to that of the S&P 500. There are 34 funds besides Communications & Information within the Seligman family. Overall, the fund family's risk adjusted performance can be described as fair.

Tax Minimization   ★★★★★
During the past five years, a $10,000 initial investment dropped in value. This means that investors in this fund had a taxable loss. A loss means that there were no negative tax consequences. Since a loss does not result in any kind of tax liability, technically the fund's tax efficiency, not performance, has been excellent.

Expenses   ★★★★★
Seligman Communications & Information A's expense ratio is 1.4 percent; it has averaged 1.4 percent annually over the past three calendar years. The average expense ratio for the 355 funds in this category is 2.0 percent. This fund's turnover rate over the past year has been 123 percent, while its peer group average has been 215 percent.

Summary
Seligman Communications & Information A has done surprisingly well during the most recent bear market. Returns over the last three years look terrible, but not when compared to its 350+ category average. Risk has been comparatively low, although one needs to understand that this group sports tremendously high volatility. Still, the long-term investor who can live with the inevitable ups and downs of this kind of offering should be rewarded.

Profile
minimum initial investment $2,500
subsequent minimum investment . . $100
available in all 50 states . . . . yes
telephone exchanges . . . . yes
number of funds in family 35

IRA accounts available . . . . yes
IRA minimum investment $1,000
date of inception . . . . Jun. 1983
dividend/income paid . . . . annually
largest sector weighting . . . technology

Utility Stock Funds

Utility stock funds look for both growth and income, investing in common stocks of utility companies across the country. Somewhere between one-third and one-half of these funds' total returns come from common stock dividends. Utility funds normally stay away from speculative issues, focusing instead on well-established companies with solid histories of paying good dividends. The goal of most of these funds is long-term growth.

Utility, metals, natural resources, health care/biotech, and technology funds are the only sector, or specialty, fund categories in this book. Most investors should avoid funds that invest in a single industry, or sector, for two reasons. First, you limit the fund manager's ability to find attractive stocks or bonds if he or she is only able to choose securities from one particular geographic area or industry. Second, the track record of sector funds as a whole is pretty bad. In fact, as a general category, these specialty funds represent the worst of both worlds: above-average risk and substandard returns. If you find the term *aggressive growth* unappealing, then the words *sector fund* should positively appall you.

Utility funds are the one exception. They sound safe and they are safe. In fact, over the past 10 years (ending December 31, 2002), this category has only experienced three down years (-9 percent in 1994, -21 percent in 2001, and -24 percent in 2002). Any category of stocks that somewhat relies on dividends generated automatically has a built-in safety cushion. A comparatively high dividend income means that you have to worry less about the appreciation of the underlying issues.

Four factors generally determine the profitability of a utility company: (1) how much it pays for energy, (2) the general level of interest rates, (3) its expected use of nuclear power, and (4) the political climate.

The prices of oil and gas are passed directly to the consumer, but the utility companies are sensitive to this issue. Higher fuel prices mean that the utility industry has less latitude to increase its profit margins. Thus, higher fuel prices can mean smaller profits and/or dividends to investors.

Next to energy costs, interest expense is the industry's greatest expense. Utility companies are heavily debt-laden. Their interest costs directly affect their profitability. When rates go down and companies are able to refinance their debt, the savings can be staggering. Paying 7 percent interest on a couple of hundred million dollars' worth of bonds each year is much more appealing than having to pay 9 percent on the same amount of debt. A lower interest-rate environment translates into more money being left over for shareholders.

Depending on how you look at it, nuclear power has been an issue or problem for the United States for a few decades now. Other countries seem to have come to grips with the matter, yet we remain divided. Although new power plants have not been successfully proposed or built in this country for several years, no one knows what the future may hold. Venturing into nuclear power always seems to be much more expensive than anticipated by the utility companies and the independent experts they rely on for advice. Because of these uncertainties, mutual fund managers try to seek out utility companies that have no foreseeable plans to develop any or more nuclear power facilities. Whether this will help the nation in the long run remains to be seen, but such avoidance keeps share prices more stable and predictable.

Finally, the political climate is an important concern when calculating whether utility funds should be part of your portfolio. The Public Utilities Commission (PUC) is a political animal and can directly reflect the views of a state's government. Utility bills are something most of us are concerned with and aware of; the powers that be are more likely to be re-elected if they are able to keep rate increases to a minimum. Modest, or minimum, increases can be healthy for the utility companies; freezing rates for a couple of years is a bad sign.

Nearly 110 funds make up the utilities category. More than 88 percent of a typical utility fund's portfolio is in common stocks, with the balance in bonds, convertibles, and money market instruments. The typical utility fund has about 11 percent of its holdings in foreign stocks.

Over the past three years, utility funds have had an average compound return of *negative* 13.2 percent per year; the annual return for the past five years has been -2.0 percent. For the past 10 and 15 years, these funds have averaged 4.8 percent and 7.8 percent, respectively. The standard deviation for utility funds has been 15.3 percent over the past three years. This means that these funds have been less volatile than any other stock category except real estate (14.1 percent) and equity-income funds (15.1 percent). The average annual expense ratio for this category is 1.5 percent and the typical yield is 2.5 percent.

Usually, utility stock prices closely follow the long-term bond market. If long-term interest rates go up, utility stock prices are likely to go down. Utility stocks are also vulnerable to a general stock market decline, although they are considered less risky than other types of common stock because of their dividends and the monopoly position of most utilities. Typically, utilities have fallen about two-thirds as much as other common stocks during market downturns.

Worldwide, there is a tremendous opportunity for growth in this industry. The average per-capita production of electricity in many developing countries is only one-fifth that of the United States. The electrical output per capita in the United States is 12,100 kilowatt-hours, compared to 2,500 kilowatt-hours for developing nations. This disparity may well be on the way out. All over the world, previously underdeveloped countries are making economic strides as they move toward free market systems.

When emerging countries become developed economically, their citizens demand higher standards of living. As a result, their requirements for electricity, water, and telephones tend to rise dramatically. Moreover, many countries are selling their utility companies to public owners, opening a new arena for investors. The net result of all of this for you, the investor, is that fund groups are beginning to offer global utility funds. This increased diversification—allowing a fund to invest in utility companies all over the world instead of just in the United States—coupled with tremendous long-term growth potential should make this a dynamic industry group. Utility funds are a good choice for the investor who wants a hedge against inflation but is still afraid or distrustful of the stock market in general.

Beta, which measures the market-related risk of a stock, is only 0.6 for utility funds as a group (compared to 1.0 for the S&P 500). This means that when it comes to stock market risk, utilities have only 60 percent the risk of the S&P 500. Keep in mind, however, that other risks, such as rising interest rates, also need to be evaluated whenever utilities are being considered.

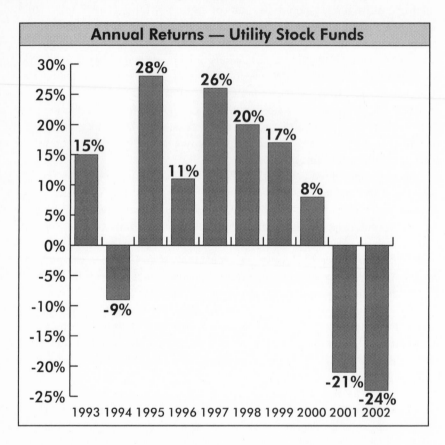

AXP Utilities A

IDS Tower 10
Minneapolis, MN 55440
(800) 328-8300
www.americanexpress.com

total return	★★★★
risk reduction	★★★
management	★★★★
tax minimization	★★★★★
expense control	★★★★
symbol INUTX	20 points
up-market performance	good
down-market performance	good
predictability of returns	good

Total Return   ★★★★

Over the past five years, AXP Utilities A has taken $10,000 and turned it into $9,800 ($7,340 over three years and $19,710 over the past 10 years). This translates into an annualized return of 0 percent over the past five years, -10 percent over the past three years, and 7 percent for the decade. Over the past five years, this fund has outperformed 35 percent of all mutual funds; within its general category it has done better than 75 percent of its peers. Utility stock funds have averaged -2 percent annually over these same five years.

Risk/Volatility   ★★★

Over the past five years, AXP Utilities A has experienced average risk for its category. Over the past decade, the fund has had three negative years, while the S&P 500 has had three (off 9 percent in 2000, 12 percent in 2001, and 22 percent in 2002). The fund has underperformed the S&P 500 seven times in the past 10 years. Consistency of *overperformance* for this fund has been very good.

	last 5 years		last 10 years	
worst year	-21.5%	2002	-21.5%	2002
best year	22.8%	1998	29.0%	1997

During the past five years, the fund's three worst months have been June 2001 (-8 percent), January 2001 (-7 percent), and August 1998 (-5 percent). During the same period, the three best months have been August 2000 (9 percent), March 1998 (8 percent), and September 2000 (7 percent). In the past, AXP Utilities A has done better than 40 percent of its peer group during the most recent bull market and outperformed 50 percent of its peer group during the most recent bear market. Consistency, or predictability, of returns for AXP Utilities A can be described as good. This fund's risk-adjusted return over the past three/five years ranks in the top-three quintiles.

Management   ★★★★
There are 80 stocks in this $790 million portfolio. The average utility stock fund today is $130 million in size. Close to 90 percent of the fund's holdings are in stocks. The stocks in this portfolio have an average p/e ratio of 19 and a median market capitalization of $8 billion. The 10 largest holdings compose 35 percent of the fund's total assets. The portfolio's equity holdings can be categorized as mid-cap and value-oriented issues.

Bern Fleming has managed this fund for the past eight years. Management is considered fairly conservative, yet the portfolio includes electric utilities as well as telecom. This rather broad exposure has helped out the fund at times when other utility offerings have not fared so well. The fund's share price movement has no correlation to that of the S&P 500. There are 48 funds besides Utilities within the American Express Financial family. Overall, the fund family's risk adjusted performance can be described as between fair and good.

Tax Minimization   ★★★★★
During the past five years, a $10,000 initial investment dropped in value. This means that investors in this fund had a taxable loss. A loss means that there were no negative tax consequences. Since a loss does not result in any kind of tax liability, technically the fund's tax efficiency, not performance, has been excellent.

Expenses   ★★★★
AXP Utilities A's expense ratio is 1 percent; it has averaged 1 percent annually over the past three calendar years. The average expense ratio for the 100 funds in this category is 1.5 percent. This fund's turnover rate over the past year has been 85 percent, while its peer group average has been 108 percent.

Summary
AXP Utilities A has turned in negative results over the last three and five years, but the returns have still been better than its peer group. Risk levels have been average, while expenses and turnover have been on the low side. The fund has virtually no correlation to that of the general stock market, making this a fine addition to a diversified portfolio.

Profile
minimum initial investment $2,000	*IRA accounts available* . . . . yes
subsequent minimum investment . . $100	*IRA minimum investment* $100
available in all 50 states . . . . yes	*date of inception* . . . . Aug. 1988
telephone exchanges . . . . yes	*dividend/income paid* . . . . quarterly
number of funds in family 49	*largest sector weighting* . . . . . industrial cyclicals

Morgan Stanley Global Utilities B
P.O. Box 2798
Boston, MA, 02208
(800) 869-3863
www.deanwitter.com

total return	★★★★★
risk reduction	★★★★
management	★★★★
tax minimization	★★★★★
expense control	★★★
symbol GUTBX	21 points
up-market performance	poor
down-market performance	very good
predictability of returns	excellent

Total Return   ★★★★★
Over the past five years, Morgan Stanley Global Utilities B has taken $10,000 and turned it into $10,920 ($6,350 over three years). This translates into an annualized return of 2 percent over the past five years and -14 percent over the past three years. Over the past five years, this fund has outperformed 45 percent of all mutual funds; within its general category it has done better than 90 percent of its peers. Utility stock funds have averaged -2 percent annually over these same five years.

Risk/Volatility   ★★★★
Over the past five years, Morgan Stanley Global Utilities B has experienced average risk for its category. Over the past decade, the fund has had two negative years, while the S&P 500 has had three (off 9 percent in 2000, 12 percent in 2001, and 22 percent in 2002). The fund has underperformed the S&P 500 six times in the past 10 years. Consistency of *overperformance* for this fund has been very good.

	last 5 years		last 10 years	
worst year	-24.3%	2001	-24.3%	2001
best year	37.6%	1998	37.6%	1998

During the past five years, the fund's three worst months have been August 1998 (-10 percent), June 2001 (-9 percent), and June 2000 (-7 percent). During the same period, the three best months have been March 1998 (10 percent), October 1999 (7 percent), and April 2001 (6 percent). In the past, Morgan Stanley Global Utilities B has only done better than 15 percent of its peer group during the most recent bull market but outperformed 65 percent of its peer group during the most recent bear market. Consistency, or predictability, of returns for Morgan Stanley Global Utilities B can be described as excellent. This fund's risk-adjusted return over the past three/five years ranks in the top-two quintiles.

Management   ★★★★
There are 40 stocks in this $340 million portfolio. The average utility stock fund today is $130 million in size. Close to 95 percent of the fund's holdings are in stocks. The stocks in this portfolio have an average p/e ratio of 18 and a median market capitalization of $8 billion. The 10 largest holdings compose 40 percent of the fund's total assets. The portfolio's equity holdings can be categorized as large-cap and value-oriented issues.

Edward F. Gaylor and Andrew Arbenz have managed this fund for the past six years. Management is not afraid to embrace a theme, be it a heavy weighting in global issues or telecom and then abandoning such themes when it feels the time is right. The fund's share price movement is only modestly correlated to that of the S&P 500. There are 63 funds besides Global Utilities within the Morgan Stanley family. Overall, the fund family's risk adjusted performance can be described as good.

Tax Minimization   ★★★★★
During the past five years, a $10,000 initial investment grew to $13,200 after taxes, assuming a 40 percent income tax bracket (state and federal combined) and a capital gains rate of 20 percent. This means that investors in this fund were able to preserve 72 percent of their total returns. Compared to other funds in its category, this fund's tax savings are considered to be excellent.

Expenses   ★★★
Morgan Stanley Global Utilities B's expense ratio is 1.8 percent; it has averaged 1.8 percent annually over the past three calendar years. The average expense ratio for the 100 funds in this category is 1.5 percent. This fund's turnover rate over the past year has been 19 percent, while its peer group average has been 108 percent.

Summary
Morgan Stanley Global Utilities B is only one of four utility funds to make the book and it is the only one with a global emphasis. The fund's five-year track record is one of the best of the bunch while its risk level has been below average. In fact, over the last three years the portfolio's risk level has ranked the lowest. Consistency of returns is also better than any of its contemporaries. Tax efficiency has been super.

Profile
minimum initial investment $1,000
subsequent minimum investment . . $100
available in all 50 states . . . . yes
telephone exchanges . . . . yes
number of funds in family 64

IRA accounts available . . . . yes
IRA minimum investment $1,000
date of inception . . . . Jun. 1994
dividend/income paid . . . . quarterly
largest sector weighting . . . . . industrial
cyclicals

Prudential Utility A
One Seaport Plaza
New York, NY 10292
(800) 225-1852
www.prudential.com

total return	★★★★
risk reduction	★
management	★★★
tax minimization	★★★★★
expense control	★★★★★
symbol PRUAX	18 points
up-market performance	very good
down-market performance	fair
predictability of returns	fair

Total Return   ★★★★
Over the past five years, Prudential Utility A has taken $10,000 and turned it into $9,390 ($8,370 over three years and $19,730 over the past 10 years). This translates into an annualized return of -1 percent over the past five years, -6 percent over the past three years, and 7 percent for the decade. Over the past five years, this fund has outperformed 30 percent of all mutual funds; within its general category it has done better than 65 percent of its peers. Utility stock funds have averaged -2 percent annually over these same five years.

Risk/Volatility   ★
Over the past five years, Prudential Utility A has experienced average risk for its category. Over the past decade, the fund has had three negative years, while the S&P 500 has had three (off 9 percent in 2000, 12 percent in 2001, and 22 percent in 2002). The fund has underperformed the S&P 500 eight times in the past 10 years. Consistency of *overperformance* for this fund has been fair.

	last 5 years		last 10 years	
worst year	-26.0%	2002	-26.0%	2002
best year	40.0%	2000	40.0%	2000

During the past five years, the fund's three worst months have been September 2001 (-14 percent), November 1999 (-11 percent), and August 1998 (-8 percent). During the same period, the three best months have been September 1998 (9 percent), August 2000 (8 percent), and April 1999 (8 percent). In the past, Prudential Utility A has done better than 80 percent of its peer group during the most recent bull market but outperformed just 25 percent of its peer group during the most recent bear market. Consistency, or predictability, of returns for Prudential Utility A can be described as fair. This fund's risk-adjusted return over the past three/five years ranks in the top-two quintiles.

Management   ★★★
There are 95 stocks in this $2 billion portfolio. The average utility stock fund today is $130 million in size. Close to 100 percent of the fund's holdings are in stocks. The stocks in this portfolio have an average p/e ratio of 19 and a median market capitalization of $5 billion. The 10 largest holdings compose 35 percent of the fund's total assets. The portfolio's equity holdings can be categorized as mid-cap and value-oriented issues.

David A. Kiefer and Shaun Hong have managed this fund for the past nine years. Management looks to companies trading at discounts to their industry peers. A buy-and-hold strategy is frequently maintained. The managers stay conservative by favoring companies with healthy balance sheets and strong earnings growth. The fund's share price movement has very little correlation to that of the S&P 500. There are 36 funds besides Utility within the Prudential Funds family. Overall, the fund family's risk adjusted performance can be described as good.

Tax Minimization   ★★★★★
During the past five years, a $10,000 initial investment dropped in value. This means that investors in this fund had a taxable loss. A loss means that there were no negative tax consequences. Since a loss does not result in any kind of tax liability, technically the fund's tax efficiency, not performance, has been excellent.

Expenses   ★★★★★
Prudential Utility A's expense ratio is 0.8 percent; it has averaged 0.8 percent annually over the past three calendar years. The average expense ratio for the 100 funds in this category is 1.5 percent. This fund's turnover rate over the past year has been 40 percent, while its peer group average has been 108 percent.

Summary
Prudential Utility A has been a leader when it comes to keeping overhead costs down. The fund's turnover rate is well under half its group's average. Price movement has very little correlation to that of the overall market, making this a smart choice for portfolio diversification and risk reduction. The fund's value approach coupled with management's philosophy makes this a good choice for the traditional conservative utility investor.

Profile

minimum initial investment $1,000	*IRA accounts available* . . . . yes
subsequent minimum investment . . $100	*IRA minimum investment* $100
available in all 50 states . . . . yes	*date of inception* . . . . Jan. 1990
telephone exchanges . . . . yes	*dividend/income paid* . . . . quarterly
number of funds in family 37	*largest sector weighting*. . . . . industrial cyclicals

Strong Dividend Income
P.O. Box 2936
Milwaukee, WI 53201
(800) 368-1030
www.strongfunds.com

total return	★★★★★
risk reduction	★★★★
management	★★★★★
tax minimization	★★★★★
expense control	★★★★
symbol SDVIX	23 points
up-market performance	good
down-market performance	excellent
predictability of returns	good

Total Return   ★★★★★
Over the past five years, Strong Dividend Income has taken $10,000 and turned it into $10,980 ($9,070 over three years). This translates into an annualized return of 2 percent over the past five years and -3 percent over the past three years. Over the past five years, this fund has outperformed 90 percent of all mutual funds; within its general category it has done better than 95 percent of its peers. Utility stock funds have averaged -2 percent annually over these same five years.

Risk/Volatility   ★★★★
Over the past five years, Strong Dividend Income has experienced below average risk for its category. Over the past decade, the fund has had three negative years, while the S&P 500 has had three (off 9 percent in 2000, 12 percent in 2001, and 22 percent in 2002). The fund has underperformed the S&P 500 seven times in the past 10 years. Consistency of *overperformance* for this fund has been very good.

	last 5 years		last 10 years	
worst year	-19.8%	2002	-19.8%	2002
best year	27.3%	2000	37%	1995

During the past five years, the fund's three worst months have been December 1999 (-13 percent), February 2000 (-9 percent), and January 2001 (-6 percent). During the same period, the three best months have been March 2000 (11 percent), April 1999 (10 percent), and September 1998 (9 percent). In the past, Strong Dividend Income has done better than 50 percent of its peer group during the most recent bull market and outperformed 85 percent of its peer group during the most recent bear market. Consistency, or predictability, of returns for Strong Dividend Income can be described as good. This fund's risk-adjusted return over the past three/five years ranks in the top quintile.

Management ★★★★★

There are 70 stocks in this $160 million portfolio. The average utility stock fund today is $130 million in size. Close to 95 percent of the fund's holdings are in stocks. The stocks in this portfolio have an average p/e ratio of 18 and a median market capitalization of $35 billion. The 10 largest holdings compose 35 percent of the fund's total assets. The portfolio's equity holdings can be categorized as large-cap and value-oriented issues.

A team has managed this fund for the past 10 years. Management likes to own inexpensive, dividend-paying stocks from a number of different industry groups. The fund's share price movement has almost no correlation to that of the S&P 500. There are 58 funds besides Dividend Income within the Strong family. Overall, the fund family's risk adjusted performance can be described as good.

Tax Minimization ★★★★★

During the past five years, a $10,000 initial investment grew to $10,830 after taxes, assuming a 40 percent income tax bracket (state and federal combined) and a capital gains rate of 20 percent. This means that investors in this fund were able to preserve 85 percent of their total returns. Compared to other funds in its category, this fund's tax savings are considered to be excellent.

Expenses ★★★★

Strong Dividend Income's expense ratio is 1.1 percent; it has averaged 1.1 percent annually over the past three calendar years. The average expense ratio for the 100 funds in this category is 1.5 percent. This fund's turnover rate over the past year has been 77 percent, while its peer group average has been 108 percent.

Summary

Strong Dividend Income is not only just one of four utility funds to be included in the book, its overall ranking makes it the best choice. Returns over the last five years have been positive, even though its peer group average has been negative. The fund's performance over the past three and five years have beaten out those of its colleagues. Risk over the last half decade has been below average and again has been better than its competitors. Tax efficiency has been excellent.

Profile

minimum initial investment $2,500
subsequent minimum investment . . . $50
available in all 50 states . . . . yes
telephone exchanges . . . . yes
number of funds in family 59

IRA accounts available . . . . yes
IRA minimum investment $1,000
date of inception . . . . Jul. 1993
dividend/income paid . . . . quarterly
largest sector weighting. . . . . industrial
cyclicals

World Bond Funds

Global, or world, funds invest in securities issued all over the world, including the United States. A global bond fund usually invests in bonds issued by stable governments from a handful of countries. These funds try to avoid purchasing foreign government debt instruments from politically or economically unstable nations. Foreign, also known as international, bond funds invest in debt instruments from countries other than the United States.

International funds purchase securities issued in a foreign currency, such as the Japanese yen or the British pound. Prospective investors need to be aware of the potential changes in the value of the foreign currency relative to the U.S. dollar. As an example, if you were to invest in U.K. pound-denominated bonds with a yield of 15 percent and the British currency appreciated 12 percent against the U.S. dollar, your total return for the year would be 27 percent. If the British pound declined by 20 percent against the U.S. dollar, your total return would be -5 percent (15 percent yield minus 20 percent).

Since foreign markets do not necessarily move in tandem with U.S. markets, each country represents varying investment opportunities at different times. According to Salomon Brothers, the current value of the world bond market is estimated to be over $24 trillion. About 40 percent of this bond marketplace is made up of U.S. bonds; Japan ranks a distant second.

Assessing the economic environment to evaluate its effects on interest rates and bond values requires an understanding of two important factors: inflation and supply. During inflationary periods, when there is too much money chasing too few goods, government tightening of the money supply helps create a balance between an economy's cash resources and its available goods. Money supply refers to the amount of cash made available for spending, borrowing, or investing. Controlled by the central banks of each nation, the money supply is the primary tool used to manage inflation, interest rates, and economic growth.

A prudent tightening of the money supply can help bring on disinflation—decelerated loan demand, reduced durable goods orders, and falling prices. During disinflationary times, interest rates also fall, strengthening the underlying value of existing bonds. While such factors ultimately contribute to a healthier economy, they also mean lower yields for government bond investors. A trend toward disinflation currently exists in markets around the world.

As the United States and other governments implement policies designed to reduce inflation, interest rates are stabilizing. This disinflation can be disquieting to the individual who specifically invests for high monthly income. In reality, falling interest rates mean higher bond values, and investors seeking long-term growth or high total returns can therefore benefit from declining rates. Inflation, which drives interest rates higher, is the true enemy of bond investors. It diminishes bond values and, in addition, erodes the buying power of the interest income investors receive.

Income-seeking investors need to find economies in which inflation is coming under control, yet interest rates are still high enough to provide favorable bond yields. An investor who has only U.S. bonds is not taking advantage of such opportunities. If global disinflationary trends continue, those who remain invested only in the United States can lose out on opportunities for high income and total return elsewhere. The gradually decreasing yields on U.S. bonds compel the investor who seeks high income to think globally.

While not all bond markets will peak at the same level, they do tend to follow patterns. Targeting those countries in which interest rates are at peak levels and inflation is falling not only results in higher income but also creates significant potential for capital appreciation as rates ultimately decline and bond prices increase.

Each year since 1984, at least three government bond markets have provided yields higher than those available in the United States. With more than 60 percent of the world's bonds found outside the United States, investors must look beyond U.S. borders to find bonds offering yields and total returns that meet their investment objectives.

According to Salomon Brothers, over the past three years, international bonds have underperformed U.S. bonds by an average of 4.1 percent per year; the figure drops to 1.8 percent over the past five years. Over the past 10 years, the figure drops to an average of 0.9 percent per year and then rises to 1.3 percent per year over the past 15 years (all periods ending December 31, 2002).

Even with high income as the primary goal (these funds have a typical yield of roughly 4.9 percent annually), investors must consider credit and market risk. By investing primarily in mutual funds that purchase government-guaranteed bonds from the world's most creditworthy nations, you can get an extra measure of credit safety for payment of interest and repayment of principal. By diversifying across multiple markets, fund managers can significantly reduce market risk as well. Diversification is a proven technique for controlling market risk.

The long-term success of a global bond manager depends on expertise in assessing economic trends from country to country, as well as protecting the U.S. valuation of foreign holdings. The most effective way to protect the U.S. dollar value of international holdings is through active currency management. Although its effects over a 10-year period are nominal at best, currency fluctuations can help returns over a one-, three-, or five-year period.

In the simplest terms, effective currency management provides exposure to bond markets worldwide, while reducing the effects of adverse currency changes that can lower bond values. If a portfolio manager anticipates that the U.S. dollar will strengthen, he or she can lock in a currency exchange rate to protect the fund against a decline in the value of its foreign holdings. (A strong dollar means that other currencies are declining in value.) This strategy is commonly referred to as hedging the exposure of the portfolio. If, on the other hand, the manager expects the U.S. dollar to weaken, the fund can stay unhedged to allow it to benefit from the increasing value of foreign currencies. As good as hedging sounds, there is a cost to hedging and, on balance, this cost over time more than wipes out any benefit.

Investing in global bonds gives you the potential for capital appreciation during periods of declining interest rates. An inverse relationship exists between bond values and interest rates. When interest rates fall, as is the case in most bond markets in the world today, existing bond values climb. Conversely, as interest rates rise, the value of existing bonds declines (they are less desirable since "new" bonds have a higher current yield).

Over the past three and five years, global bond funds have had an average compound return of 6.7 and 4.7 percent per year, respectively; the annual returns for the past 10 and 15 years have been 6.2 for both periods. The standard deviation for global bond funds has been 8.3 percent over the past three years. This means that these funds have been less volatile than any equity fund but more than twice as volatile than any other bond category except high-yield (standard deviation of 9.4 percent). Just 190 funds make up the global bond category. These funds have an average expense ratio of 1.4 percent, a 4.9 percent yield, and an annual turnover rate of a staggering 230 percent.

Global bond funds, particularly those with high concentrations in foreign issues, are an excellent risk-reduction tool that should be utilized by a wide range of investors.

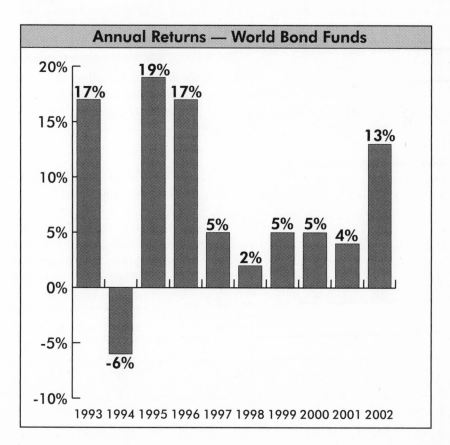

Credit Suisse Global Fixed-Income
466 Lexington Avenue
New York, NY 10017
(800) 927-2874
www.csam.com

total return	★★★★★
risk reduction	★★★★
management	★★★★★
current income	★★★★
expense control	★★★★
symbol CGFIX	22 points
up-market performance	good
down-market performance	good
predictability of returns	excellent

Total Return   ★★★★★
Over the past five years, Credit Suisse Global Fixed-Income has taken $10,000 and turned it into $13,280 ($12,200 over three years and $19,560 over the past 10 years). This translates into an annualized return of 6 percent over the past five years, 7 percent over the past three years, and 7 percent for the decade. Over the past five years, this fund has outperformed 70 percent of all mutual funds; within its general category it has done better than 60 percent of its peers. World bond funds have averaged 5 percent annually over these same five years.

During the past five years, a $10,000 initial investment grew to $11,200 after taxes, assuming a 40 percent income tax bracket (state and federal combined) and a capital gains rate of 20 percent. This means that investors in this fund were able to preserve 69 percent of their total returns. Compared to other funds in its category, this fund's tax savings are considered to be very good.

Risk/Volatility   ★★★★
Over the past five years, Credit Suisse Global Fixed-Income has experienced below average risk for its category. Over the past decade, the fund has had one negative year, while the Lehman Brothers Aggregate Bond Index has had two (off 3 percent in 1994 and 1 percent in 1999); the Salomon Brothers World Government Bond Index also fell twice (off 4 percent in 1999 and less than 1 percent in 2001). The fund has underperformed the Lehman Brothers Aggregate Bond Index seven times and the Salomon Brothers World Government Bond Index four times in the past 10 years. Consistency of *overperformance* for this fund has been good.

	last 5 years		last 10 years	
worst year	0.4%	1999	-5.5%	1994
best year	10.2%	2002	19.6%	1993

During the past five years, the fund's three worst months have been December 2001 (-3 percent), May 1999 (-2 percent), and December 1998 (-2 percent). During the same period, the three best months have been September 1998 (2 percent), November 1998 (2 percent), and April 1999 (2 percent). In the past, Credit Suisse Global Fixed-Income has done better than 45 percent of its peer group during the most recent bull market and outperformed 55 percent of its peer group during the most recent bear market. Consistency, or predictability, of returns for Credit Suisse Global Fixed-Income can be described as excellent. This fund's risk-adjusted return over the past three/five years ranks in the top-two quintiles.

Management ★★★★★
There are 205 fixed-income securities in this $110 million portfolio. The average world bond fund today is $100 million in size. Close to 65 percent of the fund's holdings are in bonds. The average maturity of the bonds in this account is eight years; the weighted coupon rate averages 5 percent. The portfolio's fixed-income holdings can be categorized as intermediate-term, medium-quality debt.

Charles C. Van Vleet has managed this fund for the past five years. Management tends to buy beaten-down issues. Foreign bonds are often hedged so that there is little currency risk. The fund's price movement is only modestly cor-related to that of the Lehman Brothers Aggregate Bond Index. There are 34 funds besides Global Fixed-Income within the Credit Suisse family. Overall, the fund family's risk adjusted performance can be described as good.

Current Income ★★★★
Over the past year, Credit Suisse Global Fixed-Income had a 12-month yield of 7.3 percent. During this same 12-month period, the typical world bond fund had a yield that averaged 4.9 percent.

Expenses ★★★★
Credit Suisse Global Fixed-Income expense ratio is 1 percent; it has averaged 1 percent annually over the past three calendar years. The average expense ratio for the 190 funds in this category is 1.4 percent. This fund's turnover rate over the past year has been 144 percent, while its peer group average has been 227 percent.

Summary
Credit Suisse Global Fixed-Income ties for first place as the safest of the global income funds. The fund's overall ranking makes it the second-best choice for its entire category. No other funds in this group have had lower risk; consistency of returns has been excellent. The portfolio's expenses are about 40 percent less than average while turnover has also been about 40 percent less. Management looks for severely discounted issues, making this a fine choice for the conservative investor who is looking for additional diversification.

Profile

minimum initial investment $2,500	IRA accounts available . . . . yes
subsequent minimum investment . . $100	IRA minimum investment $500
available in all 50 states . . . . yes	date of inception . . . . Nov. 1990
telephone exchanges . . . . yes	dividend/income paid . . . . quarterly
number of funds in family 35	average credit quality . . . . A

Fidelity New Markets Income

82 Devonshire Street
Boston, MA 02109
(800) 544-8888
www.fidelity.com

total return	★★★★★
risk reduction	★★★
management	★★★★
current income	★★★★★
expense control	★★★
symbol FNMIX	20 points
up-market performance	excellent
down-market performance	fair
predictability of returns	poor

Total Return   ★★★★★

Over the past five years, Fidelity New Markets Income has taken $10,000 and turned it into $14,500 ($13,660 over three years). This translates into an annualized return of 8 percent over the past five years and 11 percent over the past three years. Over the past five years, this fund has outperformed 96 percent of all mutual funds; within its general category it has done better than 85 percent of its peers. World bond funds have averaged 5 percent annually over these same five years.

During the past five years, a $10,000 initial investment grew to $11,200 after taxes, assuming a 40 percent income tax bracket (state and federal combined) and a capital gains rate of 20 percent. This means that investors in this fund were able to preserve 69 percent of their total returns. Compared to other funds in its category, this fund's tax savings are considered to be very good.

Risk/Volatility   ★★★

Over the past five years, Fidelity New Markets Income has experienced average risk for its category. Over the past decade, the fund has had two negative years, while the Lehman Brothers Aggregate Bond Index has had two (off 3 percent in 1994 and 1 percent in 1999); the Salomon Brothers World Government Bond Index also fell twice (off 4 percent in 1999 and less than 1 percent in 2001). The fund has underperformed the Lehman Brothers Aggregate Bond Index five times and the Salomon Brothers World Government Bond Index five times in the past 10 years. Consistency of *overperformance* for this fund has been good.

	last 5 years		last 10 years	
worst year	-22.4%	1998	-22.4%	1998
best year	36.7%	1999	41.4%	1996

During the past five years, the fund's three worst months have been August 1998 (-37 percent), May 1999 (-6 percent), and May 1998 (-5 percent). During the same period, the three best months have been April 1999 (10 percent), March 1999 (8 percent), and September 1998 (7 percent). In the past, Fidelity New Markets

Income has done better than 90 percent of its peer group during the most recent bull market but outperformed just 30 percent of its peer group during the most recent bear market. Consistency, or predictability, of returns for Fidelity New Markets Income can be described as poor. This fund's risk-adjusted return over the past three/five years ranks in the top-two quintiles.

Management   ★★★★
There are 120 fixed-income securities in this $400 million portfolio. The average world bond fund today is $100 million in size. Close to 80 percent of the fund's holdings are in bonds. The average maturity of the bonds in this account is 10 years; the weighted coupon rate averages 9 percent. The portfolio's fixed-income holdings can be categorized as below investment grade.

John H. Carlson has managed this fund for the past eight years. Management looks for companies that attract foreign investment. Only a small number of countries dominate the portfolio, mostly emerging markets. The fund's price movement has zero correlation to that of the Lehman Brothers Aggregate Bond Index. There are 76 funds besides New Markets Income within the Fidelity family. Overall, the fund family's risk adjusted performance can be described as very good.

Current Income   ★★★★★
Over the past year, Fidelity New Markets Income had a 12-month yield of 9.0 percent. During this same 12-month period, the typical world bond fund had a yield that averaged 4.9 percent.

Expenses   ★★★
Fidelity New Markets Income's expense ratio is 1 percent; it has averaged 1 percent annually over the past three calendar years. The average expense ratio for the 190 funds in this category is 1.4 percent. This fund's turnover rate over the past year has been 259 percent, while its peer group average has been 227 percent.

Summary
Fidelity New Markets Income is the five-year performance leader. The fund also sports the best current income figures. Management has been able to keep overhead costs low while keeping tax efficiency high. This is one of the few top-rated funds that specializes in emerging markets debt. It is a fine addition for any investor seeking this kind of global exposure. The fund's overall risk level is high, but quite mild when compared to stock funds.

Profile
minimum initial investment . . . . . $2,500   IRA accounts available . . . . yes
subsequent minimum investment . . $250   IRA minimum investment $500
available in all 50 states . . . . yes   date of inception . . . . May 1993
telephone exchanges . . . . yes   dividend/income paid . . . . monthly
number of funds in family 77   average credit quality . . . . BB

Payden Global Fixed-Income R

333 South Grand Avenue, 32nd Floor
Los Angeles, CA 90071
(800) 572-9336
www.payden.com

total return	★★★★★
risk reduction	★★★★
management	★★★★★
current income	★★
expense control	★★★★★
symbol PYGFX	21 points
up-market performance	poor
down-market performance	fair
predictability of returns	excellent

Total Return   ★★★★★

Over the past five years, Payden Global Fixed-Income R has taken $10,000 and turned it into $13,870 ($12,490 over three years and $20,710 over the past 10 years). This translates into an annualized return of 7 percent over the past five years, 8 percent over the past three years, and 8 percent for the decade. Over the past five years, this fund has outperformed 95 percent of all mutual funds; within its general category it has done better than 90 percent of its peers. World bond funds have averaged 5 percent annually over these same five years.

During the past five years, a $10,000 initial investment grew to $11,200 after taxes, assuming a 40 percent income tax bracket (state and federal combined) and a capital gains rate of 20 percent. This means that investors in this fund were able to preserve 74 percent of their total returns. Compared to other funds in its category, this fund's tax savings are considered to be excellent.

Risk/Volatility   ★★★★

Over the past five years, Payden Global Fixed-Income R has experienced below average risk for its category. Over the past decade, the fund has had two negative years, while the Lehman Brothers Aggregate Bond Index has had two (off 3 percent in 1994 and 1 percent in 1999); the Salomon Brothers World Government Bond Index also fell twice (off 4 percent in 1999 and less than 1 percent in 2001). The fund has underperformed the Lehman Brothers Aggregate Bond Index six times and the Salomon Brothers World Government Bond Index five times in the past 10 years. Consistency of *overperformance* for this fund has been good.

	last 5 years		last 10 years	
worst year	-0.5%	1999	-3.0%	1994
best year	11.7%	1998	18.0%	1995

During the past five years, the fund's three worst months have been December 1998 (-4 percent), December 2001 (-3 percent), and February 1999 (-2 percent). During the same period, the three best months have been September 1998

(3 percent), August 1998 (2 percent), and November 2000 (2 percent). In the past, Payden Global Fixed-Income R has only done better than 10 percent of its peer group during the most recent bull market but outperformed 65 percent of its peer group during the most recent bear market. Consistency, or predictability, of returns for Payden Global Fixed-Income R can be described as excellent. This fund's risk-adjusted return over the past three/five years ranks in the top quintile.

Management   ★★★★★
There are 65 fixed-income securities in this $250 million portfolio. The average world bond fund today is $100 million in size. Close to 95 percent of the fund's holdings are in bonds. The average maturity of the bonds in this account is seven years; the weighted coupon rate averages 7 percent. The portfolio's fixed-income holdings can be categorized as intermediate-term, high-quality debt.

A team has managed this fund for the past 10 years. Management prefers high-quality government bonds from the U.S. and abroad. A fair degree of hedging helps fight any currency risk. There is no emerging markets debt in the portfolio. The fund's price movement is highly correlated to that of the Lehman Brothers Aggregate Bond Index. There are 13 funds besides Global Fixed-Income within the Payden family. Overall, the fund family's risk adjusted performance can be described as good.

Current Income   ★★
Over the past year, Payden Global Fixed-Income R had a 12-month yield of 3.9 percent. During this same 12-month period, the typical world bond fund had a yield that averaged 4.9 percent.

Expenses   ★★★★★
Payden Global Fixed-Income R's expense ratio is 0.5 percent; it has averaged 0.5 percent annually over the past three calendar years. The average expense ratio for the 190 funds in this category is 1.4 percent. This fund's turnover rate over the past year has been 110 percent, while its peer group average has been 227 percent.

Summary
Payden Global Fixed-Income R throws off little current income, but the more important total return figures are quite good. The fund has managed to outperform 95 percent of the entire fund universe as well as 90 percent of its peers. The portfolio tends to do best during bear markets, making it a nice defensive play. Tax minimization has been outstanding. The fund's overall risk level makes it the number one choice for the nervous investor.

Profile

minimum initial investment $5,000	*IRA accounts available* . . . . yes
subsequent minimum investment . . $1,000	*IRA minimum investment* $2,000
available in all 50 states . . . . yes	*date of inception* . . . . Sept. 1992
telephone exchanges . . . . yes	*dividend/income paid* . . . . monthly
number of funds in family 14	*average credit quality* . . . . AAA

T. Rowe Price Emerging Markets Bond
100 East Pratt Street
Baltimore, MD 21202
(800) 638-5660
www.troweprice.com

total return	★★★★★
risk reduction	★★★★
management	★★★★★
current income	★★★★★
expense control	★★★★
symbol PREMX	23 points
up-market performance	excellent
down-market performance	fair
predictability of returns	poor

Total Return   ★★★★★
Over the past five years, T. Rowe Price Emerging Markets Bond has taken $10,000 and turned it into $13,050 ($13,790 over three years). This translates into an annualized return of 5 percent over the past five years and 11 percent over the past three years. Over the past five years, this fund has outperformed 85 percent of all mutual funds; within its general category it has done better than 50 percent of its peers. World bond funds have averaged 5 percent annually over these same five years.

During the past five years, a $10,000 initial investment grew to $11,200 after taxes, assuming a 40 percent income tax bracket (state and federal combined) and a capital gains rate of 20 percent. This means that investors in this fund were able to preserve 68 percent of their total returns. Compared to other funds in its category, this fund's tax savings are considered to be very good.

Risk/Volatility   ★★★★
Over the past five years, T. Rowe Price Emerging Markets Bond has experienced average risk for its category. Over the past decade, the fund has had one negative year, while the Lehman Brothers Aggregate Bond Index has had two (off 3 percent in 1994 and 1 percent in 1999); the Salomon Brothers World Government Bond Index also fell twice (off 4 percent in 1999 and less than 1 percent in 2001). The fund has underperformed the Lehman Brothers Aggregate Bond Index three times and the Salomon Brothers World Government Bond Index four times in the past 10 years. Consistency of *overperformance* for this fund has been good.

	last 5 years		last 10 years	
worst year	-23.1%	1998	-23.1%	1998
best year	23.0%	1999	36.8%	1996

During the past five years, the fund's three worst months have been August 1998 (-37 percent), May 1999 (-6 percent), and May 1998 (-5 percent). During the same period, the three best months have been November 1998 (8 percent), September 1998 (7 percent), and February 2000 (5 percent). In the past, T. Rowe

Price Emerging Markets Bond has done better than 85 percent of its peer group during the most recent bull market but outperformed just 30 percent of its peer group during the most recent bear market. Consistency, or predictability, of returns for T. Rowe Price Emerging Markets Bond can be described as poor. This fund's risk-adjusted return over the past three/five years ranks in the top-three quintiles.

Management ★★★★★
There are 75 fixed-income securities in this $200 million portfolio. The average world bond fund today is $100 million in size. Close to 90 percent of the fund's holdings are in bonds. The average maturity of the bonds in this account is 13 years; the weighted coupon rate averages 7 percent. The portfolio's fixed-income holdings can be categorized as intermediate-term, low-quality debt.

A team has managed this fund for the past eight years. Management maintains a conservative bent as it seeks out broadly-diversified emerging markets debt. Currency hedging further helps reduce risk. Lead manager Mike Conelius is considered a cautious investor who takes a long-term approach. The fund's price movement is not correlated to that of the Lehman Brothers Aggregate Bond Index. There are 85 funds besides Emerging Markets Bond within the T. Rowe Price family. Overall, the fund family's risk adjusted performance can be described as very good.

Current Income ★★★★★
Over the past year, T. Rowe Price Emerging Markets Bond had a 12-month yield of 8.1 percent. During this same 12-month period, the typical world bond fund had a yield that averaged 4.9 percent.

Expenses ★★★★
T. Rowe Price Emerging Markets Bond's expense ratio is 1.2 percent; it has averaged 1.2 percent annually over the past three calendar years. The average expense ratio for the 190 funds in this category is 1.4 percent. This fund's turnover rate over the past year has been 76 percent, while its peer group average has been 227 percent.

Summary
T. Rowe Price Emerging Markets Bond ranks as the number one choice in a category of 190 contenders. The fund's total point score is a near-perfect 23 out of 25. Current income is quite high, almost twice that of its category average. Three-year performance figures have been amazingly good while risk has ranged between average and below average. The portfolio also has the lowest turnover rate for its group.

Profile

minimum initial investment $2,500	*IRA accounts available* . . . . yes
subsequent minimum investment . . $100	*IRA minimum investment* $1,000
available in all 50 states . . . . yes	*date of inception* . . . . Dec. 1994
telephone exchanges . . . . yes	*dividend/income paid* . . . . monthly
number of funds in family 86	*average credit quality* . . . . BB

XII.
Summary

Aggressive Growth Funds
Ariel
ARK Small Cap Equity A
Bjurman, Barry Micro-Cap Growth
Fidelity Low-Priced Stock
Pennsylvania Mutual Investor
Quaker Aggressive Growth A
Royce Micro-Cap
Royce Opportunity
Royce Total Return
Smith Barney Aggressive Growth A

Balanced Funds
American Funds American
Balanced A
Calamos Convertible Growth &
Income A
Dodge & Cox Balanced
First Eagle Global A
FPA Crescent Institutional
Franklin Income A
MFS Total Return A
Oakmark Equity & Income I
Vanguard Wellesley Income

Corporate Bond Funds
Dodge & Cox Income
Fidelity Short-Term Bond
Fremont Bond
Janus Short-Term Bond
TIAA-CREF Bond Plus
Vanguard Intermediate-Term Bond
Index

Financial Funds
FBR Small Cap Financial A
Hancock Regional Bank B

Global Equity (Stock) Funds
American Funds Capital World
Growth & Income A
American Funds New Perspective A
First Eagle Overseas A
Julius Baer International Equity A
Matthews Asian Growth & Income
Matthews Pacific Tiger
Tweedy, Browne Global Value

Government Bond Funds
American Century Ginnie Mae
Investor
ING GNMA Income A
Sit U.S. Government Securities
Vanguard GNMA
Vanguard Short-Term Federal

Growth Funds
Calamos Growth A
Clipper
Hartford Midcap A
Longleaf Partners
Lord Abbett Mid-Cap Value A
Mairs & Power Growth
Merger
Meridian Value
Yacktman

Growth and Income Funds
American Century Equity Income
American Funds Capital Income
Builder A
Ameristock
Dodge & Cox Stock
FPA Perennial
Franklin Rising Dividends A

Prudential Jennison Equity
   Opportunities A
Scudder Dreman High Return
   Equity A
Van Kampen Equity and Income A

Health Care Funds
   Eaton Vance World Health A
   Vanguard Health Care

High-Yield Corporate Bond Funds
   Janus High-Yield
   Lord Abbett Bond-Debenture A
   T. Rowe Price High-Yield
   Vanguard High-Yield Corporate
   Waddell & Reed Advisor High-
      Income A

Metals and Natural Resources Funds
   American Century Global Gold
      Investments
   First Eagle Gold
   Oppenheimer Gold & Special
      Minerals A
   State Street Research Global
      Resources A

Money Market Funds
   Dreyfus Basic Money Market
   Federated Liquid Cash Trust
   Federated Short-Term Government
      Trust
   Strong Municipal Money Market
   Scudder Tax Exempt Money
   Scudder Yieldwise Money
   TIAA-CREF Money Market
   USAA Tax-Exempt Money Market
   Vanguard Federal Money Market
   Vanguard Prime Money Market
   Wells Fargo National Tax-Free
      Money Market Fund

Municipal Bond Funds
   American Century California High-
      Yield Municipal Investor
   American Funds Limited-Term
      Tax-Exempt Bond Fund of
      America
   American Funds Tax-Exempt Bond A
   Fidelity Advisor Municipal Income T
   Franklin Federal Tax-Free Income A
   USAA Tax Exempt Intermediate-
      Term
   Vanguard Intermediate-Term Tax-
      Exempt
   Vanguard New York Long-Term
      Tax-Exempt Investor
   Vanguard Short-Term Tax-Exempt

Real Estate Funds
   Security Capital U.S. Real Estate
   Vanguard REIT Index

Technology Funds
   Icon Information Technology
   Seligman Communications &
      Information A

Utility Stock Funds
   AXP Utilities A
   Morgan Stanley Global Utilities B
   Prudential Utility A
   Strong Dividend Income

World Bond Funds
   Credit Suisse Global Fixed-Income
   Fidelity New Markets Income
   Payden Global Fixed-Income R
   T. Rowe Price Emerging Markets
      Bond

Appendix A
Glossary of Mutual Fund Terms

advisor—The individual or organization employed by a mutual fund to give professional advice on the fund's investments and asset management practices (also called the "investment advisor").

asked or offering price—The price at which a mutual fund's shares can be purchased. The asked, or offering, price means the current net asset value per share plus sales charge, if any.

BARRA Growth Index—An index of 152 large-capitalization stocks that are all part of the Standard & Poor's 500, specifically those with above-average sales and earnings growth.

BARRA Value Index—An index of 363 large-capitalization stocks that are all part of the Standard & Poor's 500, specifically those with above-average dividend yields and relatively low prices considering their book values.

bid or sell price—The price at which a mutual fund's shares are redeemed (bought back) by the fund. The bid or redemption price usually means the current net asset value per share.

board certified—Designation given to someone who has become certified in insurance, estate planning, income taxes, securities, mutual funds, or financial planning. To obtain additional information about the board-certified programs or to get the name of a board-certified advisor in your area, call (800) 848-2029.

bottom up—Refers to a type of security analysis. Management that follows the bottom-up approach is more concerned with the company than with the economy in general. Analysis is based on things such as a company's financial strength, competitive strength, and potential for growth in earnings and cash flow. (For a contrasting style, see top down.)

broker/dealer—A firm that buys and sells mutual fund shares and other securities to the public.

capital gains distributions—Payments to mutual fund shareholders of profits (long-term gains) realized on the sale of the fund's portfolio securities. These amounts are usually paid once a year.

capital growth—An increase in the market value of a mutual fund's securities, as reflected in the net asset value of fund shares. This is a specific long-term objective of many mutual funds.

cash reserves—Short-term, interest-bearing securities that can easily and quickly be converted to cash. Some funds keep cash levels at a minimum and always remain in stocks and/or bonds; other funds hold up to 25 percent or more of their assets in cash reserves (money market instruments) as either a defensive play or as a buying opportunity to be used when securities become depressed in price.

CFS—Also known as Certified Fund Specialist, this is the only designation awarded to brokers, financial planners, CPAs, insurance agents, and other investment advisors who either recommend or sell mutual funds. Fewer than 7,000 people across the country have passed this certification program. To obtain additional information about the CFS program or to get the name of a CFS in your area, call (800) 848-2029.

CPI—The Consumer Price Index (CPI) is the most commonly used yardstick for measuring the rate of inflation in the United States.

custodian—The organization (usually a bank) that keeps custody of securities and other assets of a mutual fund.

derivatives—A financial contract whose value is based on, or "derived," from a traditional security, such as a stock or bond. The most common examples of derivatives are futures contracts and options.

diversification—The policy of all mutual funds to spread investments among a number of different securities in order to reduce the risk inherent in investing.

dollar-cost averaging—The practice of investing equal amounts of money at regular intervals regardless of whether securities markets are moving up or down. This procedure reduces average share costs to the investor, who acquires more shares during periods of lower securities prices and fewer shares during periods of higher prices.

EAFE—An equity index (EAFE stands for Europe, Australia, and the Far East) used to measure stock market performance outside the United States. The EAFE is a sort of Standard & Poor's 500 Index for overseas or foreign stocks.

exchange privilege—An option enabling mutual fund shareholders to transfer their investment from one fund to another within the same fund family as their needs or objectives change. Typically, funds allow investors to use the exchange privilege several times a year for a low fee or no fee per exchange.

expense ratio—A figure expressed as a percentage of a fund's assets. The main element is the management fee. Administrative fees cover a fund's day-to-day operations, including printing materials, keeping records, paying staff, and renting office space. Sometimes administrative fees are included in the management fee; a number of funds list such fees separately. Roughly half of all funds charge a 12b-1 fee, which pays for a fund's distribution and advertising costs. The 12b-1 fee can be higher than the management or administrative fee.

indexing—In contrast to the traditional approach to investing that tries to outperform market averages, index investing is a strategy that seeks to match the performance of a group of securities that form a recognized market measure, known as an index.

investment company—A corporation, trust, or partnership that invests pooled funds of shareholders in securities appropriate to the fund's objective. Among the benefits of investment companies, compared to direct investments, are professional management and diversification. Mutual funds (also known as open-ended and close-ended investment companies) are the most popular type of investment company.

investment objective—The goal that the investor and mutual fund pursue together (e.g., growth of capital or current income).

large-cap stocks—Equities issued by companies with a net worth of at least $7.5 billion.

long-term funds—An industry designation for funds that invest primarily in securities with remaining maturities of more than one year. In this book, the term means 15 years or more. Long-term funds are broadly divided into bond and income funds.

management fee—The amount paid by a mutual fund to the investment advisor for its services. The average annual fee industrywide is about 0.7 percent of fund assets.

"market-neutral" funds—A strategy that seeks to neutralize market movements by running two portfolios simultaneously: One buys stocks that are predicted to rise, and the other invests an equal amount in a similar assortment of other stocks that are predicted to decline.

mid-cap stocks—Equities issued by companies with a net worth between $1 billion and $7.5 billion.

mutual fund—An investment company that pools money from shareholders and invests in a variety of securities, including stocks, bonds, and money market instruments. A mutual fund stands ready to buy back (redeem) its shares at their current net asset value; this value depends on the market value of the fund's portfolio securities at the time of redemption. Most mutual funds continuously offer new shares to investors.

net asset value per share—The market worth of one share of a mutual fund. This figure is derived by taking a fund's total assets—securities, cash, and any accrued earnings—deducting liabilities, and dividing by the number of shares outstanding.

no-load fund—A mutual fund selling its shares at net asset value without the addition of sales charges.

passive management—A portfolio that tries to match the performance of a target index, such as the Standard & Poor's 500.

portfolio—A collection of securities owned by an individual or an institution (such as a mutual fund). A fund's portfolio may include a combination of stocks, bonds, and money market securities.

portfolio diversification—The average U.S. stock fund has about 30 percent of its assets invested in its 10 largest holdings.

prospectus—The official booklet that describes a mutual fund; it must be furnished to all investors. The prospectus contains information required by the U.S. Securities and Exchange Commission on subjects such as the fund's investment objectives, services, and fees. A more detailed document, known as "Part B" of the prospectus or the "Statement of Additional Information," is available at no charge on request.

redemption price—The amount per share (shown as the "bid" in newspaper tables) that mutual fund shareholders receive when they cash in the shares. The value of the shares depends on the market value of the fund's portfolio securities at the time. This value is the same as net asset value per share.

reinvestment privilege—An option available to mutual fund shareholders in which fund dividends and capital gains distributions are automatically turned back into the fund to buy new shares, without charge (meaning no sales fee or commission), thereby increasing holdings.

Russell 2000—An index that represents 2,000 small domestic companies (less than 8 percent of the U.S. equity market).

sales charge—An amount charged to purchase shares in many mutual funds sold by brokers or other sales agents. The maximum charge is 8.5 percent of the initial investment; the vast majority of funds now have a maximum charge of 4.75 percent or less. The charge is added to the net asset value per share when determining the offering price.

short-term funds—An industry designation for funds that invest primarily in securities with maturities of less than one year; the term means five years or less in this book. Short-term funds include money market funds and certain municipal bond funds.

small-cap stocks—Equities issued by companies with a net worth of less than $1 billion.

top down—Refers to a type of security analysis. Management that follows the top-down approach is very concerned with the general level of the economy and any fiscal policy being followed by the government (see bottom up).

transfer agent—The organization employed by a mutual fund to prepare and maintain records relating to the accounts of its shareholders. Some funds serve as their own transfer agents.

turnover—The percentage of a fund's portfolio that is sold during the year, a percentage rate that can range from 0 percent to 300 percent or more. The average turnover rate for U.S. stock funds is approximately 80 percent (10 percent for domestic stock index funds).

12b-1 fee—The distribution fee charged by some funds, named after a federal government rule. Such fees pay for marketing costs, such as advertising and dealer compensation. The fund's prospectus outlines 12b-1 fees, if applicable.

underwriter—The organization that acts as the distributor of a mutual fund's shares to broker/dealers and investors.

value stocks—Stocks that most investors view as unattractive for some reason. They tend to be priced low relative to some measure of the company's worth, such as earnings, book value, or cash flow. Value stock managers try to identify companies whose prices are depressed for temporary reasons, and that may bounce back strongly if investor sentiment improves.

■ ■ ■

The Securities Act of 1933 requires a fund's shares to be registered with the Securities and Exchange Commission (SEC) prior to their sale. In essence, the Securities Act ensures that the fund provides potential investors with a current prospectus. This law also limits the types of advertisements that may be used by a mutual fund.

The Securities Exchange Act of 1934 regulates the purchase and sale of all types of securities, including mutual fund shares.

The Investment Advisors Act of 1940 is a body of law that regulates certain activities of the investment advisors with regard to mutual funds.

The Investment Company Act of 1940 is a highly detailed regulatory statute applying to mutual fund companies. This act contains numerous provisions designed to prevent self-dealing by employees of the mutual fund company, as well as other conflicts of interest. It also provides for the safekeeping of fund assets and prohibits the payment of excessive fees and charges by the fund and its shareholders.

Appendix B
Who Regulates Mutual Funds?

Mutual funds are highly regulated businesses that must comply with some of the toughest laws and rules in the financial services industry. All funds are regulated by the U.S. Securities and Exchange Commission (SEC). With its extensive rule-making and enforcement authority, the SEC oversees mutual fund compliance chiefly by relying on the four major federal securities statutes mentioned in Appendix A.

Fund assets must generally be held by an independent custodian. There are strict requirements for fidelity bonding to ensure against the misappropriation of shareholder monies. In addition to federal statutes, almost every state has its own set of regulations governing mutual funds.

Although federal and state laws cannot guarantee that a fund will be prof-itable, they are designed to ensure that all mutual funds are operated and managed in the interests of their shareholders. Here are some specific investor protections that every fund must follow:

- Regulations concerning what may be claimed or promised about a mutual fund and its potential
- Requirements that vital information about a fund be made readily available (such as a prospectus, the "Statement of Additional Information," also known as "Part B" of the prospectus, and annual and semiannual reports)
- Requirements that a fund operate in the interest of its shareholders, rather than any special interests of its management
- Rules dictating diversification of the fund's portfolio over a wide range of investments to avoid too much concentration in a particular security

Appendix C
Dollar-Cost Averaging

Investors often believe that the market will go down as soon as they get in. For these people, and anyone concerned with reducing risk, the solution is dollar-cost averaging.

Dollar-cost averaging is a simple yet effective way to reduce risk, whether you are investing in stocks or bonds. The premise behind dollar-cost averaging (DCA) is that if several purchases of a fund are made over an extended period, the unpredictable highs and lows will average out. The investor ends up buying some shares at a comparatively low price, others at perhaps a much higher price.

DCA assumes that investors are willing to sacrifice the possibility that they bought all their shares at the lowest price for the certainty that they did not buy every share at the highest price. In short, investors are willing to accept a compromise—a sort of *risk-adjusted* decision.

DCA is based on investing a fixed amount of money in a given fund at specific intervals. Typically, an investor will put a few hundred dollars at the beginning of each month into the XYZ mutual fund. DCA works best if you invest and continue to invest on an established schedule, *regardless of price fluctuations*. You will be buying more shares when the price is down than when it is up. Most investors do not mind buying shares when prices are increasing, since this means that their existing shares are also going up. When this program is followed, losses during market declines are limited, while the ability to participate in good markets is maintained.

Another advantage is that DCA increases the likelihood that you will follow an investment program. As with other aspects of our lives, it is important to have goals. However, DCA is not something that should be universally recommended. Whether you should use dollar-cost averaging depends on your risk level.

From its beginnings well over 100 years ago, the stock market has always had an upward bias in performance. More often than not, the market goes up, not down. Therefore, it hardly makes sense to apply dollar-cost averaging to an investment vehicle, knowing that historically you would be paying a higher and higher price per share over time.

Studies done by the Institute of Business & Finance (800-848-2029) show that over the past 50 years, a dollar-cost averaging program produced inferior returns compared to a lump-sum investment. The institute's studies conclude the following: (1) a DCA program is a good idea for a conservative investor (the person or couple who gives more weight or importance to risk than reward); (2) for investors whose risk level is anything but conservative (an immediate, one-time investment resulted in better returns the great majority of the time); and (3) there have certainly been periods when a DCA program would have benefited even the extremely aggressive investor—but such periods have not been very common over the past half-century and have been quite rare over the past twenty, fifteen, ten, five, and three years.

Example of Dollar-Cost Averaging
($1,000 invested per period)

period (1)	cost per share (2)	number of shares bought with $1,000 (3)	total shares owned (4)	current total amount invested (5)	net gain value of shares (2) x (4) (6)	or loss (percentage) (6) x (5) (7)
1	$100	10.0	10.0	$1,000	$1,000	0
2	$80	12.5	22.5	$2,000	$1,800	-10.0
3	$70	14.3	36.8	$3,000	$2,576	-14.1
4	$60	16.7	53.5	$4,000	$3,210	-19.7
5	$50	20.0	73.5	$5,000	$3,675	-26.5
6	$70	14.3	87.8	$6,000	$6,146	+2.4
7	$80	12.5	100.3	$7,000	$8,024	+14.6
8	$100	10.0	110.3	$8,000	$11,030	+37.9

Appendix D
Systematic Withdrawal Plan

A systematic withdrawal plan (SWP) allows a check for a specified amount to be sent monthly or quarterly to you, or to anyone you designate, from your mutual fund account. There is no charge for this service.

This method of getting monthly checks is ideal for the income-oriented investor. It is also a risk reduction technique—a kind of dollar-cost averaging in reverse. A set amount is sent to you each month. In order to send you a check for a set amount, shares of one or more of your mutual funds must be sold, which, in turn, will most likely trigger a taxable event, but only for those shares redeemed.

When the market is low, the number of mutual fund shares being liquidated will be higher than when the market is high, since the fund's price per share will be lower. If you need $500 a month and the fund's price is $25 per share, 20 shares must be liquidated; if the price per share is $20 per share, 25 shares must be sold.

Here is an example of a SWP from the Investment Company of America (ICA), a conservative growth and income fund featured in previous editions of this book. The example assumes an initial investment of $100,000 in the fund at its inception, the beginning of 1934. A greater or smaller dollar amount could be used. The example shows what happens to the investor's principal over a 68-year period (January 1, 1934, through February 28, 2003). It assumes that $10,000 is withdrawn from the fund at the end of the first year. At the end of the first year, the $10,000 withdrawal *is increased by 4 percent each year thereafter* to offset the effects of inflation, which averaged less than 4 percent during this 67-year period. This means that the withdrawal for the second year was $10,400 ($10,000 multiplied by 1.04), for the third year $10,816 ($10,400 multiplied by 1.04), and so on.

Compare this example to what would have happened if the money had been placed in an average fixed-income account at a bank. The $100,000 depositor who took out only $9,000 each year would be in a far different situation. His (or her) original $100,000 was fully depleted by the end of 1948. All the principal and interest payments could not keep up with an annual withdrawal of $9,000.

The difference between ICA and the savings account is nearly $13 million. The savings account had a return of $26,300 (plus distribution of the original $100,000 principal); the ICA account had a total return of $13,059,680 ($3,493,180 distributed over 69 years plus a remaining principal, or account balance, of $10,231,000). This difference becomes even more disturbing when you consider that the bank depositor's withdrawals were not increasing each year to offset the effects of inflation. The interest rates used in this example came from the *U.S. Savings & Loan League Fact Book*.

SWP from the Investment Company of America (ICA)
initial investment: $100,000
annual withdrawals of: $10,000 (10 percent)
the first check is sent: 12/31/34
withdrawals annually increased by: 4 percent

date	amount withdrawn	value of remaining shares
12/31/34	$10,000	$109,000
12/31/35	$10,400	$185,000
12/31/40	$12,700	$153,000
12/31/45	$15,400	$247,000
12/31/50	$18,700	$212,000
12/31/55	$22,800	$374,000
12/31/60	$27,700	$465,000
12/31/65	$33,700	$679,000
12/31/70	$41,000	$742,000
12/31/75	$50,000	$669,000
12/31/80	$60,700	$1,007,000
12/31/85	$73,900	$1,790,000
12/31/86	$76,900	$2,104,000
12/31/87	$79,900	$2,136,000
12/31/88	$83,100	$2,336,000
12/31/89	$86,500	$2,936,000
12/31/90	$89,900	$2,865,000
12/31/91	$93,500	$3,525,000
12/31/92	$86,500	$3,673,000
12/31/93	$101,200	$3,997,000
12/31/94	$105,200	$3,897,000
12/31/95	$109,400	$4,981,000
12/31/96	$113,780	$5,830,000
12/31/97	$118,330	$7,448,000
12/31/98	$123,060	$9,026,000
12/31/99	$127,987	$10,386,000
12/31/00	$133,107	$10,649,000
12/31/01	$138,431	$10,159,100
12/31/02	$143,969	$9,715,100
3/31/03	————	$9,566,500

If the ICA systematic withdrawal plan were 8 percent annually instead of 10 percent (but still increased by 4 percent each year to offset the effects of inflation), the investor would have ended up with remaining shares worth nearly $100 million, plus withdrawals that totaled $2.8 million.

So, the next time some broker or banker tells you that you should be buying bonds or CDs for current income, tell him or her about a systematic withdrawal plan (SWP), a program designed to maximize your income and offset something the CD, T-bill, and bond advocates never mention: inflation.

Appendix E
Load or No-Load—Which Is Right for You?

As the amount of information available on mutual funds continues to grow almost exponentially, the load versus no-load debate has intensified. What makes the issue difficult to evaluate is the continued absence of neutrality on either side. Before you learn the real truth, let us first examine who is advocating what, what their biases are, and how each side argues its point.

A number of publications, including *Money, Forbes, Fortune, Kiplinger Personal Investor*, and *BusinessWeek*, favor the no-load camp. Although these publications appear neutral, they are not. First, each one derives the overwhelming majority of its mutual fund advertisements from funds that charge no commission. Second, these publications are trying to increase readership; they are in the business of selling copy, not information. A good way to increase or maintain a healthy circulation is by having their readership rely on them for advice—instead of going to a broker or investment advisor.

On the other side is the financial services industry, whose most vocal load supporters include the brokerage, banking, and insurance industries. That's not much of a surprise. These groups are also biased. Like the publication that only makes money by getting you to purchase a copy or having an editorial board whose policy favors no-load funds, much of the financial services community supports a sales charge because that is how they are compensated.

No-load proponents argue that a fund that charges any kind of commission or ongoing marketing fee (which is known as a 12b-1 charge) inherently cannot be as good as a similar investment that has no entry or exit fee or ongoing 12b-1 charge. On the surface, this argument appears logical. After all, if one investor starts off with a dollar invested and the other starts off with somewhere between 99 and 92 cents (commissions range from 1 to 8.5 percent; most are in the 3 to 5 percent range), all other things being equal, the person who has all of his money working for him will do better than the person who has an initial deduction. The press and the no-load funds say that there is no reason to pay a commission because you can do as well or better than the broker or advisor whose job it is to provide you with suggestions and guidance.

The commission-oriented community says you should pay a sales charge because you get what you pay for—good advice and ongoing service. After all, brokers, financial planners, banks that include mutual fund desks, and insurance agents are all highly trained professionals who know things you do not. Moreover, they study the markets on a continual basis, ensuring that they have more information than any weekend investor. In short, they ask, Do you want someone managing your money who has experience and works full-time in this area, or someone such as yourself who has no formal training and whose time and resources are limited?

There is no clear-cut solution. Both sides raise valid points. To gain more insight into what course of action (or type of fund) is best for you, let us take a neutral approach. I believe I can give you valid reasons why both kinds of funds make sense, because I have no hidden agenda. True, I am a licensed broker and branch manager of a national securities firm; however, the great majority of my compensation is based on a fee for service, meaning that clients who invest solely in no-load funds pay me an annual management fee.

First, you should never pay a commission to someone who knows no more about investing than you do. There is no value added in such a situation, except perhaps during uncertain or negative periods in the market. (This point will be discussed later.) After all, if your broker's advice and mutual fund experience are based solely on the same financial publications you have access to, you are not getting your money's worth by paying a sales charge. I raise this point first because the financial services industry is filled with a tremendous number of inexperienced and ignorant brokers. These people may make a lot of money, but this is usually the result of their connections (they know a lot of people) or marketing skills (they know how to get new business)—neither of which has anything to do with your money.

Brokerage firms, banks, and insurance companies hire stockbrokers based on their sales ability, not on their knowledge or analytical ability. The financial analysts at the home office are the ones involved in research and managing money. The fact that your broker has a couple of dozen years' experience in the securities industry or is a vice president may actually be hazardous to your financial health. Extensive experience could mean that the advisor is less inclined to learn about new products or studies, because he or she already has an established client base. Brokers obtain titles such as "vice president" because they outsell their peers. Contests (awards, trips, prizes, and enhanced payouts) are based on how much is sold, period. There has never been an instance of a brokerage firm, bank, or insurance company giving an award to someone based on knowledge or how well a client's account performed.

Second, if your investment time horizon is less than a couple of years, it is a mistake to pay anything more than a nominal fee, something in the 1 percent range. Even though the advice you are receiving may be great, it is hard to justify a 3 to 5 percent commission over the short haul. Sales charges in this range can only be rationalized if they can be amortized over a number of years. Thus, worthwhile advice becomes a bargain if you stay with the investment, or within the same family of mutual funds, for at least three years.

Third, if you are purchasing a fund that charges a fee, find out what you are getting for your money. Question the advisor; find out about his or her training, experience, education, and designations. Equally important, get a clear understanding about what you will be receiving on an ongoing basis. What kind of continuing education does the broker engage in (attending conferences, reading books, seeking a designation, and so forth)? Finally, make sure your advisor or broker tells you how your investments will be monitored. It is important to know how often you will be contacted and how a buy, hold, or sell decision will be made.

So far, it looks as if I've been pretty tough on my fellow brokers. Well, believe me, I'm even harder on about 99 percent of those do-it-yourself investors. I have been in this business for close to 20 years, and I can tell you that I have rarely met an investor who was better off on his or her own. Here's why.

First, it is extremely difficult to be objective about your own investments. Decisions based on what you have read from a newsletter or magazine or what you learned at a seminar are often a response to current news, such as trade relations with Japan, the value of the U.S. dollar, the state of the economy, or the direction of interest rates. This kind of knee-jerk reaction has proved to be wrong in most cases.

Mind you, out of fairness to those who manage their own investments, amateurs aren't the only ones who make investment errors. As an example, the majority of the major brokerage firms gave a sell signal just before the 1991 war in the Persian Gulf. It turned out that this would have been about the perfect time to buy. E. F. Hutton was forced to merge with another brokerage firm because they incorrectly predicted the direction of interest rates (and lost tens of millions of dollars in their own portfolio).

The mutual fund industry itself deserves a healthy part of the blame, as evidenced by their timing of new funds. Take my advice: When you see a number of new mutual funds coming out with the same timely theme (government plus or optioned-enhanced bond funds in the mid-1980s, Eastern European funds after German reunification, health-care funds a few years ago, derivatives and hedge funds more recently), run for cover. By the time these funds come out, the party is about to end. Investors who got into these funds often do well for a number of months but soon face devastating declines.

Your favorite financial publications are also to blame. Their advice is based on a herd instinct: What do our readers think? Instead of providing leadership, they simply reinforce what is most likely incorrect information. For example, for over a year after the 1987 stock market crash, the most popular of these mainstream publications, *Money*, had cover stories that recommended (and extolled the virtues of) safe investments. For almost a year and a half after the crash, this magazine was giving out bad advice. When something goes on sale (stocks, in this case) you should be a buyer, not a seller. Since *Money* routinely surveys (or polls) their readers for feature articles, such behavior (the herd instinct) is understandable but not forgivable.

Besides the lack of objectivity and the constant bombardment of what I call "daily noise" (what the market is doing at the moment, comments from the financial gurus, etc.), there is also the question of your competence. Presumably, you and I could figure out how to fix our own plumbing, sew our own clothes, fix the car when it breaks down, or avoid paying a lawyer by purchasing "do-it-yourself" books. The question then becomes whether it is worth going through the learning curve, and, even supposing we are successful, whether the task would have been better accomplished by someone else—perhaps for less money or better use of our own time. I think the answer is obvious. Each of us has his or her own area or areas of expertise or skill. You and I rely on others either because they know more than we do about the topic or task at hand or because having someone else help is a more efficient use of our time.

If you're going to seek the services of an investment advisor or broker, it should be because he or she knows more than you do, because he or she is more objective, or because you can make more money doing whatever you do than taking the time to make complex investment decisions yourself. This is what makes sense. The fact that there are brokers and advisors who put their interests before yours is simply a reality that you must deal with. And the proper way to deal with these conflicts of interest or ignorant counselors is by doing your homework. Ask questions. Just as there are great plumbers, mechanics, lawyers, and doctors, so, too, are there exceptional investment advisors and brokers. Your job is to find them.

Eliminating load or no-load funds from your investing universe is not the answer. If you are determined never to pay a commission, then you may miss out on the next John Templeton (the Franklin-Templeton family of funds), Peter Lynch (Fidelity Magellan Fund), or Jean-Marie Eveillard (First Eagle Funds). You will also miss out on some of the very best mutual fund families: American Funds (large), Fidelity-Advisor (medium), and First Eagle (small). A better way to proceed is to try to separate good funds from bad ones. After all, an investor is clearly far better off in a good load fund than in a bad no-load one.

The bottom line is that performance, as well as *risk-adjusted returns*, for load funds often exceeds the returns on no-load funds, and vice versa. The "top ten" list (or whatever number you want to use) for one period may have been dominated by funds that charge a commission, but in just a year or two the top 10 list may be heavily populated by mutual funds with no sales charge or commission.

It might seem strange to be questioning the benefits of financial planning when our society places professions like law and accountancy in such high regard. And certainly I am not suggesting that investors should consider only load funds. But with all the load-fund bashing in recent years, it is important to recognize that no-load funds are not the perfect answer for a large percentage of investors. Approaching the mutual fund industry with an "us versus them" mentality results in a great deal of misleading information and unfairly discredits the work of skilled financial planners and brokers.

Appendix F
The U.S. Market Compared to Foreign Markets

Investing worldwide gives you exposure to different stages of economic market cycles, which has given international investors an advantage in the past. Foreign equities and bonds have generally offered higher levels of short-, intermediate-, and long-term growth than their domestic counterparts. Not once during the past 14 years was the U.S. stock market the world's top performer (all figures are in U.S. dollars).

Historically, Europeans have invested most of their money in gold and bonds. Today, lower interest rates, the privatization of state assets, and pension reform are providing renewed interest in common stocks for the Continent, where levels of equity ownership are a very small percentage of what they are in the United States and the United Kingdom.

Top-Performing World Stock Markets
A 14-Year Review: 1987–2000

year	1st	2nd	3rd	4th	5th
2000	Denmark 22%	Switzerland 16%	Venezuela 12%	Ireland 7%	Norway 2%
1999	Finland 153%	Malaysia 110%	Singapore 99%	Sweden 80%	Japan 62%
1998	Finland 121%	Belgium 68%	Italy 52%	Spain 50%	France 42%
1997	Portugal 47%	Switzerland 45%	Italy 36%	Denmark 35%	USA 34%
1996	Spain 37%	Sweden 35%	Finland 32%	Hong Kong 29%	Ireland 29%
1995	Switzerland 44%	USA 37%	Sweden 33%	Spain 30%	Netherlands 28%
1994	Finland 52%	Norway 24%	Japan 22%	Sweden 19%	Ireland 15%
1993	Malaysia 114%	Hong Kong 110%	Finland 101%	Singapore 62%	Ireland 60%
1992	Hong Kong 37%	Switzerland 17%	USA 6%	Singapore 6%	France 3%
1991	Hong Kong 43%	Australia 39%	USA 30%	Singapore 23%	France 16%
1990	United Kingdom 6%	Austria 5%	Hong Kong 4%	Norway (1%)	Denmark (2%)
1989	Austria 105%	Germany 49%	Norway 46%	Denmark 45%	Singapore 42%
1988	Belgium 54%	Denmark 53%	Sweden 48%	Norway 42%	France 38%
1987	Japan 43%	Spain 41%	United Kingdom 35%	Canada 14%	Denmark 13%

The U.S. stock market has ranked among the five top performers only four times in this 14-year period. During this same period, the U.S. bond market has never claimed the number-one spot against other world markets.

Appendix G
Growth Stocks versus Value Stocks

Throughout the different equity sections (growth, growth and income, global equity, etc.), the end of each stock fund's "Management" paragraph often mentions whether the fund manager seeks out "growth" or "value" issues. The differences and possible consequences of these two forms of equity selection are shown in the following table.

Value means that the stocks are inexpensive relative to their earnings potential. *Growth* refers to stocks of companies whose earnings per share are expected to grow significantly faster than the market average.

As you can see by the table, the performance of these two types of stocks can vary from year to year. On a monthly or quarterly basis, the difference is often much more significant than on an annual basis.

The following table shows performance of large company value stocks (dividends reinvested in both indexes). Over the past 13 years, an investment in both growth stocks and value stocks would have been less volatile than an investment in only one equity style.

year	growth	value
1990	3%	-5%
1991	45%	24%
1992	4%	16%
1993	3%	24%
1994	1%	0
1995	41%	52%
1996	25%	23%
1997	36%	50%
1998	81%	22%
1999	27%	31%
2000	-22%	-15%
2001	-20%	-10%
2002	-21%	-21%

Although growth stocks have outperformed value stocks during the 1990s, value was the winner in the 1970s and 1980s.

Appendix H
Stock Market Declines

If you are a relatively new investor, you may not have had firsthand experience with a bear market. Since corrections are a natural part of the stock market cycle, it is important to ask yourself how you would react. Would you panic or would you be patient? It is difficult to know for sure. Stock market fire drills do not really work, because it is one thing to ponder your reaction to a market meltdown—another to live through one with your financial goals at stake. However, a historical perspective may help you gain a better perspective and, even more important, remain patient.

The following table shows all of the periods when the U.S. stock market dropped 15 percent or more from 1953 through the end of 2000 (a "bear market" is defined as a drop of 20 percent or more; a "correction" is a decline of 10 percent or more). Of these 14 down markets, the worst took place during the 1973–1974 recession, resulting in the greatest loss since the Great Depression. Surprisingly, half of the 48 percent loss that took place during the 1973–1974 decline was recovered within five months after the drop.

U.S. Market Declines of 15% or More (1953–2000)

bear year	% decline	# of down months	months to recovery
1953	15%	9	6
1956–1957	16%	6	5
1957	20%	3	12
1961–1962	29%	6	14
1966	22%	9	6
1968–1970	37%	18	22
1973–1974	48%	21	64
1975	15%	2	4
1977–1978	18%	14	6
1978	17%	2	10
1980	22%	2	4
1981–1982	22%	13	3
1987	34%	2	23
1990	20%	3	23
1998	15%	2	5
2000	13%	3	?
average	**23%**	**7**	**14**

During the 1998 calendar year, the S&P 500 dropped 15.4 percent from the end of June through the end of August. It took just four months (end of November) for the market to recover this loss and move on to yet another high. For 1999, the market had a positive return of 21 percent, but it had a negative return of 9.1 percent for the 2000 calendar year, followed by a loss of 11.9 in 2001.

One possible strategy to avoiding market declines is to sit on the sidelines until the volatility passes. According to a study by the University of Michigan, this is a bad idea. An investor who was on the sidelines during the best 1 percent of all trading days from 1963 to 2000 missed 95 percent of the market's gains. According to figures from Micropal, missing the best 15 months of the market from June 1980 to June 2000 resulted in foregoing 75 percent of the market's gain (as measured by the S&P 500). A $100 investment in the S&P 500 grew to $613 if all 15 months were missed, versus $100 growing to $2,456 if one were fully invested from June 1980 to June 2000.

These included investors who were sidelined in 1995 by the poor showing in 1994 for both stocks and bonds as well as those stock market investors who bailed out in 1996 because the 38 percent gain in 1995 made them nervous about a downturn. Investors who bailed out in 1997 because the 23 percent gain in 1996 made them nervous missed a 29 percent gain in 1998 and a 21 percent gain in 1999!

Being in the market when it falls is not the greatest risk most stock investors face; it is being out of the market when it soars. The best strategy is to keep investing through any market environment.

The problem is that no one rings a bell when the market hits bottom. Similarly, there is no advance notice that the market is turning around. Stocks tend to gain significant ground in short periods; missing out on the first, brief phase of a recovery can be costly. For example, when the stock market took off in August 1982, ending years of mediocre performance, the market jumped 42 percent in just three months. From the October low of the 1987 crash to the end of December, just two months later, stocks rebounded 22 percent. And in the four months after the October 1990 Gulf War low, with the United States still mired in recession, the stock market shot up more than 30 percent.

Trying to get out of the market and get back in calls for two right decisions. There is no evidence that professional investors, market timers, brokers, financial analysts, or anyone else can get these calls right with any degree of consistency. One bad market timing call can seriously handicap lifetime performance.

The question then becomes, If stock prices fall hard, should you cut your losses and play it safe? Of all the options that investors have, this one may be the worst solution and the most devastating. An investment of $10,000 in common stocks, as measured by the S&P 500, on the day before the October 1987 crash would have fallen to $7,995 in a single day. Leaving the account intact would have resulted in a whopping 746 percent gain through December 31, 2001. Taking the $7,995 and reinvesting it in U.S. Treasury bills would have resulted in a gain of just 98 percent over the same period.

Moving from the S&P 500 to the Dow Jones Industrial Average, and changing the perspective somewhat, a review of the declines in the Dow may be an insightful comparison. Since 1990, a "routine" decline (a loss of 5 percent or more) has happened about three times a year, and it has taken about forty-eight days for half of the decline to be recouped. A "moderate" decline (a loss of 10 percent or more) has happened about once a year, and it has taken about 114 days for half of the decline to be recouped. A "severe" decline (a loss of 15 percent or more) has happened about once every two years, and it has taken about 219 days for half of the decline to be recouped. A "bear market" decline (a loss of 20 percent or more) has happened about once every three and a half years, and it has taken about 340 days for half of the decline to be recouped.

Appendix I
A Reason Not to Index

Appendix D showed a systematic withdrawal program (SWP) for Investment Company of America (ICA), a growth and income portfolio from the American Funds Group, starting with its first full year through the first two months of 2003. Let us now look at two more examples of an SWP, comparing results from the S&P 500 versus Washington Mutual, another growth and income fund offered through the American Funds Group.

For this example, a different time frame (January 1, 1973 through February 28, 2003) will be used, showing radically different results. Like the ICA example, it is assumed that a single $100,000 investment is made and that all capital gains and dividend payments are automatically reinvested into the fund. Also less money is taken out in this example (8 percent, or $8,000 per year).

As you can see, applying an SWP to the S&P 500 results in the investor being flat broke by December 1996 (all of the $100,000 and its resulting growth has been depleted). Yet, by using professional management like that found with Washington Mutual (abbreviated as WM), not only are the cumulative distributions greater ($240,000 versus $188,700), so is the remaining principal ($659,030 versus zero).

Systematic Withdrawal Program Using a
Growth & Income Fund (Washington Mutual) versus the S&P 500
$100,000 Invested in Each Portfolio on January 1, 1973

date	cumulative withdrawal from WM	cumulative withdrawal from S&P 500	remaining value of Washington Mutual (WM)	remaining value of S&P 500
01/01/73	0	0	$100,000	$100,000
12/31/73	$8,000	$8,000	$79,280	$76,890
12/31/74	$16,000	$16,000	$57,460	$48,370
12/31/75	$24,000	$24,000	$74,830	$58,050
12/31/80	$64,000	$64,000	$89,980	$52,930
12/31/85	$104,000	$104,000	$170,740	$42,890
12/31/90	$144,000	$144,000	$260,020	$28,520
12/31/95	$184,000	$184,000	$503,180	$3,910
12/31/96	$192,000	$188,700	$596,530	$0
12/31/97	$200,000	$787,050		
12/31/98	$208,000	$931,140		
12/31/99	$216,000	$933,800		
12/31/00	$224,000	$1,009,930		
12/31/01	$232,000	$829,440		
03/31/02	$240,000	$698,270		
02/28/03	———	$659,030		

For the S&P 500, the average annual total return for this illustration was 6.0 percent (January 1, 1973 through December 15, 1996, when the money ran out). For Washington Mutual Fund (WM), the average annual total return for this illustration was 12.5 percent (January 1, 1973 through February 28, 2003).

Two conclusions can be reached from this illustration. First, there is a benefit to professional management versus a passively managed portfolio such as the S&P 500 (which as an index fund is also considered to be a growth and income fund). Second, moderate gains or advances in some early years can make a great difference later on (compare the value of both portfolios at the end of 1974 and 1975 with what happened in later years, such as 1980 and 1985, when the gaps become huge due to earlier gains by Washington Mutual).

Appendix J
A Benefit of Balanced Funds

Prudence can pay off. Even though stocks usually outperform bonds, there have been extensive periods when a balanced portfolio (30 percent to 70 percent in bonds and the balance in stocks) can be a better way to go than a pure stock portfolio (represented by the S&P 500 here)—especially when current income is needed.

The following table shows a systematic withdrawal program (SWP) for Income Fund of America (a balanced portfolio from the American Funds Group) versus a similar SWP using the S&P 500. Both withdrawal programs assume a one-time investment of $200,000 made on January 1, 1974, annual withdrawals made at the end of each year, and a first-year withdrawal of $15,000 (7.5 percent of $200,000) that is then increased by 3.5 percent for each subsequent year (in order to offset the effects of inflation). As you can see, the balanced fund comes out ahead.

Systematic Withdrawal Program Using a Balanced Fund (IFA) and the S&P 500 ($200,000 Invested in Each Portfolio on January 1, 1972)

date	cumulative withdrawal from IFA	cumulative withdrawal from S&P 500	remaining value of IFA	remaining value of S&P 500
01/01/74	0	0	$200,000	$200,000
12/31/74	$15,000	$15,000	$165,240	$131,834
12/31/75	$30,525	$30,525	$208,287	$164,740
12/31/76	$46,593	$46,593	$265,307	$187,368
12/31/80	$116,691	$116,691	$248,709	$191,095
12/31/85	$219,029	$219,029	$488,588	$221,773
12/31/90	$340,574	$340,574	$632,843	$257,400
12/31/95	$484,932	$484,932	$1,067,108	$347,972
12/31/96	$516,905	$516,905	$1,197,075	$394,987
12/31/97	$549,997	$549,997	$1,428,937	$493,109
12/31/98	$584,247	$584,247	$1,529,268	$597,424
12/31/99	$619,696	$619,696	$1,501,077	$686,033
12/31/00	$656,385	$656,385	$1,612,601	$586,516
12/31/01	$679,360	$679,360	$1,596,644	$493,746
12/31/02	$703,130	$703,140	$1,526,871	$384,678

For the S&P 500, the average annual total return was 11.6 percent (January 1, 1974 through February 28, 2003) and 8.7 percent for the past 10 years. For Income Fund of America (IFA), the average annual total return for this illustration was 12.5 percent and 8.8 percent for the past 10 years.

Appendix K
Asset Categories: Total Returns for the Past 16 Years

The following table shows the year-by-year returns for eight different asset categories. All of the returns are in U.S. dollars, expressed as percentages, and include the reinvestment of any dividends, interest, and capital gains. The boldface type indicates the best-performing category for the year.

category	'87	'88	'89	'90	'91	'92	'93	'94	'95	'96	'97	'98	'99	'00	'01	'02
S&P 500	5	17	32	-3	31	8	10	1	38	23	33	29	21	-9	-12	-22
small U.S. stocks	-9	25	16	-20	46	18	19	-2	28	17	22	-3	30	-4	23	-13
foreign stocks (EAFE)	25	28	11	-24	12	-12	33	8	11	6	2	20	27	-14	-21	-16
emerging market stocks	14	58	55	-30	18	0	68	-1	-13	8	-15	-25	74	-31	-4	N/A
U.S. gov./corporate bonds	3	8	15	9	16	7	10	-3	19	4	10	10	-1	12	8	10
high-yield bonds	5	13	1	-10	46	16	17	-1	19	11	13	4	5	-5	6	3
foreign government bonds	35	2	-3	15	16	5	15	6	20	4	-4	18	3	-3	-4	20
U.S. T-bills	6	7	8	8	5	4	3	4	5	5	5	5	5	6	4	2

Source: Micropal

Appendix L
Stock Gains, Losses, and Averages

In the five calendar years ending December 1932, the S&P 500 had a cumulative loss of almost 49 percent. Although this is quite a depressing figure (particularly since similar losses took place during the 1973–1974 recession), basing your stock market strategy on a couple of terrible periods is foolish.

To get a better feel for the likely range of returns you will experience, let us examine what happens when you throw out the worst 10 percent and best 10 percent of the years and then look at performance for the remaining 80 percent of the time. Here is what you would find, looking at rolling calendar-year periods from 1871 through 1998 (all figures are from *Stocks for the Long Run* by Jeremy Siegel and the Institute of Business & Finance):

- For five-year periods (124 observations) and then eliminating the 12 best and 12 worst such periods, annualized returns ranged from 0.1 percent to 18.5 percent
- For 10-year periods (119 observations), annualized returns ranged from 2.8 percent to 15.9 percent
- For 20-year periods (109 observations), annualized returns ranged from 5.3 percent to 13.8 percent
- For 30-year periods (99 observations), annualized returns ranged from 6.0 percent to 11.8 percent

Note: If you earned 5.3 percent per year for 20 years, your money would grow 181 percent. If you earned 6.0 percent per year for 30 years, you would end up with 474 percent.

Looking at returns and variability from a different perspective, Jeffrey Schwartz, a senior consultant at Ibbotson, provides an even wider range of returns. According to his figures, since the end of World War II (throwing out the best 5 percent and the worst 5 percent of the years):

- Five-year returns vary from 2.5 percent to 22.7 percent per year
- 10-year returns vary from 4.0 percent to 20.4 percent per year
- 20-year returns vary from 6.0 percent to 15.8 percent a year

The Siegel and Schwartz figures are slightly more positive if you include 1999 and 2000 figures.

Appendix M
Individual Stocks versus Mutual Funds

If you believe recent headlines, you might think that mutual funds are a thing of the past, and that today's investors prefer to choose individual stocks for their portfolio. However, as you will see in the following table, funds are more relevant now than they were in 1924, when MFS invented the mutual fund. Unlike individual stocks, funds provide active management with the risk-reduction benefit of diversification. Perhaps no other investment has provided a better balance of risk and return.

Did you know:

- Over the past five years, from September 30, 1995, to September 30, 2000, 39 percent of stocks produced negative annualized total returns as compared to less than 1 percent of equity mutual funds?
- In 1999, the standard deviation of individual stocks was 229, while it was only 37.3 for equity mutual funds?
- Historically, individual stocks have had higher annualized average returns over the one-year period, but equity mutual funds produced higher returns over the three-, five-, and 10-year periods ending September 30, 2000?

individual U.S. stocks	1 year (2000)	3 years (1998–2000)	5 years (1996–2000)	10 years (1991–2000)
# stocks in existence	6,375	5,424	4,408	2,524
average annualized return	32%	-3%	5%	12%
highest return per year	5,569%	395%	179%	94%
lowest return per year	-97%	-83%	-76%	-35%
# stocks with negative annualized return	3,137	3,103	1,711	420
% stocks with negative annualized return	49%	57%	39%	17%

U.S. equity mutual funds	1 year (2000)	3 years (1998–2000)	5 years (1996–2000)	10 years (1991–2000)
# funds in existence	2,683	2,110	1,565	778
average annualized return	28%	14%	17%	17%
highest return per year	264%	88%	56%	41%
lowest return per year	-75%	-18%	-17%	-8%
# funds with negative annualized return	116	140	13	1
% funds with negative annualized return	2%	3%	0%	0%

Appendix N
Decades at a Glance (1930–1999)

The following text and figures cover the past seven decades (1930–1999). The summary information is useful in gaining a historical perspective of the market. Perhaps more important, it shows that despite a number of catastrophic events, the U.S. stock market has continued to trend upward.

DECADE AT A GLANCE (the 1930s)

Economic distress swept the nation after the October 1929 stock market crash. The Great Depression, which lasted from 1930 to 1936, bottomed in 1933, when *one-fourth* of the civilian labor force was unemployed.

index	average annual total return
Standard & Poor's 500 Index	-0.1%
long-term U.S. government bonds	4.9%
U.S. Treasury bills	0.6%
	average for the decade
short-term interest rates	1.5%
annual inflation rate	-2.1%
unemployment rate	18.2%

DECADE AT A GLANCE (the 1940s)

Japan's attack on Pearl Harbor on December 7, 1941, thrust the United States into World War II and a wartime economy. In the midst of price controls and consumer goods shortages, upward trends marked the stock market from 1943 to 1946, with a vigorous bull market in 1945 as the war ended.

index	average annual total return
Standard & Poor's 500 Index	9.2%
long-term U.S. government bonds	3.2%
U.S. Treasury bills	0.4%
	average for the decade
short-term interest rates	1.6%
annual inflation rate	5.4%
unemployment rate	5.2%

DECADE AT A GLANCE (the 1950s)

While Eisenhower guided America through the early years of the Cold War, the stock market made gains, and by year-end 1954, stock prices had reached their highest levels since 1929. This exuberance was followed by a bear market lasting 18 months, from April 1956 through October 1957, during which the S&P 500 declined 19.4 percent.

index	average annual total return
Standard & Poor's 500 Index	19.4%
long-term U.S. government bonds	0.1%
U.S. Treasury bills	1.9%
	average for the decade
short-term interest rates	3.2%
annual inflation rate	2.2%
unemployment rate	4.5%

DECADE AT A GLANCE (the 1960s)

American culture, long restrained by the sense of team spirit and conformity induced by the crises of depression, war, and the ongoing Cold War, broke loose in a multitude of swift changes. The economy was equally turbulent, and the stock market cycles recorded three bear markets. In 1963, President Kennedy submitted a federal budget with the then-largest deficit in history, $10 billion.

index	average annual total return
Standard & Poor's 500 Index	7.8%
long-term U.S. government bonds	1.5%
U.S. Treasury bills	3.9%
	average for the decade
short-term interest rates	5.3%
annual inflation rate	2.5%
unemployment rate	4.8%

DECADE AT A GLANCE (the 1970s)

When the Organization of Petroleum Exporting Countries (OPEC) quintupled oil prices in 1973, a deep recession hit America. The stock market plunged 45.1 percent from January 1973 through December 1974. Unemployment reached 8.7 percent in March 1975, the highest level since 1941. In 1979, commercial banks raised their prime rates to a whopping 15.7 percent.

index	average annual total return
Standard & Poor's 500 Index	5.9%
long-term U.S. government bonds	5.5%
U.S. Treasury bills	6.3%

	average for the decade
short-term interest rates	8.1%
annual inflation rate	7.4%
unemployment rate	6.2%

DECADE AT A GLANCE (the 1980s)

President Reagan signed extensive budget- and tax-cutting legislation in 1981, and sweeping tax-reform legislation in 1986. The Black Monday stock market crash of October 19, 1987, became the largest one-day stock market decline on record, as the Dow Jones Industrial Average fell an astounding 508.32 points.

index	average annual total return
Standard & Poor's 500 Index	17.6%
long-term U.S. government bonds	12.6%
U.S. Treasury bills	8.9%

	average for the decade
short-term interest rates	11.8%
annual inflation rate	5.1%
unemployment rate	7.3%

DECADE AT A GLANCE (the 1990s)

From November 1990 through the end of 1999, stock market investors were rewarded by the longest bull market in history: "The current bull market has added about $7.2 trillion to households' balance sheets." The Asian Economic Crisis briefly shook U.S. investor confidence as the Dow Jones Industrial Average experienced the single-biggest point loss ever on October 27, 1997. The decade ended with technology stocks fueling the NASDAQ Index to its highest close ever on December 31, 1999.

index	average annual total return
Standard & Poor's 500 Index	18.2%
long-term U.S. government bonds	8.8%
U.S. Treasury bills	4.9%

	average for the decade
short-term interest rates	8.0%
annual inflation rate	2.9%
unemployment rate	5.8%

About the Author

Gordon K. Williamson, JD, MBA, MS, CFS, CLU, ChFC, AEP, CSC, CLTC, CEPP, RP, is one of the most highly trained investment counselors in the United States. Williamson, a former tax attorney, is a Certified Fund Specialist and branch manager of a national brokerage firm. He has been admitted to the Registry of Financial Planning Practitioners, the highest honor one can attain as a financial planner. He holds the two highest designations in the life insurance industry: Chartered Life Underwriter and Chartered Financial Consultant. Gordon is an Accredited Estate Planner, Certified Senior Advisor, and certified in long-term care. He is also a real estate broker with an MBA in real estate.

Mr. Williamson is the founder and executive director of the Institute of Business & Finance, a fourteen-year-old professional education program that leads to the designations "CFS" and "Board Certified" (800-848-2029).

He is also the author of more than thirty books, including *Building & Managing an Investment Portfolio, Making the Most of Your 401(k), The 100 Best Annuities You Can Buy, All about Annuities, How You Can Survive and Prosper in the Clinton Years, Investment Strategies under Clinton/Gore, The Longman Investment Companion, Investment Strategies, Survey of Financial Planning, Tax Shelters, Advanced Investment Vehicles and Techniques, Your Living Trust, Sooner Than You Think, Getting Started in Annuities, Big Decisions—Small Investor, Building & Managing an Investment Portfolio, Low Risk Investing,* and *First Time Investor.* He has been the financial editor of various magazines and newspapers and a stock market consultant for a television station.

Gordon K. Williamson is located in La Jolla, California. The firm specializes in financial planning and investments for individuals and institutions ($100,000 minimum account size). Additional information can be obtained by phoning (800) 748-5552 or (858) 454-3938.

100 BEST STOCKS YOU CAN BUY, 2004

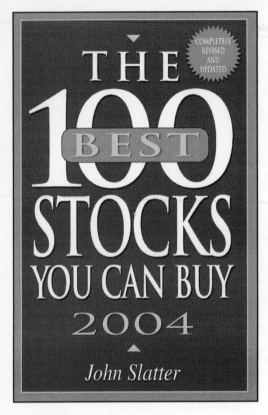

Stocks remain the most popular form of investment. However, in today's volatile climate choosing the right stock isn't easy. In fact, it can be a risky, stressful, and time-consuming experience.

In *The 100 Best Stocks You Can Buy, 2004*, investment analyst John Slatter helps you minimize your risk by narrowing the options down to the 100 stocks you can't afford to miss. Mr. Slatter has painstakingly researched thousands of stocks to bring you those that demonstrate the best potential for both long- and short-term growth. The 100 best are companies with innovative marketing, great products, cutting-edge research, sound management, financial strength, and consistent growth.

The 100 Best Stocks You Can Buy, 2004 brings you the best choices for the following investment strategies:

- ✦ Income
- ✦ Conservative Growth
- ✦ Growth
- ✦ Aggressive Growth

Each stock listing includes invaluable background on the company, contact information, stock and ticker symbols, Web site address, S & P rating, plus insider tips on reasons to buy, potential shortcomings to bear in mind, and a snapshot of company financials. *The 100 Best Stocks You Can Buy, 2004* is the guide you'll rely on—year after year.

Trade Paperback, $14.95
6" x 9 ¼" 352 pages
ISBN: 1-58062-926-1

To order, call 1-800-872-5627, or visit us at *www.adamsmedia.com*!